Intersectionality in Intentional Communities

Intersectionality in Intentional Communities

The Struggle for Inclusivity in Multicultural U.S. Protestant Congregations

By Assata Zerai

LEXINGTON BOOKS
Lanham • Boulder • New York • London

Published by Lexington Books
An imprint of The Rowman & Littlefield Publishing Group, Inc.
4501 Forbes Boulevard, Suite 200, Lanham, Maryland 20706
www.rowman.com

Unit A, Whitacre Mews, 26-34 Stannary Street, London SE11 4AB

Copyright © 2016 by Lexington Books

All rights reserved. No part of this book may be reproduced in any form or by any electronic or mechanical means, including information storage and retrieval systems, without written permission from the publisher, except by a reviewer who may quote passages in a review.

British Library Cataloguing in Publication Information Available

Library of Congress Cataloging-in-Publication Data

Names: Zerai, Assata, 1964- author.
Title: Intersectionality in intentional communities : the struggle for inclusivity in multicultural U.S. Protestant congregations / by Assata Zerai.
Description: Lanham : Lexington Books, 2016. | Includes bibliographical references and index.
Identifiers: LCCN 2016008408 (print) | LCCN 2016009341 (ebook) | ISBN 9781498526418 (cloth : alkaline paper) | ISBN 9781498526425 (Electronic)
Subjects: LCSH: Church and minorities—United States—Case studies. | Multiculturalism—Religious aspects—Christianity—Case studies. | Protestant churches—United States—Case studies.
Classification: LCC BR517 .Z47 2016 (print) | LCC BR517 (ebook) | DDC 280/.4080973—dc23 LC record available at http://lccn.loc.gov/2016008408

∞™ The paper used in this publication meets the minimum requirements of American National Standard for Information Sciences Permanence of Paper for Printed Library Materials, ANSI/NISO Z39.48-1992.

Printed in the United States of America

Dedicated to my parents, and Rev. Keith Harris, and Rev. Heidi Weatherford, gentle soldiers leading the march toward justice and peace.

Contents

Acknowledgments	ix
Introduction: The Struggle for Inclusive Multicultural U.S. Protestant Congregations	1
1 Intersectionality: A Feminist Interpretive Methodology	11
Part I: Developing a Theory of Intersectionality in Inclusive Churches	19
2 Afrocentricism, Color-Blind Ideology, and Intersectionality : Three Models of Internal Christian Congregational Cohesion	21
3 Christian Evangelical Internal Discussions of the 2008 Presidential Election	39
4 An Africana Feminist Critique of American Christian Antiwar (Dis)engagements	47
Part II: Becoming Inclusive in a Presbyterian Church : 1940 to 1980	69
5 A Presbyterian Campus Church: 1940 to 1953	71
6 McKinley, UPCUSA, and Civil Rights: 1953 to 1967	99
7 Growing Pains of a Social Justice Ministry: 1968 to 1973	113
8 The Dawning of More Light Presbyterianism at McKinley	123
Conclusion: New Definitions of the Inclusive Social Justice Church and a Theory of Intentional Institutional Social Change	131
Appendix: PC(USA) Precursors and McKinley Memorial Presbyterian Church Timeline 1789–1983, Including Sources.	143
References	157
Index	169
About the Author	173

Acknowledgments

I am deeply grateful to the many friends and family who have supported me as I have sought a deeper understanding of issues of diversity and inclusion in church settings. First of all, my parents and grandparents, aunts and uncles were my first role models of service, dedication, sacrifice, and benevolence. I remember playing at age eight in my grandparents' living room as my grandfather sat at his desk, doing his work as treasurer of the Friendship Baptist Church in Memphis, Tennessee.

Years later, when I was in high school, as I practiced aerobics moves in my parents' family room—preparing to lead a joint Bible study and fitness class for women at our church, I can now still glimpse the image of my dad, our church's treasurer, always present, but also consistently engaged in service, dutifully reconciling the checkbook for Westlane Christian Church. I remember the many missionaries who would come through Westlane to share stories of their service in inner city neighborhoods, and to collect goods to take back to families in need, and how my mom would make up our bunk beds and provide hospitality during their visits. I remember how happy my dad would become at "get acquainted time" after church—the excitement of welcoming new visitors and catching up with friends fueled by the Taylor Bakery cakes my mom would have picked up the night before. These images of my childhood church experiences probably sound like those of many readers from religious backgrounds, but the difference for me, an African-American woman, is that during my formative years at Westlane Christian Church, half of our ministers were white and half were African-American. Given the itinerant nature of ministers' appointments, the elders and effective leadership of my church, was diverse. The minister who most influenced me, who served during my middle and high school years when I became serious about Bible study and came to embrace a progressive theology, was an African American man who was married to a white woman. So, growing up at Westlane, I both enjoyed a diverse and inclusive church environment, while at the same time holding an awareness that our wider non-denominational Christian sect was largely white.

Despite this knowledge, I was still shocked when I arrived to Anderson College in Anderson, Indiana, surrounded by music, happy young women in my dorm, and embedded in my new found love—my lifelong love affair with my discipline of sociology, to learn in Dr. Scott Chesebro's sociology of religion class, that "11:00 a.m. is the most segregated hour in America" (quote attributed to Dr. M. L. King, Jr.). We looked at the data on this fact. And I was shaken.

Skipping forward past my graduate school years and the beginning of my career, once tenured, I began to find my sociological imagination focused on the issue of diversity and multiculturalism in churches once again. Due to some personal trials, I sought refuge in a familiar place, in multicultural church communities, and as I visited several, I found wide variation in how each "did church" and also in how each "did diversity." Some were more intentional in how they handled issues of diversity, and some were less so. I noticed that some seemed to have leaders and members who thought through and carried out a more intersectional understanding of their members' and attenders' social identities. So I began taking notes and analyzing what I was seeing.

In those many years of visiting churches, taking and transcribing fieldnotes, and getting to know members, I was the recipient of amazing hospitality. For three of the churches in this study, I became deeply embedded, serving on committees, participating in and/or leading Bible studies, teaching Sunday School, and attending *weekly*, or even at times finding myself at church multiple times in a week. To protect the confidentiality of the many generous individuals I have encountered, I have chosen to focus on formal interviews, sermon content and the more public representations (e.g., weekly bulletins, websites, newsletters, and artwork) of the churches I examined. And the church I attended during most of the data collection in the churches aside from McKinley Presbyterian, is not included in this analysis. And though I attend McKinley, my analysis is focused on its past. I profoundly appreciate each person who shared their stories with me, and their lives throughout the decade that I gathered data. The countless pastors, elders, deacons, and everyday people who counseled and inspired me hold a special place in my heart.

Colleagues and friends have provided succor and sustenance. Our Africana women's writing group at the University of Illinois offers good cheer, reassurance, and help to me as well collectively navigate the meaning and experiences of serving as women of color in the Midwest at an institution where the challenges of diversity and inclusion often weigh on us heavily. I especially appreciate my dear colleagues, Ruby Mendenhall, and Merle Bowen, Faye V. Harrison, and Karen Flynn. We have many allies in the fight for justice and peace. Several have paved the way for me, including Antoinette Burton, Sarah Lubienski, Tim Liao, Asef Bayat, Menah Pratt Clark, Reginald Alston, Craig Koslofsky, and our late colleagues, Nancy Abelmann and Jorge Chapa. Our former Provost Ilesanmi Adesida also provided generous advice to me, and institutional support to my department. My former heads of the Department of Sociology, Tim Liao, Anna-Maria Marshall, and Antoinette Burton provided research support and teaching releases to give me more time to gather and analyze my ethnographies. And all of my colleagues, my former students who are now working as professional sociologists, and our awesome current students at Illinois have been so gracious as to hear and comment on my nascent ideas as this work has matured over time. I must make special recognition to Dr. Sandra Weissinger, Dr. Torrence Sparkman, Dr. Courtney Cuthbertson, and Dr. Jovaughn Barnard, former students, of whom I am immensely proud. I also recognize colleagues in my professional networks, Paul Gundani, Michael West, and Osageyfo Sekou. And I thank Kathryn Tafelski, acquisitions editor at Lexington Books, for her faith in me and my project.

I was fortunate enough to have a manuscript workshop in May 2015. I thank our campus Research Board for funding. I have so much gratitude for the workshop participants, Tim Liao, Ruby Mendenhall, Keith Harris, Molly Bentsen, and Joanna Perez. And the reviewers who traveled to campus, Marj DeVault and Mary Romero, gave of their time, humor, creativity, and labor to help me to strengthen my manuscript. I am forever grateful.

My copy-editor, Molly Bentsen has been a constant source of encouragement and assistance. Even during a very difficult time, Molly worked diligently to format the text and to help me express myself in the best way possible. Thank you, Molly!

I extend a special thanks to Heidi Weatherford and Keith Harris, pastors at McKinley Presbyterian Church, to Dave Bechtel, McKinley's historian, to Bill Capel, who supplied the beautiful inclusiveness window image for the book's cover, and to additional members who kindly gave of their time and talent, relaying to me their recollections of church history and sharing with me their experiences: Marlyn Rhinehart, Jane Cain, Jill Mulder and Paula Wells, Tom Seals, Linda and Grear Kimmel, Andrea and Elaine Mitchell-Miller, and Judi Geistlinger.

I gratefully acknowledge Professor Jean Belkhir, editor of the journal *Race, Gender, and Class*, and Professor David Downing, editor of the journal *Works and Days*. Portions of chapters two and three originally appeared in *Race, Gender, and Class*, and portions of chapter four originally appeared in *Works and Days*. Both are printed with permission. I also acknowledge the Presbyterian Historical Society, Philadelphia, Pennsylvania for granting me permission to print the Presbyterian Family Connection—Family Tree of Presbyterian Denominations.

Finally, I express thanks to my children who inspire me to create a better world for them and for those who follow.

Introduction

The Struggle for Inclusive Multicultural U.S. Protestant Congregations

"34,000 Black Churches Break Ties With Presbyterian Church USA"
—National Black Church Initiative Statement, March 2015

In 2015, the General Assembly of the Presbyterian Church (USA) voted to allow pastors discretion in performing same-sex marriage. This long and hard-won fight began within this mainstream denomination in 1974, at the unofficial start of the movement of More Light Presbyterians[1] (MLP). During a session of the denomination's 1974 General Assembly,[2] David Sindt held up a sign: "Is anyone else out there gay?" Having felt the call to ministry, Sindt had struggled for more than a decade to have his spiritual call recognized by the wider Presbyterian Church.[3] He established the Presbyterian Gay Caucus in 1974, which would later seed MLP. From 1974, the incremental moves in the Presbyterian Church (PCUSA)—from first embracing LGBTIQ[4] members and ordaining LGBTIQ elders and clergy all the way to, more than forty years later, approving the performance of same-sex marriage ceremonies by PCUSA clergy—chart for us a route to greater diversity and inclusion in the denomination. But contestation and conflict both within the PCUSA and from external forces are crucial aspects of the movement toward inclusivity among the denomination and its congregations.

The opening quote refers to the response of the National Black Church Initiative (NBCI) to the PCUSA's 2015 stance on gay marriage (Evans 2015). In a press release dated March 29, 2015, the NBCI states that as "a faith based coalition of 34,000 churches comprised of fifteen denominations and 15.7 million African Americans, [NBCI] has broken fellowship with Presbyterian Church (USA) following its recent vote to approve same sex marriage." The NBCI charges the PCUSA with "deliberately [changing] the Word of God and [its] interpretation of holy marriage between one man and one woman" (nationalblackchurch.com).

Given that 3.6 percent of the American adult population is gay, the purported 15.7 million African Americans claimed by the NBCI could include about 500,000 (out or closeted) LGBTIQ individuals, and likely many allies.[5] The reality of intersectional identities is not attended to by NBCI's stance. On the other hand, while mainstream denominations are beginning to embrace LGBTIQ members, they often are not culturally welcoming to underrepresented racial and ethnic minority (URM) groups. Some denominations may have a congregation that is predominantly African American or Latina/Latino in urban areas, but most congregations have 1 percent or fewer URM members. Gender hierarchies still do not affirm women's contributions in many churches. Additionally, financial resources correlate with power and hierarchy in church settings, as in other complex organization. Sitting at the intersections of race, class, gender/heterogender, and sexuality, women of color who are LGBTIQ struggle to find a place in communities of faith. As one African American church member I interviewed stated, "As a Christian, you can either be black and not gay, or gay and not black" (Andrea Miller interview, 2015).

While LGBTQI individuals may struggle to find their place in church, many congregations struggle for survival. Confidence in religion is at an all-time low in the United States, especially among white Protestant Americans.[6] And church affiliation among mainline Protestants has dropped 3.4 percent, while the number of Americans with no religious affiliation has grown by 6.7 percent (2007–2014)—they now outpace mainline Protestants.[7] One important potential source of new members in mainstream churches is expansion from predominantly white middle class or working class populations as they embrace greater levels of demographic diversity and inclusion. On the basis of five case studies conducted over a decade, in this book I examine the struggle for racial, gender, and sexuality inclusivity[8] in multiracial/multiethnic congregations in the United States.

Social institutions in the United States reproduce heteronormativity and the dominant racial, gender, and class structures of capitalist society (Marx 1867, Du Bois 1946, Foucault 1973, Omi and Winant 1986, Smith 1987, Collins 1990, Ingraham 1996, Bonilla-Silva 1997).[9] Examining postsecondary education, we see that despite deep commitment and herculean efforts on the part of many, together with dedication of significant resources, African American youth still struggle with the standardized testing that continues to serve as a gatekeeper to accessing the most prestigious collegiate institutions.[10] African American infants, even those birthed by middle class women, are *still* twice as likely to die within the first year of life relative to white American infants (Loggins and Andrade 2014).[11] Queer youth still must go through the stage of questioning their sexuality, because heteronormativity demands that if American youth are not heterosexual, they are still considered deviant.[12] Though levels of physical activity decline during adolescence into adulthood for all youth, declines are more marked among girls during middle school and beyond (Lam and McHale 2015); many drop out of sports[13] in middle school to maintain the falsehoods of hegemonic femininity (Slater and Tiggeman 2010, Zapico et al. 2012), which puts them on the path to weight imbalance, eating disorders, and a lifetime of struggle with body and even sense of self. These dominant structures of racism, class, sexism, and heteronormativity are challenged by the agency of parents and guardians who want better for those in their care; by youngsters who insist that, despite external forces, they must be free to simply be; and by the many movements connected to authentic representations of selves and cultures.

In this book, I examine Christian communities, characterized as volitional communities, that to varying degrees intentionally strive for gender inclusivity, to build multiracial alliances, and to create welcoming environments to sexual minorities; some attempt a more passive route that requires marginalized members to adapt and assimilate to old ways of doing church, and others work to undo dominant structural edifices and carry out an equitable and new ethic. I examine this phenomenon in a least likely, yet perhaps most likely, space[14] —in mainline and evangelical Christian churches. A religious congregation can be a natural crucible in which to observe how previously segregated volitional communities struggle to become more inclusive.

During a decade of research conducting case studies of five multicultural Protestant churches in sites across the United States, I have observed both incremental moves toward inclusiveness and strategies employed to accomplish long-term changes. With an interpretive approach, I explore these centers of worship and theorize the conditions under which progressive social change occurs in some U.S. Protestant congregations. Understanding the daily practices of change and entrenchment in Protestant congregations and the intentional work to replace dominating structures with liberating ones may provide keys to creating multicultural, antiracist, feminist, and sexually inclusive volitional communities more broadly.

Making a significant advance toward inclusion requires change in the underlying social structures of racism, sexism, heteronormativity, class, and other marginalizing influences. In order to isolate this phenomenon, I have conducted fieldwork and archival research in one African American and four multiracial U.S. churches. Different from a university or other public institution in which members are legally required to support diversity and related values, volitional communities may provide a best-case scenario for how, motivated by higher ideals, members may find ways to create inclusive communities. My research has a broad empirical base, encompassing five sites: site 1 is a largely African American urban megachurch in the Midwest; site 2 is a large midwestern multiracial/multicultural church; site 3 is a large urban multiracial/multicultural church in the eastern United States; site 4 is a small, suburban midwestern multiracial church; and site 5 is an inclusive midwestern college town church.

INTERSECTIONALITY, STRUCTURE, AND AGENCY IN VOLUNTARY ASSOCIATIONS

Colleagues in social science and humanities disciplines have bravely fought the intellectual battles that cleared the way for twenty-first-century theorizing to elucidate not only the lofty concepts of structuration (Giddens 1971, 1973, 1976, 1979, 1984) and situated agency (Foucault 1991), but also the realities in multiracial spaces that hold practices of "racism without racists" (Bonilla-Silva 2003), the intersectional matrix of domination (Lorde 1984; Collins 1990, 1998, 2006), heteronormativity (Ingraham 1996), gender as social structure (Guillaumin 1995, Risman 2004), and multicultural alliances (Robnett 1997, Jung 2006, Jung and Kwon 2013). Building on these works, I analyze the social organization of especially race, gender, and sexuality in churches—as antecedents to change in those communities, and as either seriously impeding change or facilitating change in keeping with the values of peace, justice, and equity. In fact, I examine what I believe to be a convergence leading to *both* entrenchment and change. Just as race, class, gender, and sexuality structures occur simultaneously, the realities of conservative values, ideas, and ideologies coexist with those possibilities that are progressive in the volitional communities under examination.

Why do the conservative and progressive coexist? They coexist because of the meaning that members attach to both tradition and change. For example, the long-official, now-retired pseudo–Indian chief sports mascot at the University of Illinois is held fast with white knuckles by some alumni and their legacy. Of course, there may be those who are entirely insensitive to the racial overtones of this contested symbol. But most supporters likely "honor the chief" because the totem symbolizes their families' connections with the Urbana campus. It is, for them, a reminder of happy days from the past and verification of their entitlement to the good things of life. *"I went to Illinois; I worked hard; I graduated, and this is why I deserve...."* For others, *protesting* the "chief" mascot is the way we began to feel a connection to a space that would attempt to marginalize us.[15] As others have argued, poor conditions, marginality, and oppression are the stimuli to change (Marx 1867).[16] And as social analysts have observed, attempts to effect change are often the antecedents to further entrenchment (e.g., Collins 1990, 1998, 2006).

Similarly, in the congregations I study, intersecting structures of domination are produced and reproduced continually. This work aims to illuminate the intersecting racial, gender, sexuality, and class structures embedded in African American and multiracial churches in the United States and to help explain multiracial churches' struggles with the issue of diversity and inclusion. By working intersectionally, I aim to contribute to the many literatures cited above. Questions this research addresses follow: How are churches attempting to build cohesion in the face of racial and ethnic differences? How do members resolve political differences and agree on collective political activities and activism? If the social structures of American society, of which Christian churches are a microcosm, reflect intersections of race, class, gender, and sexuality, how have some progressive churches been able to approach and overcome challenges with regard to gender, sexuality, and race? In what ways might a theory of organizational change in these settings be generalized to other volitional communities and beyond?

A SUSTAINED ETHNOGRAPHY OF MULTIRACIAL CONGREGATIONS

I conducted case studies of congregations to understand what is happening in churches in regards to race, gender, class, and sexuality. I explore the churches' outreach efforts and examine evidence of ways that various groups have been excluded. I examine the underlying social systems in these voluntary associations and how they have changed over time. I explore discursive structures that facilitate communication and cooperation among groups with competing interests in these institutions. I unveil the new structures promoting multicultural alliances that have been built over time and expose the costs of building inclusivity. Africana feminism (Zerai 2014), Black feminist thought (Collins 1990), and the intersectional framework (Crenshaw 1989, Uttal and Cuadraz 1999, Zerai 2000a, Zerai and Banks 2002a) are conversant with the sociological literature addressing multiculturalism (Lentin and Titley 2011) and religion in the United States (see Zerai 2010a, 2010b, 2011). These are appropriate perspectives from which to study multiculturalism and religion because they are uniquely poised to examine multiplicative and intersecting privileges and inequities emanating from the structures of race, class, gender, and sexuality.

In this work, I seek to enlighten our understandings of the problems of race/racism, gender/sexism, and sexuality/heterosexism for inclusivity in volitional public settings. The intersectional methodological approach for this study is, of course, heavily influenced by the ethnographic method (Emerson, Fretz, and Shaw 2011, Creswell 2013), feminist ethnography (Smith 1987, DeVault 1999), and institutional ethnography (Smith 2005, Diamond 1992). I use a four-step research design that entails (a) identifying relevant contextual factors by perusing church documents, media sources, government policy concerning diversity in public institutions, and the history of inclusion in surrounding institutions; (b) presenting members' words about their experiences; (c) contextualizing members' descriptions to trace the intricate connection between biography and history (Mills 1959); and (d) linking local events and specific outcomes to more distant social forces and more remote consequences (Smith 2005, DeVault 1999).

Congregations

To aid the reader, I have chosen descriptors for the five congregations (four are anonymous; the fifth has agreed to be named[17]). I examine the first three congregations (sites 1, 2, and 3) in chapters 2 and 3. I explore sites 1, 3, and 4 in chapter 4. And I focus on site 5 in chapters 5 through 8. I refer to sites sometimes by number and other times by descriptor:

Site 1. "Afrocentric and Evangelical" megachurch in a Midwest city
Site 2. "Friendliest Place in College Town USA," a large Midwest church
Site 3. "Oasis in the City," a large urban church in the East
Site 4. "Leadership and Congregation at Odds," a small church in a Midwest suburb
Site 5. "Inclusive Presbyterian Church" (McKinley Memorial Presbyterian Church), a medium-size congregation in a Midwest college town

IMPLICATIONS FOR POLICY

Apropos to step 3 of my research design (see chapter 1 for a fuller description), I not only analyze congregations to identify their successes and failures in becoming more inclusive in regards to race, sexuality, and gender, but I also identify the indicators of those successes and failures so that shapers of other public and private institutions might apply the lessons these congregations have learned in order to make their contexts more diverse. "Race, class and gender intersectionality's analytic power manifests itself in its ability to help us change society. Remaining true to the promise of intersectional analysis means using it to liberate, because this is where its genesis lies. To stop short of liberatory activity is to stop short of duly and properly utilizing the race/class/gender framework" (Zerai 2000a, 212). Some volitional institutions beyond churches that may benefit directly from my case studies include but are not limited to service organizations (such as YMCAs, YWCAs, Boys and Girls Clubs), feminist political organizations and support groups, antiracist political and social organizations, activist groups promoting marriage equality, and campus social organizations promoting diversity.

Guided by current theories of race, racism, heteronormativity, gender, inclusion, and impediments to multiracial/ethnic/gender/sexuality organizational success that are salient to contemporary sociologists, I evaluate churches' moves toward inclusivity. I utilize the case studies of African American and multiracial congregations, volitional organizations whose stated mission is inclusion, in order to contribute to current understandings of multiracial/multicultural organizational change and power relations. It is my hope that this work has the potential to contribute powerfully to social policy. If we can begin to identify the keys to accomplishing the goal of inclusivity in multiracial/multicultural volitional communities, perhaps we can affect a sea change in the lives of those who continue to languish on the margins. A theory of change in volitional communities is timely and offers an important intervention for democratic institutions.

A MAP OF MY ETHNOGRAPHIC JOURNEY

In chapter 1, "Intersectionality: A Feminist Interpretive Methodology," I discuss my qualitative research design. In qualitative research, it is important to delineate theoretical framework, study design, and data analysis plan. I provide details of my research design because I believe my methodology, informed by *Black feminist thought* (Collins 1990, 2000) and *dehumanizing discourse* (Zerai and Banks 2002a), to be distinctive in the context of sociological studies of race and Christianity.

Part I includes chapters 2 through 4. In chapter 2, "Afrocentrism, Color-Blind Ideology, and Intersectionality: Three Models of Internal Christian Congregational Cohesion," I discuss multiracial/multicultural congregations as the fastest-growing type of large Christian church in the United States today (Yancey 2003). I compare three churches to explore diverse meanings of church unity in the context of American color-blind society (Bonilla-Silva 2007), distinguished by coherence around black liberation theology, practicing color-blind approaches, and maintaining multiracial/multicultural identity through a more intersectional approach to unity. The availability of resources for understanding, expressing, and mediating racial identity shapes the choices of members in these church settings concerning addressing cultural difference. And local context, educational attainment, and exposure of ministers and parishioners, all indicators of social isolation (as discussed by Emerson and Smith 2000), contribute to this resource base. Despite efforts to build internal cohesion, some analysts may continue to criticize multiracial churches' slow progress toward eradicating color-blind racism.

In chapters 3 and 4 I examine two tests for multiracial congregations, composed of potentially explosive conflicts within American politics and the ways churches under examination handle volatility. In chapter 3, "Christian Evangelical Internal Discussions of the 2008 Presidential Election," I examine the phenomenon of active participation by Christian denominations and individual parishes in the public debate and outcomes during the 2008 election season. As expected, there were clear divergences in political opinion among churchgoers that appeared to divide by race. In this chapter, I complicate commonly held views of evangelical Christians in American society by conducting a comparative analysis of three of the churches in my sample regarding the extent to which they address issues of political salience, and in particular the 2008 election, a watershed event in the American political landscape. In this first of two "volatility" tests that I explore, I ask the following: Is the election discussed in the pulpit or in smaller group discussions among church members? What political activities were encouraged and carried out in the name of religious values and dictates?

The three congregations I compared differed widely in their views on the best presidential candidate and how to handle differences of political opinion within the church. The operation of the intersection of race, class, gender, and nation in American society helps to explain these distinctions.

In chapter 4, "An Africana Feminist Critique of American Christian Antiwar (Dis)engagements," I discuss the strong tradition of antiwar sentiment within various Protestant African American and progressive white churches. Considering the role of patriarchy, I conduct a comparative analysis of predominantly African American Protestant evangelical ministers and their parishioners as contrasted with white Protestant evangelical leaders and multiracial members in regards to the extent to which they address U.S. aggression in the Middle East in their words and actions. In this second of two "volatility" tests, I ask how church members with varying views on the U.S. wars in Iraq and Afghanistan worked through their differences of opinion. Are these issues taken up in the pulpit or smaller group discussions among church members? What humanitarian, activist, or other activities are encouraged and carried out in the name of religious values and dictates? An analysis that considers the intersection of race, class, and gender within American society helps to answer these questions. I explore nationally representative data sets and opinion polls to establish variations on views according to respondents' race and religious denomination. And I use the intersectional perspective to conduct participant observation analysis in a sample of black and multiracial churches, along with analyzing transcripts of sermons and conducting content analysis of church websites and weekly bulletins.

In Part II, "The Struggle for Inclusivity in a Presbyterian Church: 1940–1980," which includes chapters 5 through 8, I provide a social history of cohesion around creating an inclusive environment supportive of lesbian, gay, bisexual, transgender, intersex, questioning/queer (LGBTIQ) communities and concomitant racial, gender, and class diversity in a Presbyterian college-town congregation. The More Light Presbyterians–affiliated church examined in chapters 5 through 8 is well known for its support and sustenance of a movement among "More Light Presbyterians . . . to work for the full participation of lesbian, gay, bisexual and transgender people of faith in the life, ministry and witness of the

Presbyterian Church (USA)" (MLP.org). For over 15 years, McKinley Memorial Presbyterian Church has been headed by vibrant and engaging LBGTIQ and LGBTIQ-allied leaders. It is the struggle to become an open, welcoming, and multiracial congregation, a struggle that has embroiled the Presbyterian Church (USA) denomination since the 1940s, which is the focus of Part II. Examining internal church documents, conducting oral history interviews with current and past staff and older members, and examining documentation of the church's board of elders and the national PCUSA denomination provide primary source material to craft a social history of this Presbyterian congregation located within a multidimensional context that includes the history of race, gender, and sexuality in America; the history of race, gender and sexuality in the Midwest; and churches as a microcosm of that history that weave an intricate tapestry.

Finally, in my conclusion, "New Definitions of the Multicultural/Social Justice Church and a Theory of Intentional Institutional Social Change," I revisit my examination of the ways in which the multiplicative, simultaneous, relational operation of race, class, gender, and sexuality structures shows up in volitional communities. I argue that the daily practices of change and entrenchment in volitional communities and the arduous intentional work to overcome dominant structures with liberatory ones is the key to creating institutions that are multicultural, multiracial, nonheteronormative, feminist, and nonhierarchical. The push and pull are both necessary. A volitional community full of yes-women and yes-men who agree with every change, where there is never any pushback, is a false community. Real change can happen only if members voice their differences of opinion, challenge one another, and work to create common solutions that ultimately uphold ethics of accountability, inclusivity, caring, and other values agreed upon by the group.

NOTES

1. More Light Presbyterians work for the full inclusion of lesbian, gay, bisexual, transgender, intersex, and queer/questioning members into the life and ministry of the PCUSA.

2. The General Assembly meeting (then annual, now held every other year) is an international convention of a representative body of thousands of teaching and ruling elders of the PCUSA, where policy is decided, trainings are held, and networking happens among regional presbyteries and leaders of the denomination.

3. For over a decade until his death in 1986.

4. LGBIT is short for lesbian, gay, bisexual, transgender, intersex, and queer/questioning.

5. According to a recent Gallup poll, in 2012–14, 3.6 percent of adults nationwide considered themselves lesbian, gay, bisexual, or transgender (http://www.gallup.com/poll/182051/san-francisco-metro-area-ranks-highest-lgbt-percent-age.aspx?utm_source=Social%20Issues&utm_medium=newsfeed&utm_campaign=tiles).

6. The percentage of Americans with "quite a lot" or "a great deal" of confidence in organized religion fell to 42 percent in 2014 (http://www.gallup.com/poll/183674/

confidence-religion-new-low-not-among-catholics.aspx?utm_source=church%20affiliation&utm_medium=search&utm_campaign=tiles).

7. These data from the Pew Research Center for Religion and Public Life compare 2007 to 2014 (http://www.pewforum.org/2015/05/12/americas-changing-religious-landscape).

8. Inclusivity is deliberately broad. However, in this book, I focus on intersectionalities of race, gender, and sexuality.

9. This familiar premise can be found in the ideas of many notable in the field of sociology, including Karl Marx (1867), WEB DuBois (1903, 1946), Michel Foucault (1965, 1973), Michael Omi and Howard Winant (1986), Dorothy Smith (1987, 1999, 2005), Patricia Hill Collins (1990), Chrys Ingraham (1994), and numerous other insurgent scholars.

10. Nichols et al. (2012) analyze student achievement as measured by the National Assessment for Education Progress (NAEP) in reading and math and find that high-stakes testing accountability pressure does not increase student achievement. The correlations between math standardized testing and math achievement, for example are lowest among African American children (Nichols et al. 2012). So results of standardized tests, known for cultural biases that undermine scores of African American students by and large (Williams 1983) tell us the least about the actual educational *achievement* of these students. Yet standardized testing is a requirement (and serves as a gatekeeper) to enter private and specialized secondary schools and undergraduate and graduate institutions (Grodsky et al. 2008).

11. According to the National Vital Statistics Report (Murphy, Xu, and Kochanek 2012), the 2010 U.S. infant mortality rate is 5.37 for whites and 11.02 for African Americans. These differences persist or increase across regions of the United States (Hirai et al. 2014).

12. Though the American Psychiatric Association repudiates conversation therapy, lawmakers now must adjudicate bans, given the prevalence of attempts to convert homosexuality. Further, youth risk behavior surveys indicate that "all sexual minority youths [SMY] had increased odds of suicide ideation," and most "had increased odds of suicide attempts," compared to non-SMY (Stone et al. 2014, 262).

13. The literature further provides numerous examples of girls who want to be physically active, but who are provided limited opportunities to engage in desirable activities (e.g., Burk and Shinew 2013; Clark 2012).

14. Churches are a "least likely" space historically to struggle for inclusion, due to their histories in supporting slavery and segregation (Emerson and Smith 2000). But churches today may become a "most likely" space, as mainline congregations tend to promote a social gospel in line with an ethic of diversity and inclusion.

15. For decades, the University of Illinois campus has been embroiled in contestation over the racist depiction of American Indian groups by its fictive sports mascot. The NCAA sanctioned UIUC, and in 2007 the university finally retired its former mascot. Students, faculty, staff, and community members participated in numerous protests against the use of the mascot before it was retired. Tremendous backlash occurred against supporters of and participants in various forms of campus protest. Still today, merchants, alumni, and some students persist in reproducing and displaying the offensive image (Cohen 2013).

16. Of course the social movements literature has offered an analysis of the complex resources and processes that contribute to social change. Here I simply acknowledge the dialectical relationship between the discontent, agency, and oppression of marginalized groups that facilitates their desire for social change, and the enjoyment of advantages that create inertia on the part of dominant group members who may, when feeling threatened, move to consolidate their privilege.

17. McKinley Memorial Presbyterian Church has agreed to be named in this book, as approved by the University of Illinois Institutional Review Board.

ONE

Intersectionality

A Feminist Interpretive Methodology

To theorize the conditions under which progressive social change occurs in U.S. Protestant congregations, I analyze race, gender, class, and sexuality structures in these religious communities, as both promoting and preventing progress. In this chapter I provide more details of the case studies of the five U.S. churches in which I analyze the daily practices of change and entrenchment and the hard work of replacing dominant structures with liberating ones.

In exploring discursive structures that facilitate communication and collaboration among groups with competing interests in these institutions, I ask (as noted before): What are the new structures that promote multicultural cooperation that have been created, and what have been the costs of building inclusivity? Africana and Black feminist thought and intersectionality offer exceptional advantages for examining intersecting privileges and inequities. Past congregational studies have provided knowledge about race, class, gender, and sexuality as simple discrete binaries or dyads: for example, examinations of racial harmony and discord among congregants (Emerson and Smith 2000, Emerson and Kim 2003, Yancey 2003, Marti 2012, Matsuoka 1998); reports of the prevalence of monoracial church realities (Chaves 2004, Chaves and Anderson 2008, Barnes 2009, Emerson and Smith 2000, Priest 2007, Edwards 2008); work on race and political activism within churches (Beyerlein and Chaves 2003, McRoberts 2003, Findlay 1993); analyses in which churches are welcoming or not to LGBTIQ congregants (Fillmore 2010, Sumerau 2013); and multiple treatises on the role of women in churches (Dodson 1988, Barnett 1989, Higginbotham 1993, Wiggins 2005, Gilkes 2001; Prelinger 1992). However, they fail to explain how *structures* intersect and result in multiplicative advantages to some groups but relational privilege and oppression to others. Utilizing analytic and methodological approaches offered by Africana feminism, I deliver the first sustained intersectional ethnography of multiracial congregations that also considers influences of gender and sexuality, with the hope to enlighten our understandings of the problem and possibilities of race/gender/sexuality and inclusivity in volitional public settings.

Progress toward multicultural society requires successful multicultural, multiracial, integrated organizations that are not ordered solely by class, gender, sexuality, or other dominant social categories. For example, the activism of multicultural political organizations has resulted in many successful legal challenges and changes in policy. These legal contests have resulted in substantial improvements in the lives of many and have provided access to American institutions such as civil service, public education, public goods and services, and the like. Their accomplishments have been a necessary but insufficient advance toward equity and access and eventual true inclusiveness for marginalized groups. So, for example, due to Section 504 or the Rehabilitation Act, students with disabilities have academic accommodations at many public and private universities, but efforts to truly integrate students with disabilities into the social life of campuses are deficient (Buckley-Shaklee 2009). As we continue to fight legal battles for equity and access (e.g., in the vein of *San Antonio Independent School District v. Rodriguez* [1973], in which the Supreme Court ruled that Rodriguez did not sufficiently prove that education is a fundamental right) in this era of "postracial" democracy, it is important to explore other fronts in which strategic strides toward democratic ideals result in better inclusiveness overtime.[1]

I examine whether and how some churches defy the dominant racial, class, gender, and sexuality structures in the United States, and analyze their efforts to build volitional communities that intentionally practice undoing these edifices and building something equitable and new. I believe religious environments to be a natural laboratory in which to observe how previously segregated volitional communities become more inclusive. Absent this intentionality and strategic moves to break down racial, gender, class, and other dominant structures within these institutions, multiracial/multicultural churches will continue to struggle with the issue of diversity. Some questions I pose: What incremental moves toward inclusiveness do we observe, and what strategies seem to work to accomplish long-term and standing changes toward inclusiveness? What lessons can be learned from these previously intransigent sites about institutional change in volitional communities?

In order to get at this phenomenon of diversity and inclusivity, I have conducted unobtrusive ethnographies of five churches in multiple sites over a ten-year period. With this interpretive approach, I have sought to understand the experiences of the church going and church belonging and have unveiled the underlying social systems of these congregations by attending and sometime participating in services and events, writing field notes, analyzing websites and sermon content, and examining the histories, leadership, and decision-making structures of these places of worship.

METHODOLOGICAL CONSIDERATIONS

In qualitative research, it is important to delineate the theoretical framework, study design, and data analysis plan. Here I provide more details because I believe my methodology to be unique in the context of sociological studies of race and Christianity. The theoretical framework combines the lens used to understand the phenomenon under study and the methodological approach. The lens used in this book is Africana feminism (Zerai 2014), which encompasses Black feminist thought (Collins 1990, 2000) and other diaspora feminisms (e.g., Mama 2002). These Africana women–centered perspectives and their analytic and methodological vehicle, intersectionality (Crenshaw 1989, 1995; Uttal and Cuádraz 1999; Zerai and Banks 2002a), provide a critique of multiculturalism and religion (see Zerai 2010b, 2011). These are appropriate perspectives from which to study multiculturalism and religion because they are poised to examine multiplicative and intersecting privileges and inequities emanating from the structures of race, class, gender, and sexuality. Africana feminist perspectives, and intersectionality in particular, hold promise. These analytic and methodological approaches may shed light on the intractable problem of race in Christian churches that may help to further elucidate issues of race in other public settings.

The methodological approaches for this book are ethnography (Emerson, Fretz, and Shaw 2011; Creswell 2013; Taylor and Bogdan 1998), feminist ethnography (DeVault 1999), and institutional ethnography (Smith 1987, 1999, 2005; DeVault 1999; Diamond 1992). Below I elucidate some important features of an intersectional analysis. Details of the discrete thematic analyses and congregational makeup of those on which I focus are provided in subsequent chapters.

The Promise of Intersectional Analyses

The value of intersectionality is its practical use in liberation struggles. Race, class, and gender analysis cannot remain at the descriptive level. Intersectionality is an analytic tool (Uttal and Cuádraz 1999). As I have argued elsewhere, the precursors and practitioners of this framework give us practical suggestions for ways that race, class, and gender analysis should promote social change with research. Activist research agendas are important because they make scholarly work relevant to the people in the trenches, making social change happen (Kuumba 2002). Below I summarize ways to accomplish an intersectional praxis.

In work on scholar-activism, I argue that *academic work should have practical relevance* (Zerai 2000a). We should make the relevance of our research explicit throughout the research process, by writing to and presenting to multiple audiences. The potential audiences for this manuscript vary. It is my hope that analysts with an interest in the study of race and racism will find the book to offer interesting and useful case studies in the practice of multicultural inclusiveness. Queer theorists may find the book useful. Scholars, practitioners, and students of intersectionality who want to move beyond using the tool as just a framework to building intersectional theory and methods will find this manuscript to offer numerous robust examples. An important audience is the plethora of multiracial churches that are struggling to stay afloat, that are in crisis due to conflict within their congregations, or that seek to expand already healthy-sized memberships and are looking for practical strategies for building internal cohesion among parishioners and are open to making structural changes to become more inclusive. Finally, students of sociology of religion; race, class, and gender intersectionality; race and racism; and racial and ethnic relations are a crucial audience.

I further argue that *intersectional analyses should connect local struggles to the international humanist struggle* (Zerai 2000a). When possible, international connections should be made to local struggles so that we can see how local struggles are tied to the worldwide humanist movement.[2] The interconnections between gender oppression, racism, heterosexism, and class oppression—including imperialism as interlocking systems of domination on a world scale—should be basic to this analysis. Notable activists worldwide have devoted their lives to the world humanist struggle. Women recognized as activist intersectional thinkers, such as Anna Julia Cooper, Ida Wells Barnett, Amy J. Garvey, and Rose Brewer, continually reminded the male-centered "humanists" in their midst of the importance of integrating a gendered analysis. Audre Lorde and others worked to integrate an analysis of heterosexism in liberatory scholarship and activism in order to promote a more comprehensive notion of humanism. In examining defiance against intersecting structures of domination within the five churches, I pay attention to internationalism and to the social locations of marginalized groups.

Intersectionality examines relational difference (Zerai 2000a, Zerai and Banks 2002a, Zerai 2014). Audre Lorde showed how examining difference as relational is an effective method for carrying out intersectional analysis. Elsa Barkley Brown has written a brilliant essay using jazz and quilting as metaphors for the way to understand intersectionality (1992). I utilize this tool to uncover the operation of power in congregational spaces that serve to privilege certain members at the expenses of excluded and relegated members.

Subjugated knowledges are the starting point of intersectional analysis (Zerai 2002a). The beauty of my analysis is that it is written in the tradition of liberating feminisms, creating knowledge by women *for women* (Smith 1999). Looking from the margin inward (Smith 1999), I seek to bring African American women, LGBTIQ groups, and individuals with insufficient access to financial resources out of the shadows and to place their experiences at the forefront. Many top-down perspectives on churches exist in religious practitioner literature, studies of pastors and executive leaders in denominations, and the like. I carry out a methodology in which I pay explicit attention to those hangers-on who are more likely to eventually leave church settings so that we can learn how to better serve marginalized groups and to better center their needs, perspectives, gifts, and lives in the work of the church. If churches can learn to reach out and to integrate subjugated knowledges, perhaps this may provide needed input instructive to other voluntary associations that seek to be inclusive.

Activism is an important vantage point from which to understand domination and resistance (Zerai 2000a). Activists need not be only beneficiaries of intersectional research. Scholars should avail themselves of the tremendous resources that activists offer. Their day-to-day work in the trenches provides a perspective on domination and resistance that is still woefully missing (Kuumba 2002, Cohen 1999). Activists abound in four of the five churches studied. Their strategies to affect social change in both their communities and wider society, as well as within their own church cultures, are instructive to analysts' understandings of organizational change.

Scholarly rigor is important to activist agendas. Multiple precursors and practitioners of intersectionality exemplify the importance of scholarly rigor. From Ida B. Wells Barnett's statistical analysis of lynching that provided evidence of the magnitude of this social problem to Anna Julia Cooper's pursuit of doctoral studies that were completed in her 60s to Cheikh Anta Diop's three dissertations, only one of which was finally accepted but all of which were eventually published; from W.E.B. Du Bois's copious documentation of the plight of Africana peoples in his hundreds of publications to Zora Neal Hurston's very serious interest in anthropology[3] —precursors of race, class, and gender intersectional work provided stellar examples of the importance of scholarly rigor to activist agendas. Practitioners of race, class, and gender analysis understand that their scholarly work has repercussions for more than themselves and that they have a special responsibility to provide the facts, figures, and analyses that might one day make the difference between liberation and its alternative (Zerai 2000a).

The Research Design

I conducted ethnographies of congregations to understand what is happening in churches in regards to race, gender, class, and sexuality specifically. What are the racial, gender, class, and sexuality structures in these voluntary associations? What discursive structures exist to facilitate communication and cooperation among groups with competing interests in these institutions? What are the new structures that promote inclusivity that have been built over time? What have been the costs of building these inclusive structures?

I utilize the tool of intersectionality to examine the ways in which social phenomena mutually construct one another (Zerai and Banks 2002a). In identifying structural forces at work, it is not enough to identify that racism has an impact; intersectional researchers look for how racism experienced is supplemented or supported by sexism or classism (Zerai and Banks 2002a). And finally, I not only analyze congregational shifts to becoming more inclusive in regards to race, sexuality, and gender, but I also identify the most important factors that brought about that shift so that shapers of other public institutions might apply the lessons these congregations have learned in order to make their contexts more diverse.

Settings and Variation in Denominations

According to the Pew Research Center (2015), 71 percent of Americans are Christian by tradition, family, or denomination. In the United States, 25 percent of Americans are evangelical Protestant, 15 percent are mainline Protestant, and 6.5 percent are "historically Black Protestant." The Pew Research Center's designation of these categories may obscure the experiences of African Americans who participate in inclusive Protestant churches that are racially and ethnically diverse. In this manuscript, I explore the rituals and experiences of Protestants in two evangelical and three mainline congregations representing five distinct denominations. Site 1, the "Afrocentric" megachurch in a Midwest city is mainline (Congregationalist); Site 2, the "Friendliest Place in College Town USA," a large Midwest church, is evangelical (Pentecostal); Site 3, "Oasis in the City," a large urban church in the East, is mainline (Reformed); Site 4, "Leadership and Congregation at Odds," a small church in a Midwest suburb, is evangelical (nondenominational); and Site 5, the medium-size "Inclusive Presbyterian Church" in a Midwest college town, is mainline (Presbyterian).

The racial makeup of mainline and evangelical Protestants is relevant. The majority in both groups are white: 76 percent of evangelical Protestants (6 percent are African American) and 86 percent of mainline Protestants (3 percent are African American). As may be expected, in "Historically Black" Protestant denominations, 94 percent are African American (2 percent are white).[4]

Mainline and evangelical Protestants differ in their religious theology and political ideology, though there is variation within each group (there are conservative mainline Protestants and liberal evangelicals). To articulate ideal types of the two: evangelical denominations promote literal interpretations of the Bible, whereas mainline denominations challenge literal interpretations. Evangelicals embrace the idea of a "personal relationship" with Jesus and focus on spiritual aspects of Christianity, including their personal spiritual growth, and outward manifestations of their spirituality, such as speaking in tongues. Mainline denominations instead embrace the social gospel and manifest their religiosity in doing good works that better conditions for those in greatest need.

Historically Black Protestant denominations, a cross-section of the dimensions of mainline and evangelical Christianity, are characterized as interpreting the Bible literally, yet their Democratic political leanings are consistent with the social gospel. Though African American Protestants may promote some literal interpretations of the Bible, particularly in regards to marriage and even sometimes the role of women, they argue for alternative understandings of slavery.[5] The issue of inclusion is very relevant among these three groupings, as racial minorities are underrepresented in evangelical denominations and even more severely underrepresented in mainline denominations.

And given their literal interpretations of the Bible, historical Black Protestant denominations are likely to exclude out and/or "unrepentant"[6] LGBTIQ members and especially feminist women. Taken together, evangelical and historically African American denominations comprise the majority of Protestants. Despite their numerical majority, they perceive themselves to be countercultural[7]—they (at least ideally—in their view) do not participate in aspects of American culture that they believe are inconsistent with their beliefs. Examples for adults include choosing not to watch R-rated movies or drink alcoholic beverages; they also may take pride in waiting until being married (to someone of the opposite sex) to engage in sexual intercourse.[8] Belongingness is deepened by their collective decisions and support of one another around a countercultural identity. They cohere around a shared sense of mission in a world they believe is much in need of their message. They pattern themselves after their interpretations of the apostle Paul, who once was lost but now is found. As such, they hold a special place for those who eschew the old life "of sin" and resolve to come into the fold and become countercultural. They see themselves as speaking truth to power in the world.

Evangelicals have been labeled by mainline Christians as "anti-intellectual" (as they promote literal interpretations of the Bible).[9] Though they promote the idea that the Bible is the inerrant word of God, I found them to also be deeply studious—which troubles the notion of anti-intellectualism. Many devout evangelical members who interpret the Bible literally attend churches with very active small groups and Bible study groups where members engage, often weekly, in collective exegesis of biblical passages (which may range from a sermon-type explanation of passages by a minister to smaller meetings in which members read passages and explore their meanings). Labeling evangelicals as "anti-intellectual" is inaccurate; I found the evangelical churches to include higher percentages of members engaged in serious study of the Bible. A better descriptor is that with regards to biblical interpretation they are anti-liberal, or anti-post-enlightenment intellectual traditions.

In subsequent chapters, I describe each church setting and identify descriptive themes. In part I (chapters 2 through 4), I discuss social cohesion in churches, political activism, and the influence of racial strife in contemporary churches. In part II (chapters 5 through 8), I examine the history of an inclusive church to identify moments of honest disagreement, discussion, and change leading to eventual positive structural transformation. The intersectional Africana feminist interpretive method permeates these analyses.

NOTES

1. I realize that I am emphasizing the positive here. I will discuss the challenges for each of these congregations in respective chapters. I believe that emphasizing the positive has merit because the successes of these churches were hard won, and I choose to celebrate them!

2. "PanHumanism . . . refers to the kinship of the dispossessed and the degraded and . . . this includes but goes beyond people of African descent" (Gbadegesin 1996, 225).

3. Though Hurston was trained in English, taught writing, and is well known as a novelist, she obtained fellowships to study anthropology in order to do background research for her powerful novels.

4. Source: http://www.pewforum.org/religious-landscape-study/racial-and-ethnic-composition.

5. See Swartley (1983) for a discussion of disparate interpretations of biblical passages concerning slavery, women, and marriage. Also see Emerson and Smith (2000) for a discussion of southern Christians' biblical justifications for slavery and a summary of "Evangelical Racial Thought and Practice, 1700-1964" (pp. 21–49), including a Baptist minister's treatise, "Why Christians Should Support Slavery" (p. 35).

6. Many evangelicals believe their congregations *are* welcoming to LGBTIQ members, but they believe that LGBTIQ identities are sinful. They welcome, as they define them, "sinners" of all kinds—so long as sinners are willing to repent and change.

7. The idea and value of being countercultural was repeated on multiple occasions in the various evangelical church services I attended over the past decade. The literature also speaks to this issue (Sanders 1996; Paris 1982).

8. In fact, at one of the evangelical churches I examined, some members took pride in never even kissing their betrothed before marriage.

9. See Giberson and Stephens 2011; Enns 2013.

Part I

Developing a Theory of Intersectionality in Inclusive Churches

As I noted in chapter 1, cohesion is important to churches' countercultural identity, especially in evangelical settings. However, belongingness in heteronormative, androcentric, and predominantly white churches is an impediment to inclusion of LGBTIQ members and women and to racial/ethnic diversity. In part I, I examine the first four congregations: two multiracial evangelical settings and two mainline settings—one largely African American and the other diverse. Chapter 2 begins my exposition of the theory of intersectionality in intentional communities. I explain why an inclusive church must be a social justice–oriented church, not only holding social justice among its ideals, but also integrating principles of social justice in its organizational structure (intentionally communicating its social justice values, of which inclusiveness is a part, in the way it carries out its work on a daily basis). After arguing that the inclusive church must cohere around ideas of social justice, intentionally embued values in its organizational structure, and engage in political education and discussion around those values, I move to chapters 3 and 4 on politics and political engagement. There I examine how churches fare in the context of two volatility tests especially relevant and appropriate for intersectional analysis—the 2008 election period and race for the Democratic Party presidential nomination, and the U.S. engagement in Iraq and Afghanistan and antiwar activism. In the first case, this potential conflict between supporters of Barack Obama and of Hillary Clinton exposed divergent racial and gender cleavages within churches. In the second, church members and leadership sometimes differed in their views concerning antiwar activism. In part I, the theory developed by observing sites 1 through 4 is that inclusive churches need four components: (a) a nonhierarchical structure, at minimum one that intentionally includes men and women and multiple racial/ethnic groups; (b) a social justice orientation; (c) political education to expose majority members to the realities of the social injustices impacting marginalized groups and to create a shared vocabulary to discuss these realities; and (d) unique expressions of cultural identity that honor majority and minority groups within a congregation. Part II allows me to further develop this theory by examining the incremental moves in a mainline church toward becoming more inclusive over a forty-year period. I return to this theory of intersectionality in intentional communities in the book's conclusion.

TWO

Afrocentricism, Color-Blind Ideology, and Intersectionality

Three Models of Internal Christian Congregational Cohesion

Some argue that multiracial/multicultural congregations are the fastest-growing type of large Christian church in the United States today (Yancey 2003). According to Michael Emerson, "Large Protestant churches (more than 1,000 regular attenders) are more than twice as likely to be multiracial now compared to a decade ago" (2010). In this chapter, I compare three churches to explore diverse meanings of church unity in the context of American "color-blind" society. Site 1 ("Afrocentric and Evangelical") is an African American Protestant evangelical megachurch distinguished by its practice of black liberation theology. Site 2 ("Friendliest Place in College Town USA") is evangelical Protestant, with predominantly white leadership but a multiracial flock. Site 3 ("Oasis in the City") is an inclusive, urban, multiracial church with multiracial pastoral staff with both an evangelical and social justice mission. I conducted unobtrusive participant observation analysis in these churches in the U.S. Midwest and East along with analyzing their web presence (newsletters and websites), sermon transcripts, and weekly bulletins.

HERMENEUTICAL DIFFERENCES

Divergence in political and social views among African American Christians (Gay and Lynxwiler 2010) and between white and African American evangelicals has been well documented (Emerson and Smith

2000, Gay and Lynxwiler 2010, Zerai 2010b). Yet the growth of multiracial and evangelical churches has joined together groups with some of the most contradictory political and social viewpoints. Consider the following excerpt from Christian scripture:

> After fasting 40 days and enduring temptation from Satan and prevailing, the beginning of Jesus' public ministry commences. He enters the temple in Nazareth, opens a scroll and reads from Isaiah 61, "The Spirit of the Lord is on me, because he has anointed me to preach good news to the poor. He has sent me to proclaim freedom for the prisoners and recovery of sight for the blind, to release the oppressed, to proclaim the year of the Lord's favor" (Luke 4:18-19). He continues, "Today this scripture is fulfilled in your hearing" (Luke 4:21b). And "all . . . were amazed" (Luke 4:22a). [NIV]

Reminiscent of President Abraham Lincoln's words during his second inaugural address (1863), one theologian who teaches in South Africa says, "Two groups can read the same text and interpret it differently. It is not the text, but the *hermeneutics*, the *understanding* of the text that is under contention" (Professor Paul Gundani, personal communication 2010; emphasis added). For many marginalized individuals, the scriptural text is an endorsement of the *social gospel*. It underlies an understanding of Jesus as a radical, as one who sought to make foundational changes in humans' relationships to God and to each other. Conversely, for many white conservative Christians, this text references the proclamation of Jesus's reign over our hearts and the coming of a spiritual kingdom, rather than proclaiming a call to change living conditions, to recognize and eradicate racism, sexism, class exploitation, and the other social ills that marginalized folk "complain about."[1]

In this chapter, I look at different understandings of church cohesion and how congregations attempt to accomplish church growth in the context of so-called color-blind society. I argue that this herculean task cannot succeed without an acknowledgment of the racism hidden away in the edifice of American capitalism. And recognition of "polite" racism, or "color-blind" racism (Bonilla-Silva 1997), requires multiracial churches to work to dismantle racism both overt and "polite" racism at the core of the Americanism reproduced in their religious institutions. So my ultimate question is, *How do we get there from here?* How are churches attempting to build cohesion, reduce systemic racism from the American volitional institutions of Christianity, and forge ahead to a unified destiny?

BACKGROUND

In groundbreaking work in the field of sociology of religion, Emerson and Smith (2000) argue that white American evangelical churchgoers are likely to blame African Americans themselves for a lack of educational and economic advancement and that white conservative Christians' cultural toolkit not only promotes antistructural explanations for inequality but actually perpetuates economic inequality in American society. They explain that within the white evangelicals' worldview, "the racialized system itself is not directly challenged. What is challenged is the treatment of individuals within the system" (p. 75). Therefore, "individualism and defective personal relationships were constants in evangelicals' assessment of the race problem" (p. 75). And "by not seeing the structures that impact on individual initiative, such as access to quality education, segregated neighborhoods that concentrate the already higher black poverty rate and lead to further social problems, and other forms of discrimination, the structures are allowed to continue unimpeded" (p. 75). Because white evangelicals who hold the "individualist perspective 'rarely if ever examine the innumerable cases in which black people do act on the Protestant ethic and still remain at the bottom of the social ladder' (West 1993, 13, as quoted in Emerson and Smith 2000), they continue to champion effort, and in so doing, 'inadvertently contribute' (West 1993, 13, as quoted in Emerson and Smith 2000) to racialization" (in Emerson and Smith 2000, 112). Racial inequality is thus perpetuated in the following actions: voting an antistructuralist viewpoint, keeping exclusive social practices, and socializing new generations of white evangelicals into this individualistic perspective.

African American evangelicals, on the other hand, are more likely to embrace structural explanations for social inequality (Emerson and Smith 2000). The joining together of religious Americans within the Christian church has not encompassed viewpoints so diverse since the time of slavery, when white land-owning slaveholders required their enslaved African workers to attend church with them (Emerson and Smith 2000). During the antebellum period, landowners and African workers also derived divergent messages from the biblical texts read in church. Landowners viewed the spiritually focused utterances regarding prosperity as evidence that their lifestyle was ordained by God. But enslaved African workers and their families understood the biblical text and the hymns differently, as a pathway to freedom, both spiritual and temporal (Emerson and Smith 2000). Is a similar phenomenon going on in multicultural settings today?

Current research on church growth shows that internal conflict among congregation members may be the most important factor impeding growth (Willimon 2007, 14). With so many congregations concerned with promoting internal cohesion, how are large African American–led and multiracial churches able to maintain internal unity despite observed differences among congregants? To begin to address the cohesion of large congregations from a sociological perspective, I examine three church settings that exemplify unique pathways to interchurch unity: a Midwest Afrocentric mainline church,[2] a Midwest college-town evangelical congregation, and a liberal church in the East. Site 1 allows me to examine cohesion among African American evangelical Christians. Site 2 allows me to address multiracial church unity in a setting that includes members with conflicting political opinions—where Democrats and Republicans worship together amid a volatile political environment on the national landscape.[3] And site 3 allows me to consider a liberal fellowship that recognizes multiple oppressions but in which individual members might believe that one system of inequality supersedes another in importance. I describe the three church settings, analyze the ways they intentionally and perhaps unintentionally create internal social cohesion, evaluate their relative successes and failures at achieving unity in light of current theories of congregational growth and color-blind racism, and recommend future research on internal social cohesion. This work makes potentially significant contributions to social scientific studies of multiracialism and interracial cooperation.

METHODS

I have examined a wealth of data from the three sites, including ethnographic field notes and website content. I analyze sermon notes and bulletins from sites 1 and 3 collected less systematically than from site 2. However, I analyze weekly e-newsletter content for over 100 issues from site 1, spanning August 2008 through January 2015, and weekly sermon notes from site 2, spanning January 2004 through June 2010. I analyze the content of twenty-five monthly newsletters from site 3, spanning January 2008 through January 2014.

Site 1: "Afrocentric and Evangelical"

Site 1 is a resource-rich and vibrant congregation known for its exuberant worship and Afrocentric flair, located in a large midwestern city. Its lead pastor and his long-time predecessor are both recognized for their social activism and charismatic preaching. The church has thousands of members, and they are active; there are thirty-nine ministries concerning deepening faith, twenty focused on transforming the community, and thirteen charged with increasing awareness of the African diaspora. The music ministry alone is quite extensive: there are six choirs, including a women's chorus and sanctuary choir with over 200 members each, a men's chorus, and children's choirs. The African American male senior pastor has excellent academic training, having earned a graduate degree at an Ivy League institution and a doctoral degree at a progressive school of theology. And the eight highly educated individuals who compose the pastoral staff, seven of them women, all have degrees in relevant fields, with most earning a master's of divinity and one a doctoral degree.

In this site, both heavily centered on African culture and strongly evangelical, many of the ministries, choirs, and programs have names derivative of African languages. African American heritage is spotlighted in every aspect of this church's program, worship celebration, community outreach, and ministry.

Site 1 has an extensive web presence. Their website includes pictures and biographies of pastoral staff and a pictorial telling of the history and values of the church, its many ministries, and resources available to the congregation. The website also includes information on assistance with educational and job placement, complete with an online application process, offered to individuals who have been members of the church for at least one year.

The digital outreach for site 1 includes not only their extensive website, but also weekly e-newsletters mailed to members and anyone else who requests them, a Facebook page, and a Twitter account. Online media present a clear focus on faith in Christ, family values, Africana-centered ethos, and maintaining a connection to the black community.

When attending services at site 1, I was struck by the African clothing that adorns the choir and many members. I myself am a middle-aged African American woman, and I don dreadlocks. Whenever I attend this upper-middle-class church, I feel very much at home, a rare experience since I grew up in a conservative multiracial church in the Midwest, and I currently live in a small midwestern city. It was a breath of fresh air to look around and see women whose body type was similar to mine, whose clothing choices I identified with, and whose hair was styled naturally (without processed chemicals or wig attachments). The age of most attenders also captured my attention. I have two children, and when they attended with me, we were one of few families with youth sitting near the front on the main floor. The average age of individuals attending and singing in the choir appeared to be sixty-five to seventy, especially at the earlier of the two Sunday services. I suspect that the retired long-time lead pastor drew in members mostly from his age cohort and that their presence has persisted. Site 1 has a much older membership than site 2 (which appeals to college students and young families) or site 3 (which encompasses young urban professionals and other urban singles and couples).

Site 2: "The Friendliest Place in College Town USA"

Site 2 is located in a prominent college town in the Midwest. Though situated on the edge of town, it is proximate to graduate student campus housing and a newly sprawling suburban neighborhood. Its growth has been precipitous. Over 1,000 people attend weekly worship services. Though the sermon is the same in every service, the four services cater to the different social groups who attend. An early Sunday morning service held in the sanctuary appeals to elderly members; more traditional hymns are sung, and there is no extensive use of percussion instruments. Two services held near a café offer continental breakfast, coffee, and other beverages in a laid-back atmosphere that appeals to many families with younger children and to college students. The later-morning service in the sanctuary offers a traditional setting but modern-day praise music of the type played on the local contemporary Christian music station, complete with drum set, synthesizer, and electric guitars. The same upbeat music is played in the café services. It is common for congregants to stand during the times of singing praises to clap their hands, sing expressively, and even sometimes dance. Shouts of "hallelujah!" are common in these charismatic worship services, which feel like a rock concert. People hold their hands up in praise and often just sway to the beautifully moving music. The contemporary services also include a sophisticated media display, with projections of song lyrics and sermon points. The straightforward sermon messages deal with practical issues in life. Series examples include such topics as family, marriage, the miracle of Jesus's birth, God's grace, and the seven deadly sins.

Finally, a video, often humorous, is typically shown during announcement time to round out the services' multimedia presentations. My favorite was a video styled as a public service announcement one year when the church was preparing for Easter. The announcer politely asks members to park off-site to accommodate the expected crowd. The announcer further asks members to obey the lot attendants and park where they are told. So we then see a shot of harried attendants trying to direct the traffic, and drivers are behaving erratically, ignoring the frustrated attendants. Next, someone dressed in a bunny costume walks out onto the lot, baseball bat in hand, slowly and deliberately hitting his hand with the bat, threatening various drivers. "Park where you are told, or the Easter Bunny will get you!" says the voiceover. The video incited laughter, as the "announcement" videos often did. This example really gives a good sense of the College Town site: very relaxed, sometimes corny, with staff and members endeavoring to make people feel comfortable and welcome.

Though this site is located in a college town, the educational attainment of its pastoral staff does not match the other two sites, and it is clear that formal education is less important than a perceived anointing of the Holy Spirit. Though education levels of staff members are not listed on the site 2 website, I know that most of the pastors have at least a bachelor's degree, because they would occasionally discuss their undergraduate encounters during services in an effort to relate to the university students, faculty, and staff in the audience. Two of the pastoral staff had master's degrees.

Site 3: "Welcoming, Artistic, and Inclusive"

The site I describe as an "Oasis in the City" is located in the artistic, academic, and commercial center of a highly visible Eastern city. Jazz, gospel, traditional church music, Broadway show tunes, liturgical dance, and drama enliven this bold, committed congregation and pastoral staff. It appears that there is something for everyone with a progressive politic and liberal Christian theology at site 3. In one newsletter entry, for example, a member congratulates the congregation, saying she is writing to "highlight the achievements of my Asian brothers and sisters in the congregation" ("Oasis in the City" newsletter, February 2010, p. 2). And she notes "we have an Asian American on the Consistory [elected church leaders]" as being another accomplishment (p. 2). An Asian American visitor to the church who is Unitarian Universalist and atheist was so enthralled by the welcome she received that she admits considering "defecting" to site 3 even though it is unabashedly Christian. Weekly activities include gatherings of several special-interest groups, including men of color, women over forty, a sexual identity/coming-out group, a fellowship for homeless LGBTIQ youth, an African dance class, and a dance prayer meeting. The church distributes meals to the neighborhood homeless after Sunday services, makes low-cost groceries available to members and neighborhood residents, has a clothing ministry, and provides social work services weekly. Site 3 celebrates Pride Week annually with a Pride Sunday service, participation and a float in the city's Pride March, and preparatory events to raise money for the float. In anticipation of Pride Sunday, their website provides inspiration for participating in the march: "We're going to leave [site 3] after worship, and bring justice to the streets!"

The weekly music offerings vary from contemporary gospel and hip hop to classical orchestral movements. A gospel choir sings two Sundays during most months, and a professional choir[4] sings the other Sundays. A summer choir sings during July and August. The director of music notes that the professional choir is diverse in their offerings; within one month, for example, they presented excerpts from *Jesus Christ, Superstar*, offered an composition by the church's organist, featured a soprano soloist who masterfully delivered an operatic piece, and performed John Coltrane's *Love Supreme*.

During the time of my ethnographic research, the staff at the "Oasis in the City" site 3 church included a vivacious African American female senior minister, two or three associate ministers (one white and the other one or two African American), an African American director of the gospel choir, a white director of music, and a white director of the arts center, among other positions. One of the associate ministers is an African American woman, and the executive minister is gay. The executive minister explains his role at site 3 as working to create collaborations with groups that are aligned with the church's mission. The sexual identity/coming out program hosted by the "Oasis in the City" church is supported by funds the executive minister was able to secure from the United Way. He has also been involved in pastoral care, preaching and worship, bolstering the security of the church grounds, overseeing building improvements, and working with accountants to streamline the church's finances.

The various governing and visionary bodies of the church reflect diversity. Site 3's vision team is "a commissioned cross section of our congregation" charged with writing a five-year plan for the church. The consistory is a grouping of elders and deacons that sees to the congregation's spiritual growth and day-to-day concerns. Both bodies, as well as the staff and congregation at large, include a healthy representation of African Americans, progressive whites, and Latinos as well as a cross-sectional representation of sexualities. I have not, however, been able to get as good a sense of the representation of economically marginalized individuals in the governing and decision-making bodies of site 3. One newsletter entry is authored by a man who first came to site 3 when he was homeless. He writes about how he was welcomed by the members and eventually served on the consistory. But my sense has been that the church's leadership is largely highly credentialed[5] individuals, due at least in part to the vast and rich human resources of the city and neighborhood in which site 3 is situated. In chapter 1, I argue that this site characterizes an intersectional organization because minority women are part of the top leadership, the organization is somewhat nonhierarchical, a shared leadership structure is evident, and members and leaders utilize an integrated analysis (that recognizes multiple and intersecting spheres of domination within American society) in order to promote strategies to effectively include all members.[6]

REAL COHESION OR COLOR-BLIND IDEOLOGY?

Race and racism are among the most divisive issues in American society. And as a microcosm of society, multiracial churches are bound to be plagued by racial issues. In studying the three church sites, I uncover three different types of social cohesion. Black liberation theology offered a unifying worldview to participants in site 1, where racial issues were less salient because the congregation is 99 percent Africana (a majority are urban African American, though members with Afro-Caribbean, continental African, and multiracial backgrounds may be present). Routes to internal cohesion in the two multiracial churches diverge, however. I argue that site 2 practices a color-blind approach and site 3 an intersectional approach.

Eduardo Bonilla-Silva (2003) discusses the operation of color-blind racism. He notes that *all* individuals are affected by racial ideology (p. 76) and that although "blacks have historically internalized white supremacist standards . . . [and] . . . stereotypes developed by whites about blacks, nevertheless, groups subordinated along racial, class or gender lines develop oppositional views . . . and even counter cultures" (p. 77). In Bonilla-Silva's view, social actors either accept the status quo and practice the dominant racial ideology in their daily lives or they develop oppositional views. These views and the countercultures that grow out of them create a possibility for real social change. Bonilla-Silva explains that "when the counter views of oppressed groups match periods of deep sociopolitical crisis and social upheaval, they can produce fundamental breaks and even revolutionary transformations in the social structure" (p. 77).

In the following section, I examine data sources from each site in order to examine their challenges and acquiescence to color-blind racism. To the extent that there are challenges to dominant racial ideology, members in the settings will be involved with creating oppositional views to color-blind racism and countercultures. And where color-blind racism is evident, there will be acquiescence to the status quo, practice of the dominant racial ideology, and no effort to change the racial hierarchy in American society.

Challenges to Color-Blind Racism in Site 1 ("Afrocentric and Evangelical")

The Afrocentric urban church regularly challenged and worked to eradicate color-blind racism and its co-conspirator, classism. Its typical church bulletin has abundant entries concerning social justice. For example, an article entitled "To Do Justice" mentions the congregation's connection to ministries in the African Diaspora, including in Venezuela. The author discusses the liberation struggles of Afro-Venezuelans, with systemic analysis evidenced by statements referring to past attempts to "privatize oil, electricity, schools, food production and other industries; thereby draining Venezuela of natural resources and leave large segments of Venezuelans without proper education" ("Afrocentric and Evangelical" newsletter, June 2010, p. 12). An article titled "Witness for Justice" criticizes labor and sex traffickers who brought young women and girls to South Africa to work in brothels or on the street in anticipation of tourists expected for the 2010 World Cup. In the e-mailed announcements that same week, the senior pastor asks readers to pray for those living in the Gulf of Mexico who are impacted by the oil spill and to "pray for . . . the protection of all persons impacted by environmental injustices" ("Afrocentric and Evangelical" e-newsletter, June 24, 2010). A link encouraging readers to donate to Haiti relief efforts had been in the e-newsletters since the country's earthquake in January 2010. The "Afrocentric and Evangelical" church's focus on social justice, its systemic analysis of Venezuela and the visibility of Venezuelans of African ancestry, and its concern with the plight of girls and young women in South Africa and with environmental justice in the Gulf and Haiti are all indicators of a social justice-oriented counterculture.

Site 1's efforts to defy color-blind racism were also evident in their articulation of core beliefs. Along with evangelical statements of commitment to worshipping God, to eternal salvation, and to biblical education, core beliefs state that the pastors and membership are committed to "liberation, restoration, and to working towards economic parity." In their mission statement they affirm that they are "called to be agents of liberation not only for the oppressed, but for all of God's family." They further address racism and class exploitation specifically, proclaiming in their mission statement that they are "agents of change for God who is not pleased with America's economic mal-distribution! W.E.B. Du Bois indicated that the problem in the 20th century was going to be the problem of the color line. He was absolutely correct. Our job as servants of God is to address that problem and eradicate it in the name of Him who came for the whole world" ("Afrocentric and Evangelical" website). Their viewpoints opposing dominant racial and class ideology are evident in these statements.

Importantly, in the Afrocentric and Evangelical church, the ministries level a sound attack against color-blind racism. As noted before, there are twenty ministries devoted to "the transformation of our Community," including, for example, the Church in Society (CIS) ministry. They describe their mission "to identify and to address political justice and social justice issues which have particularly adverse effects on the lives and rights of persons of African descent in the United States and throughout the Diaspora." They further explain that "CIS has both a political justice and a social justice committee which are committed to educating and empowering the individual and the community to improve our world by standing up to injustice" ("Afrocentric and Evangelical" website). Their work includes direct social protest: "whether it is a march on City Hall protesting inadequate housing, conducting town hall meetings on poverty and welfare reform, hosting forums for voters from the congregation and community, so they may ask questions to potential candidates' seeking political offices, CIS is committed to educating and empowering the community," according to their website.

Another site 1 example is the "People's Legal Ministry" (a pseudonym), whose mission is "to advance civil and human rights through education and Christian activism." Quoting Micah 6:8— "He has told you, O mortal, what is good; and what does the Lord require of you but to do justice, and to love kindness, and to walk humbly with your God?"—they explain that "we assist the Church and its members in meeting the call to be agents of liberation for the oppressed and all of God's children" ("Afrocentric and Evangelical" website). Social change is at the forefront of their agenda. Working "in service to the Church and the surrounding community, the [People's Legal Ministry] seeks to: Advance civil and human rights [and] improve the administration of justice by increasing the participation of African Americans throughout the legal system."

A final example of the many social justice-oriented ministries in site 1 is the "Economic Viability" ministry (again, a pseudonym). Their purpose statement follows: "The [Economic Viability] ministry exists to implement programs and services that promote the spiritual, economic, social and political viability of the African American community. In so doing, the [Economic Viability] ministry seeks to create close ties between [site 1] church and the communities it serves. This will be accomplished through constant exchange and activism within our communities, around those issues that most affect African Americans" ("Afrocentric and Evangelical" website). Again, members in this site are clearly oriented toward an African-centered counterculture and a commitment to values that oppose racism and promote progressive social change.

Lack of Recognition of Color-Blind Racism in Site 2, the "Friendliest Place in College Town USA"[7]

Members in site 2, the college-town church, desired to be antiracist, I believe, but evidence of color-blind racism is clear there. Emerson and Smith succinctly describe the features of white evangelical churchgoers' views in regards to race in America, arguing that they by and large do not believe that racial inequality is a real problem, do not adopt structural understandings of society, and embrace individualist explanations of social phenomena, and thus blame African Americans for their lack of educational and economic advancement, inadvertently perpetuating economic inequality in American society. Eduardo Bonilla-Silva explains that "racial ideology provides basic rules of engagement for racial actors" that he refers to as "racial etiquette" (2003, 75). The lack of structural analysis, individualist explanations, and racial etiquette are characteristics of the white evangelical worldview and of discussions of race in site 2.

Dominant racial ideology is evident in the "Friendliest Place in College Town USA" sermon content, focus for leadership development, and structure. Systemic racial inequality was not addressed in sermons over a six-year period. Race is hardly ever mentioned directly, except for statements that the church is multiracial. (And publicly available documents normally refer to the congregation as multi*cultural* or multi*ethnic*, due to racial etiquette.) The occasional nod to race is a quote of Dr. Martin Luther King, Jr. added to the sermon notes. When the race issue (never referred to as *racism*) is addressed directly, it is referred to as an individual problem with a spiritual solution. For example, only one sermon within a twenty-eight-month span focused on "diversity." Others focused on some aspect of the evangelical message.[8] In the sermon on diversity—"People Matter Most: Breaking Through Tolerance and Embracing Love"—the importance of accepting and loving one another is stressed. The sermon is described as a summary of "Bible thoughts on diversity." The lesson is basically that Jesus surrounded himself with a diverse group of people and that God is love, so followers of Jesus in present times should show God's love to everyone, including people from a diversity of backgrounds. Though the audience is multiracial, it appears that the sermon is addressed to whites. And further, in the sermon, diversity is expanded to include global diversity. The importance of spreading the gospel of Jesus Christ to other nations is addressed, as shown in this quote from the sermon notes: "The blood of Jesus *'purchased for God people from every tribe and language and people and nation'*" (Revelations 5:9). So site 2 lacks progressive social change, an acknowledgment of racism, and even a forum in which whites in the church can come to appreciate the "divergent views" and "experiences" of African Americans as a subordinate social group in the "racial order" (Bonilla-Silva 2003, 77).

Another example emanating from the teaching content in site 2 is leadership development efforts. In upcoming seminary studies and other training promoted by site 2, the church focuses on preparing evangelists to save the spiritually lost through mission work and through building or contributing as staff in American or missionary churches. The aim of these studies is personal spiritual growth and evangelism, not addressing the social gospel.

The pastoral staff of site 2 is not very racially diverse. Pointedly, the senior pastor is white, the executive pastor is white, the music director is white, and two youth pastors are white. Only the college pastor and the francophone pastor are nonwhite. There are no African American pastors on the staff, though at least 30 percent of the congregation is black. The replacement of previous African American youth and music directors, who served as volunteers, with salaried white personnel was met with some consternation by black and multiracial families within the congregation.

The most painful example of color-blind racism is shown in the handling of changes in the church's music director. When the African American–led choir was replaced by a multicultural worship team led by a newly hired white music pastor, former choir members, many of whom were African American, were instructed by the lead pastor "not to talk about" the dismissal of the choir director or the dispersal of the choir. The new choir director incorporated contemporary Christian music into the church's repertoire, both some of the music that the former choir sang and new music marketed to a growing demand for choices that can appeal to younger and multiracial churchgoers. So when potentially interracial conflict was repeatedly squelched,[9] some middle class African

American and multiracial families found this use of color-blind ideology offensive and eventually chose to leave site 2.

Site 3's Intersectional Approach to Acknowledging and Challenging Color-Blind Racism

In site 3, the progressive "Oasis in the City," members worked tirelessly to acknowledge and challenge color-blind racism and to make sexism, classism, and heterosexism visible. For example, site 3 hosted and staffed a home-grown leadership conference with core concepts including "Leading with Vision for a Just Society; Deepening Understanding of Systemic Injustice and Congregational Ethics as Speaking Truth to Power; [and] Leading Social Justice in the Public Square" ("Oasis in the City" website). The planners noted that "worship will focus on congregations as instruments for justice," and in describing "Leading Social Justice in the Public Square," they noted that "participants will be challenged to explore their skills in the service of the common good, to explore a focus for social engagement, to apply a personal ethic to view social justice from the perspective of the marginalized and to create an action plan that gathers information, organizes resources and people and uses power constructively to create change." The goal of the conference was to develop leaders for a just society. And the "Site 3 Project," a group that largely consists of members of site 3, takes this mission a step further: "The [Site 3] Project prepares ethical leaders for a just society in which all people are welcomed and endowed with equal rights." It "unites progressive leaders who are ready for a revolutionary and prophetic way of using power, information, and resources to act . . . to heal the human family . . . and to advocate for those on the margins: the poor, the working poor, the diminishing middle class, and those who are marginalized by racial and gender/sexual injustice" ("Oasis in the City" executive summary, p. 2).

Another example of challenging the invisibility of race appeared in site 3's February 2010 newsletter. Haiti is referred to, but not just as a place that needs donations after a devastating earthquake. The country's history is retold by the senior minister. It is a story resplendent with references to race—that Haiti's land was "tilled by kidnapped Africans," that the country abolished slavery in 1794, ushering in the first "Black independence" after the Atlantic slave trade era in 1804. She further relates how Jean Baptiste Point Du Sable, "a free black man, the son of . . . an African-born slave mother," founded Chicago. She asks, "How will they speak about this Haitian American hero?" Returning her gaze to American shores, the senior minister muses about how race is storied in the U.S., and she notes that "race . . . become[s] a sign for who is privileged and who is not, who holds power and who does not" ("Oasis in the City" newsletter, February 2010, p. 1). Her words are underscored by a call to cancel Haiti's debt to U.S. financial institutions and to provide the country struggling with the aftereffects of the earthquake with grants to rebuild, not loans. A congratulatory post was added to the senior minister's blog when the U.S. Treasury Department announced its support for debt cancellation and agreement to provide grants, not debilitating loans, to Haiti.

Values opposing color-blind racism and other injustices are found in the social justice actions promoted by site 3 staff. For an event titled "Phone Call for Social Justice," congregants were invited to brunch and to participate in making calls from a phone bank in support of GENDA (the Gender Expression Non-Discrimination Act), "which would make it illegal in their state to discriminate on the basis of gender identity and expression in the areas of employment, housing, public accommodations, education and credit" ("Oasis in the City" newsletter, March 2010, p. 5).

Another mark of oppositional culture in site 3 was the call for direct social protest by members promoting the "Peace Tax." An article promoting the tax appeared in the church's newsletter. The author writes, "I live much of my life celebrating peace . . . and yet part of what I earn actually funds, through my taxes, war. About half our government spending is military related. I will not do this anymore. I do not want my tax money supporting war in any form" ("Oasis in the City" newsletter, May 2010, p. 3). And the National War Tax Resisters Coordinating Committee in New York organized an event at site 3 in which they showed the film *Death and Taxes* and described ways they withdraw financial support from military spending by the U.S.

Congruous with a commitment to social action is the congregation's support of multiracial church growth in South Africa. The senior minister discusses her work with the Uniting Reform Church in South Africa: "I . . . want[ed] to help the church to feel relevant, to have skills and capacities for worship, education and leadership development, all of which can transform lives and systems. This is a mission opportunity for [site 3 church]" ("Oasis in the City" newsletter, May 2010, p. 1). Notice that the senior minister sees the opportunity to transform lives and systems in South Africa in ways that are "relevant" to the millions of marginalized citizens there, a majority of whom are dispossessed black Africans, and that she does not even mention Christian evangelism to save souls. Her commitment is clearly about progressive social action. In her blog, she comments regarding South Africa, "When I preach against racism, it is my passion for a world free of racism that is on the table" (May 10, 2010). So racism is explicitly named in site 3, and there are multiple and consistent attempts to address racism at both the individual and systemic levels.

EVALUATING A SITE'S COHESION

It is possible that the availability of resources for understanding, expressing, and mediating racial identity shapes the choices of members in these church settings. One main resource is relative social embeddedness (versus social isolation). As I noted before, site 1 members cohered around evangelical religious philosophy and a progressive African-centered cultural ethos. Site 2, however, located in the midwestern college town, had the biggest obstacles to overcome. The political differences among its congregants were the greatest. While the college town is somewhat racially diverse (though less so than the other two sites), whites in site 2 are more socially isolated relative to the other sites. Emerson and Smith (2000) argue that the degree of social isolation will be related to the practice of color-blind ideology. In the college town, education, household income, and wealth are structured along lines that reproduce racial hierarchy, so neighborhoods and friendship circles are less diverse relative to site 3, for example, and the degree of social isolation among whites is greater than in site 3. The degree of social isolation as indicated by whites' racially homogenous friendship circles and segregated neighborhoods is related to the practice of color-blind ideology (Bonilla-Silva 2003). I argue that the pastoral staff in site 2 approached multiracialism from a color-blind perspective. It did not work in the college town church. The leadership at site 2 wanted to minimize conflict, but their method was to avoid conflict; this pattern showed up in their handling of internal disagreements. The flip side to this is that they also minimized identity expression. So racism was not discussed, and worship styles were streamlined. Eventually, many middle-class African American members, who felt that their roles had been marginalized, resigned their memberships in this church during the time I observed. Finally, in site 3, intersectional thought provided a common perspective from which race, class, educational, and cultural differences could be attended to and patriarchy and heterosexism could be challenged.

"Colorblind racism is a racial ideology that has emerged as a central mechanism for supporting and reproducing the racial structure of the U.S." (Bonilla-Silva 2003). What follows from the works of Bonilla-Silva and Emerson and Smith is that, due to isolation (Emerson and Smith 2000), all white evangelical congregations are guilty of perpetuating color-blind racism, and unless multiracial congregations are actively involved in dismantling racial hierarchy of the United States, they are practicing color-blind racism (Emerson and Smith 2000; Bonilla-Silva 1997, 2003). Congregations that are majority African American will normally not practice color-blind racism, though they may be guilty of practicing sexism, heterosexism, ageism, classism, and other social inequalities. Churches interested in building a cohesive multiracial congregation cannot ultimately be effective unless they acknowledge racism generally—

color-blind racism in all U.S. institutions, including but not limited to the church, education, politics, and economics—and begin to work toward a unified vision of what it means to build God's kingdom here on earth. Here I part from Yancey (2003). His keys to congregational growth are inclusive worship, diverse leadership, an overarching goal, intentionality, personal skills, location, and adaptability. But these factors are only partial in the context of a multiracial congregation. What is missing is active work to dismantle racism, sexism, ableism, heterosexism, classism, and other aspects of the matrix of domination (Collins 1990, 2000). If these aspects of American society are not addressed, the implicit (and sometimes explicit) expectation of majority members (whites, those who enjoy racial privilege in this society) is that marginalized folk will "go with the flow." But is it right, is it brotherly (or sisterly), selfless, and God-centered for white conservative Christians to expect their black counterparts to "hush up" about politics and not rock the boat? Emerson explains that structural bases of social phenomenon abound within the biblical text, but white evangelicals have been socialized not to see them. They are blinded by their privileged positioning and perspectives.

About her Universalist congregation, an Asian woman writes, "To some of my fellow Unitarian Universalists [UU] I was the congregant who brought race into the church and disturbed their conflict-free existence" (Lin, 2010, p. 2). She further states, "Like many UUs of color, sometimes I wonder whether there's really a place for us in this faith. . . . I realize that UU churches don't recognize all of me" (p. 3). It is not more consonant with Unitarian values than it is with Christian values to place the burden on the oppressed to simply bear their pain in silence. That is not Christian brotherhood/sisterhood. That is oppression.

DISCUSSION

Bonilla-Silva's criticism (2003) that color-blind racism can be eradicated only if attacked at the systemic level is well founded. He makes these policy prescriptions: "reparations for past and present racial injustices to all minorities," "social protest," and "a new Civil Rights movement that strives for equality of *status* among the races, that is a movement to extend the substantive benefits of citizenship for all Americans" (p. 80). He further argues that anything short of this "will reproduce the second-class citizenship of all racial minorities" (p. 80). But there is a lack of connection between the present-day engagements of individuals who uphold this view and a clear path to effecting real systemic change.

What is happening at the congregational level is that antiracist churches are working to attack the ideological foundations of color-blind racism by dispelling its stereotypes, stories, and lore among their members and within their community (so at the individual level) and also by building institutions that are actively working to exemplify antiracism, antisexism, anticlassism, and antiheterosexism in their daily practices and avoid the reproduction of hegemony within their small-scale church "system."

This is happening at "Oasis in the City," except that I do not find abundant references to its work to address disability. And this is happening at least partially at site 1, "Afrocentric and Evangelical," where racism is attacked and undercut by the church's Afrocentric philosophy. Further, classism is challenged, at least to some extent. In site 3, however, I am less convinced about the feminist posture and more suspicious of the heteronormative posture, as well as about any redress to disability.

Site 3 goes even farther in the journey to break down racism at the systemic level by training up a new generation of leaders sensitive to the need to eradicate racism in all of its forms, including color-blind racism, by building up institutions now and in the next generation that do not reproduce systemic inequality.

So the problem remains of a disconnect between the valiant efforts carried out by trailblazers—such as the founders and sustainers of progressive agendas at the site 1 and site 3 churches and notable ministers including James Forbes, Bishop Desmond Tutu, Reverend Allan Boesak, Delores S. Williams, Jacquelyn Grant, and others—and the necessary step of eradicating the systemic practice and reproduction of racism. My question is, How do we get from here to there? In subsequent work, I want to interview visionary Christian leaders to understand their transformative work.

In summary, I believe that churches such as site 1 and site 3 are on the right track. They are training up and socializing their youth into a different ideology. They are making their small but significant triumphs available to the public utilizing media and face-to-face encounters through conferences and training workshops. What is more, they are working hard to practice what they preach in their everyday lives, and they have institutional support to sustain their vision. So for this historic moment, they are among the churches setting the standard for building antiracist Christian institutions.

It is my hope that we can support their impressive work, learn from their examples, and continue to create sites of multiracial antiracist (and of course antisexist, anticlassist, antiheterosexist, and antiableist) contestation of global hegemony and systemic racism in the United States. And to carry this struggle a step forward, what is needed is to create a base for social protest and a new Civil Rights movement that will work "to extend the substantive benefits of citizenship for all Americans" (Bonilla-Silva 2003, 80). In the following two chapters I examine two tests provided by the realities of conflict within American politics emanating from two contested terrains, the election of Barack Obama into the White House and activism to promote the withdrawal of forces from Iraq and Afghanistan.

The ability to overcome the potential volatility offered by these tests provides evidence of congregations' successes and failures in building inclusive volitional institutions.

NOTES

1. I attended a worship service in which a white pastor dismissed black congregants' concerns by referring to them as "complaints about" racism.
2. Though this African American site is part of a mainline denomination, I describe the church members and staff as evangelical in their outlook.
3. See chapter 3 for an extended analysis of evangelicals' internal political discussions of the 2008 election.
4. The wealth of resources in this church's city enables the church to hire professional singers to provide music ranging from baroque selections to show tunes to jazz scores. The gospel choir, on the other hand, consisted of unpaid church members who donated their time.
5. The African American female senior minister has obtained many degrees, including a master's in divinity from an Ivy League institution and an M. Phil and a PhD in religion. One of the associate ministers has a doctoral degree and the other has an M. Div. A staff member who teaches dance and leads dramaturgy has had experiences performing on Broadway, and the site 3 choir includes professional singers.
6. Please see chapter 4 for further elaboration of intersectional organizations and site 3 church examples.
7. My goal is not to level a debilitating critique of color-blind churches, but to attempt to make them see (Exodus 33–34; Isaiah 61; Luke 4)! I am committed to the project of multiracial cooperation, envisioned by my parents and others in their generation.
8. The crux of the evangelical message is that all people are sinners and have fallen short of the glory of God. We therefore cannot earn our way to heaven. Once we accept Jesus as our personal Lord and Savior, salvation is a gift. Other tenets are that the Bible is the inerrant Word of God, that we are called to live life in community (by joining a local church and becoming active there), and that we are called to tithe and share our spiritual gifts with the church.
9. This was one of many potentially explosive changes that occurred at site 2 in a short time period. Many changes were viewed by some as disenfranchising to African American members.

THREE
Christian Evangelical Internal Discussions of the 2008 Presidential Election

Though the separation of church and state is touted as the American democratic "way of being," Christian denominations and individual parishes were active participants in the public debate and outcomes during the 2008 election season. Interestingly, there were clear divergences in political opinion among churchgoers that appeared to divide by race. In this chapter, I complicate commonly held views of evangelical Christians in American society by conducting a comparative analysis of the three churches examined in chapter 2 regarding the extent to which they address issues of political salience, and in particular the 2008 election. In this first of two volatility tests that I explore, I ask the following: Was the election discussed in the pulpit or in smaller group discussions among church members? What political activities were encouraged and carried out in the name of religious values and dictates? These three congregations differed widely in their views on the best presidential candidate and how to handle differences of political opinion within their church. The operation of the intersection of race, class, gender, and nation in American society helps to explain these distinctions.

BACKGROUND: THEOLOGY OF BLACK LIBERATION AND ALTERNATIVE PERSPECTIVES

There is an observable, palpable, and missional tradition of progressive social activism at the foundation and within the defining moments of many African American Protestant congregations (as discussed in several works, including Burrow et al. 2002, Barnett 1989, Sekou 2009, Frederick

2003, and McRoberts 2003, to name a few). This tradition is stimulated by African Americans' social placement in U.S. society. According to James Cone, "The difference in the form of Black and White religious thought is . . . sociological" (1970). Harry Singleton argues, as have many other black theologians (Pinn 2007), that a primary preoccupation of the black theologian has been to assert her humanity and to proclaim an understanding of Christianity that is consonant with black liberation (2008). However, social scientists have identified heterogeneity among African American churches. McClerking and McDaniel (2005), Barnes (2009), Reese, Brown, and Ivers (2007), Lee (2003), and others argue that some churches, identified as political black churches, are more likely to stimulate electoral activity compared with other churches that are less political.

Singleton describes the ontological anguish experienced by the confessional black theologian, who on one hand has to contend with marginalization in the white supremacist theological establishment in U.S. seminaries and on the other hand has to fight for legitimacy among black church leaders who perceive seminary-trained theologians to be too heady and not submissive to spiritual direction and ecclesial leadership. He describes three areas of importance that the black theologian must begin to reassess (2008). A black theology for the twenty-first century, according to Singleton, is one that *challenges* "the Western intellectual tradition" (p. 25), *defies* "ecclesial approaches that equate myopic thinking with divine wisdom" (this includes debunking "the myth that spiritual endowment is compromised by theological preparation at White institutions") (p. 26), and *commits* to "the destruction of White supremacy and its impact on the academy and the church" (p. 28). This present-day understanding of black theology is instructive, and I use it as a point of departure to analyze the theology of the churches under examination.

While there have been several studies of Black church political participation using national data sets and other quantitative data, there is a limit to the types of political participation that can be captured in these generalizable data (Sherkat and Ellison 1991, Barnes 2009). I collected ethnographic data to provide a more in-depth look at theology, culture, and political participation in a smaller group of Christian churches. In my qualitative analysis of three churches I begin to explore the extent to which sentiments are communicated from the pulpit to support a particular political candidate or promote participation in electoral activities. Further, I examine whether such a perspective is addressed in church bulletins, newsletters, and web presence. Finally, I look at whether there is evidence of political activism. I observed several multiracial congregations from 2004 to 2014. For this chapter, I analyze the same three congregations as in chapter 2. Site 1 ("Afrocentric and Evangelical") is considered African American and the other two sites are multiracial, but further explanation is in order. The multiracial "Oasis in the City" has an African American female lead pastor, but most of the associate pastors are white, and the leadership board is mostly white. The membership is about 50 percent African American. "Friendliest Place in College Town USA" is multiracial. Except at the "Oasis in the City" site, all lead pastors are men, and most associate pastors are men.

I have chosen sites for the wider study because they represent three different types of nonmajority congregations (at least 50 percent nonwhite) in which I can observe how issues of race, class, and gender are addressed. I chose the specific three to be examined because the 2008 presidential election was discussed directly in each church. The data collection for this chapter was unobtrusive, so gaining access to these sites was fairly straightforward, as I explored publicly available documents and attended services that were open to the public.[1]

An African American Community of Faith

Site 1 is located in a historical African American community that is part and parcel of a Midwest city. It is one of the largest churches in its denomination, with a reported membership exceeding 8,500. While the wider denomination is predominantly white, this congregation is African American. The lead pastor is an African American man, and his leadership team includes a number of African American women. Afrocentric culture and content permeate the building structure, the Sunday morning service, church programs, and the appearance of members. Jesus and all of the biblical characters depicted in the stained glass windows have brown skin. Many members wear African garb and hairstyles (ones that do not require chemical processing, such as cornrows, dreadlocks, and shaved heads) on Sunday morning and during the weekly events. The choir follows suit in this regard. The names of many church programs and the bookstore are taken from African languages and dialects. The "African Family values" to which the church ascribes were articulated by a committee of church members. These values are consonant with many "family values" touted in evangelical rhetoric, such as commitment to God, community, and family. However, the values espoused by this congregation unabashedly challenge racial prejudice and racially biased aspects of American politics. Among other tenets, they include a commitment to "adherence to the black work ethic" (quoting II Thessalonians 3:7–12, they insist that African Americans must be productive members of the workforce) and "disavowal of the pursuit of 'middle-classness'" (i.e., members are encouraged to reject the notion that they are better than their African American counterparts simply because they have a higher socioeconomic status). Clearly this congregation practices black theology as described by James Cone (2001) and more recently by Harry Singleton (2008). It is a theology that critiques white supremacy, supports the intellectual contributions of university-trained black theologians such as Jeremiah Wright and James Forbes, and challenges the mainstream Western intellectual tradition.

A Place for the Unchurched

The second site is "Friendliest Place in College Town USA," also described in chapter 2. It has grown rapidly in the last fifteen years. The lead pastor is white; an Asian American associate pastor leads the college ministry housed in a separate building, and an African associate pastor leads a Congolese congregation that uses the church's facilities. However, the associate pastors who interact regularly with the congregation are white, and they hold paid positions. In the past, when some of these positions were held on a voluntary basis, a number of African Americans filled posts. This change has brought discomfort for some members of this multiracial congregation. Though some prominent middle-class African American and multiracial families have since left, other working-class African Americans have begun attending the church, so the racial balance of attenders has remained somewhat stable. On the other hand, the balance in formal and informal leadership has subsequently skewed toward an almost all-white leadership.

The church is Pentecostal; for example, at the conclusion of Wednesday night Bible study, with forty or more listeners in pews, all participants are invited to (and expected to collectively gather at) the altar to pray out loud (everyone praying their own prayers at the same time), and participants are encouraged to speak "in tongues"[2] while they pray.

In this site, the church leadership ignores black theology as they "conceive of the theological task as other-worldly, and conceive of the theological task independent of Black oppression" (Singleton 2008). For example, during Wednesday night services one season, the church screened a video series derived from *The Bait of Satan* by John Bevere (1994), written in the Christian self-help genre. To help readers "escape the victim mentality," the author promotes the idea that a person who "takes offense" at being mistreated is not living in line with biblical dictates. Adherents are instructed to forgive their offenders. This series has been marketed to churches as a way to contain internal disagreement, but its lessons have unhealthy implications for coping with intimate partner violence, sexism more generally, homophobia, ableism, and racial offenses. Avoiding disagreement and forgiving without addressing the offense helps to keep sexism, patriarchy, violent relationships, heteronomativity, ableism, and white privilege intact. The offended individual is marginalized as simply "bitter."

A Dynamic Urban Ministry

Site 3, or "Oasis in the City," also described in chapter 2, is located in a prominent neighborhood of a city in the East, a desirable location resulting from its proximity to commerce, higher education, and conventional and alternative cultural outlets. Famous parks are interspersed in the web of neighborhood buildings. The church's vivacious staff is led by an African American female minister and a number of associate ministers. The church is well endowed by its denomination to provide for opportunities to do inner-city ministry. The diverse and "dynamic ministry" provides clothing and food to the significant homeless population in the neighborhood. They employ a minister of social justice, and social justice-oriented work and events predominate, including movie series and other cultural events that feature political genre, gatherings that provide opportunities to express a progressive social agenda to civic leaders, and workshops devoted to eradicating racism. One of the associate ministers, who holds executive duties, is gay. The inclusive congregation has a specific LGBTIQ ministry and hosts events to promote awareness, education, and an open and welcoming environment. Several programs are organized at the church to make it an inclusive congregation. The pastor does not use gender- specific pronouns when referring to God, and the messages are universalist.[3] While the theology of site 3 is consistent with some aspects of a liberation theology in the way that Singleton describes black theology, its stance on the preoccupations and lives of its adherents is much more broadly conceived. It is pointedly concerned with the promotion of progressive feminist values, inclusiveness, and the dismantling of heterosexism, in addition to some of the concerns with race and class addressed in black theology.

ASSUMED UNITY IN THE AFRICAN AMERICAN CONGREGATION AND HOW MULTIRACIAL CONGREGATIONS HANDLE POLITICAL DIFFERENCES AMONG MEMBERS

Concurrent with the theology of each observed congregation, I found three distinctive positions on political engagement during the 2008 presidential election. Each of the parishes examined represents one of these distinct positions:
- "Afrocentric and Evangelical": Barack Obama as heir apparent to the dream of Dr. Martin Luther King, Jr.
- "Friendliest Place in College Town USA": Don't ask, don't tell.
- "Oasis in the City": The "morning after."

Barack Obama as Heir Apparent to the Legacy of Dr. Martin Luther King, Jr.

I attended worship at site 1 in August 2008, right after Barack Obama was declared the Democratic Party's nominee for the presidential election. Clad in their clothing inspired by Africa and its diaspora and in Obama political attire, the congregation was jubilant. The lead pastor spoke of the "unfinished cathedral of American democracy" and the contributions of Frederick Douglass, Shirley Chisholm, and Jesse Jackson and how these individuals paved the way for Barack Obama. He said the nomination of Obama "is a down payment on the dream" of Martin Luther King, Jr. "It doesn't mean that all the problems are solved, but God is moving in our lives!" He spoke of the history of black political participation in America, the limitations imposed by institutional racial discrimination generally, and specific ills such as the poll tax and the mishandling of the Mississippi Freedom Democratic Party at the 1964 Democratic National Convention. Jazz played in the background while the pastor mused about Dr. King's powerful role in building the edifice of American democracy. My field notes from that day include these words:

> The worship celebration is aptly named today. As the choir sings their selections, the crescendo of their voices and energy is matched and surpassed by the choir director who jumps up and down, his long dreadlocks dancing, swinging back and forth, as he directs syncopated tempo and punctuates the choir's words with his baton. The tempo speeds faster and faster until the exhausted choir ends the selection. But excitement remains in the air and the choir picks up the song again, joining in on the musical accompaniment in the background. People just shout out in praise when the Reverend begins to speak (Zerai field notes, November 2, 2008).

At site 1, members see themselves as being in line with the Civil Rights objectives expressed by the late Dr. Martin Luther King, Jr. and carried out by now-President Barack Obama. Electoral political activity is normative in this congregation. On November 2, 2008, a three-page "Litany of Faith" was included in the Sunday bulletin that promoted voting and reminded the congregation that African American ancestors made sacrifices to make November 4, 2008 possible: the day that an African American man would run for the U.S. presidency on behalf of the Democratic Party. This was one of three separate reminders to vote published in that day's bulletin.

Don't Ask, Don't Tell

In the 2008 election season, both during the primaries and in the months preceding the election, the site 2 senior pastor proclaimed that he would not discuss politics and that he forbade church members from bringing cars with campaign stickers into the church parking lot or wearing buttons in support of particular political candidates. I must say that in surveying cars in the church parking lot, I saw very few sporting John McCain/Sarah Palin stickers, though I was aware that a majority of white members supported this ticket for its antiabortion stance. At one meeting, I saw a "Colin Powell for President/Condoleezza Rice for VP" sticker on the faded, barely running Mazda belonging to a white middle-aged female member whom many parishioners considered "liberal."

The lead pastor took heat for his stance to leave politics at the door. He reported that politically conservative members of the church argued with him about this position. However, he related that he feared that discussing politics would "turn off" potential adherents. Believing that his mission was to reach out to the "unchurched," his goal was to make everyone feel welcome. Ultimately, his actions demonstrate his view that politics are secondary to a focus on spiritual growth and development. And it was, he felt, God's leading that empowered him to take a courageous stance in the face of opposition.

The "Morning After"

While site 3 sees political engagement as central to the church's mission, their political activity includes issues of local importance to the church's residents, mission work in the Gulf Coast and in Ghana, special events focused on dismantling white privilege and promoting the Gay Rights Movement, poetry readings to promote social change, and an active outreach to depressed individuals. The red-hot issue of the 2008 Democratic Party presidential nomination was not addressed in any of their written documents. The church could not risk divisiveness between pro-Obama and pro-Clinton supporters. Even after Obama was chosen as the Democratic nominee, he was not discussed formally. The November 2008 newsletter (published in late October) includes an inspiring article by the senior minister entitled "There's Got to Be a Morning After," in which she dares the congregation to "find our identity beyond American, beyond [site 3] Church. . . . Find an . . . identity that is deeper. . . . This identity comes from centering ourselves in our faith" ("Oasis in the City" newsletter, November 2008, p. 1). Clearly, site 3 strikes a balancing act to honor the multiple voices within its community and maintain harmony. It recognizes differences in political opinion but holds that ultimately all members are focusing on the same goal in the end, defined by the senior minister as "rehearsing for the Reign of God here on earth!"

DISCUSSION

I have found that the three identified church sites differ greatly in their demography, culture, and theology and in internal discussions of the

2008 presidential election. These sites represent diverse approaches to electoral politics. Site 1, a predominantly African American Protestant evangelical congregation distinguished by its black liberationist theology, has members who are exuberant supporters of President Barack Obama. They actively promoted voter registration and created an environment in which electoral participation was normative.

Site 2, a Protestant evangelical church with predominantly white leadership and a multiracial flock, had a hands-off policy on discussions of the election. However, this policy reflected a general avoidance of conflict at this Pentecostal church, a pattern that showed up in their handling of other internal disagreements. Only in site 1 is Black liberation theology found to be a contributor to lively discussion and enthusiastic support of candidates who are viewed to be in accord with some of its principles.

Finally, site 3, an inclusive multiracial church with a multiracial ministry team, worked hard at maintaining its multiracial/multicultural identity with respect to the presidential election of 2008, which led to a muted engagement. Discussion of the Democratic Party primaries and the general presidential election was off-limits until after the election, when congregants reasserted the values that unite them.

It is possible that the availability of resources for understanding, expressing, and mediating racial identity shapes the choices of members in these church settings. Black liberation theology offered a unifying worldview in site 1, but this viewpoint is not salient in the other two sites. In future work, I plan to address how the church members in these three sites put their resources to work to address conflict and forge congregational unity. It is possible that local context, educational attainment, and exposure of ministers and parishioners all contribute to this resource base.

This analysis not only has exposed some approaches to political discussions in churches but has provided a more complicated picture of evangelicals than is commonly understood. This analysis reveals evangelical congregations to contain diverse groups of individuals with varied opinions concerning politics in the United States.

NOTES

1. I submitted an Institutional Review Board protocol to ensure ethical oversight over data collection and reporting of my human subjects research.

2. Speaking "in tongues" is the practice of praying out loud so fervently as to invite the Holy Spirit to take over; if it is done correctly, the prayer is spontaneously spoken in another language—even, and especially, in a language not known to the speaker.

3. Universalist theology adheres to the doctrine of universal salvation. While the "Oasis in the City" church is more universalist in its theology, its wider denomination is somewhat evangelical in doctrine.

FOUR

An Africana Feminist Critique of American Christian Antiwar (Dis)engagements

There is a strong tradition of antiwar sentiment within various Protestant African American and progressive white Protestant churches. Considering the societal role of patriarchy, I conducted a comparative analysis of predominantly African American Protestant evangelical ministers and their parishioners (site 1) as contrasted with white Protestant evangelical leadership and multiracial flock (sites 2 and 3) regarding the extent to which they address U.S. aggression in the Middle East in their words and actions. Are these issues taken up in the pulpit or smaller group discussions among church members? What humanitarian, activist, or other activities are encouraged and carried out in the name of religious values and dictates? An analysis that considers the intersection of race, class, and gender within American society helps to answer these questions. In this chapter, I analyze nationally representative data sets and opinion polls to establish variations on views according to respondents' race and religious denominations. And I use the intersectional perspective to conduct participant observation analysis in a sample of black and multiracial churches, along with analyzing transcripts of sermons and conducting content analysis of church websites and weekly bulletins during the period of 2005 to 2010 to examine antiwar activism during the era of the wars in Iraq and Afghanistan.[1]

Several years after former President George W. Bush had declared "Mission Accomplished," in 2009 the United States still had 174,200 troops deployed in Iraq (U.S. Department of Defense 2009), and a peak of 100,000 American troops in Afghanistan in 2010 (Thompson 2014). Over 1 million were deployed to the Middle East, with most of them sent to Iraq and Afghanistan (U.S. Department of Defense 2009, Kane 2006). In 2009 legislation was approved to support President Barack Obama's request for continuing military and diplomatic operations in Iraq and Afghanistan. According to AP sources, "As Obama [sent] more than 20,000 additional troops [to Afghanistan], the annual cost of the war in Afghanistan exceeded the cost of fighting in Iraq. . . . War funding [boosted] total approved spending for the Iraq and Afghanistan wars above $900 billion" (AP, May 21, 2009). This happened while poor and working class communities in the United States languished.

Unemployment hit 9.4 percent in May 2009 (U.S. Bureau of Labor Statistics 2009). The entire nation suffered from the effects of the recession, but African Americans were disproportionately affected. The unemployment rate among African Americans was already in the double digits at 15 percent in May 2009 (Parker 2009), and both underclass and middle-class African Americans were—and continue to be—overrepresented among the unemployed. "Between 2007 and 2011, the gap in unemployment between [African American and white college grads] nearly doubled, rising from 3.7 to 7.0 percentage points" (Jones and Schmitt 2014, 4), and it was even higher in 2014, at 12.4 percent for African American college grads, compared with 5.6 percent for all graduates (Ross 2014). While the economic prospects for most in the United States have improved, African Americans still find themselves in dire recession-like straights.

Nevertheless, the public outcry over continuing U.S. deployments to the Middle East had waned since the 2008 presidential election. And Christian religious groups' voices were especially absent from the public domain in regards to U.S. government spending in the Middle East and U.S. involvement in Iraq, Afghanistan, and other potential sites.

BACKGROUND LITERATURE AND NEW QUESTIONS

In "Beyond Vietnam: A Time to Break Silence," delivered April 4, 1967, at a meeting of Clergy and Laity Concerned at Riverside Church, New York City, Dr. Martin Luther King Jr. states the following:

> Since I am a preacher by calling, I suppose it is not surprising that I have seven major reasons for bringing Vietnam into the field of my moral vision. There is at the outset a very obvious and almost facile connection between the war in Vietnam and the struggle I, and others, have been waging in America. A few years ago there was a shining moment in that struggle. It seemed as if there was a real promise of hope for the poor—both black and white—through the poverty program. There were experiments, hopes, new beginnings. Then came the buildup in Vietnam, and I watched this program broken and eviscerated, as if it were some idle political plaything of a society gone mad on

war, and I knew that America would never invest the necessary funds or energies in rehabilitation of its poor so long as adventures like Vietnam continued to draw men and skills and money like some demonic destructive suction tube. So, I was increasingly compelled to see the war as an enemy of the poor and to attack it as such.

The tradition of antiwar sentiment has been taken up by a new generation of clergy, who echoed King's statements against the war in Vietnam in a fight to end wars in Afghanistan and Iraq and to prevent a war in Iran (Sekou 2009). While literature has begun to address the new militancy of post–Civil Rights African American clergy (Lee 2003; Brown 2006; Reese, Brown, and Ivers, 2007; McRoberts 2003; Barnes 2008) and political activism within congregations (Beyerlein and Chaves 2003), antiwar activism of these clergy has received scant attention in the social science literature (exceptions are Zerai 2011; R. Brown and K. Brown 2013).

I explore fascinating differences between African American and white Protestant churches. Studying antiwar and prowar sentiment within churches necessitates acknowledging what is going on in evangelical circles.[2] Popular understandings of evangelicalism often get reduced to white, politically conservative, proselytizing religion.[3] Here I continue to trouble oversimplifications by offering a corrective that considers how the intersection of race, class, gender, and other spheres of inequality informs cleavages within evangelical communities.

Antiwar engagement is not a given among Protestants. Though the majority of Americans did not support fighting wars in Iraq or Afghanistan, very few were involved in active protest. The extent of even passive protest from a visible minority in the United States was often limited to wearing the peace sign. But to take activism to the arena of public discourse is rare, especially during the presidency of Barack Obama. According to many religious organizations and social movement theorists (Salime 2005, Calhoun-Brown 2001, Myers 2005), certain physical and ideological resources are necessary precursors to specific outcomes of interest. Analogously, I theorize that certain activism-promoting institutional structures are important antecedents of antiwar activism in the post-9/11 era. In this chapter I look at one characteristic of those structures that I believe is strongly connected to social activism: fundamentals of Africana feminist organizational methods. I theorize that to the extent that religious organizations have elements of an Africana feminist organizing structure, they were apt to tackle militarism and protest the "war on terror."

MY THEORY

I argue in this chapter that Africana feminist elements of organizational structure, including the structure of religious organizations, lend themselves to progressive activist output, and in particular antiwar activism in the last decade. It is my belief that, conversely, religious organizations that reflect a patriarchal structure will more likely be aligned with individuals (leadership and members) who are conservative and who would not become involved with progressive activism of any kind. Elsewhere I have argued that Africana feminist methods of organizing have distinct features (Zerai 2000a, 2002b, 2005; Zerai and Salime 2006). These include a nonhierarchical leadership structure (Zerai and Campbell 2005), use of integrated analysis in program and day-to-day discussions, a recognition of relational difference, an attention to local and global issues, strategies that are dynamic and ever-changing, and a focus on outcomes that are rooted in everyday people's experiences and desires (Zerai and Salime 2006).

In previous work Zakia Salime and I ask, "What are the contributions of black feminism to methods of organizing to end oppression, and specifically against war, racism, and repression?" (Zerai and Salime 2006). We analyzed discussions from the Women of Color Resource Center located in the Bay area of northern California and INCITE! websites, the Black Feminist Caucus, the Black Radical Congress, and *War Times* to provide evidence of Africana feminist analysis and organizing methods among Africana feminists, women of color, and progressives in the antiwar movement of 2001 to 2004. The features of Africana feminist organizing delineated above are discussed in detail in this and other work (Zerai and Salime 2006, Zerai and Campbell 2005). Briefly, in analyzing the operation of the Black Radical Congress Convention of June 2003, Campbell and I found that a nonhierarchical, collective approach ensued. Three co-chairs organized the convention, giving rise to some conflict but also an opportunity for input and participation by numerous constituencies. A nonhierarchical structure is one that emphasizes democratic participation (Zerai and Campbell 2005). Integrated analysis is a hallmark of black feminism. This integrated analysis is referred to by many names, most notably "race, class, gender" analysis or intersectionality (Collins 1990, 1998, 2000). "The most important analytic tool of Black feminist thought is intersectionality—a paradigm for reconceptualizing oppression and resistance" (Zerai and Banks 2002a, 12). "Race, class, and gender intersectionality is a framework for analyzing ways that various spheres of inequality work together to simultaneously affect social life" (Zerai and Banks 2002a, 12).

A recognition of relational difference, one aspect of an intersectional analysis, means moving beyond recognizing differences only between individuals who occupy different social locations to seeing how the social location of privileged groups is enabled by the oppression of dominated groups. Put simply, differences in access to power influence social locations (see Brown 1995, Zerai and Banks 2002a, Zerai and Banks 2002b, and Zerai 2008). An attention to local and global issues and using strategies that are dynamic and ever-changing are both features of black feminism that were articulated in Patricia Hill Collins' *Black Feminist Thought* (1990). Finally, Africana feminist organizing is organically tied to and representative of multiple distinct groupings within Africana communities and rooted in everyday people's experiences and desires (Collins 1990, Zerai and Campbell 2005, Zerai and Salime 2006). Organizing starts with the knowledge base and experiences of community members. The voices of even the most marginalized should be reflected. There is no room for exclusionary practices among African, African American, or Caribbean men; LGBTIQ groups; middle-class African Americans; or Christians (see also Zimm et al. 1986). The features discussed are all integral to black feminism because each is articulated in the seminal works on black feminism and is present in subsequent analyses that consider the tenets of Africana feminist organizing.[4]

POLITICAL CLEAVAGES AMONG PROTESTANTS

The findings reported in this chapter come from the analysis of four sources: (1) my analysis of nationally representative and opinion poll data to establish variations in antiwar sentiment according to respondents' race and religious denomination, (2) unobtrusive participant observation of a sample of black and multiracial churches, (3) transcripts of sermons, and (4) content analysis of church websites and weekly bulletins.

Several articles have addressed political cleavages within Protestant and other religious congregations in the United States since the late 1990s (for example, Beyerlein and Chaves 2003). Much of this work has been stimulated by the availability of data from the National Congregation Survey (NCS), created in cooperation with the General Social Survey.[5] It is the first nationally representative sample of U.S. congregations. Mark Chaves spearheaded this effort (Chaves et al 2000; Chaves, Giesel, and Tsitsos 2002; Chaves and Anderson 2008). Data sets were collected in 1998, 2007, and 2012.

In analyzing nationally representative and opinion poll data from the American National Election Study (ANES) 2006 and 2012, I examine the distribution in opinion on the "War on Terror" (2006) and President Barack Obama's foreign relations policies (2012).[6] Assessment of former President George W. Bush's work in foreign relations shows that white Protestants, most of whom are evangelical in their leanings, were three times as likely to approve of Bush's handing of foreign relations in 2006 relative to African Americans—37.6 percent of white Protestants approved, compared with 11.7 percent of African American Protestants. A CBS News/*New York Times* opinion poll asked "how it was going for the U.S. in Iraq, and Bush's antiterrorism efforts in 2007."[7] The poll found stark and revealing differences by race: white evangelical Christians were more than three times as likely as African American evangelicals to support Bush's handling of terrorism and five times as likely to support his handling of the war in Iraq. In asking whether the Iraq action was the "right thing to do," white evangelicals were almost *nine* times as likely to agree with this statement as were African American evangelicals.

In analyzing ANES data (2007 and 2012), I found that though African American and white parishioners may agree on fundamental principles of Christian faith (e.g., the view that Jesus is the Son of God) and are similarly actively engaged in church activities, they by and large are in complete disagreement regarding U.S. domestic and foreign policy prior to Barack Obama's presidency. Regarding the Obama White House, overall confidence in the U.S. presidency is at an all-time low (11 percent, according to Bump 2015). But a racial gulf remains, with only 10 percent of white Americans expressing great confidence in the Obama presidency compared with twice as many African Americans (20.7 percent). The gap is even wider among Protestant Americans, as 7 percent of white Protestants and three times as many African American Protestants (21.5 percent) express great confidence in the executive branch of the U.S. government (analysis of GSS 2014). Interestingly (and unlike in 2007), confidence in the U.S. military converged among African American and white Protestants nearing the end of the War in Afghanistan (in 2014). A slim majority of Protestants (54.3 percent of whites and 54.7 percent of African Americans) held great confidence in the military, according to the 2014 General Social Survey (GSS).

CASE STUDIES AND THE PRESENCE OR ABSENCE OF AFRICANA FEMINIST ORGANIZATIONAL CHARACTERISTICS

Given a dearth of national data sets addressing antiwar activism within churches, in my qualitative analysis of three sites I explore the extent to which antiwar (or prowar) sentiments were communicated from the pulpit and in church bulletins, newsletters, and web presence by church members in from 2005 to 2010, at the height of the recent U.S. wars in the Iraq and Afghanistan. Further, I look for evidence of activism within these sites to end these wars. The three sites I analyze for this chapter include sites 1 and 3, as described earlier, and a new site 4:[8]

- Site 1, "Afrocentric and Evangelical"—located in a major metropolitan area in the Midwest, an African American congregation with African American leadership that is part of a predominantly white denomination.
- Site 3, "Oasis in the City"—a multiracial congregation with multiracial leadership located in the heart of a major city in the East.

- Site 4, "Leadership and Congregation at Odds"—a multiracial congregation with multiracial leadership located in the Midwest that is part of a predominantly white denomination.

By leading notions in the social scientific literature of what constitutes African American congregations, where 75 percent to 80 percent of membership is African American (Beyerlein and Chaves 2003, Chaves 2004), two of my sites are African American while one is multiracial. The multiracial church (site 3) has an African American female lead pastor, but most of the associate pastors are white and the leadership board is mostly white. The membership in site 3 is about 50 percent African American. The congregation in site 1 is over 90 percent African American. Site 4, the new church under analysis, is considered African American by membership, though the pastor is white and the denomination is largely white. With the exception of site 3, all lead pastors are men, and most associate pastors are men.[9]

I chose these sites for this analysis because, of the dozen churches at which I had conducted fieldwork before Obama withdrew forces, they were the only ones to directly address the Iraq/Afghanistan wars and/or the "War on Terror" from the pulpit, in special events at parishes, or in any publications. I do not present these three settings as ideal types for engagement in antiwar work. At least two of the sites, in fact, are extremely unique in their identity, program, resources, and membership. Rather than being concerned with representativeness and generalizability, I hoped to capture a valid picture of antiwar work, given that antiwar work in evangelical churches is so rare.

Site 1: Afrocentric Rhetoric Meets Evangelical Message

Site 1, located in a historical African American community that is part and parcel of a major city in the Midwest, is one of the largest churches in its mainline denomination). While its larger denomination is a predominantly white denomination, this congregation is not only African American, but Afrocentric. Afrocentric cultural indicators richly texture the church edifice, programs, and member interactions. For example, the website background features African patterns and colors and the caption "Imagine a place where Africa is part of one's theology." In website descriptions of the congregation's various ministries, the Counseling Ministry is distinguished as "grounded in the Black Value System." One writer describes this church by saying that the "colors of Africa" are dominant in the Sunday morning services (Mansfield 2008). The 200-member choir wears not traditional European-style robes but African garb on Sundays. The choir sits behind the pulpit, so the "colors of Africa"—*kente* oranges; rich blues, yellows, and greens; mudcloth chocolates—dominate in this church's services. The budget for the church comes predominantly from member donations. Membership size is purported as upwards of 8,500 (Keogh 2007), but service attendance is somewhere around 500 and 1,000 at the two Sunday Services. This cutting-edge church has several associate pastors, including one whose focus is drama ministry. The services are well choreographed, culminating in a twenty-minute message by the lead pastor that is basically evangelical in tone, though he often refers to his children, the black community, and issues of political relevance during his sermons.

The denomination is mainline while this congregation expresses a more evangelical orientation. "Evangelical Christianity includes denominations such as Methodists and Baptists [and] is marked by its emphasis on conversion" (Robbins 2004, 119). Adherents must "'voluntarily' choose Evangelical faith on the basis of a powerful conversion experience"; in other words, they must be "born again" (Robbins 2004, 120). This religious tradition is taken up in full force in site 1, though they also strongly identify with the denomination. In all of their publications and their church's website, the wider denomination's emblem is featured. The church sponsors a biblical studies institute, established for students to be "transformed to serve," as captured in a New Revised Standard Version Bible verse on the church website that introduces the institute: "I appeal to you therefore, brothers and sisters, by the mercies of God, to present your bodies as a living sacrifice, holy and acceptable to God, which is your spiritual worship" (Romans 12:1–21).

Several African American women serve as associate pastors in site 1, but the lead pastor is male, and the church has been traditionally associated with its well-known pastor emeritus, who is also male. Afrocentric theory and cultural forms have been associated with a *male-centered discourse*, which black and Africana feminists have challenged in theoretical works and in practice (Sudbury 1998, Collins 2006, Davies 1994, Kuumba 2002). Site 1 has a strong pastor model and is somewhat *hierarchical*. The church is led by a team of pastors, but the focus is on the lead pastor on Sunday morning and in public presence. The lead pastor preaches most Sundays, unless a guest (usually a male pastor from another congregation) preaches. The elaborate elements of the service all build to the male lead pastor's sermon, the clear climax of the Sunday worship experience. The website features pictures of the lead pastor and his words, including a prominent link to download audio from his sermons. A weekly email newsletter features numerous pictures of the lead pastor (for example, in one 8-page message, as many as four pictures are typical). The associate pastors are almost never featured in these weekly emails. This church demonstrates very few characteristics that would distinguish it as having an Africana feminist organizing structure.

Site 3: An Urban Oasis

Site 3 is in the middle of a major eastern city, a busy hub connected to commerce, higher education, and the best and worst of post-modern American society. The church property is adjacent to well-known parks, called home by a number of homeless individuals.

A vibrant group of well-resourced staff provide a labor of love at this church, which I characterize as an oasis in the urban environment. The lead minister has a number of associate ministers with whom she works, and the church is well endowed, receiving the majority of its budget from the denomination. Site 3 is thus poised to do inner city ministry, which provides a number of unique opportunities for the congregation. They have a respectable outreach to the homeless population in the immediate community, providing clothing and food on a regular basis. They normally employ a minister of social justice. And one of the associate ministers is gay; several programs are organized to make the church a truly opening and welcoming congregation. Their advertisements feature a plus sign to symbolize they are an inclusive space. The lead minister does not use gender-specific pronouns when referring to God, and the messages are universalist in their content and delivery.

The religious tradition is liberal. And this congregation parts from their denomination on some matters of importance. For example, site 3 has been sanctioned by the wider denomination for their liberal stance on gay marriage. In one issue of the newsletter, a member writes that he does not accept the Bible as the inerrant word of God: "Belief in the inerrancy of scripture . . . has given rise to a narrow, exclusive, and dogmatic social agenda" ("Oasis in the City" newsletter, June 2009, p. 5). And the church proclaims an acceptance of Jesus's humanity, another indicator of a liberal theology. The senior minister explains a passage in scripture, writing, "Even Jesus could be entrapped by our human tendency to withhold love and care and compassion for the 'other'" (p. 5). However, while this church is not theologically fundamentalist, different from its denominational counterparts, it does have some Pentecostal elements in worship provided by its gospel choir, which sings every other Sunday.[10]

As far as incorporating principles of Africana feminist organizing in its structure, this site stands at the forefront among the three under examination. The lead minister and one of the associate ministers are African American women.[11] This is the only church of sites 1, 3, and 4 in which the top leaders are women. But this is not enough to ensure elements of an organizational structure that is not patriarchal. The leadership is *nonhierarchical* to some extent, in that a board of elders makes decisions on hiring, pay rates for staff, and other such matters. Another element of a *shared leadership* structure is that there is not just one voice that speaks for the congregation in the pulpit and in the public domain. The various ministers take turns preaching so that in a typical month, the lead minister preaches only two or three times, and associate ministers or guests preach the other weeks. In site 3's main publication, a monthly newsletter that is distributed in hard copy and posted on the church's website, the lead minister has a standing column; however, two or three associate pastors also have columns every month, and members contribute regularly. There is even a section in which members are invited to share their vision of what it means to belong to their church. So the vision of this church is rooted in *everyday people's desires* and experiences. All of the characteristics of Africana feminist organizing structure are present in this church. *Integrated analysis* that considers the intersection of race, class, gender, and sexuality is a mainstay of the congregation's public discourse and analysis of social problems. For example, regular workshops are held on white privilege, sharing of power (which addresses relational difference[12]), "puzzling passages" in the Bible in regards to homosexuality,[13] what it means to be an inclusive space, and opportunities to "heal" "scars from racial, ethnic, gender and sexual orientation differences" and "celebrate [the] gifts" of diversity [quoted phrasing is from the congregation's website). The *local and global* are addressed in benevolence, political events, and activism. This is the most progressive of the three sites I analyzed regarding Africana feminist organizational characteristics. Their motto is "come as you are" (site 3 website).

Site 4: Leadership and Congregation at Odds

This church in a midsize Midwest city is the least well attended of the five sites examined in this book. While it was once a thriving congregation, attendance has dwindled due to losses of key members. Though multiracial for much of its history, this church today would be considered African American by quantitative valuations; however, the church's denomination and its lead pastor are white. Notably, the denomination at large and pastor hold Republican sentiments while the African American congregants in site 4 are Democrats. From its inception, site 4 has been led by a board of male elders that excluded the minister. For a significant portion of the church's history, the lead elder was African American. However, this board of elders has largely disappeared, and membership losses have certainly decreased its power. There are no associate pastors at site 4, only a female African American education director; there is not even a secretary. There has been conflict between the white pastor and the handful of African American members remaining who have attended the church since its beginnings. The white pastor preaches pro-Bush, pro-Israel, and "antiterrorism" sentiments from the pulpit, with which a number of African American congregants disagree. Multiple members have left the church.

This church, like site 2 ("Friendliest Place in College Town USA"—not examined in this chapter), is evangelical and conservative in its theology. "Evangelicalism is a segment of Christianity that reveres the Bible, embraces a personal relationship with God through a conversion to Jesus Christ, and seeks to lead others on a similar spiritual journey" (Lindsay 2006, 208). This church fits squarely into the evangelical roots of its denomination. Its Sunday bulletin proclaims, "[Site 4's] purpose for existence is to glorify God. We are a multi-racial, multi-cultural community committed to making disciples." Indicating a *less-than-inclusive* tradition, they practice "closed" communion: "Our time of communion is open [only] to all who believe that Jesus is the Christ, the Son of God." Those welcome to join in the practice of communion, offered weekly in worship, are limited to people who have "publicly accepted Jesus Christ as their Lord and Savior" and who have participated in baptism by full immersion. Further, site 4 preaches that homosexuality is a sin. Unfortunately, its elders have actively dismissed out-LGBTQ individuals from participation unless they are willing to denounce their "lifestyle" as sinful.

This congregation has a female African American education director, the only staff member in addition to the pastor. Site 4 had past potential for a less hierarchical structure, but the board of elders is now virtually nonfunctioning. In violation of dictates from the church's own policy, the lead pastor serves as an elder now, due to paltry membership numbers. So *power is more concentrated* at site 4 relative to sites 1 and 3. The designation of "minister" versus "pastor" is significant. In the past at site 4, the worship leader's title was "minister," a word that refers to biblical interpretations describing every member of a church as a minister who shares the responsibility to live a life that is Christ-like, to spread the good news of Christ, and to attend to the needs of others. When the current minister took over the reins some years ago, he defied the tradition of the church and changed his title to "pastor." "Pastor" is a more hierarchical designation denoting a higher level of spiritual development relative to the congregation and a church leader who has the responsibility to care for "the flock," analogous to a shepherd. Some members at site 4 have taken issue with this change in title.

While at sites 1 and 3 attention is paid to relational difference, integrated analysis, and social change, at site 4 these issues are not addressed in Sunday morning worship services or in the monthly newsletter or events. Of the three sites, site 4 has the fewest characteristics of the feminist-organizing framework. In fact, women and LGBTQ members are not considered to be eligible to serve as elders in this denomination, clear evidence of a *patriarchal and heteronormative leadership* structure. And feminism is considered to be a school of thought antithetical to Christianity by numerous (especially male) adherents.

THEMES REGARDING CHURCHES' POLITICAL ENGAGEMENTS

I expected to see the three churches fall on some kind of continuum in their views on antiwar activism. Instead, I found three distinct positions on political engagement, whether activism around bringing U.S. troops home or any other issue related to social justice. The three congregations represent one of three distinct positions:

- Talk the talk, walk the walk, and don't forget to tithe! (site 1)
- "Open, inclusive, spiritual, activist" (site 3)
- Social justice as a "bunny trail" (site 4)

Site 1: Talk the Talk, Walk the Walk, and Don't Forget to Tithe!

Importance of the tithe. At site 1, "Afrocentric and Evangelical," while spiritual development is primary in the messages communicated from the pulpit, support for African heritage is a close second, imbuing every aspect of worship, weekly activities, the physical structure of the church, the bookstore, and various church subgroupings. Material concerns are quite important at site 1, which makes sense given the size of the church structure itself. Remember, this is the Afrocentric congregation with the 200-member choir. Mortgages are high for a church that can house thousands of worshippers[14] ($50,000 monthly payments are typical for a facility of this size). Concerns with meeting financial commitments are certainly an important subtext on Sunday mornings and in supplemental communications from the church. After visiting three times from over 100 miles away, I was sent an offering envelope number. I also received cards on which to commit funds for a Lent offering.

Talking the talk: expressing views consistent with African American cultural nationalist rhetoric and values. "Talking the talk and walking the walk" is another important theme for site 1, where congregants literally wear their politics on their chests. Not only does the African garb worn by the choir members and many attenders speak to an African American cultural nationalist sensibility, but parishioners wore Obama t-shirts, pins, hats, and buttons to church during the 2008 and 2012 election seasons (and subsequent to them). There was a clear expectation that the lead pastor would mention current political debates relevant to the African American community during his sermons. These utterances were encouraged with hearty "Amens," clapping hands, and other boisterous comments from the audience.

A part of "talking the talk and walking the walk" relates to the importance of promoting self-esteem of the children of church members, another Afrocentric value. I witnessed several family-oriented additions to the services over the months I attended, including an emotional Father's Day tribute in which young girls danced with their fathers while Luther

Vandross's "Dance with my Father" played in the background and a "step" presentation by mothers and their preteen children to congratulate students being promoted to high school and their mothers' efforts to help them succeed in school and in life. The dedication of babies followed an African ritual, similar to that when Alex Haley's character Kunta Kinte (in *Roots: A Saga of an American Family*) raised his son up to the sky to dedicate him to the community. African drums played softly in the background while the choir sang a mother's love song to an African cadence and rhythm. All of these activities exemplified the importance of "walking the walk" to promote African American children's positive identity.

"Walking the walk": an expression of congregants' accountability to God, country, and family. What was surprising to me at site 1 was the expression of responsibility to God, country, and family, reminiscent of white evangelical rhetoric. In describing the church's "Black Value System," site 1's website declares the following:

> Prayerfully, we have called upon the wisdom of all past generations of suffering Blacks for guidance in fashioning an instrument of Black self-determination, the Black Value System. . . . These Black Ethics must be taught and exemplified in homes, churches, nurseries and schools, wherever Blacks are gathered. They consist of the following concepts:
>
> 1. Commitment to God. "The God of our weary years" will give us the strength to give up prayerful passivism and become Black Christian Activists, soldiers for Black freedom and the dignity of all humankind.
> 2. Commitment to the Black Community. The highest level of achievement for any Black person must be a contribution of strength and continuity of the Black Community.
> 3. Commitment to the Black Family. The Black family circle must generate strength, stability and love, despite the uncertainty of externals, because these characteristics are required if the developing person is to withstand warping by our racist competitive society. Those Blacks who are blessed with membership in a strong family unit must reach out and expand that blessing to the less fortunate.

Members of site 1 further express their "accountability to God" by promoting personal spiritual growth, evidenced at least partially by tithing. They express their "accountability to country" by contributing to the electorate, as they see themselves in line with the Civil Rights objectives expressed by Dr. Martin Luther King, Jr. and now carried out by President Barack Obama, as noted in chapter 3. The congregation organized weekly voter registration drives during the 2008 election period. The pastor preached in mid-2008, "In 1888 at the Republican National Convention Frederick Douglass was nominated; he received one vote. . . . But in 2008 Barack Obama was selected as Democratic nominee for President. Look what the Lord has done!" The congregation's responsibility to family is expressed through a focus on children, with a significant additional focus on intact family arrangements. The senior pastor preaches, "Any time you become so self-serving that you forget about the God who put you in the position you are, you jeopardize family, community, and nation. Because of relationships God has not ordained, we are killing our children. You have a choice! David didn't have to sleep with Bathsheba!" The themes of God, country, and family permeate the Sunday services and sermons as well as the mission of the church and its web presence. Notably, however, site 1 articulates the church's accountability to "God, country, and family" with an Afrocentric flair.

The social gospel is key to the structure in site 1, which has a social justice pastor. The social gospel made an appearance in the content of some services, and it is promoted through the social justice pastor's column in the Sunday morning bulletin. A "Litany for Workers" insert from the Interfaith Workers for Justice was added to the Sunday bulletin one week and read aloud: "God, you stand with poor and disenfranchised, and for justice among people. Please show us how to do the same. God, hear our prayer" (Boyd 1). However, other than an occasional unison reading of social justice–promoting text and normative participation in electoral activities, site 1 evidenced no mention of antiwar activism or requirement to engage in it.

Site 3: Open, Inclusive, Spiritual, Activist

Site 3, the urban church in the East ("Oasis in the City"), addresses the social gospel, inclusion, deep engagement, and spiritual development in Sunday morning messages, newsletters, bulletins, web presence, and special events. Spiritual growth is at least partially reflected in political commitment to the downtrodden. The senior minister at site 3 states, "Our faith values: caring for the poor, putting children in the forefront of our care, welcoming everyone, and being fully inclusive, advocating social justice, and racial reconciliation." And a parishioner succinctly summarizes site 3's politic, motivated by the church's understanding of the gospel, with the phrase "open, inclusive, spiritual, activist" ("Oasis in the City" newsletter, April 2009, p. 6). Forging this identity has worked to provide cohesion among members. The senior minister explains that site 3 is no accident, as it is a "multiracial, multicultural experiment . . . clearly in the center of God's will for humanity" ("Oasis in the City" newsletter, May 2009, p. 1) She congratulates her congregation regularly for their efforts to cohere: "Thank you for rehearsing the reign of God here on earth!!" (p. 1). Dougherty and Huyser argue that creation of a congregational identity is crucial to the success of multiracial churches (2008).

According to the church's documents, site 3 sees political engagement as central to its mission. An associate minister encourages members in an issue of the newsletter that "it is time to lead the revolution through our unique voice" ("Oasis in the City" website). The political issues taken up by site 3 include local issues of importance, mission work in the Gulf Coast and in Ghana, special events focused on the Gay Rights Movement, poetry readings to promote social change, and an active outreach to depressed individuals. Another indicator of site 3's goals is reflected in the projects borne from the creative energies of their members and allies. For example, motivated by their understanding of Jesus's teachings, site 3 created a new institute, described on the church's website as a "liberationist, ecumenical and interdisciplinary [project that focuses on] progressive religion" as a vehicle for delivering the promise of a just society to everyone. They further state that they support "equal opportunity for all irrespective of race, religion, gender and sexual orientation."

This is the only site whose leadership was explicitly involved in antiwar activism. Their engagement included events hosted at the church, co-sponsorship of antiwar events in the city, and articulation of antiwar sentiments in public documents. For example, in one of four antiwar events in a six-month period, the church co-sponsored a film night to screen a movie that "gives special attention to parallels between the Vietnam war and the war in Iraq." Further, the senior minister writes, "Our leaders still think war serves as a negative good. They don't quite get it. . . . that no nation can live alone. . . . I dream of peace that comes from negotiation, from diplomacy, from prayer, through love" ("Oasis in the City" newsletter, January 2008, p. 1). While the social gospel dominated this site more than any other, ministers and congregants by and large articulated some antiwar sentiment and participated in *occasional* activism (with the exception of the social justice minister, who was more consistently involved in antiwar actions but was only briefly on staff during my observations). With all of the other work the staff, ministers, and congregants were involved in, it appears there was little time left over for extensive antiwar activism.

Site 4: Social Justice as a "Bunny Trail"

I was shocked when the pastor at site 4 actually preached on a Sunday morning that some churches are "distracted" by pet projects like social justice. "Social justice is a bunny trail" were his words. Site 4 is the smallest of the five churches under examination. Its white middle-aged pastor is completely out of touch with his African American congregation; in fact, he was demoted during my observations to a part-time status, perhaps to better reflect his efforts given to the congregation.

This pastor's sermons were repetitive. Once Obama won the presidency, they were characterized by panic-ridden themes of the "end times," coming financial tragedies for America, and the need for members to stock their pantries in preparation for mass poverty and hunger "in America," perhaps reflecting this pastor's own angst about the challenges of financial markets. A few months after President Obama's inauguration, the pastor of site 4 wrote, "This is a time when we must all look up because looking around can only cause sorrow and fear. Our economy is failing as if by design; could we be more foolish than what is already coming forth from our 'leaders'? We cannot look around and find peace. We must look up."

Another prominent theme in his messages was the threat of terrorism "in our own back yard" (as he put it). He spoke of possible terrorist cells at a campus proximate to his midsized city, racially profiling Arab students there. He is the pastor who spoke most about the "War on Terror." But he spoke *in support* of President Bush's efforts, quoting passages on the responsibility for Christians to pray for their leaders and accept their authority as an extension of God's authority. Once Obama was elected, however, he began to pray for the "misguided leaders" of this country and that those who truly have God's authority would be successful in imposing better agendas. Interestingly, this pastor perceived himself to be apolitical—and that the church was not to be involved in politics, though his conservative political commitments were clear to parishioners.

DISCUSSION

Features of an Africana feminist organizational structure—one that is nonhierarchical, that challenges patriarchy, that privileges the lives and voices of ordinary members in its vision and program, and that works for social justice with creative strategies—are coincident with a higher level of activism among church leadership and members in the three churches I have examined. However, the challenges of everyday living and the need to extend resources to address members' immediate needs divert efforts from extensive antiwar activism at even the most progressive of the three sites.

As discussed in the analysis, I found significant differences between the sites under examination. To summarize, I saw divergences in three salient areas: social location of members, the relationship between leaders and ordinary members, and variations in the centrality of social justice and activism to the church's mission.

The social location, also influenced by region, urbanity, and racial/ethnic composition, of members in each site created a context for activism to take place or not. Site 3, "Oasis in the City," was located in an eastern metropolis rife with activism. To be a member of the wider progressive community in this city was synonymous with undertaking some type of visible political activism. People on staff, on the board of elders, who led classes, and who taught Bible studies in this congregation were by and large middle-class, upper-middle-class, or wealthy individuals who saw their involvement in church activities as a way to give back to the community. They chose membership in site 3 so that they could use their access to power for the benefit of the less privileged. The rank-and-file members and attenders of site 3 included these privileged individuals as well as folks from all walks of life, including homeless men and women. The wider membership is clearly diverse, and the senior minister, other staff, and leadership board are intentional about creating a balance in leadership representation and worship style to reflect the many cultures present in the church in its collective identity.

In site 1, "Afrocentric and Evangelical," the membership consists of movers and shakers in the Midwest city as well as less influential middle-class and working-class urban African Americans. While members and leaders in site 1 share the experience of racial marginality, many represent an elite in the city's African American communities. In site 4 ("Leadership and Congregation at Odds"), on the other hand, while the membership is also largely African American, their class status, race, gender, and ability locate them socially at the margins of their city. The members of site 4 are by and large middle-class and working-class or working-poor African American women. Several members are disabled as well.

This issue of the membership's social location is related to the second distinguishing feature among the sites, the relationship between leaders and members. In site 3, "Oasis in the City," the most diverse in terms of race/ethnicity, gender, class, sexuality, and ability, the leadership mirrors the diversity of the membership in many ways (except class background and ability). And the differences among members are not ignored but embraced. The leadership works tirelessly to design programs, to fashion cultural products and a church culture that is deliberate about creating shared community. The leadership consciously engages in a daily effort to move beyond the difficulties of dissimilarity among members. The open, shared leadership style invites members to partake in the work of redefining commonality on the basis of shared ideals.

In the "Afrocentric and Evangelical" church, the leadership represents the ordinary members in many ways, except for gender, as the leadership is male-dominated and focused on the head pastor (while women predominate in the active congregation). And where leaders and members diverge, the gap is filled by expectation. The leadership represents the best of what the membership hopes to be. Leaders in addition to members are African American: a strong male pastor, with a team of capable male and female African American associate pastors. The leaders are highly educated and well connected politically and socially within the community, city, state, and nation. The leadership style and structure of site 1 are more hierarchical than shared, but this apparently suits the membership.

At site 4, "Leadership and Congregation at Odds, the class status of members has diminished over time, and with this development, the relationship between the leadership and the congregation has changed. A more inclusive leadership style characterized this congregation when more middle-class members and men attended. A pastor-concentrated leadership has evolved with the loss of class status and gender diversity among church members.

The last difference to be addressed among the sites is how they diverge on interest in activism and centrality of social justice to their mission. In site 3 ("Oasis in the City"), activism is part of their identity and thus central to their day-to-day programming. In site 1 ("Afrocentric and Evangelical"), activism is a part of their theology; a primary preoccupation of black theology has been to assert the humanity of black folk and to proclaim an understanding of Christianity that is consonant with black liberation (Singleton 2008). The pastors and members in site 1 integrate this activist worldview in words uttered from the pulpit, in publications, and in the Sunday morning liturgy, but involvement in *formal* political organizing is less central to their daily program efforts. It is important to note, however, that congregants and pastors may disagree with this statement. It is conceivable that they would define counseling with a couple considering marriage, coordinating after-school activities for youth, and planning rites of passage activities for middle school–aged children all as political acts because they are carried out in accordance with the Afrocentric "Black Family Values" articulated in the church's documents, values which at their core are political in nature. These Afrocentric values specify appropriate ways for African Americans to promote self-esteem and educational success of youth, preserve African American families, and harness power for Africana communities in the context of racism in American society. So promoting the basic survival of African American families is viewed as a political act, which is related to formal political participation (Reese, Brown, and Ivers 2007) but does not necessarily translate to immediate, visible, externally directed political activism.

Site 4, "Leadership and Congregation at Odds," has a majority of African American members who might be sympathetic to the goals of left-leaning political activism, but members and the site's pastor are on the whole somewhat ambivalent in their collective stance on political activism. Visible politically motivated efforts consistent with the social gospel are nonexistent in site 4. Given that the pastor of site 4 preaches *against* left politics, it follows that progressive political activism consonant with the views of its majority African American members is not part of this site's program. In examining its programming over the period of observation, activities centered on fellowship, Bible study for multiple age levels, and to a lesser extent, physical health of members of the congregation.

Different from site 4, which has dwindled in membership and attenders and whose pastor is paid only part-time, sites 1 and 3 are focused on bread-and-butter issues that they may feel are of more immediate importance than antiwar activism. All three churches are interested in spreading their interpretation of the message of the good news of salvation, as shown in rhetoric from the pulpit, in newsletters, and in activities that are driven by long-standing members. Reaching out and bringing in those who need the good news, another term for "the gospel," is the central concern at evangelical Christian churches by definition. So I found very little antiwar activism at these sites.

Over time, the political nature of work at "Oasis in the City" church is topical and timely. Whereas antiwar work was relevant ten years ago, over the past five years, "Oasis in the City" has been heavily engaged in #BlackLivesMatter and work against gun violence. But they have kept up their efforts on marriage equality and continued in their bread/butter/benevolence work at the same time. And they are ever working toward cooperation and inclusion among the diverse church membership.

Part of the work of diversity and inclusion in multiracial voluntary associations, including churches, is that expressions of political identity are not separated from spirituality. Political work is seen as an outgrowth of spiritual growth. And the two are seen to go hand in hand. Also, as urgent and pressing issues of the day affect members, the entire congregation expends energy to uplift offended and hurting groups and to provide support by directing most of the congregation's social justice efforts toward agreed-upon dominant themes.

For example, a survey of the "Oasis in the City" church's blogs and websites from 2011 to 2015 reveals some balance between prophetic social justice work and more spiritually oriented themes. Approximately 75 percent of posts on the lead pastor's blog include left-leaning political content. Searching under keywords such as politics, activism, and war yields the following types of posts by pastors and members, which characterize the prophetic work at site 3 in recent years:

- Performance of "After 8" to publicize the Proposition 8 trial (November 28, 2012)
- Testimony by an associate pastor before the state senate in support of legislation to ban conversion therapy (July 7, 2014)
- Involvement in the Occupy Movement (August 9, 2015)
- A Dr. Martin Luther King, Jr. intergenerational human rights teach-in held in lieu of a regular worship service (January 10, 2014)
- Multiple posts regarding church work to support #BlackLivesMatter (e.g. July 16, 2013; February, 1, 2015; August 9, 2015)
- Themes countering gun violence (January 29, 2013) and supporting the global Black Lives Matter movement (August 9, 2015)
- A standing committee, "Leadership in Arts, Education, and Activism" (noted in multiple blog entries and in every issue of the newsletter)

These posts show that activism is central to site 3's identity and that the concerns of African Americans (who are not the majority of members) are not marginalized. In fact, "activism" is the keyword with the most entries—eleven pages' worth. For "Oasis in the City," perhaps it is less about being political and more about being prophetic—living, teaching, and working toward social justice, economic justice, and racial justice. As I struggled to code a passage written by the senior minister that focused on Jesus's crucifixion, I wrote the following:

> code: (Jesus/Kingdom of God on earth as speaking truth to the modern world, including politically)

Not feeling satisfied with this characterization, I continued to write more.

> Observer comment: This passage could be read on multiple layers. One may be relevance of Jesus to modern society. And another may be Jesus's crucifixion and death as a metaphor for allowing apathy; a sense of powerlessness; and religion, only as personal piety, to die. And the minister further posits Jesus's triumph over death as a symbol of retaining/rediscovering/claiming faith as political action to flourish. The minister's final statement, "I hope we get really clear that we are not free until everyone is free" (March 26, 2013), leaves no doubt about the intention of her remarks.

A final observation is that the lack of antiwar activism in the three sites I analyzed reflected antiwar protest more broadly in the American context. There are several interreligious antiwar events and organizations, and antiwar activism has become a niche focus among activists broadly. Searches for antiwar activity from 2001 to 2015 leave me wanting. Religious advocates for peace and justice have had to find each other across denominational and religious lines to create a critical mass of individuals with whom to organize. This fact is not entirely disappointing, because models of interreligious cooperation are necessary in this conflict-ridden world. Efforts to work together by agnostic, Buddhist, Christian, Hindu, Jewish, Muslim, and other activists are a hopeful sign. And Africana feminist organizations, analysis, and methods have much to contribute.

NOTES

1. The war in Afghanistan, the longest running in the United States versus Iraq/Afghanistan conflict, occurred from October 7, 2001, to December 28, 2014 (Thompson 2014).

2. Evangelical Christianity promotes the view that the Bible is the inerrant word of God and emphasizes the importance of a personal relationship with God through faith in Jesus Christ. Another hallmark of the tradition is the charge to "spread the gospel" or the "good news" of the faith (Robbins 2004, 119). Some adherents within denominations that are traditionally considered to be evangelical do not hold fast to all of these criteria.

3. While conservative evangelical Christianity does not describe all Protestant denominations, these denominations' conservative branches accounted for 28 percent of Americans in 2014 (the latest data available) while "about one-in-five Americans identify with Protestant denominations that are not generally considered to be doctrinally conservative" (Hout and Smith 2015, 5).

4. Conversely, elements of patriarchal organizing include (a) a hierarchical structure, usually led by male members of the organization, (b) an analysis of problems and possibilities of the organization that does not consider issues of race, class, and gender and the ways that they mutually construct one another, (c) a recognition of differences between groups that does not appreciate the relational nature of those differences, (d) a lack of attention to the balance of addressing local and global issues, (e) a use of static "tried and true" strategies for accomplishing goals, and (f) a rooting more in "objective" analysis and external "standards" rather than everyday people's desires and experiences (see Zerai and Banks 2002a for further discussion).

5. The General Social Survey (GSS), first collected in 1972, uses a modified probability sample and a cross-sectional design and is housed at the National Opinion Research Center at the University of Chicago. The principal investigator is James Davis; co-principal investigators are Tom W. Smith and Peter V. Marsden. The National Congregations Study (1998, 2006–2007) was conducted in conjunction with the General Social Survey (GSS) in 1998 and 2007. The GSS asked respondents to name their religious congregation. Since the GSS is a nationally representative sample, it follows that the NCS approximates a representative sample of U.S. places of worship as well. The 2004 NCS is a replication of the 1998 NCS. For my analysis I examine preliminary data released from the 2007 wave.

6. The principal investigators of the ANES: 2006 Pilot Study are Jon A. Krosnick and Arthur Lupia. It is a follow-up to the 2000, 2002, and 2004 Full Panel Study collected by the University of Michigan, Center for Political Studies. The data are representative of U.S. citizens of voting age on or before Election Day (November 6, 2000). The sample also came from individuals who completed a valid interview in the 2004 ANES time series study. The pilot study was conducted after the 2006 midterm elections for the purpose of testing new questions and conducting methodological research to inform the design of future ANES studies. In the authors' own words: "The American National Election Studies (ANES) produces high quality data on voting, public opinion, and political participation to serve the research needs of social scientists, teachers, students, policy makers and journalists who want to better understand the theoretical and empirical foundations of national election outcomes" (ANES, http://www.electionstudies.org, 9/16/2009).

7. "This poll, fielded May 18–23, 2007, is a part of a continuing series of monthly surveys that solicit public opinion on the presidency and on a range of other political and social issues. An oversample of African Americans was conducted for this poll. Respondents were asked whether they approved of the way George W. Bush was handling the presidency and issues such as immigration and foreign policy" (http://www.icpsr.umich.edu/icpsrweb/ICPSR/studies/23444). The respondents are persons aged eighteen and over living in households with telephones in the contiguous 48 United States. The ICPSR explains that "a variation of random-digit dialing using primary sampling units (PSUs) was employed, consisting of blocks of 100 telephone numbers identical through the eighth digit and stratified by geographic region, area code, and size of place" (Description & Citation—Study No. 23444).

8. Note that site 2 ("Friendliest Place in College Town USA") is not included in this analysis. Antiwar activism was not addressed in site 2.

9. I have chosen not to identify the churches because my purpose is not to expose, to congratulate, or to vilify them for their activism or lack thereof, but to consider whether elements of Africana feminist organizing facilitate or impede antiwar work.

10. According to Robbins (2004), Pentecostalism's roots lie in the Protestant evangelical tradition (p. 119). Pentecostalism is distinguished "by a pattern of enthusiastic worship" (Robbins 2004: 120).

11. The literature shows that most female-headed congregations are urban, African American, or multiethnic, with being urban and multiethnic being true with site 3 (Konieczny and Chaves 2002).

12. So power held by persons privileged due to their gender, racial, or socioeconomic location is understood to be at the expense of marginalized individuals in society.

13. A critical literature that challenges literal interpretations of biblical passages that appear to condemn homosexuality has proliferated in modern Christianity. Workshops that address "puzzling passages" often provide LGBTIQ attenders and allies a set of tools to help them fend off dogmatic "biblical" attacks against queer identities.

14. For example, Calvary Assembly of God Church in Toledo, Ohio, held a $3.5-million mortgage (since 1984) that calls for a $41,000 monthly payment (*The Blade, McClatchy-Tribune* Information Services via COMTEX).

Part II: Becoming Inclusive in a Presbyterian Church

1940 to 1980

The next four chapters provide a social history of cohesion and contestation in a Presbyterian college-town congregation that was in the 1940s largely a heteronormative white, Republican, highly educated, middle-class congregation, which over a forty-year period became an inclusive environment supportive of lesbian, gay, bisexual, transgender, intersex, questioning/queer (LGBTIQ) communities and concomitant racial, gender, and class diversity. It is the struggle at McKinley Memorial Presbyterian Church to both survive and to embrace the principles of social justice, struggles that have embroiled the Presbyterian Church (USA) denomination since the 1950s,[1] that is the focus of Part II of this book. As I have argued in previous chapters, this underlying social system, which mirrors the racial/gender/heteronormative structure(s) of American society, is the predominant reason that multiracial churches struggle with the issue of diversity. However, as a volitional community that eventually devotes itself to progressive social change, the McKinley congregation does not remain content reproducing the status quo. The members work to overcome androcentric language and references to the divine. They have struggled within their own walls, within their presbytery, in the denomination at large, and in university and residential communities to supplant traditional gender hierarchies, make marriage accessible to all, and intentionally address issues of racism.

NOTE

1. While this chapter focuses on the 1940–1980 period, struggles within the PCUSA and its precursors around issues of race date back to the era of slavery in the United States. See Figure 5.2 for more details.

FIVE
A Presbyterian Campus Church
1940 to 1953

The More Light Presbyterians (MLP)–affiliated campus church examined in the next four chapters is well known today for its support and sustenance of a movement among "More Light Presbyterians . . . to work for the full participation of lesbian, gay, bisexual and transgender people of faith in the life, ministry and witness of the Presbyterian Church (USA)" (MLP.org). Since the 1980s, it has welcomed LGBTIQ members and celebrated its diversity in this regard. For over a decade, McKinley Memorial Presbyterian Church[1] has been headed by a vibrant and engaging LGBTIQ pastor. And even before this time, members proudly pointed to their prominent "inclusiveness" stained glass window (installed in 1997), one of the first of its kind in the United States, as evidence of their commitment to social equality (depicted in cover photo).

> "To our knowledge, this is the only stained glass window devoted to inclusiveness as a theme in America. . . . A pink triangle set against a white Celtic cross recalls the suffering and repression of GLBT persons at the hands of the Nazis in Germany in the 30's and 40's. Also included are the rainbow flag, an AIDS ribbon, and male and female hands clasping one another and supported by the hand of God."
> —Dave Bechtel, *McKinley's Stained Glass Windows: History and Tradition*

Long-time church members explain that while there was some contestation around the decision to become a "More Light" congregation, even in the era in which the larger Presbyterian Church (USA) denomination eschewed this stance, the struggles around expansion of membership to African Americans within the denomination at large drew even more fire prior to and during the Civil Rights era.

Examining internal church documents, conducting ethnographic oral history interviews with current and past staff and older members, and examining documentation of the national Presbyterian Church (USA) (PCUSA for short) provides rich primary source material from which to craft a social history of this MLP church located within a multidimensional context that includes the history of race, gender, and sexuality in America; the history of race, gender and sexuality in the Midwest; and churches as a microcosm of that history that weave an intricate tapestry. My argument is that, like in any other social institution in American society, intersecting structures of race, gender, sexuality, and class have been produced and reproduced throughout the various eras of McKinley's history. Looking at the 1940–1980[2] period, I ask what processes members and staff at McKinley Memorial Presbyterian Church used to create meaningful social justice ministries. How did they respond to the pressing social conflicts of those years? How did their internal day-to-day practices change to align with their social justice ideals?

GOVERNANCE IN THE PRESBYTERIAN CHURCH (USA)

The Presbyterian Church (USA) has undergone numerous name changes over the years, but its basic structure has remained the same for the past century. Figure 5.1 depicts a schematic of Presbyterian development in the United States (Presbyterian Historical Society 2014). The denomination met annually (and since 2004 has switched to biannual meetings) during a gathering called the General Assembly (GA). The General Assembly is the highest policymaking body in the PCUSA, and the stated clerk holds the highest office. Commissioners to GA are elected from among teaching elders (pastors) and ruling elders of the denomination. Presbyteries are regional groupings of congregations. Each presbytery is represented by its commissioners to the GA. In the local church, the leadership consists of staff (including ministers) and the board of ruling elders, referred to as the session. The session is an elected administrative body, with nominations made with an eye to having the board of ruling elders be representative of the church membership.

According to data collected by the PCUSA in 2012, the denomination held 10,262 congregations with a membership of 1,849,496 (Presbyterian Mission Agency, Research Services 2012a). In 2008, the "median presbytery has a membership of 10,081 persons, 124 ministers, and 62 churches" (Presbyterian Mission Agency, Research Services 2012b). And the racial composition of congregations in the denomination in 2012 was 90 percent white, 4 percent Africana,[3] 4 percent Asian, and 2 percent Latino. (See Table 5.1.) While the membership numbers of whites have decreased in the past four years, the percentages of Africana, Asian, and Latino mem-

A Presbyterian Campus Church: 1940 to 1953 73

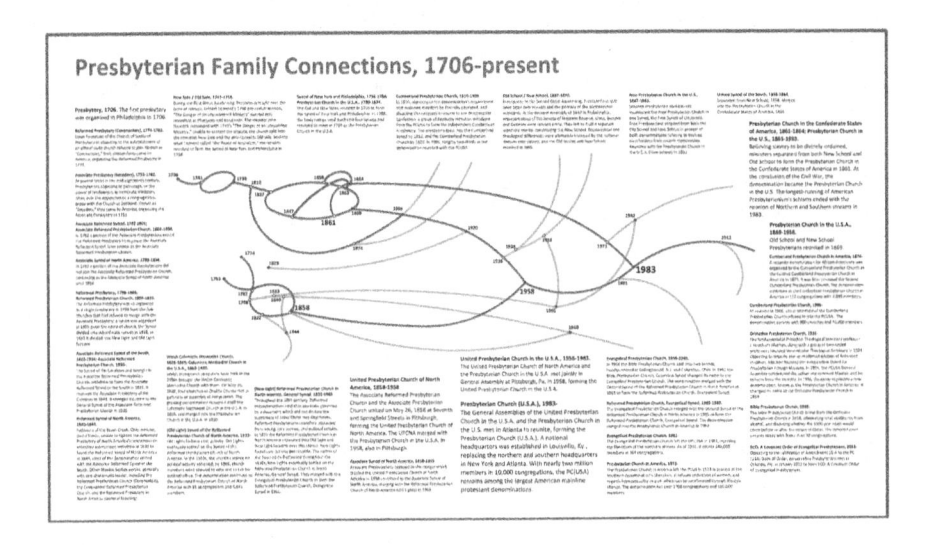

Figure 5.1. Courtesy: Presbyterian Historical Society, Philadelphia, PA. *Source: www.history.pcusa.org_sites_default_files_theme-assets_presbyterian_family_connections_ocr_2mb.*

bers have increased, accounting for *the* entire increase in overall membership in the PCUSA from 2008 to 2012.

McKinley is unique within its denomination, as it was established as a campus church, with a mission to provide for the spiritual well-being of students, faculty, and staff at the University of Illinois. The McKinley Presbyterian Student Foundation today holds an endowment and promotes social justice work. According to McKinley historian Mr. David (Dave) Bechtel (2015):

> The archives reveal a continuing tension between students and the church elders on the purpose of the ministry.... Soon after regularizing the church, in 1924, one might speculate, the church elders decided to give the students their own place and organized fundraising to build the Foundation Building. About half of the money, $200,000 came from Senator McKinley's estate and the rest was raised from around the state, primarily, from other Presbyterian churches to support a student ministry at the University of Illinois.

The focus of these chapters is McKinley Church, but its student foundation is interconnected to the church's history. Further, there was a third McKinley building: Presby House was a residence for Presbyterian female university students. Much later (in 2008), Presby House was replaced by Presby Hall, a dormitory erected by the McKinley Foundation as co-educational certified housing for University of Illinois students.

Table 5.1 Changes in Presbyterian Church (USA) Membership by Race, 2008 to 2012

Racial identity	Change in membership from 2008 to 2012	2008 membership	% of 2008 membership	2012 membership	% of 2012 membership
White	−31,764	1,693,032	92.5	1,661,268	90.2%
Africana	8,882	59,263	3.2	68,145	3.7%
Asian	26,015	43,972	2.4	69,987	3.8%
Latino	5,320	24,148	1.3	29,468	1.6%
Other	2,940	9,952	0.6	12,892	0.7%
Total	11,394	1,830,367	100	1,841,761	100%

Note: Racial identity is not reported for all members; PCUSA total membership is greater.

Sources: 2013 Research Services, Presbyterian Church (USA) Comparative Statistics 2012, p. 25; http://www.pcusa.org/site_media/media/uploads/research/pdfs/2012-cs-table13-14.pdf; 2012-cs-table1 PCUSA congreg and members.pdf; PCUSA Miscellaneous Information; http://www.pcusa.org/site_media/media/uploads/oga/pdf/2008_misc_info.pdf

METHODOLOGY

This study focuses on three distinct eras in McKinley's history that correspond with cultural changes, internal contestations, and resolutions from 1940 through 1980. They are the "pre-Civil Rights" era of 1940 to 1957, the "Civil Rights" era of 1958 to 1967, and the dawning of the "More Light Presbyterians" era from 1968 to 1980. This chapter covers the period from 1940 to 1953, focusing on analysis of ethnographic interviews, memoirs that refer to the time period, and original documents written from 1940 to 1960 (including *Daily Illini* and *News-Gazette* articles, University of Illinois Library *LibGuides* and timelines, church photographs, and McKinley session minutes).[4] I begin the study from 1940 to chart McKinley's movement from a more traditional white and upwardly mobile though college student–centered congregation to one that later embraced a social justice–oriented identity.

Documents and interviews are analyzed utilizing an intersectional framework (explained in chapter 1). In the multilayered context of McKinley Memorial Presbyterian Church, the University of Illinois, Champaign-Urbana, the Midwest, and American society, racial structures have not existed in a vacuum. They have been impacted and shaped by the multiple structures of gender, race, class, and sexuality.

Research Design and Method of Analysis

As explained in chapter 1, I use a four-step research design to discover what has happened in McKinley Church in regards to race, gender, class, and sexuality specifically. What ways have these categories been a consideration in the church's outreach efforts since 1940? Are there ways that various groups have been excluded from 1940 to 1980? What evidence exists? What was the racial structure of the church within this period, and how has it changed over time? What was the gender structure over time, and how has it changed? What about class and sexuality structures? What are evidences of the intersections of these four structures?

Step 1 of my research design is to identify relevant contextual factors by perusing church documents, *Daily Illini* and *News-Gazette* stories, government policy concerning diversity in public institutions, and the history of inclusion at the University of Illinois. For this step, I begin to answer questions about race, class, gender, and sexuality structures at McKinley by identifying aspects of its social context from internal and external documentation. The main product from this step is an extensive timeline that starts before the time period under study and follows through to about 2011. The timeline focuses on Champaign County, though it takes into account federal and state mandates and occurrences. The timeline also includes important events in the University of Illinois history of race, gender, class, and sexuality inclusion (Table 1). I also examined population data concerning racial and gender compositions of University of Illinois students and of Champaign County. I have identified notable "firsts" in the period under study (e.g., the first African American to earn a degree at the University of Illinois). Events noted by members and McKinley's staff are also recorded.

Step 2 of my research design is to authentically represent members' understandings of their experiences at McKinley. My design not only entails a study of church documents to begin to answer these questions, but also includes an analysis of ethnographic interviews conducted with older, long-time church members and current and past pastors and staff. I discuss the church activities offered by interview participants in the context of the time period when they occurred, and I identify the significance of their stories for the molding of racial, class, gender, and sexuality structures at McKinley. *Step 3* of my research design is to contextualize members' descriptions. I analyze ethnographic interview data to consider both context and the influence of structural forces. I utilize the tool of intersectionality to examine the ways in which social phenomena mutually construct one another. Finally, I link local events and specific outcomes to more distant social forces and more remote consequences (DeVault 1999). I link timeline data from church documents and exogenous sources (from University of Illinois, federal mandates, etc.) to interview transcripts.

Data Sources

I conducted qualitative interviews with thirteen participants. Before beginning the interview process, I obtained permission from the lead pastor and submitted and obtained approval for my research protocol from the Institutional Review Board (IRB) at the University of Illinois in July 2014. As a part of my IRB application, I was required to obtain written permission from the session of McKinley Church to conduct the research, which I did in August 2014.[5]

Nine interviews were conducted with women and four with men. I did not ask the sexual orientation of my respondents, but four volunteered their sexual minority status. Two of the thirteen participants are African American and eleven are white. All participants are middle-class, and the socioeconomic status of the group is largely upper-middle-class. Reflecting their college-campus congregation, all respondents are college educated, and most have advanced degrees. Most participants grew up in the Midwest of the United States; only one actually grew up in Champaign County. I conducted the interviews from November 2014 through January 2015. Posing a series of questions to each respondent, I asked when they first began attending McKinley and what attracted them there, and then I asked what they most enjoy about their experiences, as well as what they would like to see change at the church. I also asked specifically about how women's roles at McKinley have changed over time, the ways McKinley has reached out to draw in African American congregants, and McKinley's evolution toward inclusiveness. Interviews took one to three hours. To date, I have interviewed most participants once and three participants twice.

Primary document analysis is an important data source for this chapter. I read three *McKinley Minutes Books,* dated from 1942 to 1965, 1965 to 1977, and 1977 to 1989. The McKinley board of elders, termed the "session" in the Presbyterian tradition, meets about once a month, occasionally twice. The books of McKinley minutes contain a record of each meeting along with records of all congregational meetings. The clerk of session has the responsibility to compile each set of minutes during her or his term of office and ensure that a copy is placed in the minutes book. Once a decade a clerk from McKinley's presbytery (a regional grouping of the denomination's churches) checks over the minutes book. I found these records to be an invaluable resource to check members' accounts of historical events and to gain clarity on McKinley's processes, resources, procedures, personnel, conflicts, and the like.

Dave Bechtel kindly shared with me the location and organization of numerous historical church documents. Through him I was able to gain access to old photographs, which were another data source. I was also able to read various reports, such as a helpful document that Mr. Bechtel compiled on youth ministry at McKinley. Mr. Bechtel also provided clippings from a 1953–54 McKinley student newspaper and from the local *News-Gazette*. Supplementing my own *News-Gazette* and *Daily Illini* research,[6] these mainstream media sources rounded out my primary data.

I also utilized numerous secondary sources. The renowned University of Illinois library holds a cache of rare and highly valuable resources, from the IDEALS database to news databases to Ethnography of the University Initiative data sources (University of Illinois 2015). A timeline developed by library staff overviewing important historical influences in the life of the university helps to inform the McKinley and PCUSA timeline depicted in Table 5.2.[7]

Data Analysis

After conducting the interviews, typing transcripts, and reading them through, I conducted two phases of coding. First I open-coded the interview transcripts, developing inductive codes that are data-driven. For example, I sometimes used a word in phrases in the transcript to determine the code; other times I used a descriptor such as "campus ministry" as the code. After open-coding the entire set of interview transcripts, from which I generated more than 300 unique open-codes, I began to create a list of twenty broad codes that turned out to be focused codes. It was at this point in the data analysis that I decided to focus on the 1940–1980 period for the present chapter. I had so much material that I knew I could not include it all in a single chapter, and I could see a compelling story emerging about the Civil Rights and dawning MLP periods in McKinley's history. Next, I conducted focused coding on themes that helped to elucidate the 1940–1980 period.

Subsequently, I read the minutes books for 1942 to 1965, 1965 to 1977, and 1977 to 1989.[8] After reading a minutes book once, I went through it again and marked passages of high interest, similar to my focused coding from the interview transcripts. I marked all passages that had to do with the themes of student ministry, changes in leadership, Civil Rights, LGBTIQ inclusion/exclusion, conflict, cooperation, conflict resolution, gender/feminism/inclusive language, and historical/external influences on ministry, including Vietnam War protest. Then I created a grid and grouped quotes from the minutes book and from the interview transcripts under each theme. I settled on a streamlined version of these themes to provide an outline of the analysis below.

Linking Institutional Forces

Indigenous meanings are the starting point of the analysis, but it is the researcher's job to analyze what she sees, considering each member's or group's meanings as one of many perspectives that help us to identify the underlying social structure in research settings. This case study repre-

Table 5.2 PC(USA) Precursors and McKinley Memorial Presbyterian Church Timeline, 1789–1983 (sources provided in the appendix).

Year	Event
1789–1869	**Presbyterian Church in the USA (PCUSA) holds it first General Assembly (GA) in Philadelphia. (Presbyterians came to the U.S. from Scotland and Ireland.)**
1814–1887	Lifespan of church and foundation's namesake, Rev. George McKinley.
1847–1863	Free Presbyterian Church in the U.S. breaks from PCUSA in protest of PCUSA's refusal to ban slaveholders from membership.
1856–1926	Lifespan of U.S. Senator William Brown McKinley (son of George).
1858–1870	Rev. George McKinley served as Presbyterian minister in Champaign County.
1858–1958	United Presbyterian Church of North America (UPCNA) forms, uniting some previous factions of immigrant seceders, a denomination developing on a separate trajectory from the PCUSA.
1860	Abraham Lincoln is elected U.S. president.
1861–1864	Presbyterian Church of the Confederate States of America splits from PCUSA over slavery, later (after the Civil War) becoming Presbyterian Church in the U.S.
1863	President Lincoln issues the Emancipation Proclamation.
	Free Presbyterian Church in the U.S. reunites with Presbyterian Church in the USA.
1865	U.S. Congress approves the 13th Amendment to the Constitution, outlawing slavery.
1865–1983	Maintaining its split from UPCNA/UPCUSA, Presbyterian Church of the Confederate States of America becomes Presbyterian Church in the U.S. (PCUS).
1866	The Civil Rights Act confers citizenship upon African Americans and guarantees them equal rights with whites.
1867	The Illinois Industrial University is founded at Urbana; Reconstruction begins.
1869–1958	**The creation of the Presbyterian Church in the U.S.A. (PCUSA) unites Old School and New School Presbyterians.**
1870	William Brown McKinley attends the Illinois Industrial University (at age 14) for two years.
	"Trustees [of the university] agreed to admit women in a 5-4 vote." [Ed: All quotations are from the University of Illinois Library timeline.]
1871	The first female cohort is admitted to the university.
1872	The university establishes a boarding hall for women.
1873–1879	John J. Byrd is the first African American to serve as a member of the university Board of Trustees.

Year	Event
1874–pres.	Cumberland Presbyterian Church in America is established apart from the PCUSA as an African American denomination.
1874	The university's first female faculty member, Louise C. Allen, establishes a domestic science course.
1875	"Board of Trustees permitted conscientious objectors to be excused from military drill."
1877	Reconstruction ends, the result of a political deal to put Rutherford Hayes into the White House.
1881ff	Segregation of public transportation; 1882 lynchings begin.
1882	"Dora Andrus became the first woman to head the College Government."
1884	"Carlos Montezuma became the first Native American graduate of the university."
1885	Illinois Industrial University becomes the University of Illinois.
1887	Jonathan A. Rogan, the first African American student to enroll at the University of Illinois, attends for one year.
1890	The right to vote for African American males is essentially voided (the "Mississippi Plan" uses literacy tests for voting, with other states following).
1883	The Civil Rights Act is overturned, with the 1875 act declared unconstitutional; states (not citizens) are forbidden from discriminating.
1895	The university's second African American employee is also its first African American (AA) academic professional: Albert Lee, the "defacto dean of African American students," institutes the first physical education for women students.
1896	*Plessy* v. *Ferguson* challenges the validity of "separate but equal" Jim Crow segregation laws (with segregation of churches permitted as well); UIUC Women's League was established.
1898	"All women of the faculty and student body met for the first time as a Woman's Department."
1900	William Walter Smith is the university's first African American graduate.
1905	The university dedicates the Woman's Building.
1906	PCUSA Synod of Illinois establishes a U of I campus Presbyterian church by appointing T.J. Porter university pastor.
	Maudelle Tanner Brown Bausfield is the university's first female African American graduate.
1907	William Walter Smith earns his second degree from the university, a bachelor's in civil engineering.

Year	Event
1912	A donation for a campus Presbyterian church building from U.S. Senator William Brown McKinley funds the new church, named for his father, late Presbyterian pastor Rev. George McKinley. The original McKinley Presbyterian Church building is erected (completed in 1912).
	The university's first annual mass meeting of women is held.
1913	The first African American fraternity on the UIUC campus is organized.
1916–1970	Through the Great Migration, Chicago's African American population increases from 2% in 1915 to 33% in 1970.
	"On April 21st, 136 students withdrew for military and farm work. This figure grew to 1,000 by May 5th. YMCA and new women's residence used as barracks."
	"University service flag raised with 2,960 stars—one for each Illini in the service. Some 3,000 students enrolled in Student Army Training Corps (SATC)."
1918	"Woman's Residence Hall (Busey Hall) completed [ed.: the first residence hall built by the university]; Homecoming canceled because of war."
1920	Passage of 19th Amendment: "The right of citizens of the United States to vote shall not be denied or abridged by the United States or by any State on account of sex."
1922	Controversy begins as Harry Emerson Fosdick's "Shall the Fundamentalists Win?" exposes liberal and conservative differences.
1923	PCUSA General Assembly reaffirms "Five Fundamentals" to challenge ordination of ministers who could not affirm Jesus's virgin birth.
1920s–30s	Modernist–Fundamentalist controversy embroils PCUSA.
1924	McKinley Foundation is established.
1928	Record spring semester enrollment at University of Illinois.
1930	McKinley Student Ministry Foundation building is completed in midst of Great Depression.
1935	"APA and KAP establish coop African American restaurant after Boyd's Café, the only campus restaurant [ed.: except for university café] to serve AAs closed; lasted less than 1 year."
1936	Some members—many expelled from churches by liberals—leave PCUSA over Modernist–Fundamentalist controversy and form the Orthodox Presbyterian Church.
	"300 students and faculty held a strike against war"; German refugee students housed by Jewish fraternities and sororities.
1937	"Civil Rights Union and American Student Union circulated petitions protesting discrimination by campus restaurants and Champaign-Urbana theaters."
	African American university students sue Hanley-Lewis Confectionery for discrimination; circuit court judge decides for the business.

Year	Event
1939	Hilda H. Lawson is first African American woman to receive a Ph.D., in English, from U of I.
1935–1945	WWII and acceleration of the Great Migration (1940s and 1950s).
1941	"U.S. entry into World War II after Pearl Harbor greatly impacted University. Almost overnight, ratio of men to women on campus went from 3-1 to 1-4."
1942–1967	**JIM HINE ERA—McKinley is headed by Pastor/Director James R. ('Jim') Hine.**
1944	"Congress passed GI Bill offering a college education to millions of returning veterans."
1945	University sets up temporary housing to help accommodate 11,000+ veterans returning to campus following the war. Of the 20,276 U of I students who served, 738 were killed.
	Student Community Interracial Committee (SCIC) is formed to fight discrimination; campus Wesley Foundation Wescoga Women's Coop house admits an African American member.
1946	"SCIC asks restaurants to sign statement saying they don't discriminate. 6 refused. Following picketing and threatened lawsuit, they finally agreed to end discrimination."
	"Board of Trustees endorsed 'policy [to] favor and strengthen attitudes and social philosophies necessary to create [an] atmosphere in which racial prejudice cannot thrive.' "
	Residence halls open to African Americans.
1948	"SCIC helped desegregate washroom facilities for Illini Union employees. Group also protested minstrel show sponsored by the Newman Club."
1950	SCIC surveys students' opinions on desegregated housing.
1951	McKinley Church installs three "student windows": Agriculture, Arts, Engineering (dedicated to Jim Hine). Second rose window, "Christ's Call to All the World," is also installed.
1952	McKinley undertakes a building expansion of the church.
1954	In *Brown* v. *Board of Education*, Supreme Court rules that public schools separated by race are unconstitutional.
1955	*Time* magazine reports the Presbyterian Church is divided over segregation.
1955–1975	Vietnam War.
1957	Sen. John F. Kennedy addresses 1,200 U of I graduates at the midyear convocation.
1958–1983	**United Presbyterian Church of North America merges with PCUSA to form UPCUSA and enters a period of social activism; Eugene Carson Blake, the primary instigator, remains stated clerk until 1966.**

Year	Event
1959	"University recognition withheld for student organizations restricting membership on the basis of race or religion."
1960	"Committee for Liberal Action (CLA) fights student and administration apathy"; protests racial discrimination in store windows, and stages a sit-in at Walgreens.
	"Shortly before elected president, Sen. John F. Kennedy addressed 10,000 on the Quad, becoming the first presidential candidate to do so at Illinois."
1961	"Revision in state law raised drinking age for women from 18 to 21, the same age as men."
	"Committee on Student Affairs passed bill calling for end to racial discrimination in fraternities, sororities, and off-campus housing."
1963	**MCKINLEY'S ENTRY INTO CIVIL RIGHTS ERA**
1963	Jim Ray attends March on Washington.
	Blake, stated clerk of UPCUSA most well known for his stand against racial segregation, with King and eight other civil rights leaders calls for jobs and freedom at March on Washington. Group meets with President Kennedy, who marches with them, linking arms. Blake speaks to the crowd before King delivers "I Have a Dream."
	"Beginning on September 16th, students conducted week-long silent vigil memorializing four African-American youths killed in bombing of Birmingham Sunday school."
	"Some 11,500 people attended a ceremony at the Assembly Hall memorializing John F. Kennedy."
1964	Jim Ray participates in weeklong picket lines and attends SNCC court case in Hattiesburg, Mississippi.
	Students and campus ministers from various churches headed to Mississippi receive training in non-violence tactics at McKinley.
1965	Jim Ray spends 6 weeks in southern Virginia leading student group in doing voter registration and tutoring.
	Students for a Democratic Society (SDS) hold their first annual conference at McKinley Foundation (360 people/66 chapters attend).
	Confession of 1967 is penned calling for reconciliation in areas of racial discrimination, international conflict, enslaving poverty, and sexual anarchy.
1966	"Report revealed very low African-American enrollment at the University; Recognition for Dubois Club sought. Board of Trustees ultimately denied recognition for the group."

Year	Event
1967	President Lyndon Johnson issues Executive Order 11246 requiring federal contractors "to take Affirmative Action"; order is expanded to include women in 1969.
	178th GA adopts Confession of 1967, approved by 90% of presbyteries; conservatives criticize its support for universalism and interference in the political sphere.
1968	**McKINLEY'S ENTRY INTO ERA OF FEMINIST CONSCIOUSNESS AND ANTIWAR ACTIVISM**
1968–1980	Pastor/director Dick Lundy.
1968	Rev. Dr. Martin Luther King, Jr. is assassinated.
	Clarence Shelley becomes director of U of I Project 500; 252 students are arrested at sit-in to protest project's inadequacies.
1969	African American students protest racism and killings in Chicago of Black Panther leaders; UIUC chapter of the National Association for the Advancement of Colored People (NAACP) is instituted.
	Demonstrations against the Vietnam War polarize McKinley congregation.
1970	Afro-American Studies Commission and Black Law Student Association are established at the U of I; protests are held over the military–industrial complex; the first Earth Day is celebrated; U of I students strike after killings at Kent State.
	U of I Gay Liberation Front, part of the national organization, is established; university offers first women's studies course.
1972	Title IX (the Equal Opportunity in Education Act) prohibits gender discrimination in American educational institutions.
	Black Student Association becomes Afrikan People's Coalition; GLF protests bar for harassing gay patrons; 2,000 students, faculty, and community members march against Vietnam War.
1973	Conservative Presbyterian Church in America (PCA) breaks away from the PCUSA over the issues of women's ordination and a perceived drift toward theological liberalism.
	McKinley session issues a statement on behalf of the church calling for a withdrawal of troops from Vietnam.
1974	At U of I, Office of Minority Student Affairs is established and La Casa is founded; the first National Women's Music Festival is held on the U of I campus.
	At the UPCUSA GA, David Bailey Sindt holds up a sign: "Is anybody else out there gay?" His action is claimed as the unofficial start of the More Light Presbyterians movement; a Presbyterian Gay Caucus is formed.
1974–1978	UPCUSA GA does not accept reports from Presbyterians for Gay and Lesbian Concerns (new name for the caucus).

Year	Event
1974–1981	Charlie Sweitzer, associate pastor.
1975	Gay Illini is formed.
	Chief Illiniwek is criticized as offensive and removed from U of I stationery.
1976	Prodigal Child Congregation of the Metropolitan Community Church begins meeting in McKinley church basement.
	Florence C. Bailar Window is installed, with a focus on ministering to the poor.
1977	**MCKINLEY BEGINS TO BECOME INCLUSIVE IN SUPPORT OF LGBT ORGANIZATIONS AND MEMBERS**
	James R. Hine Window depicting "Presbyterian Heritage" is installed.
	Metropolitan Community Church members meet with McKinley session; session affirms commitment to hosting MCC.
	UPCUSA GA commissions study on LGBT issues; GA votes that "homosexuality is not God's wish for humanity."
	UPCUSA GA votes to welcome LGBT members but not ordain them as deacons, elders, or pastors; many churches challenge this and ordain LGBT leaders.
	West Park Presbyterian Church in New York City is the first to become a More Light Presbyterians congregation.
	The MCC holds a service of Holy Union conducted by an MCC pastor at McKinley, an event reported by National Public Radio.
1980	McKinley becomes the 13th MLP church.
	McKinley Session issues affirmative statement welcoming membership of all persons regardless of sexual orientation and extends the right to all to hold office as an ordained elder.
1983	**General Assemblies of UPUSA and PCUS meet in Atlanta to reunite and establish PC(USA).**

sents a set of perspectives presented by various members in the setting. One of the ways to go beyond indigenous meanings of just one or a few participants is to begin to triangulate experiences discussed by a number of members. It is important to get a diversity of groups in the setting represented in interview transcripts.

As a researcher analyzing the McKinley social setting, I pay attention to the actors and their viewpoint as well as to the proximate forces[9] that influence their behavior in the site to begin to understand the underlying social structure at McKinley and how it has changed over time. After starting with indigenous meanings, I triangulate the perspectives of each actor or group of actors in the site, and then I contextualize their perspectives by identifying structural forces that influence the site as well. All of this information helps to identify the underlying social structure.

Linking individual biography to sociological factors has of course been an enduring preoccupation for the social scientist. And most of us want to do this because we are interested in pointing the way toward meaningful social change for the betterment of humanity, à la C. Wright Mills (1959): "The researcher who is interested in social change wants to trace the intricate connection between biography and history." This salient goal, however, sets up a tension for the qualitative social scientist.

Part of what makes inequality such a powerful force in our society is that often people do not analyze the impact of social forces such as sexism, racism, class exploitation, environmental disability, and heterosexism. So how we do analyze our ethnographic data in a way that considers issues like context and the influence of structural forces when this explanation might not come up in informants' accounts when we interview them? Choice of site, the type of events we observe, and how we pay attention to ways informants explicitly talk about race, class, gender, and sexuality may make this easier. The problem, though, is that people don't always directly reference race, class, gender or sexuality. So it is the researcher's job to connect members' descriptions and behavior to wider social forces (Smith 2005).

Linking local events and specific outcomes to more distant social forces and more remote consequences (Emerson, Fretz, and Shaw 2011) provides a roadmap to considering the interplay between structure and agency (Uttal and Cuádraz 1999). Feminist methodologies are engaged in discussions about how to analyze these linkages in order to make the operation of hierarchy and power more visible in settings. For example, Dorothy Smith (2005) was concerned about the problem that social science research is most often conducted in service of the ruling class. She wanted to create a methodology that would place social scientific insight in the service of progressive social change. Her original audience was women. "Smith wanted a practice of sociology that would produce knowledge for women—knowledge that helps its producer understand her social world from her own location" (DeVault 1999, 47). Smith asks the relevant question, Where are the women? Following in that vein, I ask questions that highlight marginalized groups: What about race? What about ability? What about heterosexism? These criticisms suggest that " 'looking' is not so straightforward after all" (DeVault 1999, 47).

Again we come back to the problem of how to see race, class, gender, sexuality, ability, and other factors that we have been socialized to overlook. How can we see these aspects of inequality in the accounts provided by our informants when they too have been socialized not to see and certainly not to talk about these factors? Smith's solution to this problem is called "looking from the margin inward." In her work, she and others writing in feminist traditions provide an "insider's critique rooted in but extending beyond the local setting" (DeVault 1999, 48). According to Marj DeVault, it is "searching to explicate the contingencies of ruling that shape local contexts" (p. 48). So instead of producing knowledge about local contexts in order to facilitate the interests of policy makers, companies, and more powerful "others" who do not belong to those local contexts, Smith encourages us to produce knowledge for rather than knowledge about those in a particular social location. This has implications for the type of data we collect, where we publish or share our findings (outlets), and even the kind of careers we pursue.

Inspired by feminist methodologies, I attempt to determine extralocal organization of everyday activities (Smith 2005) by listing events noted by participants at McKinley and placing them in a proximate context—first by examining the minutes book to see events noted by elders that occurred in the timeframe noted by participants, then by placing events in the wider context of campus, then expanding that context to Champaign County, the state of Illinois, and the United States as a whole. Where I am able, I connect events to transnational contexts as well. So I think about informants' settings: immediate, proximate, and distal, and this allows me to identify how social forces outside the immediate setting may help to shape it. For example, in other work (Zerai 2000b), I analyze grandparents' stories about how their adult children became addicted to crack cocaine, and I link to family turmoil policy makers' decisions leading to the erosion of community programs and a lack of viable afterschool programs and other activities in inner city neighborhoods.

To summarize, here are the steps I utilize to write a case study of McKinley members' experiences from 1957[10] to 1980 that considers the impact of institutional forces. First, I identify sets of actors (groupings of individuals who have the same set of interests) and make a list. Second, I pay attention to how these individuals/groups are situated spatially and socially at McKinley and in wider contexts. For example, I examine whether there are power imbalances between individuals or groups and what accounts for them. Third, I determine the relevant proximate and distal social forces and how they are operating in the respondents' settings, remembering that distal factors are often invisible to many of the members in the setting. These are large-scale institutional and structural factors that determine a plethora of social outcomes, such as the public education system, economic factors, and public health policy. These factors may operate at the city, state, national, or global level. Finally, I analyze McKinley as a social setting, paying attention to the actors and their viewpoints as well as to the proximate forces that influence their behavior in the site to elucidate the underlying social structure at play.

Context and External Influences

Below, I place renderings in context by providing an overview of the changing world in which McKinley was embedded. External influences of the period include the Great Migration, the Protestant modernist-fundamentalist controversy, the GI Bill and the related expansion of the University of Illinois campus, federal Civil Rights legislation and the Civil Rights movement, J. F. Kennedy's visit to campus, the Vietnam War and National Guard involvement in student protest, the women's movement, and LGBTIQ consciousness raising. I start here with a brief overview of history before the period under study.

PRESBYTERIAN CHURCH (USA)[11]

The Presbyterian Church in the USA (PCUSA) was established after Presbyterians came to the United States from Scotland and Ireland. The denomination held its first General Assembly, a relatively democratic governing body, in 1789 in Philadelphia. See Table 5.2 for a timeline of McKinley's denominational heritage. Twenty-five years later, the future Reverend George McKinley was born and lived (1814–1887). He pastored a church in Champaign County (from 1858 to 1870. During his tenure as a minister, several significant historical events occurred, including the 1861 formation of the Presbyterian Church of the Confederate States of America (which split from the Presbyterian Church in the USA over slavery),[12] Abraham Lincoln's presidency, the Emancipation Proclamation (1863), the passage of the 13th Amendment to the Constitution outlawing slavery, the passage of the 1866 Civil Rights Act, Reconstruction, and the founding of the University of Illinois in 1867. George's son William Brown McKinley, a future U.S. Senator and the primary financial backer of McKinley Presbyterian Church, attended the University of Illinois from 1870 to 1872, during the time that women were first admitted to the university.[13] In 1906 he established McKinley Memorial Presbyterian Church, naming it after his father, Reverend George McKinley. The same year, Maudelle Tanner Brown Bausfield was the first African American woman to graduate from the University of Illinois (University of Illinois LibGuide 2014),[14] and the Ku Klux Klan (KKK) established a student chapter at the University of Illinois.[15] The KKK remained active and was recognized by the University of Illinois until 1923.[16] Though African American students attended the University of Illinois, their numbers were negligible in the 1910s through 1960s, amounting to only 1 percent by 1967. Despite those low numbers, Champaign County boasted an active contingent of the National Association for the Advancement of Colored People (NAACP). As early as 1927, the *Daily Illini* reports that the field secretary for the NAACP, William Pickens, was invited by the interracial commission of the University YMCA and University YWCA to speak at the Wesley Foundation. His address was "Common Interests of White and Colored Americans." The nascent Twin Cities branch of the NAACP later (in 1941) invited Madison Jones, NAACP director of youth activities, to speak; Jones noted that "The (Redress of the) Racial Problem

Is Still Only Words" in his address to an interracial and interreligious audience of 200 (*Daily Illini,* February 21, 1941). And still only words indeed, as segregation was practiced in Champaign County and continued for decades more. Housing for African Americans was confined to the "northern districts of the twin cities" (*Daily Illini,* October 16, 1959). Many businesses refused to hire African American workers (*Daily Illini,* July 11, 1963). And the Champaign Unit 4 school district was segregated (*Daily Illini,* May 29, 1953).

Segregation was also practiced on the UIUC campus. For example, before 1946, University of Illinois dormitories were not open to African American students. University restrooms were not open to African American employees.[17] Though the University of Illinois hired its first African American academic professional in 1895, very few African Americans worked in professional positions on campus. In those early days, Champaign County's African Americans comprised only 1 percent of its population, though this percentage increased to 3 percent by 1924, when the McKinley Foundation was established.

A PRESBYTERIAN CAMPUS CHURCH IN CHAMPAIGN

In 1912, the original McKinley Memorial Presbyterian Church building was erected, and its first stained glass window—the Tiffany "Good Samaritan" window—was installed. The campus church was located amid a flurry of activity, including the first mass meeting of (white) women and the establishment at the university of the country's first African American fraternity (University of Illinois 2014). The Great (African American) Migration would get underway just a few years later (1916 onward),[18] paving the way for the interstate highway, built in 1961, that linked South and North, ushering Africana migrants from mostly Louisiana and Mississippi to Chicago (U.S. Federal Highway Administration 2014). The population of Americans of African descent grew exponentially in Illinois, especially in Chicago, from 2 percent in 1915 to 33 percent in 1970. Chicago would become fertile recruiting ground to increase the number of African American students and residents in Champaign County. By 1940, African Americans in Champaign County totaled 6 percent of its population, increasing to only 7 percent by 1970 (see Table 5.3).[19]

As World War I developed, male university students withdrew to serve in the military.[20] In 1920 the 19th Amendment to the Constitution was passed (women's suffrage). And in 1922, the Protestant modernist–fundamentalist (M–F) controversy was articulated with a sermon by liberal Protestant Harry Emerson Fosdick, "Shall the Fundamentalists Win," delivered to the First Presbyterian Church in New York City (Pohlman 2012). Fosdick's sermon exposed theological differences between

A Presbyterian Campus Church: 1940 to 1953

Table 5.3 Total Populations and Percentages of African Americans in Champaign County, Illinois, and the U.S., 1850–2013

Census date	Champaign County		State of Illinois		United States	
	Total	% African American	Total	% African American	Total	% African American
1850[a]	2,649	2	851,470	1	23,191,876	16
1870[b]	32,737	1	2,539,891	1	38,555,938	13
1900[c]	47,622	1	4,821,550	2	76,212,168	12
1920[c]	56,959	3	6,485,280	3	106,021,537	10
1940[c]	70,578	6	7,897,241	5	132,164,569	10
1950[c]	106,100	7	8,712,176	7	151,325,798	10
1960[c]	132,436	5	10,081,158	10	179,323,175	11
1970[c]	163,281	7	11,113,976	13	203,211,926	11
1980[c]	168,392	9	11,426,518	15	226,545,805	12
1990[c]	173,025	10	11,430,602	15	248,709,873	12
2000[d]	179,669	11	12,419,293	16	284,121,906	13
2010[e]	201,081	12	12,830,632	14.5	308,747,716	14
2013[f] (est.)	205,761	13	12,890,552	14.7	316,128,839	15

[a] http://www.infoplease.com/ipa/A0922246.html.
[b] http://www.census.gov/prod/www/decennial.html.
[c] http://www.census.gov/population/cencounts/il190090.txt.
[d] http://en.wikipedia.org/wiki/Champaign_County, Illinois.
[e] https://www.census.gov/prod/cen2010/briefs/c2010br-06.pdf.
[f] http://quickfacts.census.gov/qfd/states/17/17019.html.

liberals within Presbyterian and other Protestant denominations that promoted a social gospel and modernist interpretations of the Bible and meaning of church, and conservative Presbyterians (and other Protestants) who believed that (liberal) politics did not belong in church and held to more literal interpretations of the Bible. Michael Pohlman explains that Fosdick, well known for his radio ministry, "contributed to secularization by facilitating a movement away from Protestant orthodoxy in America" (2012, 22). The heated M–F controversy ended in 1936 "when J. Gresham Machen and many other conservatives left the Presbyterian Church to form the Orthodox Presbyterian Church in America" (Pohlman 2012, 23).

McKinley Foundation was established in the midst of this controversy (1924), with the mission to serve students at the University of Illinois. The student ministry foundation building was completed in 1930, during the Great Depression. While some churches left the PCUSA over the modernist–fundamentalist controversy, McKinley remained with the more liberal presbyteries under the PCUSA banner.

WORLD WAR II AND PASTOR JIM HINE

World War II (1935–45) stimulated the acceleration of the Great Migration. During this time, campus officials expressed enduring concerns about the lack of housing for students.[21] For example, in 1937, discussions in the Illinois State Senate expressed this concern. A delegation was sent to Springfield on behalf of the university, and member Edgar Barton stated that "it should be made perfectly clear to the legislature that there is an urgent need for immediate construction of men's dormitories" (*Daily Illini,* May 12, 1937). In 1941, "U.S. entry into WWII after Pearl Harbor greatly impacted UIUC. Almost overnight, the ratio of men to women on campus went from 3:1 to 1:4".[22, 23] I begin my case study in 1942, when Rev. Dr. James ("Jim") R. Hine commenced his ministry at McKinley Memorial Presbyterian Church as church lead pastor and director of the McKinley Foundation. Jim served from 1942 to 1967. Campus ministry changed drastically during these twenty-five years.

A Crowded Campus and Overflowing Pews

In 1943, segregation continued to factor in the daily lives of African American students. The *Daily Illini* reports:

> Last week a senior Illini, was refused service at a major restaurant within two blocks of the campus. Why? Not because he didn't have money, or because he was a foreign agent, but solely because the accident of birth had made him a Negro. A day later two Negro girls, upon entering another restaurant located only a few yards from the center of campus were asked to retire to the kitchen if they wished to be served. . . . Our fair campus has been permeated for years with invidious prejudices of all sorts. . . . In addition to [discrimination in eating facilities and housing], there exist many other less tangible [acts of discrimination] which are nevertheless felt severely by those to whom they are directed (Browne, October 1943).

These "less tangible acts" are microaggressions, which still occur on the campus of the University of Illinois.[24]

In addition to his entering campus and community environments rife with racial discrimination, Hine began his ministry at McKinley on the cusp of WWII and the enactment of the GI Bill. In 1944, Congress passed the GI Bill, credited with creating the modern white middle class, making a college education more affordable to "millions of returning veterans" (Holley 2006). This impacted the University of Illinois significantly. After 20,276 University of Illinois students served in WWII, over 11,000 veterans returned to campus, necessitating temporary campus housing. The number of students on campus arose from 13,591 in 1940 to 16,956 in 1950.[25]

During the war and in its aftermath, the NAACP and its student allies protested discrimination against African Americans in the community and on campus. In town, housing, schools,[26] and employment opportunities continued to be segregated. And university students of color faced precarious conditions on campus. Most restaurants in campustown would not serve them, and theaters would not seat them. The Student Committee on Interracial Cooperation (SCIC) formed to fight racial discrimination. The group's tactics included picketing and threatening lawsuits. In 1946, the university's Board of Trustees endorsed policy "to create a community atmosphere in which racial prejudice cannot thrive" (*Daily Illini,* September 16, 1958). In 1946 university residence halls were opened to African Americans, and in 1948 SCIC helped desegregate restrooms for Illini Union employees. However, the local chapter of the NAACP criticized the university administration for falling short on enforcing its stated policy against racial discrimination. Private university-approved housing and Greek houses continued to discriminate against African Americans. NAACP and allies recommended that the university withdraw its official approval of these rental properties. It took several years for prominent McKinley members to join the struggle for desegregation. In fact, McKinley deacon John Bresee, the Republican Champaign County State's Attorney, was specifically called out for his lack of support for the fight to integrate Champaign-Urbana:

> A motion to picket Bresee's office will be the first order of business at a NAACP meeting today at Wesley Foundation. Members at the executive committee meeting Saturday heard a report that Bresee's office had not acted on 50 barbershop complaints of discrimination over the last three years. An informal poll of the executive committee Saturday favored picketing of the courthouse this fall if Bresee fails to bring a civil rights case after receiving complaints. However, the main decision whether or not to picket will have to be made by the entire membership (Daily Illini, September 20, 1955, p. 3).

Invited to campus by the NAACP and the local chapter of the Kappa Alpha Psi social fraternity, Chicago attorney William R. Ming expressed his outrage at the continued practice of segregation on and around the University of Illinois campus in September 1955. Jari Jackson, reporting for the *Daily Illini,* notes Ming's involvement in Supreme Court school desegregation decisions. Ming criticizes the "failure of Champaign County State's Attorney John Bresee to take action on discrimination complaints, [especially in regards to] discrimination in hiring of state employees, including those found employed the University of Illinois" (Jackson, 1955: 2).[27] Ming explains that "the University can legally disapprove private housing that practices discrimination despite opinion of its legal counsel that it cannot interfere." "If students must live in approved housing, [the University] can lay down the conditions for approving houses" (Jackson 1955). However, a full nine years after the Board of Trustees passed the University of Illinois's antidiscrimination policy, and in response to pressure from the NAACP and others calling for an end to campus discrimination, university president David Henry insisted that "the University *will not* revise its standards for approving housing because of lack of housing facilities available. He said he sees no virtue at this time to argue any legal issues involved in the granting of approval to private housing while the lack of available housing continues" (*Daily Illini,* October 11, 1955; emphasis added).

Gender ideologies were in flux following World War II. During the war, white women entered the labor force due to a vacuum created by consigned men. Examining relational differences between African American and white women, Elsa Barkley Brown notes (1995) that "we need to recognize not only differences but also the relational nature of those differences. Middle class white women's lives are not just different from working class white, Black, and Latina women's lives. . . . White women live the lives they do in large part because women of color live the ones they do" (p. 298).

During WWII, the diminished role of white middle class women in the domestic sphere and their entry into the labor force was facilitated by the work of white, Africana, and Latina working class and immigrant women in the formal and informal service sector, as well as by the exploitation of labor of women and men in the Global South.

After WWII, white women were replaced in the formal sector by men. Postwar family life featured a return to prewar ideologies of women working in the home and men fulfilling roles as primary breadwinners (Coontz 2005). This ideology was reinforced by the GI Bill, which granted access to higher education for a greater cross-section of white men. So the numbers of men on the University of Illinois campus exceeded those of women once again. The ratio of males to females on most campuses in the United States approached 1.0 (and achieved parity by 1960; Goldin 2006), but women were outnumbered at the U of I, which specialized in agricultural sciences, the physical sciences, and engineering—fields in which few women, or none, enrolled. Even as late as 1967, women were only 34 percent of the student population in Urbana-Champaign. Though women had greater access to enrolling in college, their graduation rates were a fraction of men's rates nationwide during the 1940s and 1950s (Goldin, Katz, and Kuziemko 2006, 135).[28] Many women who initially enrolled later withdrew to get married and have children (Goldin 2004; Goldin, Katz, and Kuziemko 2006). According to the U.S. Bureau of the Census (2004), in 1940 the median age at first marriage was 21.5 for women, and it dropped to 20.3 in the 1950s and early 1960s.[29] This created a fertile ground for McKinley's appeal to Republican,[30] upwardly mobile, white college students who sought guidance in early adulthood.

Dr. Hine, known for his marriage and family ministry, was a popular preacher on campus. Even after the sanctuary was enlarged to 600 seats during major renovation in the 1950s, it was filled to capacity with students. Rev. Hine comments, "Following WWII there was a tremendous return to religion on campus. It's hard to explain" (*Daily Illini,* October 10, 1967, p. 7). On McKinley Foundation's walls even today are photographs depicting hundreds of white students in the sanctuary, and archives illustrate them lined up around the building, waiting to get into church for Sunday morning's second service. The lore of this era is still alive in the memories and imaginings of current members, though very few were actually in the congregation at that time. Some say that fraternities and sororities required church attendance and that they each "had their own pews." Current member Marlyn Rinehart, who actually attended McKinley while a student in the late 1950s, indicates that Hine's popularity attracted scores of students. "The 1950s was a whole other time. People would take their dates to church" (Rinehart interview, 2014). Further, she explained the perception that Dr. Hine was the "go-to" pastor for marriage. The *Daily Illini* reports that he married 650 couples during his twenty-five years at McKinley Church (Bolster, October 1967, p. 7).

McKinley's thriving marriage and family ministry included a group called the "McKinley-Weds." Established in 1945 during Hine's tenure (session minutes, February 17, 1955) and centered on the church's middle-class families and married students, McKinley-wed couples numbered 300 in 1948. McKinley-weds were organized into fellowship units, which held small group meetings in the foundation building. They also organized monthly parties and made carpool arrangements to get families to the early service. The women in the group coordinated nursery childcare and Sunday school, and the men served as ushers for the early service (session minutes, January 26, 1950). The McKinley-weds had an active outreach component, as they engaged in "the visiting of new couples in the community" (annual congregational meeting minutes, January 14, 1949, p. 4).

Though the family and student ministries drew large crowds, the actual number of members at McKinley Church from 1947 to 1949 was 315. McKinley distinguished its "resident-members"—largely faculty and other professionals who attended McKinley and became members either by baptism or by submitting a letter of transfer from another congregation—from its "student-associates," undergraduate or graduate students who would attend McKinley and be active in its student foundation events, but who were not considered full members of the church. There were financial considerations behind these designations, as the PCUSA required all churches in the denomination to pay a tax to the denomination, determined by the number of members in the congregation. The (nonstudent) membership arose to a high of 383, as reported in 1952. McKinley's membership in 1953 was 297, but it saw record attendance (including members, student-associates, and visitors) that fall, with a high of 1,440. Former campus minister Jim Ray (2014) remembers: "I saw pictures of students standing by the hundreds outside the McKinley Church waiting to get in for the second Sunday service. The sanctuary held over 600 persons and it was packed over most of those by gone days for both services. Jim Hine was a fine preacher and drew students in" (Ray 2014).

One long-time member explained that while members of fraternities and sororities were not, as some mistakenly believe, required to attend church, all students in the mid-1960s were required to take religion courses.

> I first attended McKinley and listened to Jim Hine preach when I was an undergrad at Illinois in the middle '60s. There were hundreds of students that came to the multiple services on Sunday morning. I took one of the Religion courses . . . required by the university through McKinley. (Yes, religion courses were required by the U of I, along with PE and, for males, ROTC). The Rev. Jim Ray was my teacher. . . . Church attendance by students in general was a characteristic of the times, like required religion classes were (Dave Bechtel interview, 2015).

In the early years of Hine's tenure, three stained glass windows depicting (white) students were installed, one for agriculture, one for arts, and one for engineering.

> Above the balcony on the north wall of the sanctuary are three windows depicting students of three types of major/career choices. Much of the creativity and content included in these windows is from Jim Hine, the Pastor/Director at the time. The window on the west represents a Student in Agriculture and he is holding a growing plant. The middle window represents a Student in the Arts and she is holding bells representing music. This window is dedicated to the memory of Paul, Anna and Martha Belting by . . . Natalia Belting, a member of the church and a well-known history professor at the University. The window on the east is of a Student in Engineering and he is holding a sextant, an engineering tool. (Dave Bechtel, *McKinley Presbyterian Church's Stained Glass Windows: History and Tradition*, p. 4.)

These more traditional windows are joined by one that would later become controversial; Dave Bechtel provides a description of "Christ's Call to All the World":

> The window shows Christ surrounded by figures in a variety of clothing styles and adornments representing all nations. The Biblical admonition is ". . . Go ye therefore and teach all nations, baptizing them in

the name of the Father and the Son and the Holy Spirit, and teaching them to observe all things whatsoever I have commanded you. And lo I am with you always, even unto the end of the world" (Bechtel, p. 3.)

I am sure that in 1951, when it was installed, this window represented to the student-church its concern with the developing nations of the world and represented a desire for mission. In fact, during the height of Hine's post as pastor at McKinley, he engaged in a five-month world tour to fifteen countries "to become thoroughly acquainted with the progress and needs of Presbyterian student centers throughout the world" (*The MAC, McKinley Foundation Newspaper,* 1953–1954 school year, p. 3). But more recently a parishioner described the window as "Jesus, teaching his little brown brothers" (congregant interview, 2014). To 2015 eyes, the image appears paternalistic, challenged by the more egalitarian viewpoints held by today's congregants that there are many paths to God: "Jesus is my path, but I respect that there are other equally valid paths" (congregant interview, 2014).

I found another troubling image from the 1950s era in McKinley's archives; a cartoon depicts caricatures of two Native Americans forming the backboard of a carnival game in a photograph of white male and female students, one of them placing darts on the board. We can even see darts on the faces of the racist caricatures.

Though the window and the carnival game represent the views of the time, even in the 1950s McKinley members eschewed the dominant notions of an unquestioning faith promoted by more conservative Protestants. Barney Brantingham wrote a four-part series in the campus *Daily Illini* that addressed possible conflicts between religion and science.

> The Reverend James Hine looked out the vine-draped window of his office at the McKinley Foundation. His offhand-manner belied his reserved, dignified appearance. "I have not heard any antagonism against scientists or science. However there has been a definite feeling of, 'let's stop atomic research overseas'. . . . Scientists have to keep pursuing these matters. We should go ahead and develop atomic power and set up forces that will channel its possibilities into peaceful uses (*Daily Illini,* April 22, 1955, p. 9).

Answering Brantingham's question about whether religion conflicts with science, Dr. Hine denied that a conflict exists: "Science reinforces religion," he maintained (*Daily Illini,* April 22, 1955, p. 9). In weighing in on the modernist–fundamentalist controversy, Hine supported modernist notions that holding faith does not require abandoning reason, nor does it require refuting perceived intellectual benefits of enlightenment reasoning.

This perspective appealed to many faculty members at the University of Illinois. Several members of McKinley in the 1950s and 1960s were academic scientists. Dr. Kenneth Rinehart, the deceased husband of current member Marlyn Rinehart, was a professor of chemistry, and she remembers that her family's initial attraction to McKinley was in part its intelligentsia. Professor John C. Bailar, a McKinley member and one-time clerk[31] of session, was an organic chemist and a friend of the Rinehart family. Marlyn notes a number of other chemists who were members at McKinley, including Professor William Rose, who served on McKinley's session in the 1950s and 1960s. Many years later Marlyn and Ken visited a cathedral in Switzerland that held a science-themed stained glass window. Ken Rinehart, after becoming a McKinley elder, served on the committee developing a "science" stained glass window. In 1995, "The Celebration of Science, Faith and Reason" was installed and dedicated to Dr. John C. Bailar. Marlyn explains that Ken, influenced by their experience in Switzerland, "put a lot of thought into the design of McKinley's science window" (Rinehart interview, 2014).

Reasoning rather than a blind devotion to the conservative politics of the time influenced PCUSA to address McCarthyism and racial discrimination and to usher the denomination—at the time largely Republican[32] (Noll and Harlow 2007)—into an era of social activism. The differences between the politically conservative majority (of members and lay leaders), centrist pastors, and the more left-activist leadership in the Presbyterian denomination over time are well expressed by William (Beau) Weston (Weston 2004).

Over the past several decades, segments of the PCUSA have exhibited different theological and political tendencies. The members of local churches have tended to be traditional in both theology and politics, with the ruling elders and lay leaders being generally even more traditional. By contrast, the denomination's specialized clergy (ordained ministers who serve not in congregations but instead as teachers, chaplains, church bureaucrats, and the like) have been much more liberal in their theological and political views than either church members or ruling elders (Weston 2004).

At the helm from 1951 to 1966, PCUSA (later UPCUSA) stated clerk Rev. Dr. Eugene Carson Blake and colleagues in the General Council of the General Assembly enlivened the denomination by living and leading a fresh social justice ministry (Blake 1949, 1963, 1966, 1968, 1980).

NOTES

1. I refer to the site as "McKinley" throughout this chapter.
2. Though, on the basis of historical documents, I am able to trace McKinley's history back to 1940, I see evidence of its social justice work from about 1963 onward. Further, interviews with long-time members provide supporting accounts from about this time.
3. This includes African Americans (3.3 percent) and African immigrants (.4 percent).
4. "Session" refers to the board of elders at McKinley.

5. Unlike the other four churches covered in this book, I decided, with members' permission, to directly name McKinley. Members also agreed to be quoted directly with attribution. These permissions were indicated in my IRB documentation and respondents signed consent forms, were provided copies of quotes I planned to use, and followed up with emailed agreement to be quoted and named in this manuscript.

6. I searched *Daily Illini* issues dating from 1940 to 1980 and focused on relevant keywords, such as James Hine (along with other McKinley pastors and staff during this period), McKinley Presbyterian, Illiac IV, Martin Luther King, Jr. Project 500, black students, Vietnam War protests, and the like.

7. I have cited each source, possibly making the timeline cumbersome to read, so I have also included Table 5.2 in this chapter listing only the events, and a second timeline in the appendix that includes the data sources for each event.

8. Each McKinley minutes book generally gathers materials produced over ten or more years. They are largely broken into periods on the basis of the number of pages written.

9. I refer to the individual actors and the groups to which they belong as proximate forces. These include individuals' own life experiences, their most relevant family and community groups, and their identities that shape their behavior and their perspectives on the world.

10. Though this chapter focuses on 1940 to 1980, members' accounts date back only to about 1957. I use historical documents to trace back to 1940.

11. To avoid confusion, I will refer to the denomination by its current name, Presbyterian Church (USA) throughout the text. However, where relevant, I will indicate the historical names of the denomination.

12. The Presbyterian Church of the Confederate States of America after the Civil War became the Presbyterian Church in the U.S.

13. In 1871, the first female cohort at the University of Illinois included twenty-two women.

14. The first Native American graduated from the University of Illinois in 1884, and the first African American student enrolled in 1887.

15. http://courseweb.lis.illinois.edu/~mosucho2/klan.

16. http://courseweb.lis.illinois.edu/~mosucho2/klan.

17. See the timeline in Table 5.2 for numerous instances of discrimination and protests against it in campustown from 1935 onward.

18. http://www.encyclopedia.chicagohistory.org/pages/545.html.

19. The numbers of African Americans in Champaign County increased between 1900 and 1920 from 551 to 1,620 (*Blacks in Champaign County 1865-1970*, 1995).

20. In May 1917 "1000 students withdrew for military and farm work," and "fall 1918 enrollment was 20 percent below previous year's number" (http://archives.library.illinois.edu/slc/research-education/timeline/1910-1919).

21. From the 1890s onward, the number of students on campus grew exponentially, from 519 to 13,446 by 1930. Though men withdrew to serve in WWI, by 1940 the campus student population still totaled 14,208 (*Old Enrollment Figures for the Urbana Fall Term*, UIUC Division of Management Information, 2000).

22. http://archives.library.illinois.edu/slc/research-education/timeline/1940-1949.

23. These data refer to white students for the most part. African Americans were less than 1 percent of the University of Illinois student population in the 1930s and 1940s.

24. See *Racial Microaggressions @ University of Illinois* at Urbana-Champaign (Harwood et al., 2015 [www.racialmicroaggressions.illinois.edu/files/2015/03/RMA-Classroom-Report.pdf]).

25. http://archives.library.illinois.edu/slc/research-education/timeline/1940-1949.

26. The *Daily Illini* reported that "Mrs. Lizzie Johnson announced her resignation Monday as principal of Washington school. She said that she could not serve in a school district practicing segregation. She offered two plans for integration in Unit Four. She suggested that attendance boundaries be set throughout the unit, or that bus

transportation be provided for children in Stadium Terrace and Illini Village to schools which are how all Negro" (May 29, 1953).

27. John J. Bresee was elected on the Republican ticket as the Champaign County state's attorney for 1942 to 1956 and 1964 to 1968 (Bishop 2015). He was a member of McKinley Memorial Presbyterian Church and served on its board of deacons in the 1940s. He served as an elected McKinley elder in the 1960s. His granddaughter notes Bresee "was an engineer, architect, artist, and lawyer. Mostly though, he was a prosecutor" (Bishop 2015: 112).

28. From 1960 onward, women's college graduation rates meet and surpass those of men (Goldin et al. 2006).

29. See http://www.infoplease.com/ipa/A0005061.html and Coontz 2013, http://www.nytimes.com/2013/06/23/opinion/sunday/coontz-the-disestablishment-of-marriage.html).

30. Though it is difficult to find information confirming political party affiliation of McKinley members in the 1950s and early 1960s, it is not a stretch to assume that they were largely Republican. Most Presbyterians at that time were Republican (and are even now—Noll and Harlow 2007). McKinley elder and Champaign County state's attorney John Bresee was Republican, and a woman who was a McKinley student member in the 1960s says her mother "was probably a closeted Democrat" (congregant interview, 2014).

31. The clerk of session for each congregation in the Presbyterian Church is the lead ruling elder for the church.

32. Though PCUSA clergy are more likely to vote for Democrats than are parishioners, "they are not prone to politicize their congregants" (Weston, 2004: 69). The PCUSA/UPCUSA parishioners have by and large been Republican. For example, from 1940 to 1968 (with the exception of 1964), a large majority (at least 70 percent after 1952) of mainline Protestants voted for the Republican presidential candidate (Noll and Harlow 2007). "Even in 1964, however, Presbyterians lent a majority of their support to the Republican candidate" (p. 370). In the 1980s, 56 percent of mainline Protestants were Republican: "Among Presbyterians the proportions identifying with the GOP are even higher, with usually more than two Republicans for every Democrat" (p. 370). And today, though Republicans are now in the minority among Presbyterians, parishioners are still twice as likely as clergy to be Republican (Wisdon 2010).

SIX
McKinley, UPCUSA, and Civil Rights
1953 to 1967

In its General Assembly in 1953, the PCUSA addressed both McCarthyism and segregation. Penned by John McKay and the Princeton-educated stated clerk of PCUSA, Rev. Dr. Eugene Carson Blake, "A Letter to the Presbyterians Concerning the Present Situation in Our Country and in the World" opposed '"red scare" allegations and falsehoods as damaging to the moral ethos and democratic practices of the United States (McKay and Blake 1953). The letter, unanimously adopted by the General Council of the General Assembly, made "a concise Reformed case for the prophetic role of the church, both in public policy and civic values" (PCUSA 1953). This prophetic role would define the ministry and denominational leadership of Eugene Carson Blake, most notably in the area of civil rights (Blake 1973, 1975, 1976, 1981). McKinley members and clergy would be inspired by PCUSA leadership,[1] the Champaign County NAACP chapter, the campus Student Committee on Interracial Cooperation (SCIC), and especially students active at the McKinley Foundation to consider taking up the mantle of civil rights.

While SCIC fought racial discrimination on the University of Illinois campus, attorney Thurgood Marshall fought racial discrimination in public education all the way up to the Supreme Court, which ruled in 1954, that "separate educational facilities are inherently unequal" and that segregated public schooling was unconstitutional (*Oliver Brown, et al. v. Board of Education of Topeka, et al.*). The Presbyterian Church was embroiled in its own struggles regarding segregation. The leadership of PCUSA asserted its prophetic mission through establishing The Standing Committee on Social Education and Social Action. On the heels of the Supreme Court ruling, diversity became institutionalized as a value of the PCUSA during its 1954 General Assembly, held in Detroit. The theme for that year's GA was "Accent on the City," and the experiences of Detroit-area PCUSA churches were brought to the fore. The white flight of automobile executives and their families from urban neighborhoods to more affluent suburbs, enabled of course by the wealth produced by the labor of the working class, meant that whites' former homes in areas surrounding urban PCUSA churches were newly occupied by industrial working families, 60 percent of whom were African Americans (Taylor 2014).

Many city congregations faced the question of whether to welcome African Americans into their churches. Some congregations, such as St. Andrews Presbyterian Church, were "making noteworthy progress in race relations," despite some initial resistance and departures of white members (Taylor 2014).

The GA in Detroit endorsed the Supreme Court's Brown v. Board of Education verdict and supported the "[Standing] Committee's call to sessions, ministers, and church members to 'make it their Christian concern to communicate the claim of Christ to every person within reach of their church.... We call upon all Christians to *work* for, not *wait* for, a Church and a society which rise above racial restrictions'" (Taylor 2014). In the following year's GA, the issue of integration continued to be debated. As reported in *Time* (June 20, 1955, p. 56).[2]

> The 95th General Assembly (GA) of the Presbyterian Church in the U.S. [voted]... on the most disputed issue facing its six-day convention: a request that the assembly "reconsider and rescind" its 1954 pronouncement that "segregation is un-Christian." Pastor Shirey and six others had signed a minority report charging that the assembly erred in asking its 3,776 local churches to accept Negroes. The temper of the assembly had already become evident, and it was not in tune with the temper of Pastor Shirey. On opening night it elected as its new moderator Dr. James McDowell Richards, president of racially integrated Columbia Theological Seminary in Decatur, Georgia, and an outspoken anti-segregationist. [The GA] reaffirmed, by a vote of 293 to 109, its year-old stand against racial segregation (1954 vote: 236 to 169).

While the wider denomination supported the idea of integrating its individual churches, McKinley was slow to address discrimination in the Champaign-Urbana communities and on the University of Illinois campus.

Discrimination persisted in housing and employment in Champaign-Urbana. Students on campus faced continuing discrimination in barbershops, and the area public school systems remained segregated. In 1955, Ming, "speaking to a capacity audience at the Unitarian church" (Jackson 1955, 2), said that

12 counties in Illinois still practice segregation in their school system. Much of this results from residential segregation and is embodied in the customs and practices of the community. It is difficult to find an Illinois community of any size where residential segregation is not practiced and the colored race is not classes as black ghetto (Jackson, reporting for the *Daily Illini* 1955, 2).

Also in 1955 there was a "gentleman's agreement among realtors not to sell property outside of certain areas to Negroes" (*Daily Illini,* March 8, 1955, 7). When an immigrant family from Africa integrated a white neighborhood, "450 members of the community signed a petition for their removal," but reportedly "with the help of local clergy the petitioners changed their views" (p. 7). When called to task on the underwhelming involvement of clergy in the Champaign area civil rights struggle, McKinley's Rev. James Hine indicated "a religious foundation can't support human relations issues outside the church until it becomes interracial within itself" (p. 7).

In 1957, the local NAACP chapter conducted a housing survey to become informed about the extent of discrimination in university-approved housing. Contacting all private homes that had vacancies in August 1956 and August 1957, they found that only "24 percent of the houses contacted will admit [African Americans]" (*Daily Illini,* September 17, 1957, 5). Some of the landlords indicated that they would accept international students but not African Americans. In addition to lack of support for integration in private by the University of Illinois and the county state's attorney, the Champaign County Apartment Owners Association refused to set an antidiscrimination policy (*Daily Illini,* November 21, 1957, 11).

The PCUSA Standing Committee on Social Education and Action was not only organized at the national level; regional presbyteries had their own committees. On February 14, 1956, Rev. McClean reported for the Social Education and Action Committee of the Bloomington Presbytery at the McKinley session meeting (session minutes, February 14, 1956, 87). The committee called on local congregations to create their own Social Education and Action Committees to assist in relocating refugee families. McKinley did both.

In 1958 the United Presbyterian Church of North America merged with Presbyterian Church in the USA to form the United Presbyterian Church in the USA (UPCUSA). Almost all members of the UPCUSA (98 percent) were white, despite PCUSA's four-year-old stance in support of integration.[3] Rev. Dr. Eugene Carson Blake remained as stated clerk of the newly constituted UPCUSA until 1966.

As segregation persisted in private student housing and fraternities on the U of I campus, McKinley Foundation students were poised to address it by 1958. Perhaps inspired by Rev. Dr. Blake's 1954 "challenge to the youth to respond to the call of Christ to live adventurously"[4] (*Daily*

Illini, July 8, 1954, 3), in 1958, representatives from the Social Action and Education Committee of the McKinley Foundation Student Council sent a statement that they asked session to approve and, further, entreated Rev. Dr. Hine to read from the pulpit. To ensure a platform on which the campus NAACP chapter could be heard, the McKinley Student Council wanted McKinley Foundation and McKinley Church to apply pressure to the Interfraternity Council, a group that would not support a change in white Greek houses' practices of racial discrimination. The session response, as noted in the minutes, was that "none of the members of Session had any knowledge of the background of the situation" (March 9, 1958, 126). While no action was taken by session on the Student Council's request, Dr. Hine did promise to follow up on it.

Though McKinley elders were willing to learn more, but not perhaps prepared to act, other area churches, religious organizations, and voluntary associations continued to support the work of the NAACP to end discrimination in housing. The League of Women Voters met in 1959 to discuss the poor housing conditions for African Americans in the "northern districts" of Champaign and Urbana.

> Overcrowding in these section was . . . the prevalent reason behind the unhealthy environment which exists. Of the 68,000 white residents of Champaign-Urbana, 5 percent live in substandard housing. In comparison, more than half of the 8,000 Negro population dwell in underrated buildings. Private landowners who rent out space in the segregated areas gross [huge monthly profits] by subdividing to the point that 4 or 5 families are forced to live in a space normally take up by one. (*Daily Illini,* October 16, 1959, 2).

The McKinley Foundation's Student Council members on the Social Education and Action Committee took up the work of educating the McKinley congregation about injustices such as those taking place in private housing near the university campus. Their work would be reinforced by the social activism of the Rev. Dr. Blake and others on the SEAC at the presbytery level and nationally. Though relatively marginalized initially, beginning in 1960, the Social Education and Action Committee became a fixture of McKinley's session (session minutes, February 21, 1960).

Though—at the behest of the presbytery and the GA, as well as with the energy of the McKinley Foundation Student Council—McKinley's SEAC was organized and had representation on the church session, it took a while for the rest of the congregation and its leadership (including members of session) to embrace the committee's programs. In 1961, session liaison Robert Pearson presented a report on racial integration in Champaign-Urbana from the SEAC to session. Session minutes note that "Dr. Rose, in a courageous and forthright manner, stated his objections to the recommendations contained in the report" (March 12, 1961, 194). It is remarkable, one, that McKinley placed its SEAC within the student foundation and not as a standing committee of the church, and, further, that Dr. William Rose, a long-time session elder, professor of chemistry, and powerful member of the church, objected in 1961 and continued to voice his objections to recommendations from the McKinley student foundation's SEAC. Marlyn Rinehart explained the objections, as some members believed the church's focus should be the spiritual well-being of the congregation and "felt that it was not the church's place to be so much out in society" (M. Rinehart interview, 2014). After some discussion in the March 1961 meeting, session agreed to implement a recommendation of the report:

> Concrete steps should be taken to educate the congregation concerning the racial situation in Champaign-Urbana.
>
> 1. The information presented above,[5] and any subsequent material that becomes available should be mailed to the members of the church.
> 2. As soon as practicable, a Family Night [ought] to be devoted to information and discussion of the local racial situation.
> 3. The Session should strive to learn of members of the congregation who are particularly interested in the work of the various community organizations involved in study and action on problems related to the racial situation, seek to place such persons in those organizations, and request that they report to the Session and congregation at appropriate times in the continuing education process.
>
> It was also agreed that the community would continue discussion of this matter [at an agreed date] (session minutes, March 12, 1961, 194).

So what was the "racial situation" in Champaign-Urbana in the early 1960s? The numbers of African American students on campus were extremely low at the time. As late as 1967, only 372 (1 percent of the total student population) were enrolled. In 1960, the university finally set policy to "withhold approval from any new undergraduate rooming houses which practice discrimination" (*Daily Illini,* March 24, 1960, 5), and the American Association of University Professors (AAUP) issued a statement in support. However, the AAUP encouraged the University of Illinois to take a step further by requiring "all approved rooming houses to submit a pledge of non-discrimination within three years, [because] the University's ruling does not apply to any currently existing rooming houses as long as the present ownership continues, nor does it cover any home having fewer than four rented rooms" (*Daily Illini,* March 24, 1960, 5).

In the towns of Champaign and Urbana, discrimination existed in numerous arenas. According to the NAACP, the local hospitals practiced segregation; local dentists would not accept African American patients; "unions and employers [would not] accept African Americans into apprenticeship programs in the building trades and public utilities"; and employers, including " local banks, department store, construction companies, public utilities and other firms," did not "adopt and implement ... merit employment [policies]" (*Daily Illini,* July 18, 1963, 3). The Champaign County Board of Realtors did not recognize African Americans' "rights in their search for better housing opportunities" (*Daily Illini,* July 18, 1963, 3). Also, the NAACP exposed issues with "political patronage in civil service jobs"; they noted that recreational facilities at Douglass Center (located in the segregated African-American enclave) needed to be improved, and they further set the goal that the university would "take immediate steps to insure implementation of merit employment in non-academic job categories, especially in the hiring, training" and promotion of African American employees (p. 3).

In April 1961, the month after approving the SEAC recommendation, session continued its discussion of future plans to be adopted from the committee's other recommendations. Since first offering its recommendations to the session in March, SEAC had met with the United Church of Christ, other local Presbyterian churches, and Wesley United Methodist Church. Representatives of these congregations "enthusiastically supported suggestions" (session minutes, April 16, 1961, 198).

> After the last Session meeting the [SEA] Committee met with some of the Elders in an informal discussion of racial integration in Champaign-Urbana. This discussion and others have led the Committee to suggest that we should start with small steps and undertake a more modest program than presented last time. These steps included:
>
> - Undertaking "actions to improve the employment situation by writing to stores that we do not object to being served by persons of a different race."
> - Educating the congregation during Family Night meetings starting in the fall and then encourage them to become involved in the writing campaign named above.
> - Holding meetings with "other selected churches in the community" to formulate "a program whereby merchants in the community are encouraged to employ persons without regards to race or national origin" (session minutes, April 16, 1961, 198).

This motion carried, with a dissenting vote by Dr. Rose—his second objection voiced against SEAC's recommendations.

Less than two weeks later, immediately after SEAC's follow-up meetings with members from other churches, local merchants announced a joint agreement to carry out a nondiscriminatory employment policy with regards to hiring. Bob Pearson, reporting for SEAC, admonished McKinley's session: "Although this represents a big step for the community, [Bob] felt that the church should be leading the conscience of the community rather than following it as was the case here" (session minutes, May 14, 1961, 201). A case in point on the mixed success of the new employment policy offered by a session member was that Penney's [which had been picketed by the NAACP and allies on numerous occasions] had recently hired an African American woman to work in the men's department. This session member proceeded to complain that the woman seemed to have received inadequate training for her work (session minutes, May 14, 1961, 201).

In the same session meeting, Rev. Dr. Hine shared that concerns had been raised about a meeting about Cuba held in the foundation building. Some elders and staff had received phone calls about the group holding the meeting. Hine explained the criteria for allowing outside groups to use the building. As the request for the meeting came from the former provost of the university and other professors, one who was a department head, Hine felt that it was legitimate to allow the meeting to go forward. He further expressed that "open discussion of controversial issues should be promoted, but that allowance of such open discussion does not constitute agreement" (session minutes, May 14, 1961, 203). Session formally approved by voting the use of the foundation building for the group in question to discuss Cuba. Dr. Rose was absent for this session meeting, and there is no record of dissent on the vote.

Laying a foundation for the UPCUSA's future prophetic work, Rev. Dr. Blake, with Rev. Dr. M. L. King, Jr. and eight others, called for the March on Washington and spoke at the event. These were electric times at the University of Illinois. Senator John F. Kennedy addressed 1,200 graduates at the midyear convocation (University of Illinois 2014). And later in 1960, "shortly before [being] elected president, Senator John F. Kennedy [addressed] 10,000 on the [University] Quad becoming the first presidential candidate to do so at Illinois" (University of Illinois 2014). Stupefied by his assassination, 11,500 people attended a memorial for the slain president at the newly constructed Assembly Hall in 1963.

CIVIL RIGHTS WORK AT MCKINLEY

The entry of McKinley Church and Foundation into the Civil Rights era was solidified by their connections to the March on Washington. Rev. Dr. Eugene Carson Blake came to campus and spoken at McKinley in December 1962. By invitation, Rev. Jim Ray, one of four campus ministers at McKinley, attended the march in 1963: "I had only been on staff at McKinley, doing "student work" for about a month when I got a phone call, which was to revolutionize my life, as well as being a precursor to change on campus and the nation. A clergy friend was asking me to join him and other clergy to go to the March on Washington in August" (Ray 2014). Ray witnessed the speech by Rev. Dr. Blake to the mall, and of course he also witnessed the powerful "I Have a Dream" speech given by

Rev. Dr. M. L. King, Jr. Ray and others from McKinley were motivated to action.

Soon after the March on Washington I joined a large group of university faculty, students and staff in a protest demonstration in front of the home of the Chancellor of the University. We were there because the university was not hiring African Americans and other persons of color in the numbers that should have been in place (Ray 2014).

In addition to this demonstration, Ray and other activists held a weekly peace vigil in the center of campus.

In October 1963, the McKinley session received a report of "various race [relations] activities." "Elder Lobb reported that two meetings of Supper club had been held jointly with the AME Church[6] and some members of the staff and church have participated in the picketing of the City Building" (session minutes, October 13, 1963, 260).

The General Council of the General Assembly of the UPCUSA continued to push McKinley and other congregations to take up issues of racial discrimination in their communities. On December 15, 1963, Dr. Philip Anderson, a professor at Chicago Theology Seminary and Mr. James Coke attended the McKinley session meeting as guests to discuss the UPCUSA's ad hoc Committee on Religion and Race (session minutes, December 15, 1963). Mr. James Coke presented a proposal of the ad hoc committee re Race and religion for the action of the session. Three fields of action were recommended:

1. Education of the congregation
2. Devise appropriate action programs
3. Support community-wide programs (session minutes, December 15, 1963, 266)

Session agreed to appoint a committee on race and religion at McKinley. Further, the session members entered into a discussion and came to some agreement about operating as a church of both "custom" and "concern." In other words, they wanted to be a church of concern that remained relevant to the issues of common men and women while at the same time preserving some of the customs and rituals that upheld the traditional membership as a community (session minutes, December 15, 1963). Here they articulate a bridge between maintaining McKinley members' identity and expanding to embrace the social gospel.

While McKinley Church leaders thought through, guided, and helped the congregation along in the idea of social justice work, McKinley Foundation staff and students continued in their endeavors. Rev. Ray and Rev. Hill sought support from session and reported on their activities. Further, the GA of UPCUSA applied pressure to congregations to participate in national actions. For example, on January 19, 1964,

> Rev. Hill outlined the situation in Hattiesburg where qualified people were refused registration for voting after the courts had ruled they should be registered. The GA wants two local ministers to join an interdenominational group to be present when the people go again for registration on Wednesday January 22. The prominent churchmen will be there and the move is sanctioned by the U.S. Department of Justice (session minutes, January 19, 1964, 267).

Interestingly, even though this action was called for by the GA Committee on Race and Religion, in concert with the leadership of the UPCUSA, elders on McKinley's session did not unanimously support their teaching elders' involvement. Session "voted by a majority of nine to three to approve the trip" (session minutes, January 19, 1964, 268). Further, they decided to read a statement about the pending Hattiesburg action to the congregation and agreed that "all costs [for the trip were] to be met by private donation" (p. 268).

In the following month, Rev. Hill reported on the trip to Hattiesburg, noting that an interdenominational group of fifty-one clergy participated in the action and that activists from the Student Nonviolent Coordinating Committee (SNCC) trained African Americans who were planning to register to vote. A member of SNCC was arrested "and the ministers and a group of [African Americans] who attended the trial won the right to sit together in the court room. Mr. Hill believes this was the first desegregated courtroom in Mississippi history" (session minutes, February 2, 1964, 269). Session then approved distributing to the congregation literature on social problems and programs prepared and issued by the UPCUSA and agreed to establishing a "Religion and Race Fund" of approximately $500 (session minutes, February 2, 1964, 270). The following month, session endorsed "the 'Comprehensive Strategy of the UPCUSA in Race Relations' prepared by the Commission on Religion and Race of the UPCUSA" (session minutes, March 1, 1964, 274).

In addition to participating in week-long picket lines in Hattiesburg, Mississippi, Reverends Hill and Ray conducted trainings for organizers in nonviolent protest tactics at McKinley, led student groups to Virginia to do voter registration and tutoring, and worked toward civil rights for all Americans in myriad ways (Ray 2014). For example, Rev. Larry Hill and Rev. Jim Ray marched at Selma (Marlyn Rinehart interview, 2014). And in 1965 Students for a Democratic Society held their first annual conference at McKinley Foundation, with 360 people and sixty-six chapters attending.

McKinley session held a special meeting in regards to a joint church and community "Covenant of Open Occupancy." Session agreed to the following:

> Believing that residential segregation is contrary to God's will and the American heritage of freedom, and that every person, regardless of

race, creed, color, or national origin, has a right to make his home in our midst, with a claim upon our friendship and concern, now therefore, we the undersigned members and friends of McKinley Memorial Presbyterian Church of Champaign, Illinois, do hereby pledge to support one another in promoting open occupancy in our respective neighborhoods and throughout the community" (session minutes, March 18, 1964, 275).

Later the "Urbana [Presbyterian Church] adopted the Covenant on Open Occupancy, [and the] Ministerial Association agreed to urge the adoption of the covenant by all churches" and synagogues (session minutes, April 19, 1964, 280). An Interfaith Council on Fair Housing with 22 churches was formed by July 1964.[7] A dozen of the churches had "presented covenants on open housing to their memberships, and about 1200 non-students and 600 students [had] signed them" by that time (session minutes, July 12, 1964, 283). Next, neighborhood councils were formed to further open occupancy work beyond religious communities. As McKinley members signed the covenant, they also checked "boxes to indicate whether the person signing was a property owner, resident member or student" (session minutes, April 19, 1964, 280).

Though session agreed to the open occupancy covenant (with no dissenting votes mentioned in the minutes), disagreement was expressed about a plan for Rev. Ray, at the request of the UPCUSA, to go to Hattiesburg for a second national action, to participate in picketing and further trainings with potential African American voters to assist them in passing their voter registration examination. A number of elders objected either in person or through letters read on their behalf. And "a letter from a group of students favored [Ray's] going" (session minutes, March 18, 1964, 275). In the end, seven of those present voted in favor and two against sending Rev. Ray to Hattiesburg. Votes from absent session members were one for and one against.

McKinley's Committee on Religion and Race (CORR) met and reported to session monthly in the 1960s. The committee's work touched many in the congregation; for example, "101 students and 60 non-student signatures had been secured to the open occupancy pledge" by May 1964 (session minutes, May 6, 1964, 281–2). And a year later, "Elder Hodgman reported the completion of four Sunday A.M. meetings on race relations with 40-50 at each meeting. Information on local housing opportunities is going to local Negroes" (session minutes March 7, 1965, 1). In 1960, only 5 percent of Champaign County residents were African American, increasing to 7 percent by 1970. The committee reported their priorities for McKinley Church, including the more general (such as "housing for Negroes," employment, student involvement in race relations, and education of the congregation) and the very specific ("get more Negroes into McKinley Church"—especially "going after new students" and those "with no church affiliation" and asking "employment practices of suppliers to church"; session minutes, April 4, 1965, 4–5). While integrating McKinley's own congregation was a decades-long task, session minutes show that inquiries into the employment practices of suppliers happened immediately. The church decided to boycott suppliers who discriminated against African Americans and refused to hire African American workers.

The larger UPCUSA remained active in working for civil rights. The Confession of 1967,[8] penned in 1965,

> "declares: 'To be reconciled to God is to be sent into the world as God's reconciling community.' ... The Confession states, 'In each time and place, there are particular problems and crises through which God calls the church to act.' Then it describes the crises that were urgent in 1967: 'racial discrimination, peace among nations, enslaving poverty in a world of abundance, and relationships between women and men' (Whitt 2009).
>
> In 1967 there were factions in the denomination who opposed the new confession. An article in the New York Times described the Confession of 1967 as the "first theological statement from the Reformed or Calvinistic branch of Protestantism to discuss social ethics and support church participation in social issues." This raised the opposition of Presbyterians who believed that ... the church should not involve itself in social issues (Rev. Dr. Joanne Whitt, sermon, August 23, 2009).

While the confession was a step forward in many ways, affirming the denomination's 1954 prointegrationist stance and declaring its commitment to fighting racial discrimination, resolving international conflict, and "enslaving poverty," it was at best less clear on its support for sexual minorities. Its statement that "anarchy in sexual relationships is a symptom of man's alienation from God, his neighbor, and himself" (*Confession of 1967*, Section 9.47d) was ambiguous, if not outright condemning of LGBTIQ persons' right to exist and serve in Presbyterian contexts. Further, it did not address gender, other than to promote heteronormative family arrangements, by proclaiming that sexual anarchy occurs when sex takes place outside the confines of marriage and the purpose of procreation, stating that "the church comes under the judgment of God ... when it fails to lead men and women into the full meaning of life together" (*Confession of 1967*, Section 9.47d).

The 178th General Assembly of UPCUSA adopted the Confession of 1967, with 90 percent of presbyteries voting to approve it. In 1965 McKinley's session had studied the proposed confession over several months, then voted in January 1966 to support it (Session minutes, October 31, 1965; congregational meeting minutes, November 9, 1965; session minutes, December 12, 1965; session minutes, January 9, 1966).

Civil rights work continued at the federal level after Kennedy's assassination. In 1967 President Lyndon Johnson issued Executive Order

11246, requiring federal contractors "to take Affirmative Action" to end discrimination. McKinley was already actively involved in efforts to integrate housing, ensure nondiscriminatory employment practices, and integrate the university campus.

HOUSING INTEGRATION

McKinley became a part of the local Interfaith Council on Fair Housing that worked toward integrating Champaign County neighborhoods (session minutes, March 7, 1965). For several months, the church contemplated participation in a program under Section 221-D-3 of the National Housing Act to work with other local churches (both African American and white congregations) to purchase land and build a fully integrated housing development in south Champaign (session minutes, March 6, 1966, and October 23, 1966). After months of deliberation, session voted to go ahead with the project (Session minutes, December 11, 1966). At the February 17, 1967, annual congregational meeting, session members explained the project, and the board of deacons agreed to conduct a campaign to raise pledges for the $3,000 buy-in required of each congregation. Impressively, less than one month later, Mr. Philip Morgan of McKinley Foundation reported "that the $3,000 goal of McKinley Church was reached as of today" (session minutes, March 5, 1967, 58). In the following year, a result of the work of the NAACP, the three-year old Interfaith Council on Fair Housing, and other advocates, the Champaign City Council passed what was reportedly "the state's strongest open housing ordinance on April 30, 1968" (*Daily Illini,* June 1, 1968, 5).[9]

Dr. Jim Hine was supportive of the integrated housing initiative, but he focused on fulfilling his role as pastor and spiritual leader to the McKinley congregation and encouraged his associate pastors' work as advocates for civil rights (congregant interview, 2014). Hine's vibrant marriage ministry touched not only student and "resident" members of McKinley; he also received national recognition from the UPCUSA denomination for this work. In April 1966, Dr. Hine was featured in the national *Presbyterian Life;*[10] the article "Making Marriage Last" "describ[ed] the work being done by Dr. Hine here at McKinley in marriage counseling" (session minutes, April 3, 1966, 27). Hine was praised for his counseling, for a "course on marriage for which academic credit is given at the University" of Illinois, for two books distributed nationwide by McKinley Publications (one titled *Alternative to Divorce)*, and for being the "star of a TV show widely watched in Champaign-Urbana" (Hoffman 1966, pp. 5–6). The tempered but traditional nature of Hine's ministry was reflected in the statement that Hine "never advises divorce" (p. 6). However, in his deliberate manner, Hine eschewed some gender norms in marriage. "I don't like the concept of 'man's work' and 'women's work'. If the husband is a better cook and enjoys preparing meals—why not?" (p. 6). As reported to session, "Already many letters have come from all over the country to Dr. Hine, following the publication of the article" (session minutes, April 3, 1966).

CHANGING STUDENT MINISTRY

Despite Hine's well-known work in marriage counseling and the social justice–oriented work of the McKinley congregation, largely led by CORR efforts, by the early 1960s student participation at the church began to dwindle. Weekly attendance fell from 600 or more to "250 to 300" by 1963 (according to Jim Ray). The Church Members and Students Committee expressed "the problem of students losing their identity on the big campus.... Many who were Presbyterians at home go to no church after coming here" (session minutes, March 7, 1965). The McKinley session, deacons, and staff scrambled to rebuild student participation by asking Presbyterian "pastors in the state to send names of their student members who are coming to Illinois this fall" (session minutes, April 4, 1965). Session engaged in much contemplation during meetings as to whether the style of worship, relevance of church activities, or even sermon topics might influence participation rates (session minutes, March 6, 1966). Rev. Hine reasoned, "The student in the 40s was more apt to accept religious teaching. The student of the 60s is more apt to question and doubt. They have to solve things for themselves now" (*Daily Illini,* October 10, 1967, 7). Finally McKinley elected to expand "its ministry throughout the University campus and not just within the walls of its buildings" (session minutes, November 11, 1966).

Here student ministry took a turn. It became campus ministry, more activist-focused, following students' interests and activities of the time (Tom Seals interview, 2014). Shortly after McKinley raised the $3,000 buy-in for the public housing project, the church's lead pastor, Dr. James Hine, resigned his position to accept a new appointment as professor of family and consumer resources at the University of Arizona and to pursue his marriage and family ministry as associate pastor and director of counseling at Trinity Presbyterian Church in Tucson, Arizona (Erickson 2006), leaving the Champaign congregation in November 1967. One member noted that Dr. Hine was a great preacher, but that he "did not appeal to radical students" (congregant interview, 2014).

"Dr. Hine left at a good time because it would have been uncomfortable for him to be forced into (social justice) ministry, and his reputation would have suffered. He left on a very good note" (congregant interview, 2014).

McKinley's nascent social justice orientation necessitated new leadership.

NOTES

1. In 1954, the PCUSA's "Westminster Fellowship National Council, composed of Presbyterian youth representing each state synod convened at McKinley Foundation for a five-day policy making session" (*Daily Illini*, July 8, 1954, 3). Rev. Dr. Eugene Carson Blake delivered an inspiring message to the group's National Assembly. He stated, "We are in one of the finest periods in the history of the Presbyterian Church. In the last 10 years we have made tremendous forward strides" (*Daily Illini*, July 8, 1954, 3).

2. While the 1954 admonishment of racial segregation was significant, the issue of race and religion had been consistently debated throughout the existence of the dominant Presbyterian denomination, including the 1861 split of the Presbyterian Church of the Confederate States of America from the Presbyterian Church USA over the issue of slavery. The 1865 formation of the PCUS, and the 1874 formation of Cumberland Presbyterian Church in America. Each of these events is highlighted in Table 5.2.

3. Data on racial-ethnic makeup of UPCUSA is difficult to find. One report indicated that from 1977 to 1997 "almost all Presbyterians [98%] list their racial-ethnicity as white" (*Presbyterian Panel* 1997-1999, 12, https://www.pcusa.org/site_media/media/uploads/research/pdfs/1997_99_full_bgrndreport.pdf). The racial-ethnic identity of McKinley's members was 99 percent white through 1980, and its staff was 100 percent white until 2004.

4. Rev. Dr. Eugene Carson Blake addressed a national gathering of Presbyterian youth in 1954 when he delivered the closing address to 1,700 for the National Assembly of the Westminster Fellowship at McKinley (*Daily Illini*, July 8, 1954, 3).

5. This "information presented above" is not included in the minutes.

6. The African Methodist Episcopal Church in Champaign-Urbana is part of an African American denomination.

7. Two of the churches in the Interfaith Council on Fair Housing were African American (session minutes, July 12, 1964, 283).

8. UPCUSA/PC(USA) "confessions" are statements of faith adhered to by the entire denomination. Confessions are proposed to the General Assembly, edited by commissioners, and then voted on by presbyteries before they are adopted. Confessions are "historical statements of what we as a church believe" (http://www.pcusa.org/resource/book-confessions).

9. The *Daily Illini* further claimed that the Champaign City Council open housing ordinance "was one of the strongest such ordinance in the nation as well" (June 1, 1968, 5).

10. *Presbyterian Life*, published by the General Assembly of the PCUSA/UPCUSA (1948–1972), had a wide readership, as every household of members in the denomination was eligible to receive the magazine.

SEVEN
Growing Pains of a Social Justice Ministry

1968 to 1973

After a short period of discernment, McKinley narrowed the pool of Pastor Information Forms (the application for a job as pastor of a Presbyterian congregation) from forty-five applicants to five finalists; out of that group it hired Reverend Richard Lundy. "When Lundy was hired, he was much more social justice–minded [than Jim Hine]" (congregant interview, 2014). Reverend Lundy and his wife, Mary Ann Lundy, arrived in Champaign during turbulent times in the summer of 1968, after Rev. Dr. Martin Luther King, Jr. had been assassinated.

In 1966, a report called attention to the low numbers of African American students on the University of Illinois campus. Students, faculty, and staff worked for "Project 500" to recruit more African American undergraduates (Eisenman 1968, 13); scholars trace "the origins of race-based admissions in higher education to . . . a time of political upheaval" (Lipson 2011, 133).

With the passing of the Affirmative Action legislation and the assassination of King, students demanded more effective recruitment efforts and better support to African American students. Project 500 was borne of these efforts, with the initial purpose of increasing enrollment of black students by matriculating a cohort of 500 in the fall of 1968. When results of Project 500 fell short of expectations, 252 students were arrested during protests in the fall of 1968. One of few African American regular attenders at the time,[1] Clarence Shelley was well known for his support of African American students and his work with Project 500. He served as the director of the Special Educational Opportunities Program and through the years was appointed to several administrative posts, including special assistant to the chancellor.[2]

The increase in African American undergraduates from 1 percent in 1967 to 4 percent by 1970 resulted from the Project 500 initiative and the pressure applied by protesting students to garner more resources for the program. African Americans comprised 3 percent to 4 percent of the U of I student population in the 1970s and 1980s, with an increase to a stable 6 percent from 1990 until 2008. The current proportion of African American students at the University of Illinois is still only 5 percent. See Table 7.1 for details.

The Vietnam War well underway, students on campus participated in antiwar protest in the late 1960s. Ministry at McKinley included support for students generally, including their antiwar protest, and continued civil rights work in the community. For example, Errol Rohr was invited to continue to serve as assistant pastor, and session agreed that his work as chairman of the Economic Opportunity Council of Champaign, a group in charge of the local poverty program, was an important aspect of his ministry (session minutes, April 13, 1969). The following year session voted to direct their purchases to suppliers who were equal opportunity employers (session minutes, March 1, 1970). They also voted to purchase two properties as "rent supplement housing" in conjunction with the County Housing Authority (session minutes, May 3, 1970) to help ensure integration of Champaign-Urbana neighborhoods.

Lundy was a good fit for the congregation. He was "very social justice–oriented," according to one congregant. Another said, "Dick Lundy turned out to be very successful. He was fearless when came to [political] causes. He was an excellent preacher. He had new insights to bring to new topics." Lundy led not only from the pulpit. He also engaged in activities and raised consciousness among congregants and students. For example, during the university winter break in 1969–70, Lundy led a group of students to New York City, where they met with lawyers from the American Civil Liberties Union and the Equal Opportunity Commission, attended an address by Black Panthers, learned about drug addiction and treatment, learned about poverty in the Bronx, and attended six plays (session minutes, February 15, 1970.) This trip would fuel Lundy's revolutionary ministry of welcome to the marginalized. During the years following, the PCUSA, testing its own bounds of radicalism, became embroiled over conflict regarding funding to the Angela Davis defense fund. Also, the McKinley session issued a statement calling for withdrawal of troops from Vietnam, and the congregation was involved in supporting refugee families.

Due to the church's record of involvement in civil rights, McKinley was approached by the university about "making both floors of the Foundation open to black students of the community for social functions on Friday and Saturday nights" (session minutes, February 8, 1970, 149). The

Table 7.1. Total, African American, and Female Students at the University of Illinois, 1967–2014

Year	Total students	African Americans		Females	
		Number	Percentage	Number	Percentage
1967	30,407	372	1	10,234	34
1970	34,018	1,251	4	11,978	35
1975	35,004	1,254	4	13,609	39
1980	34,686	1,219	4	14,253	41
1981	35,006	1,188	3	14,676	42
1983	34,548	1,185	3	14,877	43
1985	35,928	1,263	4	15,711	44
1986	36,266	1,369	4	15,731	43
1987	36,282	1,556	4	15,643	43
1989	34,972	1,896	5	14,943	43
1990	35,669	2,101	6	15,071	42
1993	36,374	2,193	6	15,700	43
1994	36,137	2,219	6	15,808	44
1995	36,395	2,292	6	16,108	44
1996	36,124	2,316	6	16,245	45
1997	35,979	2,316	6	16,480	46
1998	36,303	2,351	6	16,759	46
1999	36,690	2,382	6	17,095	47
2000	36,936	2,324	6	17,279	47
2001	37,684	2,265	6	17,606	47
2002	38,263	2,335	6	17,916	47
2003	38,872	2,522	6	18,102	47
2004	39,516	2,382	6	18,518	47
2005	40,510	2,398	6	18,894	47
2006	41,180	2,516	6	19,240	47
2007	40,923	2,467	6	19,224	47
2008	41,495	2,524	6	19,327	47
2010	41,949	2,186	5	19,169	46
2012	42,883	2,160	5	19,283	45
2013	43,398	2,172	5	19,334	45
2014	43,603	2,126	5	19,436	45

Sources: DMI, Old enrollment figures for Urbana Fall Term (2000); DMI, Student Enrollment by Curriculum, Race, Sex, Residency (2014); http://archives.library.illinois.edu/slc/oral-history-portal/project-500.

rationale for the request was that "the [Illini] Union and [Illinois Student Residence Halls] lounge can no longer adequately handle such events, and the University has not been able to provide other acceptable places." After some discussion, session approved the request (p. 149).

> As the Vietnam War escalated, so did the antiwar movement, [which] borrowed tactics from the Civil Right Movement to express dissent. Although protests in the 1960s were not popular among most Americans, . . . by 1972 the Vietnam War was highly unpopular. . . . At UIUC, early protests were led by [such groups as] the Students for a Democratic Society and the DuBois Club (University of Illinois 2014).

One McKinley member remembers that "my husband and I were working out in the yard one day and big tanks from the National Guard came barreling down Pennsylvania Avenue" (congregant interview, 2014). Nixon's invasion of Cambodia sparked protest across college campuses. At Kent State University on May 7, 1970, the Ohio National Guard responded to a student rally by firing on protestors, killing four and wounding nine. Students at the University of Illinois reacted by calling for a three-day strike [May 6–8, 1970]. 99 percent of classes were shut down and the University called in the National Guard to patrol the campus (University of Illinois 2014).

Curfews limited the mobility of students on campus, and McKinley Foundation served as a metaphorical and physical shelter. Several long-term members indicated that students were offered sanctuary by McKinley Foundation during evening curfews "so that students would not get swept up" (congregant interview, 2014).

ANTI-VIETNAM WAR SENTIMENT AND PROTEST

Session members noted their study of the conflict in Vietnam (session minutes, February 4, 1968), and in 1968, Errol Rohr and Jim Ray requested session guidance as they were asked by the Draft Resistance Union (a UIUC student protest group) "to take part in a resistance demonstration south of the Illini Union on April 3, and participate in civil disobedience" (session minutes, March 31, 1968, 93).

In June 1968, the session received a letter from a former McKinley student associate "describing his feelings about applying for the status of conscientious objector." Session "reaffirms its support of the right of each individual Christian to obey the dictates of his own conscious in such matters as participation in military service" (session minutes, June 30,

1968, 101). On April 13, 1969, McKinley established a draft counseling service for the benefit of young men locally and throughout the presbytery.

In March 1970, campus dissent took place protesting the university's decision to house the $24-million Department of Defense–owned ILLIAC IV supercomputer. Students and faculty reacted to a report in the campus newspaper: "The world's most powerful computer, scheduled to go into operation this fall at the University's Urbana-Champaign campus, will be in use approximately two-thirds of the time by the Department of Defense and will play a vital role in the development of more sophisticated nuclear weaponry" (*Daily Illini,* August 1, 1970, D1).

The *DI* reported that the protests included smashing windows and firebombing an ROTC lounge in the Armory (*Daily Illini,* March 10, 1970). Session minutes show consternation on the part of members when it was brought to their attention that ILLIAC IV protestors congregated at the McKinley Foundation building, mimeographed their flyers on McKinley equipment, noted McKinley's name in their flyers, and even posted announcements in McKinley's church bulletin! Minutes note that while "the Session commended the members of the Church and Foundation staff for action in the role of setting up first-aid facilities during the recent disorder," it "deplores acts of violence which occurred" and disavows the ILLIAC IV vigil (session minutes, March 15, 1970, p. 152).

These events rattled members of the congregation; in fact, session members discussed that "Dr. and Mrs. Bailar have been disturbed by events and happenings at the Church and Foundation over the past several years which they feel are not compatible with the mission of McKinley" (session minutes, April 12, 1970, 153) and the fact that "the Bailars are suspending their pledge to McKinley until such a time they feel more firm restrictions are placed on the use of buildings by undesirable groups have been effected and enforced" (session minutes, April 12, 1970, 154). As former clerk of session and a respected member of the university faculty, Dr. Bailar still possessed power at McKinley. Though the Bailars' objections were considered carefully, a motion presented to the board of elders "to restrict the use of the Foundation by those groups who are offensive to public morality and hostile to the program of the McKinley Foundation . . . is defeated." Later Rev. Lundy expressed his hope that Session members were not becoming "too conservative" in their viewpoints so as to restrain the church "from moving ahead into new vital areas." Session affirmed support for exploring "new ideas and possibilities." In the same month, session reaffirmed the church's and foundation's open building policy (with the exception of groups advocating campus violence) (session minutes, May 3, 1970, 156).

When the National Guard arrived on campus to quell student protest against Nixon's invasion of Cambodia, Jill Mulder remembers, "This was the first big split in the church." She felt that "we lost about half of the congregation" when McKinley became involved with the anti–Vietnam War movement. Those who left felt it was not appropriate to get involved in politics. "We had different ideas about the purpose of church," she explains (Mulder interview, 2014).

While the progressive politics of McKinley contributed to disassociation for some long-term members, many new members were drawn to McKinley's progressive theology. Linda Kimmel was looking for a church family after moving to Champaign County with her husband, Grear, and their young daughter. She says, "When you have a child, you want to give them another community" and that "I knew Grear needed something progressive. I knew he didn't take the Bible literally." She remembers Lundy as having a "presence that attracted people" (L. Kimmel interview, 2014). Grear Kimmel states that "McKinley was very active when campuses were in turmoil over Vietnam" and that it served as a recognized "sanctuary for dissidents" (G. Kimmel interview, 2014). Further, some long-time members stayed, including the Bailar family. In subsequent years, scientist Dr. John Bailar would continue to serve on session, and his memory would later be preserved by the dedication of the McKinley science window in his honor. As one member explains:

> As the student involvement [in church] diminished, McKinley redefined itself in line with the history it had charted as a civil rights church. Establishment Presbyterians left in droves and those that remained were social action people who were Presbyterians incidentally. Students may not have attended church or involved themselves in traditional church stuff, but the buildings hosted hundreds of student groups and their events and gatherings, provided a great place to study with a coffeehouse, and provided opportunities for them to "do good" by sponsoring social justice and missionary and political ministries (Dave Bechtel interview, 2015).

McKinley members continued to welcome protesting students, undertake study of the situation in Vietnam, and engage in social action. For example, a collection was taken up for four Sundays by the Ministries Committee "to receive contributions for medical supplies for civilians in North Vietnam who are in need of medical treatment as a result of American military bombing" (session minutes, January 7, 1973, 200).

On January 7, 1973, session issued a statement on behalf of McKinley Church renouncing U.S. participation in the Vietnam War. The statement was placed at the rear of the church the following Sunday for members to sign, and then was sent to Senate and House representatives and to all other churches in the Southeastern Illinois Presbytery. Members were encouraged to write President Johnson to express their disapproval of the war (session minutes, January 7, 1973, 201).

McKinley members went a step further and supported a Vietnamese immigrant family in 1975. "Dick [Lundy] reported a request from the

Westminster Presbyterian Church[3] of Champaign to co-sponsor a Vietnamese refugee family.... Together with Westminster we would be asked to provide the family's financial support for the first month, to furnish the house and provide clothing." The session heartily agreed (session minutes, June 29, 1975, 266).

THE WOMEN'S MOVEMENT AND INCLUSIVE LANGUAGE

Concurrent with the Civil Rights Movement and anti–Vietnam War activism, the women's movement came alive at McKinley. Even prior to this time, women held roles as church deacons and elders. Most long-time members whom I interviewed noted that since the 1950s, women held elected positions as deacons and elders, not a universal situation among Presbyterians.

It was not until 1930 that women were admitted as deacons and elders in the PCUSA, and not until 1962 in the Presbyterian Church U.S. And it was not until 1956 that women were ordained as clergy in the United Presbyterian Church, and not until 1965 in the Presbyterian Church U.S. (Mary Ann Lundy 1991, 55).

However, men tended to be elders and women deacons in the 1950s and 1960s. One congregant explained to me that the elders set policy and the deacons carried it out (congregant interview, 2014). In a study of women in the PCUSA, Lundy writes the following:

> It would seem that we still have a way to go toward full participation of women as policymakers in the church, particularly when we define the office of elder as that of policymaking and that of deacon as a ministry of compassion. It would seem to indicate that we have not yet overcome the stereotypes of female—and of male, for that matter—and their prescribed leadership roles (Mary Ann Lundy 1991, 56).

From the 1940s on, the women at McKinley were integral to the spiritual well-being and social organization of both resident and student members. In the 1940s, women utilized the McKinley-Weds group to set and carry out plans with regards to provision of nursery care and creation of a Sunday school curriculum. (As noted earlier, the McKinley-Weds were especially active in organizing the early service and increasing attendance at the church.) Women created two groups, the Women's Society, later referred to as the Women's Association, and the active "McWed wives," which met monthly and organized activities in 1951. Eventually, the Women's Association was split into two cooperating groups, circle 1 and circle two. In a report, they note that "the group ("McWed-wives") has now become circle two of the Women's Association" (session minutes, February 3, 1953, 52).

The last mention I found of McKinley-Weds is late 1957, when the session called for recommendations for student church officers, including a request for nominees from the McWeds (session minutes, December 2, 1957). McWed nominees are never presented to session, according to minutes. However, two groups may have supplanted needs filled by the formally active McWed-wives: the Colony Plan Committee, headed by session member Miss Barry, and Christian Education and Training, headed by Mrs. McConnell until the Christian Education Committee gained session representation.[4] The colonies were a way to organize church members into neighborhood groups to coordinate discussions about social events and long-range planning for the congregation. Session members noted reductions in student pledges by 1957, and in the fall congregational meeting, members expressed that "some action should now begin to" move away from an identity of McKinley as "solely a church for students" to also becoming "a family church" (congregational meeting minutes, October 6, 1957, 114). The session created the long-range planning committee with the understanding that "the rapidly changing times demand changing emphasis in our church work" (session minutes, December 2, 1957, 119). The colony groupings and social events appear to have taken the place of the monthly McWeds gatherings, although Family Night events continued. Both types of gathering may have facilitated civil rights work in the subsequent decade.

Ms. Mary Ann Lundy, a member of McKinley since arriving with her husband, Reverend Dick Lundy, in 1968, would become the church's director of Christian education. Mary Ann not only introduced gender-neutral language to McKinley, but she also promoted transnational political and theological influences. She organized women's study groups referred to as "Women in Conversation" in the congregation and the community. Marlyn Rinehart recalls, "We studied most of the liberation theologians" (Rinehart interview, 2014). McKinley's transnationalism was evidenced in various ways, from support of activists working against apartheid in South Africa[5] to support for the wounded in Vietnam as well as for Vietnamese and later Laotian refugees.

As a young mother, Jane Cain found McKinley to be a very attractive congregation, especially because "older women [at McKinley Church] were very progressive and lived their lives for social justice" (J. Cain interview, 2014). A long-lasting influence was the introduction of inclusive language, which is still predominant at McKinley. Members today do not think twice as they read litanies that never refer to patriarchal renderings of God as "Father" or "Lord." But in the late 1960s/early 1970s, inclusive language was a novel idea. One congregant discusses the sometimes intrusive nature of corrections he would receive from proponents of inclusive language, who interrupted him sometimes mid-sentence, "destroying anything I had in my mind" (congregant interview, 2014).

The efforts to promote the women's movement at McKinley explored practical contributions to women's liberation. In the late 1960s, members noted that the basement of the foundation building was underutilized. Later, session explored the possibility of housing a day care center there (session minutes, January 11, 1970). Plans were explained at a congregational meeting: "This endeavor will put about 40 pre-school children of working mothers in basement classrooms weekdays Monday through Friday" (congregational meeting minutes, February 15, 1970, 150). Later the Women's Liberation Program established a daycare center for nonacademic university staff at McKinley (session minutes, March 28, 1971).

Mary Ann Lundy organized study groups for the congregation's youth as well as for women. For example, in the May 7, 1972 session minutes, a young people's summer program is described in which youth studied American marginalized groups ("American Indians, migrant workers, and peoples of Appalachia," p. 192). Rewarding her creativity, ingenuity, and activism, in June 1972, Session recommended Mary Ann Lundy's appointment as director of Christian education (session minutes, June 4, 1972).

Members who knew her report that Mary Ann Lundy was a McKinley powerhouse. Jane Cain remarks that she had great respect for Mary Ann and for other women of McKinley who were so deeply committed to social justice work. She said that the women's study group addressed the hot topics of the day (J. Cain interview, 2014). Marlyn Rinehart says, "I admired [Mary Ann]. She was fearless. She was inspiring" (Rinehart interview, 2014). Linda Kimmel says that Mary Ann "was a very welcoming person and made you feel like you belong right away" (L. Kimmel interview, 2014). Linda relates that the women's discussion groups spearheaded by Mary Ann appealed to her as a new member in the Urbana community and helped her find people she could connect with and who had similar viewpoints.

One impact of the women's movement is seen in session's agreeing that the new church directory "will be printed omitting the parenthesis around the names of married women" (session minutes, December 3, 1972, 198). But not only did the women's consciousness raising introduce gender-neutral language, provide impetus to create a day care center, and create a more liberated space for women to worship at McKinley Church, it also contributed in significant ways to McKinley's ecumenicalism and members' appreciation for other religious traditions, many of which were examined during the Women in Conversation discussion and study sessions. Initially Jane Cain came to campus as a student and sought out Presbyterians; but she came to conviction in her own faith that "I am Christian, because Christ was a model for me. But there are all sorts of models to live by—King, Gandhi, and others" (J. Cain interview, 2014). This openness and claim of identity as Christian, yet somewhat universalist, is commonplace at McKinley today. And it is my conviction that this more universalist perspective was grounded by the work of Mary Ann Lundy and others in the 1970s. Lundy's mentorship of women expanded to the presbytery and the national PCUSA (Youngdahl 1996). She helped organize the feminist (and controversial) Re-Imagining Conference of the PCUSA in 1993, and though she endured criticism, she later became associate director of the World Council of Churches.

While the laudable consciousness-raising work among women at McKinley centered white women's expanded understandings of the world around them, it was less focused on welcoming women of color into the conversation, and it may have been largely unaware of the need to incorporate perspectives of lesbian, bisexual, transgender, intersex, and questioning women. In McKinley's subsequent era, the work would become intentional about welcoming sexual diversity, and it would finally break down barriers to interracialism.

NOTES

1. Long-time McKinley members whom I interviewed remember only Clarence Shelley and one other African American regular attender from the 1950s until the 1980s.

2. Clarence Shelley was also appointed to posts as dean of students, assistant vice chancellor, and associate vice chancellor for student affairs (https://localwiki.org/cu/Clarence_Shelley).

3. Westminster is another progressive area church in Champaign County. Its membership is predominantly white.

4. I do not find references to these women's first names! These were fairly formal times, and even the male session members are referred to as "Mr." and "Dr.," though their first names are also often used.

5. In 1968 Lawson Lobb, a former member of McKinley, wrote a letter to Jim Ray saying he had been involved with a small group threatened with arrest for their protest of the apartheid policies of the South African government. Announcements were then made to the Graduate Luncheon and congregation so that "concerned individuals and friends of Lawson could make an individual contribution [for legal fees] to him through Jim Ray" (session minutes, May 26, 1968, 100).

EIGHT
The Dawning of More Light Presbyterianism at McKinley

"Inclusiveness: that was Jesus's main deal!"[1]

As noted in this book's introduction, the unofficial start of the More Light Presbyterians (MLP) movement occurred in 1974 at the PCUSA General Assembly in Louisville, Kentucky, when David Bailey Sindt held up a sign asking "Is anyone else out there gay?" (More Light Presbyterians 2014). In 1975 Bill Capel, whose footprint is now well known in Presbyterian polity and in Christian LGBTIQ circles, was involved in a secular "gay consciousness-raising men's group" in Champaign County that met at a member's home. When that person eventually moved, Bill was searching for another place for the group to meet. He went to Wesley United Methodist Church, known at the time to be a liberal campus congregation. Wesley's secretary turned Capel down but directed him to McKinley, muttering, "They do stuff like that there." For ten years, the secular men's gay consciousness-raising group met at McKinley. Bill explains, "That's how I came to McKinley and became a Presbyterian" (Capel interview, 2014). Later Bill would become a lay pastor and take on various leadership roles in the regional presbytery and at the national level.

In December 1976, "[Dick] Lundy reported that two congregations have been worshipping in the Chapel of the Foundation this fall: an Eastern Orthodox congregation . . . and the Prodigal Child Congregation of the Metropolitan Community Church (MCC) each Sunday afternoon" (session minutes December 5, 1976, 283–4). Three letters written by members of McKinley expressing disapproval of the use of facilities by MCC—a "gay church"—had been received. At the December meeting, session voted to allow the groups to continue to use the facilities and planned to discuss the issue further in January (session minutes, December 5, 1976). In the meantime, session members met MCC members, at "a meeting in Dick Lundy's living room" (J. Cain interview, 2014), to jointly discuss the needs of the MCC. Dr. John Bailar, whom Cain describes as a "staunch man," was in attendance and was not initially in favor of hosting MCC.

However, as a result of the meeting, Dr. Bailar came around to supporting the "MCC for gay men, saying: 'now that I have met these people, it is ok for them to meet in the Foundation'" (J. Cain interview, 2014). In January 1977, session voted to allow both the Orthodox and the MCC congregations to worship in the foundation chapel and further "that the MCC be allowed office space" (session minutes, January 22, 1977, 285). Some years later (1979) the MCC congregation folded, and many of its members joined McKinley Church (Bechtel interview, 2015).

The decision to be welcoming of sexual minorities had an impact on LGBTIQ and allied individuals, of course. But McKinley's laid-back environment also drew families. When asked how he first came to McKinley in the late 1970s, long-time member Dave Bechtel relates the following:

> We searched for churches that had young families and children. As such we had avoided campus churches, thinking they would not have a family orientation. We had gone almost everywhere when friends told us to try McKinley because people could drink coffee in the pews and they were very laid-back. Sounded interesting, so we decided to give it a try, since, 38 years ago, no other church allowed that. We, happily, found a group of young parents like us that were also attending, and more came along after we joined. There were 10 to 12 families and 20 to 30 kids, and they became our social circle as well (Bechtel interview, 2014).

Jill Mulder remembers that at that time, there was a strong detachment between McKinley Church and Foundation and Presby House, a McKinley-affiliated residence for women students. Tom Seals indicates that Presby House was like a Presbyterian sorority (Seals interview, 2015). Some women living in Presby House did not want to be associated with the "gay church"—referring to it pejoratively as McKinley "Lesbyterian" (Mulder interview, 2014). In the next era of McKinley's history, as the church embraced the More Light Presbyterians movement and enlarged their understanding of what it means to be inclusive, they endured growing pains of rejection from their regional presbytery, conflict within the General Assembly of the PCUSA, and upheaval within their own walls.

POSTSCRIPT: 1980 TO 2015

Steadfastly, McKinley held to their newfound inclusiveness. The action of accepting members of the disbanded MCC attracted a new group of active and energetic LBGTIQ and allies whose work contributed to the persistence of the campus church and foundation even when other progressive church–foundation institutions at the University of Illinois campus folded (Seals interview, 2015). The LGBTIQ welcome matured from mere diversity among attenders to fuller inclusion. Defying presbytery and PCUSA policy, McKinley voted to accept and to nominate LGBTIQ members in their congregation to lay leadership. Congregants reported that LGBTIQ and allies in the congregation worked toward greater inclusion by organizing discussion groups to encourage interaction between members, regardless of sexuality. This important work was honored in 1997 by the dedication of the McKinley Inclusiveness stained glass window. In 2002, McKinley hired its first female lead pastor (whose partner is incidentally female). And shortly thereafter, McKinley hired its first African American associate pastor. McKinley took a public stand for students of color on campus and against the University of Illinois racist Indian-chief mascot—applying pressure with other progressives that resulted in censure by the National Collegiate Athletic Association and the campus's eventual retirement of the mascot.[2] McKinley continues to operate on the frontline of progressive struggle on campus and in the community. In concert with this congregational maturation in McKinley's social justice orientation, the PCUSA denomination stepped up—notably a few paces behind McKinley—and the GA voted to ordain LGBTIQ ruling and teaching elders in 2011, followed by a landmark vote in favor of permitting pastors to perform same-sex marriages in 2014. Fighting for gay marriage within and then alongside the denomination has led to the gratifying conclusion of seeing the success of achieving the Supreme Court's support of same-sex marriage in 2015. McKinley—transformed from a conservative, white, traditional congregation to a beacon of hope that has taken the lead for more than a decade in helping the PCUSA to embrace wider inclusiveness—is a remarkable example of the quotidian incremental moves that make up the struggle for inclusivity.

DISCUSSION: A SPIRITUAL ANCHOR TO PROMOTE SOCIAL JUSTICE AND INCLUSION AT MCKINLEY

The ebb and flow of the struggle for inclusivity is evident at McKinley Church in several arenas from 1940 to 1980, including the Protestant modernist–fundamentalist controversy, Civil Rights, student ministry, Vietnam War protest, the women's movement, and LGBTIQ consciousness raising and welcome. In each arena, getting to the end point of a categorical (though perhaps an incremental) step forward toward greater inclusivity included a push and pull among congregants, the presbytery, the larger denomination, and/or the campus context.

McKinley Church and Foundation provided spaces both physical and ideological to work through differences of opinion. One of these spaces was McKinley Foundation's coffeehouse:

> "This is the Apology," the coffeehouse run by students from McKinley Presbyterian Foundation and the Catholic Newman Center, is located on the corner of Fifth and Chalmers Streets, Champaign in the McKinley Foundation Building (*Daily Illini*, August 1, 1969, C-6).

The *Daily Illini* describes the physical environment of the coffeehouse, including walls painted black, one with handprints, and floor cushions surrounding low tables near a fireplace. This Is the Apology featured an open-mic setting where participants played "folk and folk-rock" offerings. "This is a place where you can be free," one [frequent patron] said fervently. "It is like an association where everyone belongs" (p. C-6). The article also mentions poetry readings and the political content of readings that addressed the U.S. conflict in Vietnam, poverty in America, and "other current problems" (p. C-6), though a variation in political perspectives was represented at the coffeehouse. Reverend Lundy also spoke to the cross-section of the campus and church there.

Because the congregation included opposing factions, confrontations seemed likely. But, Lundy said, McKinley was one of the few places on campus where both sides met to discuss critical issues. He said groups that usually were in violent opposition would gather in the foundation lounge after Sunday services to discuss their views as "caring, feeling human beings." "'We attempted here to be a place of dialogue,' he said, and the church worked to promote non-violence" (*News-Gazette* January 16, 1980, A-3).

In the data I have gathered from 1940 to 1980, I identify push and pull factors regarding the development of inclusivity at McKinley, which I spell out in Table 8.1.

At every stage, from theological controversies to Civil Rights and all the way to LBGTIQ welcome, church members engaged in study, political education, discussion, discernment, and decision-making to mold values about what it means to be inclusive and to adopt policy and action to support these values. The opportunity to think through, feel out, disagree, and collectively work through the meaning of church membership, support for students, and welcome to the disenfranchised has resulted in the persistence of this productive, growing, vibrant congregation to this day. These values are considered by members to be foundational to their identity. Though their understandings of the values that define what it is to be a member of McKinley Church have changed over time, in concert with the changing meanings of inclusion in society, members perceive Christian values to emanate from an unchanging God, goodness personified. The fundamental values guiding the congregation, are perceived to appear as different images made more visible depending on context—

Table 8.1. Push and Pull Factors Promoting and Challenging Inclusivity at McKinley Presbyterian Church, 1940 to 2008

Push Factors +	Pull Factors –
Civil Rights	
+ Pronouncement in 1954 by General Assembly (GA) that segregation is unchristian; reaffirmation of that stand in 1955 + Participation of church staff in 1963 March on Washington + Rev. Hine's support for civil rights work by assistant and associate pastors + McKinley's support, funding, and work for integrated housing in Champaign County + Support of civil rights in denomination's Confession of 1967 + Session's decision to provide space to black students for social functions	– National, state, and campus records of racial segregation and discrimination – Conservatives' minority report to request rescinding the 1954 statement on segregation – View of some congregants that social activism is not a legitimate purpose of the church – Departure of members who disagree with social activist pursuits – Concerns of some session members about work with other local churches to purchase land and build a fully integrated housing development – Denomination's Confession of 1967 (anti-LGBTIQ) – Congregants' worries about damage to property by black students
Vietnam War Protest	
+ Study about the situation in Vietnam + Support for students adopting conscientious objector status + Medical attention for students involved with violent campus protests + Sanctuary and medical aid for students during campus curfews + Funds for medical treatment to civilians in Vietnam + McKinley statement renouncing U.S. participation in Vietnam War + McKinley sponsorship of Vietnamese refugee family	– Session contestation over involvement of McKinley Church and Foundation in Illiac IV vigil – Long-time members' suspension of financial support until "undesirable groups" are restricted from using church and foundation buildings – Members leaving McKinley over its support for students' Vietnam War protest
Women's Movement/Internationalism	
+ Introduction of gender-neutral language + Study of liberation theologians by women's discussion group + Study of marginalized groups by youth + EOC day care center housed in church basement + Welcoming of female congregants and centering of women + Support for Laotian refugee families	– Male-centered leadership at McKinley – Programs "directed" by mostly male elders and "carried out" by mostly female deacons – Images (from 1950s) depicting marginalized groups as caricatures – The sometimes intrusive nature of applying inclusive language (e.g., interjections that "destroyed anything that I had in my mind")

Student Ministry

+ Hine's flourishing marriage and family ministry	− Focus of marriage and family ministry on white, middle class, upwardly mobile students and faculty
+ Student-centered church ministry and attendance by hundreds of students (1940s and 1950s)	− Decline of marriage and family ministry in attracting students (1960s)
+ Session contemplation about changing student ministry in 1960s	− Dwindling student membership and attendance at worship (1960s)
+ "Student ministry" becomes "campus ministry"	

LGBTIQ Consciousness and Welcome

+ Prevailing of modernists in denomination (faith + reason), challenging literal interpretations of scripture	− Fundamentalist interpretations of the Bible fueling view of LGBTIQ "lifestyles" as sinful
+ Formation of GA committee to investigate sexuality	− Denomination's Confession of 1967 statement that "anarchy in sexual relationships is a symptom of man's alienation from God"
+ Dawn of More Light Presbyterians movement	− General Assembly refuses to receive committee reports from Presbyterian Gay Caucus and Presbyterians for Gay and Lesbian Concerns (1974–78)
+ Meeting of secular gay consciousness-raising group at McKinley	
+ Hosting of gay-oriented Metropolitan Community Church at McKinley; later session vote to continue to extend McKinley's welcome	− Letters of concern from three members to session about use of McKinley facility by MCC
	− Disaffection between Presby House residents and McKinley because of church's pro-LBGTIQ stance

cloud by day and fire by night, but at the core, reflecting consistent values.

Finally, the ebb and flow occurs not only in agreements and disagreements and incremental growth in voluntary associations such as McKinley Church. It is also possibly evident in outward and inward orientation. Pastors argue that self-care fuels the congregation and prepares it for outward ministry (Heidi Weatherford interview, 2014; Jacqueline Lewis 2004). It is likely that after a period of intense outward orientation, an inward-focused self-care is necessary. For example, during the Hine phase (1942–1968), McKinley received inward self-care, given Hine's focus on growing marriages and making them strong. Before Hine left, the fruits were perhaps evident in McKinley's commitment to integrated housing and its involvement with Civil Rights marches, voter registration, and other campaigns. After Hine left, McKinley was primed for a kind of intermediate self-care that focused on the church's growing social consciousness. Mary Ann Lundy saw to this excellently. It was a period of intense political education and inward growth, especially for women in the congregation. After that period of self-care, there were multiple outward evidences of the inward growth that had been achieved, including advanced involvement in promoting civil rights,[3] Vietnam protestor support, use of inclusive language, acceptance of the Metropolitan Community Church, and finally, in 1980, openness to LGBTIQ members. I believe this era of inward growth helped to sustain McKinley during heavy onslaughts in the following twenty-five years.

In Part II I have examined the transformation of this mainline Protestant church over many decades into an LGBTIQ-affirming, social justice church. Access to interviews and internal documents provided a window into this process that enriched my analysis of inclusive congregations and may provide useful examples to other churches that wish to become inclusive. Examining this church has helped me develop my theory of the push and pull that are necessary to create balanced cohesion, inclusiveness, and the energy to fuel these endeavors in multiracial/ethnic congregations.

In my conclusion, I consider the lessons provided by the five churches under consideration in this book and summarize what they teach us about becoming inclusive and about creating diverse and productive settings in voluntary associations.

NOTES

1. This is a statement by Jill Mulder (congregant interview, 2014).
2. Zellar 2007; NCAA news release 2005; NCAA news release 2007.
3. Case in point: In the January 20, 1980, session minutes—the first meeting after the departure of Dick and Mary Ann Lundy—reports of McKinley's civil rights, human, and social justice work dominate the 3-page document. Examples: the Social Concerns Committee's "Community Conversations" focused "on the problems of racism," including "Racism and Housing, Racism and the Legal System, Racism and Education, and the U.S. and Zimbabwe"; maintenance work on the "Rent Supplement House in Urbana"; a mention of a bulletin board posting with information on a bill in the U.S. Senate to place limits on the use of the death penalty; and an announcement of McKinley's upcoming Cambodian Awareness Day.

Conclusion

New Definitions of the Inclusive Social Justice Church and a Theory of Intentional Institutional Social Change

In writing this book, I have examined Protestant churches' efforts to become inclusive, with goals of contributing to a theory of intentional institutional social change and describing and analyzing characteristics and processes in social justice congregations. Specifically, I have examined attempts to create congregational cohesion in churches that vary in their strategies for approaching internal unity; internal discussions among members of churches concerning American electoral politics and the election of President Barack Obama in 2008; antiwar activism in churches during the Iraq War; and the hard work of becoming inclusive in a campus Presbyterian church. Case studies of five congregations underlying these four topics provide examples of what it means to be inclusive or not that I argue are instructive for churches and other voluntary associations looking for best practices to enhance inclusive environments. In this chapter, I discuss common characteristics I have identified of inclusive social justice churches and a theory of intentional institutional social change.

"WE ARE DEDICATED TO CREATING A DIVERSE CLIMATE"

Current theory says that diversity that is beneficial to organizations requires inclusion, equity, and access. Citing human resource management literature,[1] the Society for Women Engineers (SWE) argues that diversity and inclusion are synergistic. Diversity does not work without inclusion (and vice versa).

> Decision-making improves when teams embrace different points of view, independence of thought, and the sharing of specialized knowledge.... Diverse groups almost always do better on sophisticated problem solving tasks than homogenous groups because accommodating different experiences breaks down the risk of groupthink.... Workgroups that make the time to openly discuss conflict and that want to learn from all perspectives can reap the greatest benefits of diversity through the development of an inclusive culture. [Organizations] suffer (turnover, [missed] opportunities, and morale) when they

lose someone's contribution because they feel they don't belong. Overlooking and underutilizing the full potential of employees ... happens when unconscious bias is at play. At their best, diversity and inclusion efforts work together cultivate an empathetic understanding in leaders and colleagues that allows them to value each other as individuals and as whole people (Society for Women Engineers and ARUP [a London-based engineering firm] 2014).

Diversity, inclusion, equity, and access are needed to avoid the pitfalls of diversity named by critical race theory, including colorblindness, interest convergence,[2] and inattention to institutional racism (Crenshaw 1995; Solorzano 1998; Castagno and Lee 2007; Abrams and Moio 2009; Elise, Rolison, and Daoud 2013; Park and Liu 2014). These theories have been developed mostly in educational settings in which institutions are legally mandated with becoming diverse. Some institutions have grown wise to the necessity and benefits of diversity (Herring and Henderson 2014).

I provide a test of current understandings of diversity in volitional environments, in which legal mandates in the public sphere may have an influence, but where some members take it upon themselves to practice creating diverse environments reflecting higher ideals. In this untested environment, I ask, absent legal requirements for diversity, what higher ideals promote diversity; how those values are agreed upon; what practices seem to work in reaching the delicate balance between diversity, inclusion, equity, and access and maintaining some semblance of congregational cohesion; and, finally, what are the indicators of a productive and inclusive diverse congregation? Examining churches as a case study provides empirical evidence on which to build a theory of intentional volitional institutional social change.

Something I have struggled with over the past year in writing this book has been this question: Is it institutional social change, or is it organizational change? My resounding conclusion: *It is both!* My precepts and examples describe the way to be intentional about making organizational changes to accomplish the goal of becoming inclusive. But I also provide principles applicable to creating changes within denominational cultures, with the goal of fomenting social change in the institution of Protestant churches in American society.

The Presbyterian denominations have an opportunity to become more inclusive. And it is in their interest to do so, given that by and large, they are losing members. If Protestant churches were more inclusive, they would gain more adherents as they expand into new populations. So, yes, to name my positionality, as in the tradition of Audre Lorde (1984), I am Africana, female, LGBTIQ-ally; I adhere to the confessional reform Christian tradition; and I am both mainline/modernist and evangelical, not in the conservative political sense, but within the pure definition of εὐαγγέλιον.[3] I have an interest in my private life to offer what I see as the *good news* of inclusive community to the untethered who seek spiritual and social refuge. It is not my view that other religious or spiritual practices do not approach a transcendent reality in appropriate ways; it is rather my view that the institution of the church has the capacity to offer accessible support, succor, resources, community, and a sense of purpose to the socially isolated, underresourced, and aimless. There are so few institutions in American society that exist to be a source of unconditional love, esteem, help, and community. And this is true in manifold ways for marginalized people. Middle-class individuals, and especially middle-class, educated white men and women, have access to many of these resources through their jobs, gyms, YMCAs/YWCAs, fraternities/sororities, families, etc.; their social networks are often extensive. Bourdieu, Coleman, Portes, Wilson and others (Bourdieu 1984, 1998; Coleman 1988; Portes 1998; Marsden 2000, 2005; Wilson 1987, 1996) demonstrate the multiplicative advantages accrued to those with such cavernous social capital.

Thinking through ways to help the institution of the Protestant denominations reach marginalized groups will help churches, but my primary interest is to promote social change that will empower the disadvantaged. Examples of benefits accruing from informal networks in churches abound. I have observed infirm, poor, and working class members call on their new friends at church to help with rent and with multiple household relocations; members have recounted successful efforts to create informal childcare cooperatives; more formalized procedures are in place at most churches to provide for meals to families during illness or death of a loved one; established members serve as job references to members and attenders with weak or fractured work histories. Members with expertise often offer their services at low cost. And members with substantial financial resources hire working poor to do contract work, odd jobs, and yard work. I myself have benefited as a single mom from the kindness of church members through the years who have offered advice, counsel and their generosity of time and labor. And in turn, I have joyfully offered my expertise free of charge and hospitality on multiple occasions. "Who you know" and information shared within social networks has a huge impact on access to jobs, education, health, housing, and the like. Segregation continues to hurt marginalized groups because it impedes their access to formal and informal knowledge and resources (Anderson 2014; Emerson and Smith 2000; Massey and Denton 1993; Wilson 1987).

THE INCLUSIVE SOCIAL JUSTICE CHURCH

The five churches examined each had distinctive definitions of their desired constituencies, or, in other words, how they expected to cast their respective nets of inclusiveness. Site 1, the "Afrocentric and Evangelical" megachurch in a Midwest city, is inclusive of working-class and middle-class people of African descent, their family members and friends, and any other like-minded individuals committed to nuevo-Black nationalist values and the well-being of site 1 and the surrounding community. Issues of poverty in the community are addressed by this site's many ministries. This site's leader is representative of both male and female middle-class congregants. It is diverse, though sexual minorities remained relatively invisible during my observations.

In Site 2, the large, midwestern "Friendliest Place in College Town USA," church members are inclusive of multicultural evangelicals and "seekers" who are willing to listen to members' messages and participate in church-driven activities. This "color-blind" site's leadership is not representative of its multiracial and multiethnic congregation. This site is largely heteronormative in its membership, ideology, and practice, and this site's view that "homosexuality is sin" is articulated in its literature. Site 2 addresses poverty through its successful and long-standing food pantry. However, the leaders of the church, different from their diverse membership, are white working-class and middle-class male individuals. Women leaders are visible only in children's ministry.

Site 3, the "Oasis in the City" large, urban church in the East, is similar to site 1 ("Afrocentric and Evangelical") in that its leadership includes highly educated women and men. It is led by a senior minister who is an African American female. Its leadership includes LGBTIQ individuals and allies. Site 3 is concerned with inclusiveness and equity. It has two choirs and includes a variety of musical genres.

Site 4, the "Leadership and Congregation at Odds" small church in a Midwest suburb, has an Africana, white, and biracial membership. While its pastor is white and male, its Christian education ministry is directed by an African American female. Similar to site 2, it practices color-blindness and it shames sexual minorities, and in fact it has dismissed outed LGBTIQ persons from membership.

Site 5, the medium-size "Inclusive Presbyterian Church" in Champaign, Illinois, is similar to sites 1 and 3 in that it is inclusive of sexual minorities. It ordained LGBTIQ members before its denomination allowed this practice. Its leadership is LGBTIQ and allies, highly educated, largely white female, though its associate pastor is an African American male.

The sites with the broadest definitions of inclusion are sites 1 ("Afrocentric and Evangelical"), 3 ("Oasis in the City"), and 5 (McKinley)—broadest in the sense that they pay attention to gender, race, and ethnicity and to varied extents to creating environments that are relatively welcoming to sexual minorities. Sites 2 ("Friendliest Place in College Town USA") and 4 ("Leadership and Congregation at Odds") articulate their exclusion of sexual minorities. LBGTIQ people are welcome only insofar as they are willing to relinquish their "deviant" sexual identity. And these two sites practice color-blind racism. Clearly these practices are outside the values of inclusive social justice churches; sites 2 and 4 provide examples of what not to do.

The literature has stalled with foci on multiracial churches, multiculturalism and churches, and exclusion of LGBTIQ members. We need to move beyond nominal demographic diversity—just letting difference in—to real inclusion, reflected in a church's values, mission, leadership, membership, and various aspects of its internal culture. To become an inclusive church takes embracing a social justice orientation. Such an orientation will drive members to learn about injustice in their communities; it will necessitate their thinking intersectionally to analyze their own social and spatial locations and to unveil the ways each contributes to oppression. This orientation will encourage the hard conversations and difficult processes to break down privilege and eliminate marginalization. It includes political education, acceptance of new members' input, and listening compassionately. As one congregant expressed in response to my question How do you bring change?: "You just have to do it, and be uncomfortable. You have to change because it has to do with ... people's rights, and not whether it makes you uncomfortable" (Mulder interview, 2014). Finally, the inclusive social justice church must address issues of equity and representation. The leadership and internal culture of an inclusive church must reflect the diversity within the congregation in terms of gender, race, age, and socioeconomic status; it must be LBGTIQ/allied. Without a social justice orientation and serious consideration to issues of equity, a congregation cannot maintain an inclusive membership.

A THEORY OF INTENTIONAL INSTITUTIONAL SOCIAL CHANGE

Multiple resources are needed to initiate and sustain intentional institutional social change in Protestant churches with a mission to expand their demographic diversity: social embeddedness; exposure and access to social groups beyond white, middle-class majorities; political education to increase understandings of marginalized groups and their relative social and spatial locations; intersectional analysis; an organizational structure with elements consistent with Africana feminist principles, including a nonhierarchical leadership structure (Zerai and Campbell 2005); utilization of integrated analysis in program and day-to-day discussions; a recognition of relational difference; an attention to local and global issues; strategies that are dynamic and ever-changing; and a focus on outcomes rooted in everyday people's experiences and desires (Zerai and Salime 2006).

Political Education, Progressive Politics, and Centering the Experiences of Marginalized Groups

In "Oasis in the City" (site 3), we see African American members exercise their agency to bring their unique sets of experiences to the center of worship. Africana sacred musical, liturgical, artistic, and poetic expressions describe the culture of site 1. This is important, that historical marginalized groups are able to share in cultural expressions within multiracial churches. In fact, conflict over musical styles can threaten multiracial churches (Marti 2012). Centering the experiences of marginalized groups, as practiced in site 1, does not begin and end with music. Sermons include historical and political references that are salient for the church's Africana, Latino and pan-Asian, and other ethnic middle-class and working-class audiences. In site 2 ("Friendliest Place in College Town USA"), some contemporary musical expressions begin to center Pentecostal African American cultural expressions, but they unfortunately stop there, at emotionalism in music, dance, and praise. To site 2's credit, working-class and poor white members' experiences are centered, and the church therefore excellently created a church home for its white congregants. The drawback is that racial politics (i.e., color-blindness) stifle site 2's ability to encompass the rich resources offered by its now-former middle-class African American participants. Site 4 ("Leadership and Congregation at Odds") is moving in the same direction as site 2, in that its color-blind approach thwarts the opportunity for political education and centering the experiences of marginalized groups, such that its leader-driven model has resulted in diminished numbers attending and threatens possibilities for longevity.

Sites 1 ("Afrocentric and Evangelical"), 3 ("Oasis in the City"), and 5 (McKinley Presbyterian Church) actively engage in political education and embrace progressive politics. Their spatial location in settings that are becoming increasingly diverse is an important resource. They have centered experiences of marginalized groups in various ways over time. This has happened through missions to students and youth, to LGBTIQ members and their communities, to international populations, to working poor communities, and to the homeless. Expansion of definitions of membership over time leads to a vibrant congregational life, friendships, and networks.

Critical Race Theory, Queer Theory, and Global Feminisms

According to critical race theory, racism is endemic in American life. Queer theory points to the oppression inherent in heteronormativity. Global feminisms provide intersectional analyses of the relative social locations of women and girls vis à vis men and the multiplicative advantages provided by class, race, gender, age, national origin, documentation status, ability, religion, and other social categories. African Americans, women, the poor, sexual minorities, and other marginalized groups experience the outsider-within phenomenon when they enter into public and privileged spaces (Du Bois 1903, Collins 1990).

An inclusive congregation pays attention to its spatial and social locations on the oppression–privilege axis and seeks to continually analyze and adopt ways to challenge dominant social hierarchies. This is the definition of fundamental integration and of true diversity with inclusion, equity, and access. In order to retain diverse members, fundamental integration into the fold must occur, where all members' contributions are respected and seen as essential to the church's mission.[4]

Critical race theory describes a convergence of interests between dominating and oppressed groups in diverse environments, a convergence that benefits dominant groups and thus puts women of color, the poor, and other marginalized groups at a disadvantage, because their interests and needs are subjugated and are met only to the extent that they further the aims of the dominating institution. So, for example, a university may encourage underrepresented minority (URM) ethnic and racial groups to apply for entry to demonstrate that they are attempting to meet legal obligations to diversify the student body. But it may then turn a blind eye to institutional racism and racial microaggressions that make the university environment unlivable and finally inaccessible for URMs. I argue that a convergence of interests is unavoidable so long as there are groups vying for scarce resources. So even in churches, there is a convergence of interests.

For example, racial-ethnic minority members who are new to a church may seek a like-minded community that reflects diverse cultural expression. And white members may seek to continue to grow their church by adding new racial-ethnic minority members, but they may prefer that new members assimilate to the traditional music styles and other forms of cultural expression. The scarce resource is availability of funds to purchase music and to hire choir directors who can recruit diverse choirs and prepare diverse musical selections to appeal to multiple audiences.

If diverse congregations want to succeed, what starts out as an interest convergence should be subsumed, and the interests of the majority will become more genuine and driven by the desire to create a truly welcoming environment. So in the "Oasis in the City" church, they prioritize maintaining two choirs—a traditional choir and a gospel choir. Thus they are able to welcome multiple groups by broadening their cultural expression.

Addressing Inevitable Conflict

A group consisting of just two people is diverse. With two people, you have two different opinions, and the need for a methodology to work out differences. So, even within an all-white-and-middle-class congregation, you have different opinions (not to mention gender, age, ability, and sexuality differences), and a need for a methodology to work out differences. And of course within an inclusive congregation, encompassing differences of race, ethnicity, class, sexuality, ability, and other categories, creating a deliberate process for working out differences will be needed. Below I list and discuss suggestions for addressing inevitable conflict within inclusive churches.

1. Nonavoidance of social conflict: It is important that members be able, even within the midst of diversity, to retain their distinctiveness of identity and the ability to express differences of opinion. Respect for differing opinions and experiences provides opportunities for congregants to learn from each other and enlarge their spheres of influence.
2. Timeliness of addressing conflicts: When conflicts arise, it is important to address them head-on in a timely manner. The timeliness of addressing conflicts depends on the culture, needs, and resources available to a congregation. Thoughtful members of the congregation itself can determine timeliness. It may mean that a meeting is set right away to address a conflict. Or if, for example, a congregation is in the midst of a member's health crisis, they may decide that addressing a brewing conflict can wait until the health crisis has passed.
3. Truth-telling and
4. Respect for differences in opinion and experience: The practice of maintaining distinctiveness on the part of members can be helpful when it comes to articulating differences of opinion and truth-telling in the midst of conflict. If members do not express their views and air them in public settings so that they are heard and addressed, disgruntled members may simply "vote with their feet" by walking away from the congregation.
5. Listening,
6. A neutral environment to listen, and
7. Creation of spaces for fun, rest, relaxation, and connecting socially: Fundamental meanings of membership, including access to unconditional support, enjoyable leisure activities, articulations of love, and the exercise of friendship, will bind members so that they can work through inevitable differences when they arise. When differences occur, it is helpful to have a neutral environment to discuss variant views. Richard Lundy describes McKinley's coffeehouse, aptly named "This is the Apology," where members convened after church during the era of the 1970s to discuss their views on antiwar activism, LGBTIQ inclusion, and other issues to learn from each other in a nonthreatening and relaxed environment. The "Oa-

sis in the City" church uses its newsletter as a forum to work through views about electoral politics, inclusion, racial politics, and other topics to establish dialogue and to collectively arrive at its version of inclusion.
8. Unconditional social and emotional support to all members, and
9. Reconciliation: Finally, reconciliation must always eventually follow periods of conflict. In site 3 ("Oasis in the City"), once conflict is worked through, members reaffirm their commitment to the mission of their church. For example, the lead minister expresses "there has to be a morning after." In site 2 ("Friendliest Place in College Town USA"), however, middle-class African American members left the congregation when it fired its volunteer African American staff and hired white staff in their place. In site 5 (McKinley), Lundy explained that some members left as a result of conflict over antiwar activism in the early 1970s. By contrast, later in the decade, McKinley members worked through conflict over housing the Metropolitan Community Church to the point of later embracing and ordaining LGBTIQ members. Coming full circle from moments of conflict means arriving to rearticulation of mission, sometimes with the mission remaining essentially the same, and other times with the mission becoming enlarged to encompass new groups, activities, or cultures. Without reconciliation of the multiple sides in a conflict, cohesion is impossible.

Social Justice: The Relentless Pursuit to Relinquish Inequity and to Ensure Inclusion, Equity, and Access

This may seem contradictory, but cohesion also requires the relentless pursuit to relinquish inequity and to ensure inclusion, equity, and access. An indicator of a growing diverse and inclusive congregation is political engagement and participation in electoral politics and activism among members, even if members do not agree with each other. In addition to political engagement, a healthy and growing diverse and inclusive congregation will increase its exposure by conducting political education. Study of the experiences of diverse groups and bringing in experts with life experience in addition to academic experts and political activists to enlarge understanding and appreciation of diverse groups will be evident. Adaptive action, an understanding that strategic planning is always only partial and that plans must be flexible enough to adapt to changing circumstances (Eoyang and Holladay 2013), is another important indicator related to the first two. An enduring characteristic of privilege is that it blinds us to the dark spaces in which oppression lives, not only in the spaces that we dare not tread, but also in our own interactions and in our midst. A strong diverse congregation will not only grow to encompass multiple groups, but it will seek out opportunities to be of service to those in need. In uncovering injustice and engaging in a cyclical process of political education, diverse congregations will find that adaptive change is necessary to welcome new previously unrecognized groups that may seek a church home. So in other words, healthy diverse congregations will also be dynamic. Their definition of diversity will change over time to include old and new groups. The character defining diverse congregations as activist, engaging in political education, and seeking out oppression for the purpose of writing wrongs is that they will embrace a social justice in their orientation and will continually seek to center the experiences of marginalized groups in order to fully welcome them, include them, and provide equitable access to the social capital provided by the church's resources.

CONTRIBUTIONS

Attending a historically black institution in the South, and finding themselves in an electric environment of lunch-counter protests and marches to promote civil rights for African Americans, my mother relates, she and a group of her college friends became inspired. They took up the mantle to carry out social action to integrate public spaces. One Saturday, my mom and her colleagues collectively entered a white Seventh-Day Adventist parish in Nashville, Tennessee. They boldly took their seats on one of the church's pews. Mom says that the ushers promptly escorted the group of African American students out of the church.

I write this book as a love letter to my parents and those in their generation who have actively worked all their lives to create inclusive environments. I use my intellectual and scholarly tools to contribute to their struggle, the struggle for inclusivity.

This work addresses the social scientific debates surrounding the failures and successes of multicultural/multiracial Christianity (Barnes 2009, Chaves 2004, Emerson 2010). My case studies of urban and "micro-urban" midwestern and eastern churches in the U.S. add to the literature, because I examine how racial, gender, and sexuality structures either in communities or within churches themselves intersect and result in multiplicative advantages to some groups and disadvantages to others, it is here that I make my contributions.

Further, I offer a novel social history of race and a campus Christian church. And I add to prominent arguments in the sociology of religion that the lack of diversity in churches results, at least partly, from segregation (Emerson and Smith 2010). My case studies and social history of congregations develop theory for understanding racial structures embedded in American churches. Theoretically and methodologically, I have applied an intersectional analysis to sites of privilege. Finally, I offer a theory of intentional institutional social change in volitional communities—in Protestant U.S. churches. It is my sincere hope that in this work, I have identified a path to creating more inclusive environments.

NOTES

1. These include James Surowiecki 2004, Howard Ross 2011, Scott Page 2007, and Robin Ely et al. 2001.

2. "'Interest convergence' or material determinism" is the idea that it is difficult to make genuine progress in eradication of racism and racial hierarchy and privilege; because racism advances the interests of both white elites (materially) and working-class people (psychically), large segments of society have little incentive to eradicate it" (Delgado and Stefancic 2006, 1). Only partial redress to racism occurs when the interests of elites and racial-minority groups converge.

3. This Greek word means "bringer of good news."

4. For example, academic departments are less likely to retain underrepresented minority faculty members if they are not seen as integral to the departments' teaching and research missions, as seen in departments where such faculty teach nonessential courses and their research is not respected (Turner 2003).

Appendix

PC(USA) Precursors and McKinley Memorial Presbyterian Church Timeline 1789–1983, Including Sources.

Year	Event	Source
1789–1869	**Presbyterian Church in the USA (PCUSA) holds its first General Assembly (GA) in Philadelphia. (Presbyterians came to the U.S. from Scotland and Ireland.)**	http://www.history.pcusa.org/sites/default/files/theme-assets/presbyterian_family_connections_ocr_2mb.pdf
1814–1887	Lifespan of church and foundation's namesake, Rev. George McKinley.	Newton Bateman and Paul Selby (eds.), 1905 *Historical Encyclopedia of Illinois*, Vol. 2, p. 988; Chicago: Munsell.
1847–1863	Free Presbyterian Church in the U.S. breaks from PCUSA in protest of PCUSA's refusal to ban slaveholders from membership.	http://www.history.pcusa.org/sites/default/files/theme-assets/presbyterian_family_connections_ocr_2mb.pdf
1856–1926	Lifespan of U.S. Senator William Brown McKinley (son of George).	http://bioguide.congress.gov/scripts/biodisplay.pl?index=M000521
1858–1870	Rev. George McKinley served as Presbyterian minister in Champaign County.	Newton Bateman and Paul Selby (eds.), 1905 *Historical Encyclopedia of Illinois*, Vol. 2, p. 988; Chicago: Munsell.
1858–1958	United Presbyterian Church of North America (UPCNA) forms, uniting some previous factions of immigrant seceders, a denomination developing on a separate trajectory from the PCUSA.	http://www.history.pcusa.org/sites/default/files/theme-assets/presbyterian_family_connections_ocr_2mb.pdf
1860	Abraham Lincoln is elected U.S. president.	https://www.whitehouse.gov/1600/presidents/abrahamlincoln
1861–1864	Presbyterian Church of the Confederate States of America splits from PCUSA over slavery, later (after the Civil War) becoming Presbyterian Church in the U.S.	http://www.history.pcusa.org/sites/default/files/theme-assets/presbyterian_family_connections_ocr_2mb.pdf
1863	President Lincoln issues the Emancipation Proclamation.	January 1, 1863; Presidential Proclamations, 1791-1991; Record Group 11; General Records of the United States Government; National Archives.
	Free Presbyterian Church in the U.S. reunites with Presbyterian Church in the USA.	http://www.history.pcusa.org/sites/default/files/theme-assets/presbyterian_family_connections_ocr_2mb.pdf
1865	U.S. Congress approves the 13th Amendment to the Constitution, outlawing slavery.	http://memory.loc.gov/ammem/aap/timeline.html

Appendix

Year	Event	Source
1865–1983	Maintaining its split from UPCNA/UPCUSA, Presbyterian Church of the Confederate States of America becomes Presbyterian Church in the U.S. (PCUS).	http://www.history.pcusa.org/sites/default/files/theme-assets/presbyterian_family_connections_ocr_2mb.pdf
1866	The Civil Rights Act confers citizenship upon African Americans and guarantees them equal rights with whites.	http://memory.loc.gov/ammem/aap/timeline.html
1867	The Illinois Industrial University is founded at Urbana; Reconstruction begins.	https://www.uillinois.edu/president/history/history_of_the_university/; http://www.history.com/topics/american-civil-war/reconstruction
1869–1958	**The creation of the Presbyterian Church in the USA (PCUSA) unites Old School and New School Presbyterians.**	http://www.history.pcusa.org/sites/default/files/theme-assets/presbyterian_family_connections_ocr_2mb.pdf
1870	William Brown McKinley attends the Illinois Industrial University (at age 14) for two years.	http://bioguide.congress.gov/scripts/biodisplay.pl?index=M000521; http://friedman.cs.illinois.edu/champaign-urbana/Chapter18.htm
	"Trustees [of the university] agreed to admit women in a 5-4 vote." [Ed: All quotations are from the University of Illinois Library timeline.]	http://archives.library.illinois.edu/slc/research-education/timeline/
1871	The first female cohort is admitted to the university.	http://archives.library.illinois.edu/slc/research-education/timeline/
1872	The university establishes a boarding hall for women.	http://archives.library.illinois.edu/slc/research-education/timeline/
1873–1879	John J. Byrd is the first African American to serve as a member of the university Board of Trustees.	http://archives.library.illinois.edu/slc/research-education/timeline/
1874–pres.	Cumberland Presbyterian Church in America is established apart from the PCUSA as an African American denomination.	http://www.history.pcusa.org/sites/default/files/theme-assets/presbyterian_family_connections_ocr_2mb.pdf

Year	Event	Source
1874	The university's first female faculty member, Louise C. Allen, establishes a domestic science course.	http://archives.library.illinois.edu/slc/research-education/timeline/
1875	"Board of Trustees permitted conscientious objectors to be excused from military drill."	http://archives.library.illinois.edu/slc/research-education/timeline/
1877	Reconstruction ends, the result of a political deal to put Rutherford Hayes into the White House.	http://www.history.com/topics/us-presidents/compromise-of-1877
1881ff	Segregation of public transportation; 1882 lynchings begin.	https://memory.loc.gov/ammem/aap/timelin2.html
1882	"Dora Andrus became the first woman to head the College Government."	http://archives.library.illinois.edu/slc/research-education/timeline/
1884	"Carlos Montezuma became the first Native American graduate of the university."	http://archives.library.illinois.edu/slc/research-education/timeline/
1885	Illinois Industrial University becomes the University of Illinois.	http://archives.library.illinois.edu/slc/research-education/timeline/
1887	Jonathan A. Rogan, the first African American student to enroll at the University of Illinois, attends for one year.	http://archives.library.illinois.edu/slc/research-education/timeline/
1890	The right to vote for African American males is essentially voided (the "Mississippi Plan" uses literacy tests for voting, with other states following).	http://www.usccr.gov/pubs/msdelta/ch3.htm
1883	The Civil Rights Act is overturned, with the 1875 act declared unconstitutional; states (not citizens) are forbidden from discriminating.	http://www.archives.gov/education/lessons/brown-v-board/timeline.html
1895	The university's second African American employee is also its first African American (AA) academic professional: Albert Lee, the "defacto dean of African American students," institutes the first physical education for women students.	http://archives.library.illinois.edu/slc/research-education/timeline/
1896	*Plessy v. Ferguson* challenges the validity of "separate but equal" Jim Crow segregation laws	http://www.nps.gov/nhl/learn/themes/CivilRights_VotingRights.pdf

Year	Event	Source
	(with segregation of churches permitted as well); UIUC Women's League was established.	
1898	"All women of the faculty and student body met for the first time as a Woman's Department."	http://archives.library.illinois.edu/slc/research-education/timeline/
1900	William Walter Smith is the university's first African American graduate.	http://archives.library.illinois.edu/slc/research-education/timeline/
1905	The university dedicates the Woman's Building.	http://archives.library.illinois.edu/slc/research-education/timeline/
1906	PCUSA Synod of Illinois establishes a U of I campus Presbyterian church by appointing T.J. Porter university pastor.	PCUSA Minutes of the Synod of Illinois, Chicago, Oct 21-23, 1902; p. 464; Monmouth, IL: Review Printing Company; http://tinyurl.com/TJPorter; Bechtel, Dave, 2008, The Centennial of McKinley Presbyterian Church and Foundation, 1906-2007; Champaign, IL.
	Maudelle Tanner Brown Bausfield is the university's first female African American graduate.	http://archives.library.illinois.edu/slc/research-education/timeline/
1907	William Walter Smith earns his second degree from the university, a bachelor's in civil engineering.	http://archives.library.illinois.edu/slc/research-education/timeline/
1912	A donation for a campus Presbyterian church building from U.S. Senator William Brown McKinley funds the new church, named for his father, late Presbyterian pastor Rev. George McKinley. The original McKinley Presbyterian Church building is erected (completed in 1912).	Daily Illini, 1911, Sept 22, Vol 16, No 4, p. 1; http://www.ilga.gov/legislation/94/HR/PDF/09400HR1567Iv.pdf
	The university's first annual mass meeting of women is held.	http://archives.library.illinois.edu/slc/research-education/timeline/
1913	The first African American fraternity on the UIUC campus is organized.	http://archives.library.illinois.edu/slc/research-education/timeline/
1916–1970	Through the Great Migration, Chicago's African American population increases from 2% in 1915 to 33% in 1970.	http://www.encyclopedia.chicagohistory.org/pages/545.html

Year	Event	Source
	"On April 21st, 136 students withdrew for military and farm work. This figure grew to 1,000 by May 5th. YMCA and new women's residence used as barracks."	http://archives.library.illinois.edu/slc/research-education/timeline/
	"University service flag raised with 2,960 stars—one for each Illini in the service. Some 3,000 students enrolled in Student Army Training Corps (SATC)."	http://archives.library.illinois.edu/slc/research-education/timeline/
1918	"Woman's Residence Hall (Busey Hall) completed [ed.: the first residence hall built by the university]; Homecoming canceled because of war."	http://archives.library.illinois.edu/slc/research-education/timeline/
1920	Passage of 19th Amendment: "The right of citizens of the United States to vote shall not be denied or abridged by the United States or by any State on account of sex."	http://www.archives.gov/exhibits/charters/constitution_amendments_11-27.html
1922	Controversy begins as Harry Emerson Fosdick's "Shall the Fundamentalists Win?" exposes liberal and conservative differences.	Pohlman 2012
1923	PCUSA General Assembly reaffirms "Five Fundamentals" to challenge ordination of ministers who could not affirm Jesus's virgin birth.	Longfield 2013
1920s–30s	Modernist–Fundamentalist controversy embroils PCUSA.	Pohlman 2012
1924	McKinley Foundation is established.	http://www.mckinley-church.org/index.php?option=com_content&view=category&layout=blog&id=21&Itemid=25
1928	Record spring semester enrollment at University of Illinois.	http://archives.library.illinois.edu/slc/research-education/timeline/
1930	McKinley Student Ministry Foundation building is completed in midst of Great Depression.	http://www.ilga.gov/legislation/fulltext.asp?DocName=&SessionId=50&GA=94&DocTypeId=HR&DocNum=1567&GAID=8&LegID=26793&SpecSess=&Session=
1935	"APA and KAP establish coop African American restaurant after Boyd's Café, the only campus	http://archives.library.illinois.edu/slc/research-education/timeline/

Year	Event	Source
	restaurant [ed.: except for university café] to serve AAs closed; lasted less than 1 year."	
1936	Some members—many expelled from churches by liberals—leave PCUSA over Modernist–Fundamentalist controversy and form the Orthodox Presbyterian Church.	http://www.history.pcusa.org/sites/default/files/theme-assets/presbyterian_family_connections_ocr_2mb.pdf
	"300 students and faculty held a strike against war"; German refugee students housed by Jewish fraternities and sororities.	http://archives.library.illinois.edu/slc/research-education/timeline/
1937	"Civil Rights Union and American Student Union circulated petitions protesting discrimination by campus restaurants and Champaign-Urbana theaters."	http://archives.library.illinois.edu/slc/research-education/timeline/
	African American university students sue Hanley-Lewis Confectionery for discrimination; circuit court judge decides for the business.	http://archives.library.illinois.edu/slc/research-education/timeline/
1939	Hilda H. Lawson is first African American woman to receive a PhD, in English, from U of I.	http://archives.library.illinois.edu/slc/research-education/timeline/
1935–1945	WWII and acceleration of the Great Migration (1940s and 1950s).	http://www.encyclopedia.chicagohistory.org/pages/545.html
1941	"U.S. entry into World War II after Pearl Harbor greatly impacted University. Almost overnight, ratio of men to women on campus went from 3-1 to 1-4."	http://archives.library.illinois.edu/slc/research-education/timeline/
1942–1967	**JIM HINE ERA—McKinley is headed by Pastor/Director James R. ('Jim') Hine.**	Bechtel, Dave, 2008, *The Centennial of McKinley Presbyterian Church and Foundation, 1906-2007*. Champaign, IL.
1944	"Congress passed GI Bill offering a college education to millions of returning veterans."	http://www.benefits.va.gov/gibill/history.asp
1945	University sets up temporary housing to help accommodate 11,000+ veterans returning to	http://archives.library.illinois.edu/slc/research-education/timeline/

Appendix 149

Year	Event	Source
	campus following the war. Of the 20,276 U of I students who served, 738 were killed.	http://archives.library.illinois.edu/slc/research-education/timeline/
1946	Student Community Interracial Committee (SCIC) is formed to fight discrimination; campus Wesley Foundation Wescoga Women's Coop house admits an African American member.	http://archives.library.illinois.edu/slc/research-education/timeline/
	"SCIC asks restaurants to sign statement saying they don't discriminate. 6 refused. Following picketing and threatened lawsuit, they finally agreed to end discrimination."	http://archives.library.illinois.edu/slc/research-education/timeline/
	"Board of Trustees endorsed 'policy [to] favor and strengthen attitudes and social philosophies necessary to create atmosphere in which racial prejudice cannot thrive.'"	http://archives.library.illinois.edu/slc/research-education/timeline/
	Residence halls open to African Americans.	http://archives.library.illinois.edu/slc/research-education/timeline/
1948	"SCIC helped desegregate washroom facilities for Illini Union employees. Group also protested minstrel show sponsored by the Newman Club."	http://archives.library.illinois.edu/slc/research-education/timeline/
1950	SCIC surveys students' opinions on desegregated housing.	http://archives.library.illinois.edu/slc/research-education/timeline/
1951	McKinley Church installs three "student windows": Agriculture, Arts, Engineering (dedicated to Jim Hine). Second rose window, "Christ's Call to All the World," is also installed.	Bechtel, Dave. 2009. *McKinley Presbyterian Church's Stained Glass Windows: History and Tradition*. Champaign, IL.
1952	McKinley undertakes a building expansion of the church.	*The MAC, McKinley Foundation Newspaper*, 1953–54 school year
1954	In *Brown v. Board of Education*, Supreme Court rules that public schools separated by race are unconstitutional.	Oliver Brown v. Board of Education of Topeka. 347 U.S. 483 (1954)
1955	*Time* magazine reports the Presbyterian Church is divided over segregation.	"Religion, Segregation and the Churches." *Time Magazine*. June 20, 1955.
1955–1975	Vietnam War.	http://www.history.com/topics/vietnam-war

Appendix

Year	Event	Source
1957	Sen. John F. Kennedy addresses 1,200 U of I graduates at the midyear convocation.	http://archives.library.illinois.edu/slc/research-education/timeline/
1958–1983	**United Presbyterian Church of North America merges with PCUSA to form UPCUSA and enters a period of social activism; Eugene Carson Blake, the primary instigator, remains stated clerk until 1966.**	http://www.history.pcusa.org/sites/default/files/theme-assets/presbyterian_family_connections_ocr_2mb.pdf
1959	"University recognition withheld for student organizations restricting membership on the basis of race or religion."	http://archives.library.illinois.edu/slc/research-education/timeline/
1960	"Committee for Liberal Action (CLA) fights student and administration apathy", protests racial discrimination in store windows, and stages a sit-in at Walgreens.	http://archives.library.illinois.edu/slc/research-education/timeline/
	"Shortly before elected president, Sen. John F. Kennedy addressed 10,000 on the Quad, becoming the first presidential candidate to do so at Illinois."	http://archives.library.illinois.edu/slc/research-education/timeline/
1961	"Revision in state law raised drinking age for women from 18 to 21, the same age as men."	http://archives.library.illinois.edu/slc/research-education/timeline/ 1960-1969/
	"Committee on Student Affairs passed bill calling for end to racial discrimination in fraternities, sororities, and off-campus housing."	http://archives.library.illinois.edu/slc/research-education/timeline/
1963	**MCKINLEY'S ENTRY INTO CIVIL RIGHTS ERA**	
1963	Jim Ray, McKinley Campus Minister, attends March on Washington.	http://ncmasages.wordpress.com/2014/06/03/creating-social-change-by-jim-ray
	Blake, stated clerk of UPCUSA most well known for his stand against racial segregation, with King and eight other civil rights leaders calls for jobs and	http://www.thekingcenter.org/archive/document/march-washington-address-eugene-carson-blake

Year	Event	Source
	freedom at March on Washington. Group meets with President Kennedy, who marches with them, linking arms. Blake speaks to the crowd before King delivers "I Have a Dream."	http://archives.library.illinois.edu/slc/research-education/timeline/
	"Beginning on September 16th, students conducted week-long silent vigil memorializing four African-American youths killed in bombing of Birmingham Sunday school."	http://archives.library.illinois.edu/slc/research-education/timeline/
	"Some 11,500 people attended a ceremony at the Assembly Hall memorializing John F. Kennedy."	http://archives.library.illinois.edu/slc/research-education/timeline/
1964	Jim Ray participates in weeklong picket lines and attends SNCC court case in Hattiesburg, Mississippi.	http://ncmasages.wordpress.com/2014/06/03/creating-social-change-by-jim-ray
	Students and campus ministers from various churches headed to Mississippi receive training in non-violence tactics at McKinley.	http://ncmasages.wordpress.com/2014/06/03/creating-social-change-by-jim-ray
1965	Jim Ray spends 6 weeks in southern Virginia leading student group in doing voter registration and tutoring.	http://ncmasages.wordpress.com/2014/06/03/creating-social-change-by-jim-ray
	Students for a Democratic Society (SDS) hold their first annual conference at McKinley Foundation (360 people/66 chapters attend).	http://ncmasages.wordpress.com/2014/06/03/creating-social-change-by-jim-ray
	Confession of 1967 is penned calling for reconciliation in areas of racial discrimination, international conflict, enslaving poverty, and sexual anarchy.	http://www.creeds.net/reformed/confess67.pdf
1966	"Report revealed very low African-American enrollment at the University; Recognition for Dubois Club sought. Board of Trustees ultimately denied recognition for the group."	http://archives.library.illinois.edu/slc/research-education/timeline/
1967	President Lyndon Johnson issues Executive Order 11246 requiring federal contractors "to take Affirmative Action"; order is expanded to include women in 1969.	http://www.civilrights.org/resources/civilrights101/affirmaction.html?referrer=https://www.google.com/

Year	Event	Source
	178th GA adopts Confession of 1967, approved by 90% of presbyteries; conservatives criticize its support for universalism and interference in the political sphere.	http://www.opc.org/nh.html?article_id=59
1968	**McKINLEY'S ENTRY INTO ERA OF FEMINIST CONSCIOUSNESS AND ANTIWAR ACTIVISM**	
1968–1980	Pastor/director Dick Lundy.	Bechtel, Dave. 2008. *The Centennial of McKinley Presbyterian Church and Foundation, 1906-2007.*
1968	Rev. Dr. Martin Luther King, Jr. is assassinated.	http://www.history.com/this-day-in-history/dr-king-is-assassinated
	Clarence Shelley becomes director of U of I Project 500; 252 students are arrested at sit-in to protest project's inadequacies.	https://localwiki.org/cu/Clarence_Shelley
1969	African American students protest racism and killings in Chicago of Black Panther leaders; UIUC chapter of the National Association for the Advancement of Colored People (NAACP) is instituted.	http://archives.library.illinois.edu/slc/research-education/timeline/
	Demonstrations against the Vietnam War polarize McKinley congregation.	McKinley session minutes, April 12, 1970, p. 153
1970	Afro-American Studies Commission and Black Law Student Association are established at the U of I; protests are held over the military–industrial complex; the first Earth Day is celebrated; U of I students strike after killings at Kent State.	http://archives.library.illinois.edu/slc/research-education/timeline/
	U of I Gay Liberation Front, part of the national organization, is established; university offers first women's studies course.	http://archives.library.illinois.edu/slc/research-education/timeline/
1972	Title IX (the Equal Opportunity in Education Act) prohibits gender discrimination in American educational institutions.	http://www.justice.gov/crt/types-educational-opportunities-discrimination

Year	Event	Source
	Black Student Association becomes Afrikan People's Coalition; GLF protests bar for harassing gay patrons; 2,000 students, faculty, and community members march against Vietnam War	http://archives.library.illinois.edu/slc/research-education/timeline/
1973	Conservative Presbyterian Church in America (PCA) breaks away from the PCUSA over the issues of women's ordination and a perceived drift toward theological liberalism.	http://www.history.pcusa.org/sites/default/files/theme-assets/presbyterian_family_connections_ocr_2mb.pdf
	McKinley session issues a statement on behalf of the church calling for a withdrawal of troops from Vietnam.	McKinley session minutes, January 7, 1973, p. 201
1974	At U of I, Office of Minority Student Affairs is established and La Casa is founded; the first National Women's Music Festival is held on the U of I campus.	http://archives.library.illinois.edu/slc/research-education/timeline/
1974	At the UPCUSA GA, David Bailey Sindt holds up a sign: "Is anybody else out there gay?" His action is claimed as the unofficial start of the More Light Presbyterians movement; a Presbyterian Gay Caucus is formed.	http://www.mlp.org/2012/12/08/david-sindts-courageous-action-started-the-conversation/
1974–1978	UPCUSA GA does not accept reports from Presbyterians for Gay and Lesbian Concerns (new name for the caucus).	http://mlporg.c.presscdn.com/wp-content/uploads/2012/05/MLhistory.pdf
1974–1981	Charlie Sweitzer, associate pastor.	Bechtel, Dave. 2008. *The Centennial of McKinley Presbyterian Church and Foundation, 1906-2007.*
1975	Gay Illini is formed.	https://oiir.illinois.edu/lgbt-resource-center/about-lgbtrc/history
	Chief Illiniwek is criticized as offensive and removed from U of I stationery.	http://www.ais.illinois.edu/mascot/news/archive/documents/Dialogue_Report.pdf
1976	Prodigal Child Congregation of the Metropolitan Community Church begins meeting in McKinley church basement.	McKinley session minutes, December 5, 1976, pp. 283–4
	Florence C. Bailar Window is installed, with a focus on ministering to the poor.	Bechtel, Dave. 2009. *McKinley Presbyterian Church's Stained Glass Windows: History and Tradition.* Champaign, IL.

Appendix 155

Year	Event	Source
	MCKINLEY BEGINS TO BECOME INCLUSIVE IN SUPPORT OF LGBT ORGANIZATIONS and MEMBERS	
1977	James R. Hine Window depicting "Presbyterian Heritage" is installed.	Bechtel, Dave. 2009. *McKinley Presbyterian Church's Stained Glass Windows: History and Tradition*. Champaign, IL.
	Metropolitan Community Church members meet with McKinley session; session affirms commitment to hosting MCC.	McKinley Session minutes, January 22, 1977.
	UPCUSA GA commissions study on LGBT issues; GA votes that "homosexuality is not God's wish for humanity."	PC(USA). 1979. "Homosexuality and the Church: A Position Paper." *Definitive Guidance: The Church's Statements on Homosexuality*. p 65.
	UPCUSA GA votes to welcome LGBT members but not ordain them as deacons, elders, or pastors; many churches challenge this and ordain LGBT leaders.	http://mlporg.c.presscdn.com/wp-content/uploads/2012/05/MLhistory.pdf
	West Park Presbyterian Church in New York City is the first to become a More Light Presbyterians congregation.	http://www.mlp.org/tag/west-park-presbyterian-church/
	The MCC holds a service of Holy Union conducted by an MCC pastor at McKinley, an event reported by National Public Radio.	Bechtel, Dave. 2008. *The Centennial of McKinley Presbyterian Church and Foundation, 1906-2007*.
1977	McKinley becomes the 13th MLP church.	Bechtel, Dave. 2008. *The Centennial of McKinley Presbyterian Church and Foundation, 1906-2007*,
	McKinley Session issues affirmative statement welcoming membership of all persons regardless of sexual orientation and extends the right to all to hold office as an ordained elder.	Bechtel, Dave. 2008. *The Centennial of McKinley Presbyterian Church and Foundation, 1906-2007*.
1983	**General Assemblies of UPUSA and PCUS meet in Atlanta to reunite and establish PC(USA).**	http://www.history.pcusa.org/sites/default/files/theme-assets/presbyterian_family_connections_ocr_2mb.pdf

References

Abrams, Laura, and Jene Moio. 2009. "Critical Race Theory and the Cultural Competence Dilemma in Social Work Education." *Journal of Social Work Education*, 45(2) (Spring/Summer): 245–61.
The American National Election Studies (ANES; www.electionstudies.org). *The 2006 ANES Pilot Study Full Release* [dataset]. Stanford University and the University of Michigan [producers and distributors].
Anderson, Elizabeth. 2014. "Why Racial Integration Remains Imperative." In *American's Growing Inequality: The Impact of Poverty and Race*, edited by Chester Hartman, 141–47. New York: Lexington Books.
Andolsen, Barbara Hilkert. 2005. *Journal of the Society of Christian Ethics*, 25(1), 249–52.
Barnes, S. L. 2009. "Enter into His Gates: An Analysis of Black Church Participation Patterns." *Sociological Spectrum*, 29(2): 173–200.
Barnett, Bernice McNair. 1989. *A Structural Analysis of the Civil Rights Movement and the Leadership Roles of Martin Luther King, Jr.* PhD diss., University of Georgia.
Bechtel, Dave. 2008. *The Centennial of McKinley Presbyterian Church and Foundation, 1906-2007*. Champaign, IL.
Bechtel, Dave. 2009. *McKinley Presbyterian Church's Stained Glass Windows: History and Tradition*. Champaign, IL.
Bechtel, Dave. 2015. *McKinley Presbyterian Church and McKinley Foundation Relationships*. Champaign, IL.
Bevere, J. 1994. *The Bait of Satan: Your Response Determines Your Future*. Lake Mary, FL: Charisma House.
Beyerlein, K., and Chaves, M. 2003. "The Political Activities of Religious Congregations in the United States." *Journal for the Scientific Study of Religion*, 42(2): 229–46.
Bishop, Jeanne. 2015. *Change of Heart: Justice, Mercy, and Making Peace with My Sister's Killer*. Louisville, KY: Westminster John Knox Press.
"Blacks in Champaign County, 1865-1970." 1995. *Through the Years: Black History in Champaign County*. http://www.usd116.org/profdev/ahtc/activities/Plaut10/EAMarticle1.JPG. Accessed April 9, 2015.
Blake, Eugene Carson. 1949. "Which Way the Presbyterian Church?" *The Princeton Seminary Bulletin* 43(1): 6–11.
Blake, Eugene Carson. 1963. March on Washington Address. Accessed March 1, 2015. http://www.thekingcenter.org/archive/document/march-washington-address-eugene-carson-blake.
Blake, E. C. 1968. "Who Speaks for the Church? A Critique of the 1966 Geneva Conference on Church and Society." *Theology Today* 25(1): 134–6. ATLA Religion Database with ATLASerials, EBSCOhost.
Blake, E. C. 1980. "Bread and Justice: Toward a New International Economic Order." *Theology Today* 37(1):134-135.
Blake, Eugene Carson. 1966. "Militant Christianity—Defense and Offense." *The Princeton Seminary Bulletin*.
Blake, Eugene Carson. 1973. "A Church Both Evangelical and Ecumenical." *The Princeton Seminary Bulletin*.
Blake, Eugene Carson. 1975. "Moral Implications of Christian Faith in God." *The Princeton Seminary Bulletin* .
Blake, Eugene Carson. 1976. "The American Dream: Two Hundred Years After." *The Princeton Seminary Bulletin* .

Blake, Eugene Carson. 1981. "The Future of the Mainline Churches." *The Princeton Seminary Bulletin*.
Bolster, Carole. 1967. "McKinley Minister to Resign." *Daily Illini*, October 27.
Bonilla-Silva, Eduardo 1997. "Rethinking Racism: Toward a Structural Interpretation." *American Sociological Review* 62(3): 465–80.
Bonilla-Silva, Eduardo. 2003. *Racism without Racists: Color-Blind Racism and the Persistence of Racial Inequality in the United States*. Lanham, MD: Rowman & Littlefield.
Bourdieu, Pierre. 1984. *Distinction. A Social Critique of the Judgement of Taste*. Translated by Richard Nice. London: Routledge & Kegan Paul.
Bourdieu, Pierre. 1998. Practical Reason: On the Theory of Action. CI, CA: Stanford University Press.
Brantingham, Barney. 1955. "None of Three Finds Reaction Against Science." *Daily Illini*, April 22.
Brown, Elsa Barkley. 1992. *Black Women in America: An Historical Encyclopedia*. 2 Vols. Edited by Darlene Clark Hine. Brooklyn, NY: Carlson Publishing. Paperback edition: Bloomington: Indiana University Press, 1995.
Brown, Elsa Barkley. 1995. "Imaging Lynching: African American Women, Communities of Struggle, and Collective Memory," 100–124. In *African American Women Speak Out on Anita Hill–Clarence Thomas*. Edited by Geneva Smitherman. Detroit: Wayne State University Press.
Brown, Elsa Barkley. 1994. "Negotiating and Transforming the Public Sphere: African-American Political Life in the Transition from Slavery to Freedom." *Public Culture*, 7(1): 107–146.
Brown, Elsa Barkley. 1992. "The Politics of Difference in Women's History and Feminist Politics." *Feminist Studies*, 18(2).
Brown, R., and K. Brown. 2013. "Religion and Military Policy Attitudes in America." *Review of Religious Research: The Official Journal of the Religious Research Association*. 55(4): 573–95.
Browne, Robert S. 1943. "Democracy Here?" *Daily Illini*, October 24.
Buckley-Shaklee, Amber. 2009. "'Disability Shock': Culture among College Students with Physical Disabilities." Paper presented at the annual meeting of the American Sociological Association, San Francisco, California, August 11.
Bump, Phillip. 2015. "Government Is America's No. 1 problem—in Part Because the Economy Isn't. *Washington Post*. [Accessed July 1, 2015.] http://www.washingtonpost.com/blogs/the-fix/wp/2015/03/12/government-is-americas-no-1-problem-in-part-because-the-economy-isnt/.
Burk, Brooke, and Shinew, Kimberly. 2013. "Factors That Impact African American Girls' Participation in Health-Promoting Leisure Activities." *Journal of Park and Recreation Administration* 31(1): 1–14.
Burrow, Rufus and Mary Alice Mulligan. 2002. *Daring to Speak God's Name: Ethical Prophecy in Ministry*. Cleveland, OH: Pilgrim Press.
Calhoun-Brown, Allison. 2001. "This Side of Jordan: Black Churches and Partisan Political Attitudes." In *Understanding Public Opinion*, edited by Barnara Norrander and Clyde Wilvox, 61–76. Washington, DC: CQ Press.
Castagno, Angelina, E., and Stacey J. Lee. 2007. "Native Mascots and Ethnic Fraud in Higher Education: Using Tribal Critical Race Theory and the Interest Convergence Principle as an Analytic Tool." *Equity and Excellence in Education*, 40(1): 3–13. DOI: 0.1080/10665680601057288.
CBS News/New York Times Monthly Poll, May 2007 (ICPSR 23444). http://www.icpsr.umich.edu/icpsrweb/instructors/studies/23444.
Chaves, M. 2004. *Congregations in America*. Cambridge, MA: Harvard University Press.
Chaves, Mark, Helen M. Giesel, and William Tsitsos. 2002. "Religious Variations in Public Presence: Evidence from the National Congregations Study." In *The Quiet Hand of God Faith-Based Activism and the Public Role of Mainline Protestantism*, edited by Robert Wuthnow and John H. Evans. Berkeley: University of California Press.

Chaves, Mark, and Shawna Anderson. 2008. "Continuity and Change in American Congregations: Introducing the Second Wave of the National Congregations Study." *Sociology of Religion* 69(4): 415–40.

Clark, Sheryl. 2012. "Being 'Good at Sport': Talent, Ability and Young Women's Sporting Participation." *Sociology* 46(6): 1178–93. DOI: 10.1177/0038038511435061.

"Coffeehouses arouse student intellect in enjoyable, unusual atmospheres." 1969. *Daily Illini*, August 8, p. C-6.

Cohen, Cathy J. 1999. *Boundaries of Blackness: AIDS and the Breakdown of Black Politics*. Chicago: University of Chicago Press.

Cohen, Jodi S. 2013. "Chief Illiniwek backers, university reach agreement on mascot." Chicago Tribune, October 23. Accessed July 6, 2014. http://articles.chicagotribune.com/keyword/chief-Illiniwek.

Coleman, James S. 1988. "Free Riders and Zealots: The Role of Social Networks." *Sociological Theory* 6(1): 52–7.

Collins, Patricia Hill. 1990. *Black Feminist Thought: Knowledge, Consciousness, and the Politics of Empowerment*. Harper Collins.

Collins, Patricia Hill. 1998. *Fighting Words: Black Women and the Search for Justice*. Minneapolis, MN: University of Minnesota Press.

Collins, Patricia H. 2006. *From Black Power to Hip-Hop: Racism, Nationalism, and Feminism*. Philadelphia: Temple University Press.

Cone, J. H. 1970. *A Black Theology of Liberation* . New York: Orbis Books Maryknoll.

Coontz, Stephanie. 2005. *Marriage, a History: From Obedience to Intimacy, or How Love Conquered Marriage*. New York: Viking.

Coontz, Stephanie. 2013. "The Disestablishment of Marriage." *New York Times*, June 22.

Crenshaw, Kimberlé. 1989. "Demarginalizing the Intersection of Race and Sex: A Black Feminist Critique of Antidiscrimination Doctrine, Feminist Theory and Antiracist Politics." *University of Chicago Legal Forum* 140: 139–67.

Crenshaw, Kimberlé. 1995. *Critical Race Theory: The Key Writings that Formed the Movement*. New York: New Press.

Creswell, John. W. 2013. *Qualitative Inquiry and Research Design: Choosing Among Five Approaches*. Thousand Oaks, CA: Sage Publications.

Davies, Carole Boyce. 1994. *Black Women, Writing, and Identity: Migrations of the Subject*. New York: Routledge.

Defense Manpower Data Center. 2009. Department of Defense Active Duty Military Personnel Strengths By Regional Area And By Country (309a). March 31. http://siadapp.dmdc.osd.mil/personnel/MILITARY/history/hst0903.pdf.

Delgado, Richard, and Jean Stefancic. 2006. *Critical Race Theory: An Introduction*. New York: NYU Press.

DeVault, Marjorie. 1999. *Liberating Method: Feminism and Social Research*. Philadelphia: Temple University Press.

Diamond, Timothy. 1992. *Making Gray Gold: Narratives of Nursing Home Care*. Chicago: University of Chicago Press.

Dodson, J. E. 1988. "Power and Surrogate Leadership: Black Women and Organized Religion." *Sage* 5(2), 37-42.

Du Bois, WEB. 1946. *The World and Africa*. New York: International Publishers.

Du Bois, WEB. 1903. *Souls of Black Folk*. Chicago: A. C. McClurg & Co.

Edwards, Kori. 2008. *The Elusive Dream: The Power of Race in Interracial Churches*. New York: Oxford.

Eisenman, David. 1968. "Project 'too great' a success." *Daily Illini*, September 11.

Elise, S., G. Rolison, and A. Daoud. 2013. "Perils, Promise and Pitfalls of Diversity: Two Steps Forward, One Step Back." *International Journal of Diversity in Education* 12(2): 93–101.

Ely, Robin J. and David A. Thomas. 2001. "Cultural Diversity at Work: The Effects of Diversity Perspectives on Work Group Processes and Outcomes." *Administrative Science Quarterly* 46(2): 229–73.

Emancipation Proclamation, January 1, 1863; Presidential Proclamations, 1791-1991; Record Group 11; General Records of the United States Government; National Archives.

Emerson, Michael O., and Christian Smith. 2000. *Divided by Faith: Evangelical Religion and the Problem of Race in America*. New York: Oxford University Press.

Emerson, Michael O., and Karen Chai Kim. 2003. "Multiracial Congregations: An Analysis of Their Development and a Typology." *Journal for the Scientific Study of Religion* 42(2): 217–22.

Emerson, Michael O. 2010. "Who's Succeeding at Making Churches More Multiracial?" Accessed February 9, 2014. https://sojo.net/articles/whos-succeeding-making-churches-more-multiracial.

Emerson, R., R. Fretz, and L. Shaw. 2011. *Writing Ethnographic Fieldnotes*. Chicago: University of Chicago Press.

Enns, Peter. 2013. "Evangelicalism and the Anti-intellectual Cult of the 'Christian Worldview'." *Patheos*. Accessed May 7, 2015. www.patheos.com/blogs/peterenns/2013/12/evangelicalism-and-the-anti-intellectual-cult-of-the-christian-worldview.

Eoyang, Glenda H., and Royce J. Holladay. 2013. *Adaptive Action: Leveraging Uncertainty in Your Organization*. Stanford, CA: Stanford University Press.

Erickson, Jane. 2006. "James Hine, Pastor and Author Is Dead at 96." *Arizona Daily Star*. Jan. 22.

Evans, Anthony. 2015. "34,000 Black Churches Break Ties With Presbyterian Church USA." *Charisma News*, March 27. Accessed April 1, 2015 http://www.charismanews.com/us/48944-34-000-black-churches-break-ties-with-presbyterian-church-usa.

Fillmore, L. 2010. *The Identity Integration Process of Christian Lesbians of Color: A Narrative Analysis Study*. ProQuest. [DAI-B 71/08, Feb 2011. http://search.proquest.com/docview/744396324].

Findlay, James. 1993. *Church People in the Struggle: The National Council of Churches and the Black Freedom Movement, 1950-1970*. New York: Oxford.

Foucault, M. 1965. *Madness and Civilization. A History of Insanity in the Age of Reason*. New York: Pantheon Books.

Foucault, M. 1973. *Birth of the Clinic: An Archaeology of Medical Perception*. London: Tavistock.

Foucault, M. 1991. "Governmentality." In *The Foucault Effect: Studies in Governmentality*. Edited by G. Burchell, C. Gordon, and P. Miller, 87–104. London: Harvester Wheatsheaf.

Frederick, Marla F. 2003. *Between Sundays: Black Women and Everyday Struggles of Faith*. Berkeley: University of California Press.

Gay, David A., and John P. Lynxwiler. 2010. "The Impact of Race on Denominational Variations in Social Attitudes: The Issue and Its Dimensions." *Sociological Spectrum* 30(1): 110–27.

Gbadegesin, Segun. 1996. *Traditional Yoruba Philosophy and Contemporary African Realities*. New York: Peter Lang.

Gbadegesin, Segun, Angelina E. Castagno, and Stacey J. Lee. 2007. "Native Mascots and Ethnic Fraud in Higher Education: Using Tribal Critical Race Theory and the Interest Convergence Principle as an Analytical Tool." *Equity and Excellence in Education*, 40(1): 3–13. DOI: 10.1080/10665680601057288.

Giberson, Karl, and Randall Stephens. 2011. "The Evangelical Rejection of Reason." *New York Times*, October 17.

Giddens, Anthony. 1971. *Capitalism and Modern Social Theory. An Analysis of the writings of Marx, Durkheim and Max Weber*. Cambridge: Cambridge University Press.

Giddens, Anthony. 1973. *The Class Structure of the Advanced Societies*. London: Hutchinson.

Giddens, Anthony. 1976. *New Rules of Sociological Method: A Positive Critique of interpretative Sociologies*. London: Hutchinson.

Giddens, Anthony. 1979. *Central Problems in Social Theory: Action, Structure and Contradiction in Social Analysis*. London: Macmillan.

Giddens, Anthony. 1984. *The Constitution of Society: Outline of the Theory of Structuration*. Cambridge: Polity.

Gilkes, Cheryl T. 2001. *If It Wasn't for the Women—: Black Women's Experience and Womanist Culture in Church and Community*. Maryknoll, NY: Orbis Books.

Goldin, C. 2004. "From the Valley to the Summit: A Brief History of the Quite Revolution that Transformed Women's Work." *Regional Review* Q4: 1–9.

Goldin, C. 2006. "Education." *Historical Statistics of the United States, Earliest Times to the Present: Millennial Edition Online*, edited by Susan B. Carter, Scott Sigmund Gartner, Michael R. Haines, Alan L. Olmstead, Richard Sutch, and Gavin Wright. New York: Cambridge University Press. Accessed July 1, 2015.

Goldin, C., L. F. Katz, and I. Kuziemko. 2006. "The Homecoming of American College Women: The Reversals of the College Gender Gap." *Journal of Economic Perspectives* 20(4): 133–56.

Grodsky, Eric, John Robert Warren, Erika Felts. 2008. "Testing and Social Stratification in American Education." *Annual Review of Sociology* 34: 385-404.

Guillaumin, Colette. 1995. *Racism, Sexism, Power, and Ideology*. New York: Routledge.

Gundani, Paul. 2010. "Interfaith Dynamics in Zimbabwe: Pre-Colonial, Colonial and Post-Colonial Times." Paper presented at the Global Studies Conference, Busan, Korea, June 10–11.

Harwood, S., S. Choi, M. Orozco, M. B. Huntt, and R. Mendenhall. 2015. Racial Microaggressions @ University of Illinois, Urbana-Champaign. Accessed May 1, 2015. http://www.racialmicroaggressions.illinois.edu/files/2015/03/RMA-Classroom-Report.pdf.

Herring, Cedric, and Loren Henderson. 2014. *Diversity in Organizations: A Critical Examination*. New York: Routledge.

Higginbotham, Evelyn Brooks. 1993. *Righteous Discontent: The Women's Movement in the Black Baptist Church, 1880-1920*. Cambridge, MA: Harvard University Press.

Hirai, Ashley H., William M. Sappenfield, Michael D. Kogan, Wanda D. Barfield, David A. Goodman, Reem M. Ghandour, and Michael C. Lu. 2014. "Contributors to Excess Infant Mortality in the U.S. South." *American Journal of Preventive Medicine* 46(3): 219-27.

Hoffman, James. 1966. "Making Marriage Last." *Presbyterian Life*, 5–7, 35. Dayton, OH: General Assembly of PCUSA/UPCUSA.

Holley, K. 2006. "Defining Governance for Public Higher Education in the Twenty-First Century." In Governance and the Public Good, edited by W. G. Tierney, 199–206. New York: SUNY Press.

Holmen, R. W. 2014. *Queer Clergy: A History of Gay and Lesbian Ministry in American Protestantism*. Cleveland, OH: Pilgrim Press.

Hout, M. and T. Smith. 2015. *Fewer Americans Affiliate with Organized Religions, Belief and Practice Unchanged: Key Findings from the 2014 General Social Survey*. Chicago: NORC.

Hout, Michael and Tom W. Smith. 2015. *Fewer Americans Affiliate with Organized Religions, Belief and Practice Unchanges: Key Findings from the 2014 General Social Survey*. Press Summary.

Ingraham, Chrys. 1994. "The Heterosexual Imaginary: Feminist Sociology and Theories of Gender." *Sociological Theory*, 12(2): 203–19.

Jackson, Jari. 1955. "Bias Not Dead Issue: NAACP." *Daily Illini*, October 11.

Jackson, Jari. 1955. "Ming Attacks UI Housing: Political Remedy Seen as Solution." *Daily Illini*, September 28.

Jackson, Jari. 1955. "Henry Replies to NAACP." *Daily Illini*, September 15.

Jones, Janelle, and John Schmitt. 2014. *A College Degree Is No Guarantee*. Washington, DC: Center for Economic and Policy Research.

Jung, M. 2006. *Reworking Race: The Making of Hawaii's Interracial Labor Movement*. New York: Columbia University Press.

Jung, M., and Y. Kwon. 2013. "Theorizing the US Racial State: Sociology since Racial Formation." *Sociology Compass* 7(11): 927–40. DOI: http://dx.doi.org/10.1111/soc4.12078.

Kane, Tim. 2006. "Global U.S. Troop Deployment, 1950-2005." The Heritage Foundation, Center for Data Analysis. http://www.heritage.org/Research/NationalSecurity/upload/97626_1.pdf.

Keogh, Diana. 2007. "Chicago's Trinity UCC Prepares to Welcome New Pastor for New Generation." October 1. http://www.ucc.org/ucnews/octnov07/chicagos-trinity-ucc.html.

Konieczny, Mary, and Mark Chaves. 2000. "Resources, Race, and Female-Headed Congregations in the United States." *Journal for the Scientific Study of Religion* 39(3): 261–71.

Krell, Cheryl. 1980. "McKinley's Reverend Lundy Reviews his Decade-Plus of Challenges." *News-Gazette.* January 16, p. A-3.

Kuumba, M. Bahati. 2002. "'YOU'VE STRUCK A ROCK': Comparing Gender, Social Movements, and Transformation in the United States and South Africa." *Gender in Society* 16(4): 504–23.

Lam, C. B. and S. M. McHale. 2015. "Developmental Patterns and Parental Correlates of Youth Leisure-Time Physical Activity." *Journal of Family Psychology*, 29(1): 100–107.

Lee, S. 2003. "The Church of Faith and Freedom: African–American Baptists and Social Action." *Journal for the Scientific Study of Religion* 42(1): 31–41.

Lentin, Alana, and G. Titley. 2011. *The Crises of Multiculturalism: Racism in a Neoliberal Age*. New York: Zedd Books.

Lewis, Jacqueline J. 2004. "Authoring Stories for a New Frontier—A Study of Clergy Who Serve in Multiracial/Multicultural Congregations." PhD diss. Drew University.

Lincoln, Abraham. 1865. Second Inaugural Address. March 4.

Lindsay, D. Michael. 2006. "Elite Power: Social Networks Within American Evangelicalism." *Sociology of Religion* 67(3): 207–27.

Lipson, Daniel N. 2011. "The Resilience of Affirmative Action in the 1980s: Innovation, Isomorphism, and Institutionalization in University Admissions." *Political Research Quarterly* 64(1): 132–44.

Loggins, S., and F. C. Andrade. 2014. "Despite an Overall Decline in U.S. Infant Mortality Rates, the Black/White Disparity Persists: Recent Trends and Future Projections." *Journal of Community Health* 39(1): 118–23.

Longfield, Bradley J. 2013. *Presbyterians and American Culture: A History*. Louisville, KY: Westminster John Knox Press.

Lorde, A. 1982. *Nami: A New Spelling of My Name*. Trumansburg, NY: Crossing Press.

Lorde, A. 1984. *Sister Outsider: Essays and Speeches*. Berkeley, CA: Crossing Press.

Lundy, Mary Ann. 1991. "Saying What We Do, Doing What We Say: Church Policies on Sexism." *Church and Society* 82(1): 55–65.

The MAC, McKinley Foundation Newspaper, 1953–54.

Mama, Amina. 2002. "Editorial." *Feminist Africa: Intellectual Politics* 1:150.

Mansfield, Stephen. 2008. *The Faith of Barack Obama*. Nashville: Thomas Nelson Publisher.

Marsden, Peter. 2000. "Social Networks." In *Encyclopedia of Sociology*. Second edition, edited by E. F. Borgatta and R. J. V. Montgomery, 2727–35. New York: Macmillan.

Marsden, Peter. 2005. "Recent Developments in Network Measurement." In *Models and Methods in Social Network Analysis*, edited by P. J. Carrington, J. Scott, and S. Wasserman, 8–30. New York: Cambridge University Press.

Marti, Gerardo. 2012. *Worship Across the Racial Divide: Religious Music and the Multiracial Congregation*. New York: Oxford.

Marx, Karl. 1867. *Capital: A Critique of Political Economy, Vol. I. The Process of Capitalist Production*. Chicago: Charles H. Kerr and Co.

Massey, D. and N. Denton. 1993. *American Apartheid: Segregation and the Making of the Underclass*. Cambridge, MA: Harvard University Press.
Matsuoka, F. 1998. *The Color of Faith: Building Community in a Multiracial Society*. Cleveland: United Church Press.
McClerking, H. K. and E. L. McDaniel. 2005. "Belonging and Doing: Political Churches and Black Political Participation." *Political Psychology* 26(5): 721–33.
McKay, John, and Eugene Carson Blake. 1953. "A Letter to the Presbyterians Concerning the Present Situation in Our Country and in the World." Philadelphia: General Council of the PCUSA.
McKinley Memorial Presbyterian Church Session Minutes Books: 1942–1965; 1965–1977; 1977–1989.
McRoberts, Omar M. 2003. *Streets of Glory: Church and Community in a Black Urban Neighborhood*. Chicago: University of Chicago Press.
Mills, C. Wright. 1959. *The Sociological Imagination*. New York: Oxford University Press.
More Light Presbyterians. http://mlp.org/history. Accessed July 3, 2014.
Murphy, S. L., J. Q. Xu, and K. D. Kochanek. 2012. "Deaths: Preliminary Data for 2010." National Vital Statistics Reports, 60(4). Hyattsville, MD: National Center for Health Statistics.
Myers, Valerie. 2005. "Black Church Culture, Social Programs and Faith-Based Policy: Using Organization Theory to Reconcile Rhetoric and Reality." *African American Research Perspectives* 11(1): 116–38.
"NAACP Charges Inaction on Bias; May Vote to Picket." 1955. *Daily Illini*, September 20.
National Black Church Initiative. http://www.natlblackchurch.com.
NCAA. 2007. Press release. Statement by Bernard Franklin, NCAA Senior Vice-President for Governance, Membership, Education and Research Services on the University of Illinois Mascot Decision. February 17. Accessed April 23, 2014. fs.ncaa.org/Docs/PressArchive/2007/Official%2BStatements/ Statement %2Bby %2BBernard %2BFranklin% 2BNCAA% 2BSenior% 2BVice-President %2Bfor% 2BGovernance% 2BMembership %2BEducation %2Band% 2BResearch% 2BServices%2Bon%2BU.html.
NCAA. 2005. Press release. Statement by Bernard Franklin, Senior Vice-President for Governance and Membership on the University of Illinois, Champaign Review. November 17. Accessed April 23, 2014. fs.ncaa.org/Docs/PressArchive/2005/ Official%2BStatements/ Statement %2Bby %2BNCAA% 2BSenior %2BVice %2BPresident %2Bfor% 2BGovernance %2Band% 2BMembership %2BBernard %2BFranklin% 2Bon%2BUniversity %2Bof%2BIllinois%2BChampa.html.
National Congregations Study [Part 1]. 1998. Duke University. Accessed June 9, 2011. http://www.soc.duke.edu/natcong/explorefrequencies2.html.
National Congregations Study [Part 2]. 2006–2007. Duke University. Accessed June 9, 2011. http://www.soc.duke.edu/natcong/explorefrequencies2_07.html.
Nichols, Sharon, Gene Glass, and David Berliner. 2012. "High-stakes Testing and Student Achievement: Updated Analyses with NAEP Data." *Education Policy Analysis Archives*, [S.l.], 20: 20. ISSN 1068-2341. http://epaa.asu.edu/ojs/article/view/1048. Accessed December 31, 2015. DOI: http://dx.doi.org/10.14507/epaa.v20n20.2012.
NIV: The Holy Bible— New International Version. 1984. Grand Rapids, MI: Zondervan.
Noll, Mark A. and Luke E. Harlow (editors). 2007. *Religion and American Politics: From the Colonial Period to the Present*. New York: Oxford University Press.
Oliver Brown v. Board of Education of Topeka. 1954. 347 U.S. 483.
Omi, Michael, and Howard Winant. 1986. *Racial Formation in the United States*. New York: Routledge.
Page, Scott E. 2007. *The Difference: How the Power of Diversity Creates Better Groups, Firms, Schools, and Societies*. Princeton, NJ: Princeton University Press.
Paris, Arthur. 1982. *Black Pentecostalism: Southern Religion in an Urban World*. Amherst: University of Massachusetts Press.

Park, Julie, and Amy Liu. 2014. "Interest Convergence or Divergence? A Critical Race Analysis of Asian Americans, Meritocracy, and Critical Mass in Affirmative Action Debate." *Journal of Higher Education* 85(1): 36–64.

Parker, Randall. 2009. "Black Unemployment Rate Hits 15 Percent." May 9. Accessed June 19, 2013. http://www.parapundit.com/archives/006189.html.

Pew Research Center for Religion and Public Life. 2015. Accessed June 1, 2015. http://www.pewforum.org/2015/05/12/americas-changing-religious-landscape.

Pinn, A. B. 2007. "Jesus and Justice: An Outline of Liberation Theology Within Black Churches." *Cross Currents* 57(2): 218–26.

Pohlman, Michael Edgar. 2012. "Broadcasting the Faith: Protestant Religious Radio and Theology in America, 1920–1950." PhD diss. Southern Baptist Theological Seminary.

"Political Ban, Prejudice Attacked." 1955. *Daily Illini,* March 8.

Portes, Alejandro. 1998. "Social Capital: Its Origins and Applications in Modern Sociology." *Annual Review of Sociology* 24: 1–24.

Prelinger, C. 1992. *Episcopal Women: Gender, Spirituality and Commitment in an American Mainline Denomination.* New York: Oxford.

Presbyterian Church (USA). https://www.pcusa.org.

Presbyterian Church (USA). *The Confession of 1967*. (Updated). http://www.creeds.net/reformed/confess67.pdf.

Presbyterian Church (USA). 1953. "A Letter to Presbyterians:" The PCUSA 1953 General Council Challenge to McCarthyism. https://www.pcusa.org/resource/letter-presbyterians-mccarthyism-1953. Accessed July 13, 2014.

Presbyterian Church (USA) Presbyterian Historical Society. *Presbyterian Family Connections, 1706-Present.* Accessed December 1, 2014. http://www.history.pcusa.org/sites/default/files/theme-assets/presbyterian_family_connections_ocr_2mb.pdf.

Presbyterian Mission Agency, Research Services. 2012a. Comparative Statistics 2012. Presbyterian Church (USA). https://www.pcusa.org/resource/comparative-statistics-2012.

Presbyterian Mission Agency, Research Services. 2012b. PC(USA) Miscellaneous Information. https://www.pcusa.org/resource/comparative-statistics-2012.

Presbyterian Panel. 1997–1999. Presbyterian Church (USA). https://www.pcusa.org/site_media/media/uploads/research/pdfs/1997_99_full_bgrndreport.pdf.

Priest, R. J., and A. L. Nieves. 2007. *This Side of Heaven: Race, Ethnicity, and Christian Faith.* Oxford: Oxford University Press.

Ray, Jim. 2014. "Creating Social Change." Accessed January 4, 2014. http://ncmasages.wordpress.com/2014/06/03/creating-social-change-by-jim-ray.

Reese, L., R. Brown, and J. Ivers. 2007. "Some children see him . . . : Political Participation and the Black Christ. *Political Behavior* 29(4): 517–37.

Reinbolt, Kathy. 1970. "Motion to Oppose Illiac Defeated: Senate Discusses CAC, Violence." *Daily Illini,* 10 March. http://www.tradingmarkets.com/.site/news/Stock%20News/2026974.

"Religion, Segregation and the Churches." 1955. *Time.* June 20.

Risman, B. J. 2004. "Gender as a Social Structure: Theory Wrestling with Activism." *Gender and Society* 18(4): 429–50. DOI: http://dx.doi.org/10.1177/0891243204265349.

Robbins, Joel. 2004. "The Globalization of Pentecostal and Charismatic Christianity." *Annual Review of Anthropology* 33: 117–43. http://www.jstor.org/stable/25064848.

Robnett, Belinda. 1997. *How Long? How Long? African-American Women in the Struggle for Civil Rights.* New York: Oxford University Press.

Ross, Howard J. 2011. *Reinventing Diversity: Transforming Organizational Community to Strengthen People, Purpose, and Performance.* Lanham, MD: Rowman & Littlefield.

Ross, Janell. 2014. "African-Americans With College Degrees Are Twice As Likely to Be Unemployed as Other Graduates." *National Journal.* Accessed January 7, 2014. http://www.nationaljournal.com/next-america/education/african-americans-with-

college-degrees-are-twice-as-likely-to-be-unemployed-as-other-graduates-20140527.
San Antonio Independent School District v. Rodriguez. 1973. 411 U.S. 1.
Sanders, C. 1996. *Saints in Exile: The Holiness Experience in African American Religion and Culture.* New York: Oxford.
Salime, Zakia. 2005. *Between Islam and Feminism: New Political Transformations and Movements in Morocco.* PhD diss. University of Illinois at Champaign-Urbana. UMI 3202166.
Sekou, Osagyefo. 2009. *Dispatches from the Religious Left: The Future of Faith and Politics in America.* New York: Ig Publishing.
Shelley, Clarence. Accessed March 11, 2015. localwiki.org/cu/Clarence_Shelley.
Sherkat, D. E., and C. G. Ellison. 1991. "The Politics of Black Religious Change: Disaffiliation from Black Mainline Denominations." *Social Forces* 70(2): 431–54.
Singleton, H. 2008. "Between Racism and Obscurity: The Black Theologian in the Twenty-First Century. *Black Theology: An International Journal* 6(1): 12–31.
Slater, Amy, and Marika Tiggemann. 2010. "'Uncool to Do Sport': A Focus Group Study of Adolescent Girls' Reasons for Withdrawing from Physical Activity." *Psychology of Sport and Exercise* 11(6): 619–26. DOI: 10.1016/j.psychsport.2010.07.006.
Smith, Dorothy. 1987. *The Everyday World as Problematic: Feminist Sociology.* Boston: Northeastern University Press.
Smith, Dorothy. 1999. *Writing the Social: Critique, Theory, and Investigations.* Toronto; Buffalo, NY: University of Toronto Press.
Smith, Dorothy. 2005. *Institutional Ethnography: A Sociology for People.* Walnut Creek, CA: AltaMira Press.
Society of Women Engineers (SWE) and ARUP. 2014. *Diversity and Inclusion.* Edited by Erin McConahey, Katherine Prater, and Jesse Vernon.
Solorzano, Daniel. 1998. "Critical Race Theory, Race and Gender Microaggressions, and the Experience of Chicana and Chicano Scholars." *Qualitative Studies in Education* 11(1): 121–36.
Stone, Deborah M., Feijun Luo, Lijing Ouyang, Caroline Lippy, Marci F. Hertz, and Alex E. Crosby. 2014. "Sexual Orientation and Suicide Ideation, Plans, Attempts, and Medically Serious Attempts: Evidence From Local Youth Risk Behavior Surveys, 2001-2009." *American Journal of Public Health* 104(2): 262.
Sudbury, Julia. 1998. *Other Kinds of Dreams: Black Women's Ogranizations and The Politics of Transformation.* New York: Routledge.
Sumerau, J. 2013. *Gendered, Sexual, and Religious Transformations in an LGBT Christian Organization.* Paper 6633. http://diginole.lib.fsu.edu/etd/6633.
Surowiecki, James. 2004. *The Wisdom of Crowds: Why the Many Are Smarter Than the Few and How Collective Wisdom Shapes Business Economies, Societies and Nations.* New York: Doubleday.
Swartley, Willard. 1983. *Slavery, Sabbath, War, and Women: Case Issues in Biblical Interpretation.* Scottsdale, PA: Herald Press.
Taylor, Steven, and Robert Bogdan. 1998. *Introduction to Qualitative Research Methods: A Guidebook and Resource.* New York: Wiley.
Taylor, Nancy. 2014. "Detroit 1954: A Tale of Two Cities." Presbyterian Historical Society. Accessed February 6, 2015. http://www.pcusa.org/news/2014/6/2/detroit-1954-tale-two-cities.
Thompson, Mark. 2014. "U.S. Ends Its War in Afghanistan." Time. December 28. Accessed January 3, 2015. http://time.com/3648055/united-states-afghanistan-war-end/?xid=emailshare.
Turner, Caroline S. 2003. "Incorporation and Marginalization in the Academy: From Border toward Center for Faculty of Color?" *Journal of Black Studies* 34(1): 112–25.
United Presbyterian Church (USA). 1967. *The Confession of 1967.*
U.S. Bureau of the Census. 2004. "Table MS-2. Estimated Median Age at First Marriage, by Sex: 1890 to Present." Accessed February 7, 2015. https://www.census.gov/population/socdemo/hh-fam/tabMS-2.pdf.

U.S. Federal Highway Administration. 2014. Highway History. http://www.fhwa.dot.gov/highwayhistory/road/s10.cfm.

University of Michigan. Institute for Social Research. American National Election Studies. ANES 2004 Time Series Study. ICPSR04245-v2. Ann Arbor, MI: Inter-university Consortium for Political and Social Research [distributor], 2015-11-10. http://doi.org/10.3886/ICPSR04245.v2.

University of Illinois. Division of Management Information, 2000. Old Enrollment Figures for the Urbana Fall Term. Accessed October 9, 2014. http://www.dmi.illinois.edu/stuenr/#historical.

University of Illinois. Ethnography of the University Initiative. Accessed November 2, 2015. http://www.eui.illinois.edu.

University of Illinois. LibGuides Timelines. Accessed October 4, 2014. http://uiuc.libguides.com/content.php?pid=557710&sid=4599292.

University of Illinois. Research-Education Timeline. Accessed October 4, 2014. http://archives.library.illinois.edu/slc/research-education/timeline/.

Uttal, Lynet, and Gloria Holguin Cuádraz. 1999. "Intersectionality and In-Depth Interviews: Methodological Strategies for Analyzing and Race, Class, and Gender." *Race Gender and Class* 6(3): 156–86.

Weston, William (Beau). 2004. Presbyterian Church (USA). In *Pulpit and Politics: Clergy in American Politics at the Advent of the Millennium*, edited by Corwin E. Smidt, 59–70 . Waco: Baylor University Press.

Whitt, Joanne. 2009. "The Confession of 1967: Reconciling the World." Sermon, August 23. Accessed July 1, 2014. http://www.togetherweserve.org/the-confession-of-1967-reconciling-the-world.

Wiggins, Daphne C. 2005. *Righteous Content: Black Women's Perspectives of Church and Faith*. New York: New York University Press.

Wilson, W. J. 1987. *The Truly Disadvantaged: The Innercity, the Underclass, and Public Policy*. Chicago: University of Chicago Press.

Wilson, W. J. 1996. *When Work Disappears: The World of the New Urban Poor*. New York: Knopf.

Williams, T. S. 1983. "Some Issues in the Standardized Testing of Minority Students." *Journal of Education* 165(2): 192–208.

Willimon, Will. 2001. "Church Growth Keys: Multiracial, Happy, More Males Active." *Christian Century*, Jan 23. Hartford Institute for Religion Research, Hartford Seminary.

Wisdon, A. 2010. "Political Gaps Strain Churches: No End in Sight to the Growing Political Rift Between Laity and Clergy in Oldline Protestantism." American Spectator, February 2. Accessed June 9, 2011. http://spectator.org/articles/40041/political-gaps-strain-churches.

Yancey, G. 2003. *One Body, One Spirit: Principles of Successful Multiracial Churches*. Downers Grove, IL: InterVarsity Press.

Youngdahl, Patricia. 1996. "Subversive Devotions: Toward a Wholehearted Practice of Christian Faith." Ph.D diss. University of Arizona. Accessed October 8, 2014. http://hdl.handle.net/10150/187495.

Zapico, B., C. Tuero, J. Espartero, and R. González-Boto. 2014. "The Socialisation Process and Gender Inequality in School Sports ." *Science and Sports* . Oct 2014 Supplement, 29: S20. DOI: 10.1016/j.scispo.2014.08.037.

Zellar, Tom. 2007. Ending a Tradition That Some Find Racist, Others Noble. *The Lede, The New York Times News Blog*. February 16. Accessed May 1, 2015. http://thelede.blogs.nytimes.com/2007/02/16/ending-a-racist-noble-tradition.

Zerai, Assata. 2000a. "Agents of Knowledge and Action: Selected Africana Scholars and their Contributions to the Understanding of Race, Class and Gender Intersectionality." *Cultural Dynamics* 12(2): 182–222.

Zerai, Assata. 2000b. "'Making a Way Outta No Way': Grandparenting Cocaine Exposed Grandchildren." In *Care Work: Gender, Labor and Welfare States*, edited by Madonna Harrington Meyer, 270–92. New York: Routledge.

Zerai, Assata. 2010a. "A Black Feminist Critique of American Religious Anti-war (Dis)engagements." *Works and Days* 57/58, 29(1–2): 241–63.

Zerai, Assata. 2010b. "To Be Politically Relevant and Tolerant: A Comparative Analysis of Christian Evangelical Internal Discussions of the 2008 Presidential Election." *Race, Gender and Class* 17(3–4):336–48.

Zerai, Assata. 2011. "An Assessment of Afro-Centricism, Color-Blind Ideology, and Intersectionality: Three Models of Internal Christian Congregational Cohesion." *Race, Gender and Class* 18(1–2).

Zerai, Assata. 2014. *Hypermasculinity and State Violence in Zimbabwe: An Africana Feminist Analysis of Maternal and Child Health.* Trenton, NJ: Africa World Press.

Zerai, Assata, and Rae Banks. 2002a. *Dehumanizing Discourse, Law and Policy in America: A Crack Mother's Nightmare.* London: Ashgate Publishing.

Zerai, Assata, and Rae Banks. 2002b. "African-American Mothers and Substance Abuse: Punishment over Treatment?" *Journal of the Sexuality Information and Education Council of the United States* 30(3): 26–29.

Zerai, Assata, and Horace Campbell. 2005. "The Black Radical Congress and Black Feminist Organizing." *Socialism and Democracy* 19(2): 147–56.

Zerai, Assata, and Zakia Salime. 2006. "A Black Feminist Analysis of Responses to War, Racism, and Repression." *Critical Sociology* 32(2–3): 503–26.

Zimm, Maxine Baca, Lynn Weber, Elizabeth Higginbotham, and Bonnie Thornton Dill. 1986. "The Costs of Exclusionary Practice in Women's Studies." *Signs: Journal of Women in Culture and Society,* 11(2): 290–303.

Index

activism, 4–5, 12, 14, 15, 19, 30, 31, 47, 49, 52, 55, 58, 60, 61, 62, 64, 66, 67n9, 121, 131, 138, 139; antiwar, 19, 47, 49, 52, 58, 60, 61, 62, 64, 66, 67n8, 78, 131, 138, 139; political, 11, 18, 37, 40, 49, 64, 65, 139; social, 24, 39, 78, 96, 102, 127
African American(s), ix, 1, 2, 3, 4, 6, 8, 10n10, 10n11, 15, 16, 17, 19, 21, 23, 24, 25, 27, 28, 30, 31, 32, 35, 38n2, 38n5, 38n9, 39, 40, 41, 42, 43, 44, 45, 47, 48, 49, 50, 51, 52, 53, 54, 55, 56, 57, 58, 61, 63, 64, 67n7, 68n11, 75, 76, 78, 87, 88, 89, 90, 92, 97n14, 97n19, 97n23, 103, 104, 108, 110, 112n6, 112n7, 113, 114, 115, 122n1, 124, 134, 136, 139, 140
Africana feminisms, 5, 8, 11, 13, 18, 49, 49–50, 50, 54, 55–56, 62, 66, 67n9, 135; Black feminism, 11, 50; black feminist thought, 5, 7, 50
Afrocentric, 6, 16, 21, 24, 29, 30, 31, 37, 40, 41, 43, 52, 53, 54, 58, 59, 63, 64, 133, 134, 136
American National Election Studies, 67n6

Bechtel, Dave, xi, 71, 73, 76, 94, 118, 124
Blake, Eugene Carson, 96, 99, 101, 102, 105, 112n1, 112n4
Bonilla-Silva, 29, 31, 35, 36, 37
Buckley-Shaklee, Amber, 12

Cain, Jane, xi, 120, 121
Capel, Bill, xi, 123
Chaves, 11, 49, 51, 53, 68n11, 140
Civil Rights, 30, 36, 37, 44, 49, 59, 71, 74, 77, 86, 87, 91, 99, 101, 103, 105, 107, 109, 110, 114, 118, 119, 125, 126, 127, 128, 129n3, 140

color blindness, 132, 134, 136
color blind racism, 22, 23–24, 29, 29–37, 135
Confession of 1967, 109, 112n8, 127
Crenshaw, Kimberlee, 5, 13, 132
critical race theory, 132, 136, 137

Daily Illini, 74, 75, 76, 87, 90, 91, 93, 95, 97n6, 97n26, 101, 102, 103, 110, 111, 112, 112n1, 112n4, 112n9, 117, 126
DeVault, Marjorie, xi, 5, 13, 75, 85, 85–86

Emerson, Michael: and Christian Smith, 7, 10n14, 11, 18n5, 21, 22–23, 31, 35, 133, 140; and R. R. Fretz and L. Shaw, 5, 85
Evangelical, 6, 7, 8, 17, 18n5, 18n6, 18n7, 18n8, 19, 21, 22, 23, 29, 30, 31, 35, 37, 38n2, 38n8, 39, 40, 41, 43, 45, 46, 46n3, 49, 52, 53, 54, 57, 58, 59, 63, 64, 66n2, 132, 133, 134, 136
evangelical Protestants, 8, 16, 17, 21, 47, 49, 51, 67n3

GI Bill, 86–87, 90, 92
Goldin, C., 92, 98n28
Great (African American) Migration, 86, 88
Gundani, Paul, x, 22

Hine, James (Jim), 90, 93, 94, 95, 97n6, 101, 102, 105, 110, 111, 113, 128

inclusiveness, xi, 3, 12, 14, 19, 35, 43, 124, 126, 133, 134
inclusivity, 1, 2, 3, 5, 6, 8, 9, 10n8, 11, 12, 14, 16, 71, 76, 123, 124, 125, 126, 140
inclusive, ix, 1, 2, 5, 6, 12, 15, 16, 18, 19, 21, 35, 43, 60, 63, 69, 77, 120, 124,

126, 128, 129, 131, 132, 133, 134, 135, 137, 139, 140
intentional, x, 3, 9, 12, 23–24, 62–63, 69, 122, 131, 132
intentional communities, 19, 140
intentionality, 35–36, 135–140
intersectionality, 6, 7, 11, 13, 14, 15, 16, 19, 50, 75

Jackson, Jari, 91, 100, 101

KKK, Ku Klux Klan, 87

Latino(s), 1, 28, 72, 136
LGBTIQ definition, 9n4
LGBTIQ/LGBT, 1, 1–2, 8, 9n1, 9n4, 9n5, 11, 15, 17, 18n6, 19, 27, 43, 50–51, 68n13, 69, 71, 77, 86–87, 109, 123, 124, 124–125, 128–129, 132, 134, 135, 136, 138–139
Lundy, Dick (Richard), 113, 114, 117, 118, 123, 126, 138, 139
Lundy, Mary Ann, 119, 120, 121, 128, 129n3

Mainline Protestant, 2, 3, 10n14, 16, 17, 19, 23, 38n2, 53, 54, 98n32, 129, 132
March on Washington, 105
marginalization, 4, 33, 35–36, 40, 42, 50–51, 66, 102, 114, 135
marginalized groups, 3, 10n16, 12, 14, 15, 19, 22, 28, 35, 35–36, 68n12, 85, 121, 132–133, 135, 136–137, 139
mascot(s) (racist), 4, 10n15, 124
McKinley Foundation, 73, 87, 88, 89, 90, 91, 93, 95, 101, 105, 110, 112n1, 117, 124, 126
McKinley Memorial Presbyterian Church, 73, 87, 90, 91, 92, 93, 95, 102, 107, 109, 119, 120, 124
McKinley Minutes Books, 76, 77, 86, 97n8, 110, 112n5
McKinley, Reverend George, 87
McKinley, Senator William Brown, 73
McKinley-Weds, McWeds, 119
microaggressions, 90, 97n24, 137, 161
Midwest, x, 3, 6, 8, 16, 23, 24, 25, 35, 41, 52, 53, 56, 63, 72, 74, 76, 133, 134, 140
Ming, Attorney William R., 91, 100

Modernist-fundamentalist controversy, 86, 88, 95, 125, 132
More Light Presbyterians (MLP), 1, 8, 9n1, 71, 74, 123, 124
multiculturalism, x, 5, 13
multiracial, 2, 4, 6, 8, 19, 31, 32, 35, 37, 38n7, 46, 53, 56, 60, 65, 140
multiracial congregations, 3, 7, 8, 11–12, 21, 35, 40, 42, 43, 47, 52, 53, 129, 134, 135
multiracial churches, 3, 4, 6, 8, 12, 14, 21–22, 22, 23, 25, 28, 34, 46, 51, 65, 69, 136

NAACP, 87, 91, 99, 101, 102, 103, 104, 110
National Congregations Survey, 51, 67n5
National Black Church Initiative (NBCI), 1
News Gazette, 74, 75, 76, 77, 102

Obama, President Barack, 19, 37, 43, 44, 45, 45–46, 47–48, 49, 51, 52, 53, 58, 59, 61, 62, 131

Presbyterian Church (USA), PCUSA, 1, 72, 73, 77, 87, 89, 93, 96, 98n32, 99, 100, 101, 106, 112n1, 112n10, 114, 119, 121, 123, 124
PCUSA General Assembly (GA), 1, 9n2, 72, 87, 96, 99, 100, 106, 109, 112n1, 112n8, 112n10, 123, 124
Presbyterian Family Connections, 73
Presbyterian Gay Caucus, 1
Presbyterian Historical Society, 72, 73
Presbyterian Mission Agency, 72, 73

race, class, and gender, 2, 8, 8–9, 13, 14, 15, 39, 41, 47, 49, 50, 67n4, 69, 134, 135, 136; and heterogender, 1; and sexuality, 1, 2, 4, 5, 6, 8–9, 11, 12, 13, 16, 56, 63, 72, 75, 85, 137
Ray, Jim, 93, 105, 106, 107, 108, 111, 116, 122n5
relational, 9, 11–12, 67n4–67n5, 92
relational difference, 14, 49–50, 50, 55–56, 57, 92, 135

Sindt, David Bailey, 1, 123
Site 1. Afrocentric and Evangelical megachurch in a Midwest city, 3, 6, 16, 19, 21, 23, 24, 25, 28, 29, 30, 31, 35, 37, 40, 41, 44, 45, 46, 47, 52, 53, 54, 55, 58, 59, 60, 63, 65
Site 2. Friendliest Place in College Town USA, a large Midwest church, 3, 6, 16, 19, 21, 23, 24, 25, 26, 28, 31, 32, 35, 42, 43, 44, 46, 57
Site 3. Oasis in the City, a large urban church in the East, 3, 6, 16, 19, 21, 23, 24, 27, 28, 33, 34, 35, 37, 45, 46, 47, 52, 53, 55, 58, 60, 62, 63, 64, 65, 66
Site 4. Leadership and Congregation at Odds, a small church in a Midwest suburb, 3, 6, 16, 19, 52, 53, 56–57, 58, 61, 63, 64, 134
Site 5. Inclusive Presbyterian Church a medium-size congregation in a Midwest college town, 3, 6, 16. *See also* McKinley Memorial Presbyterian Church
Smith, Dorothy, 2, 5, 10n9, 13, 15, 85, 86
social justice, x, 4, 9, 19, 21, 27, 29, 30, 31, 33, 34, 36, 43, 55, 58, 60, 61, 62, 64, 65, 66, 69, 72, 73, 96, 102, 106, 111, 113, 118, 120, 121, 124, 125, 129, 129n3, 131, 133, 134, 135, 139
Society for Women Engineers (SWE), 131
stained glass, 41, 71, 88, 94, 95, 124

United Presbyterian Church of North America (UPCUSA), 96, 98n32, 101, 105, 106, 107, 108, 109, 110, 112n3, 112n8, 112n10
University of Illinois, 4, 10n15, 73, 74, 75, 76, 77, 86, 87, 88, 89, 90, 91, 92, 94, 95, 97n13, 97n23, 99, 100, 101, 105, 110, 113, 114, 116, 124

Weatherford, Heidi, xi, 128
World War II (WWII), 90, 92–93

Yancey, G., 7, 11, 35–36
Youndahl, Patricia, 121–122

Zerai, Assata, 5, 6, 7, 13, 14, 15, 16, 21, 44, 49, 50, 67n4, 86, 135

About the Author

Assata Zerai currently holds positions as associate dean for Educational Equity programs in the Graduate College, director of African Studies, and associate professor of sociology at the University of Illinois (Urbana-Champaign). Serving as faculty in the Department of Sociology at Illinois since 2002, Zerai's research interests have included Protestant Christianity, maternal and child health, and the social demography of Africa and in the African Diaspora. She has published *Dehumanizing Discourse* (with Rae Banks (Ashgate, 2002); *Hypermasculinity and State Violence in Zimbabwe: An Africana Feminist Analysis of Maternal and Child Health* (Africa World Press, 2014); and *Safe Water, Sanitation and Early Childhood Malnutrition in East Africa: An Africana Feminist Analysis of the lives of Women and Children in Kenya, Tanzania and Uganda,* and is currently under contract with Lexington Books.

CPSIA information can be obtained at www.ICGtesting.com
Printed in the USA
BVOW08*1448230716

456537BV00003B/42/P

f², devoted to novels-in-progress
F Magazine, Inc.

Editor
John Schultz

The *f* issues are published twice yearly by F Magazine, Inc., 1405 W. Belle Plaine, Chicago, Illinois, 60613. F Magazine, Inc., is a not-for-profit corporation under the laws of the State of Illinois. Currently the *f* series is devoted to sections of novels-in-progress, or other longer works of imaginative prose. The editor invites submissions of excerpts of reasonable length. No manuscripts will be returned unless accompanied by a stamped, self-addressed envelope. All manuscripts accepted for publication become the property of F Magazine, Inc., unless otherwise indicated. Copyright © 1986 by F Magazine, Inc. All rights reserved. The views expressed in this magazine are to be attributed to the writers, not the editors or sponsors. Printed in the United States of America.

The publication of *f²* was made possible by grants and gifts from:

    The Illinois Arts Council, chairman's grant
    Erwin A. Salk
    Mirron Alexandroff, Columbia College
    Yale Wexler
    Media Graphics, for portion of typesetting

and by contributions of up to $100 by:

    Herman Bingham
    Robert Boone
    Susan Rue Braden
    Betty Brisch
    Mary Brophy
    Rita Ann Bubacz
    William Burck
    Richard Cantrall
    Peter and Meredith Christensen
    John F. Howe
    Kathryn E. Jonas
    Mary Zoe Keithley
    Richard Riemer
    Richard and Ruth Talaber
    Maureen Ann Tarpey
    Mary Walker

The editor extends special thanks to Fred Shafer for his readings of and responses to the essay "The Author is Dead! Long Live the Author!"

Cover Photo: Bill Burck
Cover Design: Gerry Gall

ISBN 0-936959-00-2

EDITORIAL INTRODUCTION

F Magazine, with the publication of f^2 and subsequent book-issues, seeks to be the spearhead for novels-in-progress that will emphasize story—content, imagery, character, voice—and a rich exploration of points of view and style and dimensions of time, dramatic as well as self relationships, the mixing of the private and the self with the public and social and historical, the way life happens for all of us no matter how we wish it to be. Years ago, f^1 carried on its cover the audacious statement, "Here we begin again with story, image, word, and people." With f^2, we are continuing the beginning, which has become a strong movement in the writing of novels.

If you're a poet or a writer of short fiction—and these days that often means very short fiction—you may write a piece in comparatively little time and see it published, get some audience response relatively quickly, if only from the audience of your own resonating spirit. If you're a novelist you can go a long, long time in writing a novel before you get the audience and the life-giving audience response, the sort of response that can help sustain the novelist.

Historically, novelists have often had the great advantage of audience response to their novels-in-progress, published in the form of serialization or in sections. For many reasons, historical and economic, this is no longer so. If we examine even recent literary history, we find that prior publication of sections of works-in-progress has played an important part in many novelists' development and shaping of thier novels. In many cases the novels were far from finished and the prior publication stimulated the author and whetted the audience's sense of contribution.

With realism and sometimes parody, the sections of novels-in-progress published in f^2 address some of the "common secrets" of American life—of power, family, job, institutions, sex, money, class, personality, racial relations, and much more. For instance, four of the novel excerpts address the "common secret" of black-white relations and racism, which are a pervading fact and influence in American life; yet, one can read hundreds of pieces of fiction by white American writers and never find the slightest suggesttion of such awareness. The "common secrets" of our lives have always been the fascinating stuff of story.

F Magazine will be devoted to novels-in-progress that are part of a movement toward a synthesis of novelistic techniques, seeking ways to reclaim the author's function, place, potential, and responsibility in telling the dramatic tale, in this case the novel.

John Schultz
Editor

Contents
Introductory Statement

Novels-in-Progress

From *Winter House* 1
The Men Who Led Her So Far Astray
Andrew Allegretti

From *Hey, Liberal* 29
Louis
Shawn Shiflett

From *A Korean War Novel* 65
Responsibility
John Schultz

From *Marquette Park* 79
Bachelor Party
Gary Johnson

From *Failure* 117
Goldbloom's Basement
Gerald Nicosia

From *On the Seventh Day* 129
On the Seventh Day
The Miracle of Lady Kate—An Immaculate Conception
Betty Shiflett

Satire

From *The Pink Lady Primer* 169
Everything You Always Wanted to Know About
    Who and What Is and Isn't Pink
The Sunshine Inspiration Committee's Guide for
    True Ladies Everywhere
Beverlye Brown

Essay

The Author is Dead! Long Live the Author! 189
John Schultz

Winter House

Andrew Allegretti

Winter House is the story of the financial and emotional dissolution of a well-to-do Chicago family. The novel is primarily the son's story—Wyatt Parsons' story—but through a third-person story structure that employs multiple points of view, non-linear time structures, and a sustained narrative voice, which has been likened to the saddest of chamber music, it becomes the story of many people, and, in a wide sense, the story of the community to which they belong. While the social history of the book is accurate and the characters do exist in a recognizable time and place (Chicago and the Fox River Valley from 1935 to 1971), social reality is not the book's primary concern. In its broadest sense, *Winter House* is the story of the paradox of love—how love persists in the most confounding ways even while those who profess to love are injuring one another beyond repair, and probably beyond forgiveness as well.

The section that follows sets the stage for a number of the novel's themes that are developed throughout the book—Catherine Parsons' alcoholism, her relationship to her children, and generally the nature of love as it exists in the Parsons family.

Andrew Allegretti teaches fiction writing in the graduate program in writing at Columbia College. His fiction and non-fiction have appeared in numerous publications including *Angels in My Oven, The Story Workshop Reader,* and *TriQuarterly.* He was a 1985 recipient of an Illinois Arts Council Artists Fellowship Award and the winner of an Illinois Arts Council Literary Award for a short story that appeared in *Privates.*

From *Winter House*

The Men Who Led Her So Far Astray

Andrew Allegretti

The long narrow living room of the Parsons' house in the country was divided in half by a threadbare Serapi rug rolled out before a tall mirror above a chest, in front of which Catherine Parsons would try on her hats. Why she brought her hats down to the living room to put them on was a mystery to her son, but in later years it occurred to Wyatt that there, in front of that tall mirror, a woman concerned about the overall effect of her clothes could see how she looked, not against the confines of a bedroom, but head-to-toe against a large room; and once she had her hat adjusted, she could turn and look across the wide entrance hall and up two shallow steps into the dining room, where, on the opposite wall of the house, another large mirror faced her. And seeing herself across that farther room, she would compose and relax her shoulders and begin to walk toward her reflection, eyes critically watching, appraising, as a stranger or friend might see her approaching on the street. Once, in adolescence, her son Wyatt, examining in the living room mirror the peppering of pimples on his baby skin, sighed deeply, turned dramatically, and walked toward the farther glass, down two steps into the entrance hall, and up the two wide steps into the dining room, and there, eyes rolled back and breath moist, planted a brushing kiss on his own lips in the mirror. Afterwards (to his horror) he saw open lip marks on the glass, and blushing hotly, ran for a cloth.

Catherine, of course, did not kiss the mirror, but in those early years when her children were little, appraised herself critically, frowning, tipping her head, standing back, adjusting her skirt, smoothing it along her hips, turning first one way then another, while Wyatt, aged six, or perhaps seven, sat on his tricycle, his face turned up, gravely watching. Catherine, from time to time would look down at his serious little features and ask, "What do you think of this one?" And Wyatt would answer, "I don't like that one, Mommy." And Catherine would smile and laugh; and Wyatt would laugh and turn circles on his creaking tricycle and pull back up and lean on the handlebars; and Catherine, ignoring her husband Will's order not to allow the tricycle in the house among valuable things, would put on another hat and say, "What do you think of this one, my little man?" And Wyatt would lean way back on the seat holding the red handle grips with the colored streamers and say, just to be silly, "I don't like that one, either!" And Catherine would make a face at him, and Wyatt would race his tricycle to the precipice of that set of shallow steps leading down into the hall, but draw up short, clamp down on the pedals just in time to save himself, while Catherine, standing behind him, watching his tiny square shoulders in the mirror, adjusted her hat and spoke both to her son and to her eyes in her reflection, "You're going over a cliff someday if you don't watch yourself, young man." And she frowned at her reflection and took another hat from a line of hats set on the gleaming chest, and said, "Your father doesn't like you riding that tricycle in the house. If you break anything, you're on your own."

And presently there boomed the muffled thump of hard little shoes on the stairway runner and then the staccato sound of hard little shoes on wood, and Virginia, aged eleven or perhaps twelve, came stomping into the living room, and Catherine said, "Goodness, must you *march* everywhere? You sould like a bass drum!" And Virginia, all exasperated by the twisted pleats of her skirt, said, "Mom-my!" And Catherine stooped and twisted the skirt into place and pulled up the knee socks, folding them over neatly, and with her bare narrow hand dusted the patent leathers, and Virginia, regarding the hat level with her eyes, said into the feathers and velvet, or felt or satin or straw, "I like your hat, Mommy." And Catherine laughed and standing up, said, "Ah, but your brother doesn't. Your brother doesn't like my hat at all!" And Wyatt rode his tricycle in frenzied circles, wrinkling and twisting the rugs into the shape of dog beds up and down the length of the long room, and they knew they would be in hot water with Elsie Moorecraft, the housekeeper, if they left the room like that, and they dashed everywhere straightening rugs and grabbing coats and gloves and shoes and hats and purses and cigarettes, and at last Catherine said, "Ready, chicks?"

And they'd start for the train that would take them into the city.

Catherine would drive the World War II army surplus jeep like a man (which is the only way anyone can drive an army jeep), and Wyatt would ride shotgun on the seat next to his mother while Virginia was tossed to the storm in the back, and Catherine might look at her son from behind the webby black veil fitted over her face, which to her son's eyes made her look mysterious and through which, on occasion, Wyatt sometimes kissed her, making horrible faces at the feel of the netting against his lips.

From time to time Catherine stretched up a little in the seat, and searching the rearview mirror, said, "Where's our Virginia? Is she there?" And Virginia scooted forward to lean between the seats. And whizzing along, up hill and down dale and over the river and through the woods, Catherine would sing to them "Miss Otis Regrets She's Unable to Lunch Today," half-speaking, half-singing these lines:

> When she woke up and found that
>   her dream of love had gone—Madam,
> She ran to the man who led her so far astray,
> And from under her velvet gown,
> She drew a gun and shot her lover down—Madam.
> Miss Otis regrets she's unable to lunch today!

And they would take the late morning Zephyr because it ran express from Aurora to Union Station in Chicago and because it had a club car, which is where they sat—at one of the window tables. Catherine, feeling already, as she had felt every day of her life since she could remember, a kind of trepidation, dread, and peril in life, would have a late morning start-me-out drink, while Wyatt put a toy Guernsey cow into the metal drink holder attached to the window ledge with little rails like a corral and Virginia twirled the paper parasol from her drink. Presently Catherine looked at her children with her clear, rich, deep brown eyes, which promised only a world of fun, and they looked back at her with eyes containing the same richness and promise, and they laughed at the time it took her eyelid to cover her eye and open again in a wink, and they all clicked glasses: Catherine's filled with straight bourbon on the rocks, Wyatt's filled with Coke on the rocks with a twist of lemon, Virginia's with some pink concoction that threatened to mambo at any minute. And the tracks went clickity-click, clickity-click; and presently they were in the high, dim, steaming station; and holding hands all in a line, they flowed with the flow of the detraining crowds out into the dazzling sunlight and the throbbing, excited city. Catherine whistled between her teeth and threw up an arm, and they clambered into the cab, the children scrambling for the beloved jump seats, and off they went, released into the day, sprung into the glorious dirty air like a three-headed jack-in-the-box.

And—goodness!—they had to shop, shop, shop!

Up the escalators at Field's they would go and down the escalators at Field's. Wyatt always stood next to Catherine, holding her hand, feeling the strength and shape of it through the gloves she wore—gloves that smelled richly of kid leather and perfume. Wyatt enjoyed the smooth, almost imperceptible movement of the unseen machinery, never letting himself think of that inevitable moment when he would have to step off, for he was sometimes uncertain how to coordinate his feet in order to make the enormous step from moving stairs to stationary floor. He'd stare at the place where the silver escalator steps flattened and disappeared into the silver grooves, feeling the relentless movement lifting him ever closer. With his eyes fixed straight ahead, he'd feel his nerve go, and then follow an exasperated tug forward from the gloved hand of his mother and find himself on solid ground—grateful in his little soul for solid floor.

They bought their father shirts and handkerchiefs and pajamas, and Wyatt those Buster Brown shoes clunky as miniature tanks, and, depending upon the season, little suits with short, blue or brown, itchy wool pants with beanies and knee socks to match, or cool seersucker shorts and white cotton T-shirts. They might buy Catherine one of her biannual Davidow suits, and Wyatt would roll on the rug of that clothes department where his mother shopped, until Catherine, exasperated, might say over her shoulder to his reflection in the fitting room mirror, "That's enough of *that*, young man!" The seamstress always seemed to cower on her knees on the floor with pins in her mouth, and Wyatt once wondered if she ever swallowed them, and if so, did they come through like pennies do when you swallow them? Virginia sprawled in a deep fitting-room chair, her neck resting against the low back so that she watched the whole procedure all along the length of her chest and belly while her legs dangled. Wyatt rushed at her suddenly, and grasping the chair arms, leaned forward to one side of her along the length of her body close up to her face, and peering into her eyes which crossed to meet his, smelled her sweet smell, which was the smell of childhood itself. Forehead to forehead they had a gigglefest until Catherine said, "And that's enough of *that*, too!"

Then the children were absolutely, utterly and unalterably bored, bored, bored!

And then—goodness!—it was time for lunch and they might go to Jacques or the Italian Court Restaurant, and Catherine would have two martinis or sometimes three, and then—goodness!—they had more shopping to do! Sometimes Wyatt almost wet his pants and they would have to find a men's room, and he had to go in all by himself and up to the urinals that seemed big enough to drown him. And then it was time to buy Virginia her brown or blue or plaid pleated wool skirts with knee socks to match, and Buster Brown shoes clunky as miniature tanks. One year Virginia had what Catherine called a "fit of pink." Everything, from underwear to hats, had to be pink, pink, pink! so that Virginia looked like a stick of peppermint candy. But that only lasted—thank God!—about six months.

And they would avoid all the toy departments in the world!

And then Catherine would say, "Goodness! It's almost four and your father isn't out of the office until five-thirty." And they'd have a drink in the Palmer House lobby or the Drake lobby and watch the people, and Catherine often said of any provocative set of buttocks that undulated past, "I'd get that dolly into a girdle so fast her head would swim!" Of a passing fur coat Catherine might sniff scornfully and say, "Dead cat, definitely dead cat!" And she might say of a passing man, "He's so ugly he's handsome." And of another man, slightly plump, "He looks like he'd be comfortable." And to Wyatt, who was a beautiful child, "You're so homely no one could love you but your mother!" And Wyatt believed her.

Then—goodness!—it was late, and they gathered up their gear, and up they sprang and off they hurried, Catherine saying, "Goodness! it's nearly five! Let's go, chicks!" The doorman's whistle shrieked and Catherine fumbled in her purse for a coin and pressed it into Wyatt's hand and he in turn slid it into the hand of the doorman. Inside the cab the children faced their mother from the jump seats, their hearts hurrying from the flurry, and she faced them from the backseat, and inevitably she would smile that slow, sad, tired smile and say, "Mother's had it, chicks," and then gaze thoughtfully out the cab window, or light a cigarette and retreat they knew not where.

So that is how they shopped, and this is how those hectic spring or autumn shopping days always seemed to end—with Catherine's exhausted retreat, a pulling away which the children, through habit, accepted. But on this day, on this bright, clear, gentle May afternoon in 1954, Virginia, for the first time challenged her mother's right of retreat, did not, as usual, sit quietly and pleasantly respecting the distance and waiting with an anxious smile for her mother to return.

No, that day in the cab Virginia said, "What's wrong, Mommy?"

Catherine regarded her daughter from that great, sad distance and answered softly, "What make's you think something's wrong, my little lamb?"

Virginia, maintaining her courage, answered, "Because you look so sad."

Catherine said, "Ah, little lamb, I am sad but nothing's wrong. Don't you sometimes feel sad when nothing's wrong?"

Virginia held her mother's eyes, thought a moment, and with characteristic frankness, replied, "No."

Catherine betrayed nothing, but gazed at her daughter a long time before she said softly, "Well, nothing's wrong."

She looked at her son, and saw on his face the pure, unconcealed concern, and reached forward with her gloved hand and ruffled his hair, and knew that he, too, in a way more silent and oblique than that of his sister, challenged her. There was a moment of decision, only a moment, before Catherine decided not to pursue this matter of sadness and its cause. She turned to the cab window again, dismissing them utterly. Presently the children found their own distance—Virginia, the window opposite the one out of which her mother gazed; Wyatt, the rear window where the shadow play of the May sun on the cars and people absorbed him.

And then they were at Will's law office, and old Miss Strong was there in the paneled reception area where she always seemed to be, with a yellow pencil buried in pulled-back gray hair behind one ear, smiling her usual yellow horse-teeth smile, saying, "Why Wyatt Parsons! And Virginia!" And she brought from the desk drawer, as always, the slightly sticky suckers, erasure crumbs clinging to the cellophane, and Miss Strong said, "And did you all have a pleasant day?" And the children smiled and nodded, and Miss Strong laughed and said, "Hello, Catherine." And Catherine said, "Children, thank Miss Strong for the candy." And the bold children, suddenly shy, chorused timidly, "Thank you, Aunt Cissy," and Catherine asked, "Is Johnny with a client?" And Miss Strong consulted her appointment book and said, "No, he's free." As the family moved off, Narcissa Strong waved an extravagant wave, because she remembered old Eldridge Shaw, Catherine's father, and that day over twenty years ago in 1933 when the great corporate pyramid Samuel Insull had built, piling willy-nilly one corporation atop another, trembled, swayed, collapsed, the dust settling in a pall over this firm and its clients—including Eldridge Shaw, who, late one afternoon, dragged a duffle bag full of Insull stock past Cissy Strong's desk and out the door and took it home and never spoke of it again, even when they apprehended Insull and his three millions on the high seas as he was fleeing in his yacht to Greece. She waved extravagantly because she knew Frank Parsons, Will's father, the Right Honorable Franklin Parsons, Judge Retired, Superior Court of Cook County, and she respected Judge Parsons because the Williston & Strong partners who practiced before him respected him. And Cissy Strong waved extravagantly because she adored Will Parsons in the way an aged virgin of a certain worldly turn of mine will often adore a handsome man, and in her adoration will forgive him anything.

So they go through the green leather doors into the partners' corridor and down the hall past the founders' portraits in gilt frames, men dressed in black with muttonchop whiskers, always a white shirtfront bathed in light, always some touch of gold—a watch chain, a ring, a book's golden spine. The partners' secretaries look up from behind desks through the doors of the outer offices, and they wave, and Wyatt waves, and Virginia waves, and Catherine waves; and at coffee breaks and in the ladies' room ensue conversations like this:

"Kate Parsons came in a little while ago. Did you see her?"

There is a discreet little pause and then one, leaning forward to circle her mouth with lipstick, ventures, "Was she drunk?"

The other, sharing the mirror, straightens her skirt and pulls in her belly and answers, "Yes. No! Probably! Honestly, who can tell?"

There might be another little pause in which a toilet is flushed and another ventures from the stall partition, "What is it Will Parsons does to make her drink?" And laughter follows.

The one applying her lipstick finishes with it, and blotting her mouth now with a Kleenex, answers, "Good question, but he's *so* good looking! Whatever he does, I'd put up with it."

The one coming out the stall door says, "Yes, he is good looking, but she could have had Johnny Graves!"

The one who has been smoothing her skirt and now is inspecting her teeth in the mirror for tobacco shards says, "Well, count your lucky stars she *didn't* want him!"

There followed laughter, which carried the hope that one of them might land him yet, though Johnny Graves seemed chronically afflicted with bachelorhood.

Then Catherine and the children are in Johnny Graves's office, and he is pitching paper airplanes at the wastebasket placed in the center of the room, and Catherine throws herself down in one of the leather chairs at either end of the leather couch and says, "God, what a day!" And groping in her purse for cigarettes adds, "Fix me a drink, will you, Johnny? I'm done in!"

Johnny does not move, but says morosely, "Coming right up," and he goes on for a moment folding the long, yellow, legal-sized paper airplane he was folding—or about to fold—when Catherine and the children came in, giving that airplane all his attention. He varied the design and folds several times a year, then gave it up. At age sixty-five he would be dead of a heart attack. Presently, though, he brings the bourbon bottle out of a desk drawer and pours some of the liquor into a glass and gets up from behind the desk and carries it over to Catherine, saying with a morose smile, "Here, Miz Parsons."

(In love he had been with Catherine—oh, years ago! years ago!—in love in his thorough, methodical way, so distracting and maddening and plodding and predictable to Catherine. She remembered sitting at summer dusk beneath the canvas canopy of the garden glider on the lawn of her father's summer place at Green Lake in Wisconsin. Dance music drifted across the water from the hotel on the other side, and the paper lanterns glowed along the footbridge leading to the little island in the cove beneath the sloping rise on which the house stood, and with her Scottie dogs curled around her evening slippers and Johnny's pumps, she had watched, across from her on the facing seat, Johnny's squat, powerful body positively quiver with the delicate love he seemed incapable of speaking. She remembered that, and then bending down to lift Heather, the white Scottie, onto her lap, and wanting to be on the water in the little sailboat rushing under the moon toward the light on the hotel pier. She remembered asking for a cigarette and admiring Johnny's enameled cigarette case, which she had admired at least a half dozen times before—anything to put off the inevitable. A distant trombone coming from across the water began "Someone to Watch Over Me" before the full orchestra picked up the song, and she knew they were dancing over there. Then Heather had yipped and stirred in her arms and she had hushed the dog, and she had waited and waited for Johnny to get the words out, and then had known the moment at which they were coming, and just as he brought himself to say, "Kate, I love you!" she was saying aloud at the same time, "You love me, I know," so that their words crisscrossed in the night air and she finished alone, "...but I don't love you." And the glider had stopped rocking, and Angie, the black Scottie, had rolled over on her back on the slatted platform at their feet, and Johnny had uttered a little cry, stricken to his soul in that soft summer silence. Presently, though, the war had come and Johnny had written for a commission and ended up on someone's staff. He'd gotten over that summer moment somehow. And now here he was—who would have thought it!—fifteen years later handing her a glass half filled with bonded bourbon and she nearly drunk, waiting for her husband in Johnny's office on a Friday afternoon in town with two children in tow!)

She took the glass from him in the old way—with a dazzling smile worn thin. And Johnny crossed to the desk and fixed one for himself, drank deeply, went on folding the paper airplane, and then pitched it toward the wastebasket in the middle of the room, surrounded by many paper crashes fallen short of the mark.

Catherine drank deeply, hungrily, then said, "Your clients should see you now, Johnny, drinking bourbon and flinging paper airplanes all over your office!"

And Johnny, folding another airplane and suppressing a rising bitterness answered, "Yep," and he smiled at her, and raising the airplane, holding it poised to throw, glanced at the children and said, "You two study hard and maybe someday a lot of rich people will pay you a lot of money to throw paper airplanes." And he flung the plane from him and it nose-dived almost directly in front of his desk. Then he rose in his chair to peer at the floor, shook his head in mock sadness, and said, "There's another one that's bit the dust." And he sat down and began folding another, struggling as he manipulated the paper to push away the bitterness, the anger.

Catherine laughed and took a long, nervous pull on her drink.

But the children sat quietly, Virginia at the farther end of the couch that was set at a right angle to her mother's chair, Wyatt next to his sister in a tall-backed, leather wing chair opposite Catherine, with a low table between them and on it the model yawl *Irene* in a glass case. The children knew that despite the paper airplanes, this was an intensely adult moment acted in an intensely adult place and to which, for now, they were utterly incidental; and so, in the manner of all well-trained children, they did not intrude. Instead, Virginia took up a *National Geographic* from the table next to her and began to page through it, and Wyatt scooted forward on the chair, bringing himself up close to the full-rigged model, and through a trick of imagination he'd learned early, saw himself on the deck of the model ship, looking up the spar, all of his concentration there so that the room sounds became a roar of blood in his ears.

There was a long pause in which Johnny sat looking at Catherine as she lay her head back against the chair and said quietly, "Oh, Johnny, must you be so *mournful*?" And she turned her head and looked at him and added softly, "Mournful Johnny Graves," dubbed him that day with that title, which is the name that stuck. From this moment on, whenever she spoke of him, she would often preface his name with "mournful."

Johnny chuckled and, unable to keep the bitterness from his voice, said, "Here's one gal who's got my number—yes sir!" He flipped the airplane meanly from his hand; it darted fast and true toward the basket, hitting the side with an audible crack.

"Umph," Johnny said, "almost but not quite." He looked at Catherine and repeated, "Almost, but not *quite*."

In return Catherine drew an arc in the air, as though erasing a chalkboard, and took a sip of her drink. "Let's not go down that garden path again, because there ain't nuttin' there, is there, Sweet Man? And it makes us tired, doesn't it? going down that path."

At his mother's words, Wyatt looked up quickly from the ship to meet his sister's eyes over the magazine cover. Their eyes held, exchanged a secret, then slipped away, and Wyatt's eyes glanced again over the deck of the *Irene,* which, a moment before, had been stabbing her spar into a wall of waves as tall as a house. His eyes only glanced over the deck, then trailed to Catherine, who was looking at Johnny sadly, as Johnny looked down into his lap behind the desk where he held his drink. Something vibrated in the air after Catherine spoke, something that was a loose end of a thing old and unsettled between Catherine and Johnny, and the children felt it. To the children it was like lying on your back on the grass at the start of a thunderstorm—the roiling clouds moving above you and the thunder rolling in wave after wave before the rain, and three trees turning the silver bellies of their leaves skyward. Yes, there was something between Catherine and Johnny which had nothing to do with the children and from which they were absolutely excluded.

Johnny said nothing, only morosely shifted in his chair, and as Wyatt watched, the sad look on Catherine's face held, transformed to exasperation; then, in a quick shift so typical of her, she composed herself. Never dropping a stitch, they began to discuss something else—certainly not Johnny's mournfulness, certainly not garden paths.

Catherine said, "Oh, we had such a time! The stores were so crowded you'd think it was Christmas! And these two need *everything*! And I need *everything*! And these two were always disappearing on me and they're too old for leashes. When they were small, I'd put them in harness because if I turned my back for a moment, they'd be gone. Women would come up to me in the stores and say, 'How can you be so cruel putting those children on leashes like dogs!' And I'd tug 'em in and say, 'My dear woman, if they were yours, you'd have them on leashes, too!' Oh, they're the going-est kids! Aren't you kids?"

And the children smiled proudly and Catherine smiled back. Then there was a silence and Catherine buoyed herself up, took a sip of her drink. And there came the familiar sound of the antique slave bracelets, massive and weighty, bought in Jamaica in '38, slipping down her wrist as she raised the glass—that distinct, flat sound of heavy silver hitting heavy silver that would always bring Wyatt to alertness. Years later, that sound on the grown-up Virginia's wrist, after Catherine was dead, brought Catherine back, the sound making Wyatt start and remember his mother.

Then without warning, without transition, Catherine utterly forgot herself and the place and the children. She could contain herself no longer and she cried aloud, "Oh, Johnny! Johnny!" The room stopped. The desperate, frightened tone of her voice, which Wyatt knew well, pushed him down, down, down, and he had a distinct sensation of falling or fainting. Behind the magazine, Virginia's lovely eyes, fixed on a color photograph of the water gardens at Hellbrunn Palace at Salzburg, winced as though she had been stuck with a needle, for she, too, knew the tone well, and she pulled her shoulders up and dropped them as in defeat. Behind his desk, Johnny Graves's hands gripped the lip of the middle drawer, and he looked at Catherine, who had covered her eyes with one hand, looked at her thoughtfully, softly, and the bitterness went, and he thought: *Ah, she needs me. Yes, she needs me, and I am here after all.* And for the first time since Catherine and the children entered the office, he relaxed.

He said her name softly—"Catherine"—and it was musical in his voice and calming to her, and it was not that he had nothing to offer her; the difficulty was that what he had to offer she could not and would not accept.

And Johnny knew it.

And so he did not offer in the usual way an old and beloved bachelor friend offers to help a married woman snared in a troubled marriage; that is, he did not offer himself. He did not raise his eyes to meet hers, did not say, his voice trembling, "Catherine, I have loved you for years. Come away with me and I will love you and cherish you and protect you. I will give you a new life." Instead, he only said her name: "Catherine." Calmed her by saying her name.

She expelled breath, emptied her glass, smiled weakly, looked at him for a moment, then said, trying to make her voice light, "Sorry, I don't know where *that* came from!"

Johnny pushed the thin hair back from his brow and answered, "That's okay," and knew that she loved her husband, had loved Will for thirteen years now and, Johnny Graves might have guessed, would still love Will fifteen years from this moment at the moment of Will's death, and would go on loving him in all the moments left to her before her own death. Her dying words, spoken to her daughter in the twilight of a Spanish afternoon with the Castilian sun long and gold-yellow through the balcony doors, will be: "I am tired." And then she will begin: "Your father...," as if to tell Virginia an important thing. But she will stop and only repeat, "I am very tired." And close her eyes. And the death rattle will come and she will be dead.

But now Catherine sighs, turns to the children—Virginia unmoving behind the magazine, Wyatt transfixed by the model ship before him—then looks into space, idly fiddling with the glass that she holds dangling from one hand at the end of the chair arm. Johnny glanced at Wyatt and Virginia, Catherine's sweet children, Catherine's tender creatures, both of them radiating their mother in every gesture, in the very pitch and range of their voices, and he felt his barrenness, knew his barrenness, and he wondered at his indifference toward Catherine's children, and thought: I have nothing left over for them. What little I have is for their mother.

So thinking, he pulled the bottle from the desk drawer and poured himself another drink, held the bottle poised, said Catherine's name as she sat with her head back, her throat exposed. She signed suddenly, looked over at him, and letting go of whatever it was that was deviling her, said, "Yes, pour me another." She stood suddenly in a blur of skirts and a clank of bracelets, and crossed to the desk, set her glass down on the blotter next to him. Johnny poured and Catherine picked up a folded airplane, and turning toward the wastebasket and balancing in exaggerated grace on one foot, flipped it into flight and cried, "Bingo!" when, to her great astonishment—and Johnny's—it dropped in a perfect dive into the wastebasket.

Johnny looked at her in astounded, dumb admiration—the way almost any male, at some point past his puberty, looks at a woman who succeeds at a man's game.

"Good Lord," he said, "I've been pitching all afternoon and there's not a plane in that basket. How'd you do that?"

Not waiting for an answer, he tore another yellow sheet from the legal pad, quickly folded it into an airplane, handed it to her, and said, "Take another shot!" And he leaned forward in his chair, arms resting on the desk, eyes moving in excitement from Catherine to the wastebasket, from the wastebasket to Catherine.

Catherine smiled faintly at him, threw one hip onto the corner of the desk, crossed her legs at the ankles with a whisper of nylon, and aware of Johnny watching her, straightened her spine, held the plane at ear level dramatically. Abdicating the seriousness of the game, she became a woman who, thinking herself unable to win a man's game, mocks it gently, the way some women wiggle their butts when they are at bat in softball. She released the plane and it glided straight away at the level it had been tossed, glided silently, dipped a little as though in feint as it passed high above the wastebasket, and went on across the room to land with a papery plop at the feet of Wyatt, who looked up startled from his contemplation of the model ship, looked at the plane, then at Johnny, then at his mother beaming at him from across the room.

And he smiled and squirmed, thinking there was some fun brewing.

And Catherine said to her son, "The sky is falling, Chicken Little!" And she held her hands out as though testing for rain. "Here comes the sky!" she said. "Here comes the sky!"

Wyatt, pretending astonishment, threw his hands over his head as though plaster was raining down from the ceiling, while Virginia, in imitation, drew the magazine over her ears, pulling it down like a stocking cap.

Then Catherine, cocking her head to one side, fixed the children with her bright eyes and began in a low, mysterious voice, the children quickly joining in as they all recited:

> My candle burns at both ends;
> It will not last the night;
> But, ah, my foes, and, oh, my friends—
> It gives a lovely light.

And then, while Johnny watched in astonishment, all three—Catherine, Virginia, and Wyatt—laughed themselves to silence, Catherine's long sigh at the end of the laughter bringing them down, settling them before they could start up some other hilarity.

Wyatt picked up the airplane that lay at his feet. This was a fold he had never seen. Eyes intent, he gazed at the needle sharpness of the nose, the neat symmetry of the wings forming a sharp-pointed pyramid, for he loved all boy-made things that ride the air. His face serious with concentration, he flipped the plane into a neat glide that went the length of the room, where it landed with a quiet plop among the messy disorder of Johnny's legal work shoved to one side on the desk. And when he looked at his mother and Johnny, he saw something had gone out of them, saw without knowing that he had seen, knew only that the fun had vanished almost before it began, that there had come a pause and a shift, and it bewildered him; he did not know what had happened to make the fun disappear.

But Virginia did.

Knew enough, at any rate, to take all this in stride. For Virginia is serene in herself, lives contentedly, floats on the surface of things, sympathetic but detached. Even now, as her mother stares blankly at the carpet of Johnny Graves's office while Johnny pretends to read some document, Virginia twists a lock of hair in concentration as she looks at the pictures in the magazine. Her life goes on. Her life does not pause and wait breathless, as her brother's does. No, she only looks at the pictures, holds nothing off as her brother would by looking at the pictures. She has nothing on her mind but the pictures: the heavy stone cords, thick as bull snakes, in a beard on a stone face which jets water from a stone mouth into a garden pool where golden carp hover blurred just beneath the olive surface of the rippling water. She sees that, and thinks of the enormous goldfish tanks set into the walls of the stairway landings of a building in Oak Park where the dentist's office is, thinks of other fish tanks in the shape of portholes just across the swaying, rope-slung gangplank at the Cape Cod Room and how the maitre d', seeing any child in an adult party, will always tap the tank with his fingertips to make the fish come to the glass and then tell the child the fishes' names—"This is Billy and Alvin and Mean Martha," he will say to the astonished child staring open-mouthed and wide-eyed at this phenomenon of fish.

No, this shift, this pause, this silence that comes over the room does not hold Virginia in breathless, stomach-churning suspense as it holds her brother and mother and Johnny Graves. They all sit, eyes concealed or cast away, while Virginia quietly turns the page, and goes on thinking of fish and water.

But now from his vantage point behind the desk, Johnny looks at Catherine's heavy, rich hair gathered at the back of her skull; he has not touched that hair in fourteen years, and his palms tingle at the thought. Then he sees, in profile, Catherine's face suddenly drain of color and her eyes fix on some sight that is not here in this law office, and Johnny's eyes follow hers to that wide clear space of gray carpeting beyond the desk, that pond of carpeting, the midpoint of which is the green leather wastebasket and the yellow airplanes bobbing, moving on the gray shimmering surface of *things*.

And as Johnny watches, he sees her tremble through the light fabric of her daffodil yellow suit.

"Kate," Johnny says softly.

And from across the office Wyatt watches his mother's face and he knows that look. He has seen it when his mother was unaware, seen it as Catherine sat among the chairs and sofas and tables of the long living room of an afternoon in that pause in the day when Moorecraft leaves and before his father comes in from the train—a look infinitely sad, a look that remains for a second after he calls to her, then steals away as she smiles and says, "Hello, my little man!" and holds out a hand to him. And Virginia, too, has seen it, peering over the bannisters, watching her mother wearily climb the stairs, the look there on her face as she rounds the stair window landing and continues up the last flight of steps, at the top of which her daughter stands.

And then Catherine's staring eyes flicker up from the carpet and she sees them all looking at her, and her eyes flash with life, and in a sudden movement, she strides with a whip of skirts the length of the room, opens a door there at the farther end where the children sit, does not look at them as their eyes follow her, but says to Johnny in a strong, decisive voice, "Come out here, Johnny, I want to talk to you."

And the children shifted uneasily as Johnny got up from behind the desk and they watched as he followed their mother from the room, sat silently as the door closed behind Johnny and they were alone, bobbing in the wake these two striding adults left behind them.

Johnny and Catherine stood on a narrow balcony stack of the law firm library, Johnny's head almost brushing the plaster rosettes of the ceiling, enveloped in heat and the smell of calfskin rising from the stacks below—the dry, logical smell of law books, a smell that always gave Johnny great pleasure, quickened his senses, heightened his concentration, and did so now as he gazed out over the room at the blue-shaded stack lights, and the heavy, leather-topped tables, and the place where he always sat in a window alcove, his papers spread out around him, reading and dozing, sometimes far into his bachelor nights.

But now he stands just behind Catherine, who faces out over the room, her hands resting lightly on the top rail of the balcony, stands bathed on this May afternoon in the easy west light coming from the row of tall windows to one side, light that will be killing in August— harsh, hot, and yellow—but now is the gentle, soft, promising light of the season.

With a great creak of the balcony floor, Johnny comes forward beside her, and for a moment he has the distinct memory and sensation of what it was like to stand with her like this long ago at Green Lake at the rail of the long footbridge leading from the sand beach to the little island with its putting green and flag in the middle of the cove—the third hole of her father's little par-three golf course. That sensation comes back to him, and the summer smells of her dusting powder and the linen of her summer dress, and his own smell of sunburnt male flesh from a day spent on the water, rising warm and tingling from inside his shirt. How he unfolded to let the world in! How the world took his invitation and entered! And they both felt a hush and suspension in the air that brought them to peak clarity so that their senses were as sharp and clear as the air and the light. Alive they were, in an alive, animated world, and her silent smile told him she knew what he knew. And he thought then that because she felt what he felt that she should love him as he loved her. He believed then that an intensely felt and shared knowledge between a man and a woman should lead naturally to love, and most tragically, believed it now, could not stop believing to suit what the world thought he ought to believe, and he saw in the stones of her wedding band and engagement ring, and against her lovely skin and in the highlights of her hair and along the boards of the floor and here and there and everywhere in the enormous room, the terrible glinting beauty of the light.

And then he spoke. "What's this all about, Kate?" he asked.

"Will doesn't love me...," she began.

And Johnny sank.

"And he probably never did," she continued. "I was driving home a few weeks ago and it struck, just heaved up from somewhere. And a curve came up and I couldn't move my arms to turn the wheel or my legs to stop the car, and I just kept going straight into the ditch. It was so odd. I just sat there staring straight ahead thinking my husband doesn't love me and knowing the groceries were all over the back seat."

The light in this room, Johnny thought, has not changed.

"Imagine," Catherine said, "after thirteen years I suddenly realize my husband doesn't love me. Not that he's *stopped* loving me, which I suppose a lot of women realize about their husbands and in a lot less time, too, but that *he never did love me*! It's very odd, you know, to realize that. Very odd indeed."

Johnny looked at her, did not know what to say or do, except that he must not touch her under any circumstances.

"Do you know what I did, Johnny? I knelt on the front seat and reached over and began gathering up the grapefruit and apples and bananas that had flown everywhere, and suddenly I saw how ridiculous I must look and I got the giggles. I was trembling and giggling and weeping and picking up heads of lettuce and green beans and I knew I was going to have to get Mr. Jorgensen and his tractor to pull the car out. I was going to have to knock on that old reprobate's door and say, 'Dear Mr. Jorgenson, I'm in the ditch again, can you pull me out?' And he was going to mutter and sputter and damn all women allowed behind the wheels of automobiles because he's pulled me out of that ditch a lot when it's slippery—it's just an impossible curve when it's slippery because you approach it from a steep, short hill, and I always say, 'Hold onto your hats, chicks, we're going in!' And the children love it. They cheer. They call it 'Mommy's Ditch.' They get that from Will, who always slows down to show it as a point of interest to guests. 'That's my wife's ditch,' he'll say, 'where she spends her winters. Most people go to Arizona or Palm Beach. My wife goes in that ditch!'" And she sighed and looked up at Johnny for a moment and then looked out over the room as she continued, "So now I know. Now I know there's nothing I can do." And she looked at Johnny again, at his craggy face, a mass of heavy features that seemed pinched from clay by a child's fat fingers, and she saw his pained eyes and she thought: Poor man, to be subjected to this!

"Kate," Johnny said, "I'm sorry for you, Kate, I—"

But she cut him off with a toss of her head.

"No," she said, "no, I've told you more than I'd ever tell anyone and I'm not going to tell you any more."

Below them old Tommy Hauser shuffled into the stacks, nudging before him a wooden cart piled high with books, and began slowly and painfully lifting them to their places on the shelves, humming to himself as he worked—this idiot grandson of one of the firm's founders.

Suddenly Catherine said, "Be my friend, Johnny, will you? And don't ask me any questions." Her eyes sparkled and she said, "Consider this a legal consultation and send me a bill."

Smoothing her skirt, touching her hair, she drew back her shoulders and said, "Well, let's go back and wait for Will, shall we, Johnny?" Then, "You're a sweet man, Johnny, and a good man." She waited for him to open the door, which, after a pause, he did. Brushing past him, she entered the office, walked straight to his desk, turned, braced herself against the edge with two hands down at her sides, and, raising her chin, said lightly to the children, "Well, chicks, how's tricks?"

And she smiled, and smiled, and smiled, as the children chattered, and chattered, and chattered.

But Johnny stood in the open door to the library, the penetrating west light behind him and before him—light dazzling and wonderful and rich over the room and the people—and he thought that the summer lawns of fourteen years ago were at last gone and this woman had slipped away from him again. And he has been growing new skin ever since that summer she had told him she didn't love him, is, even now, growing new skin over new skin—for a moment ago, on the library balcony, she took skin from him again.

And Cathering, watching the children as they speak and laugh and squirm, thinks: They are brave little chicks. We've taught them that, I think, to be brave. And thinks: Tonight I'll say across the space of the beds, "Will, our children are very brave. We've done that right, at least. We've equipped them for the world."

And she looks at Johnny standing in the doorway and says, "Come over here, Mournful John, and pour me a drink, will you?"

Presently and without announcement, Will opened the door, stood a moment leaning into the silence of the room, his tie swaying from the open tan suitcoat, saw them all—Catherine, Johnny, Wyatt, and Virginia. Catherine turned from where she stood braced against Johnny's desk, as Will, ignoring her for a moment, looked at Johnny, who perched on a corner of the desk beyond Catherine, and said to him in the way a man says such things to another man he has seen on and off all day, "Afternoon, Johnny." Johnny nodded silently, looked down at his hands, turned them over nervously, and not knowing what to do with them, crossed them under his arms. Only then did Will look mildly and neutrally at Catherine as he said, "Cissy told me you were here." His look was cold as he thought, She is drunk already—or nearly so.

And then he called down the room to his son, "Hi, Buckaroo!" And Wyatt called, "Hi, Daddy!" And Virginia peeked over the yellow cover of the *National Geographic* she was reading, her eyes dancing, and Will drew back in mock surprise and said, "Oh, that's *Virginia* behind that magazine! For a moment I thought it was Grace Kelly descended from the clouds!"

And Virginia, delighted, covered her face with the magazine and then pulled it away and smiled, smiled, smiled. And there existed between Will and his daughter a simple, uncomplicated ease, an easy distance across which they loved, a distance that allowed delight and ease in love. In Virginia's ease Will found his own—a nonchalant love with its own rhythm.

And in a rush and flurry the children were around him, pulling him into the room, tugging his fingers, stretching for kisses, dancing in place, telling him in piping voices of their day, all in a rush, telling him of train rides and taxi rides and jump seats, and a woman they had seen with a missing nose, and a doorman with a three-note whistle, and Baked Alaska afire; and even as Will listened and touched and patted and smoothed them, he could feel his wife's eyes unwavering on him, glassy and bright, looking at him over the scramble of the children, as he said, "Yes, yes, yes, what fun! No kidding!" to their eager stories and eager questions, but knew Catherine's eyes were upon him—Catherine's eyes.

Ever since Catherine had known him, Will could not enter a room without her vivid awareness of him; at dinner parties she would find his eyes down or across the table as if to say, "Oh, yes, they've separated us, but, darling, there you are and here I am!" At her own table she was always jumping up to move the candles or the flowers, saying, "There! now I don't have to crick my neck to see you!" When that happened, he felt confined and subdued and he would do everything to avoid meeting those eyes and the sad, sweet smile she prepared just for him.

As the children continued to babble and dance, Will's eyes met his wife's and he saw the pleasure there heightened by a playful, drunken edge, and he did not know what infuriated him more: the pleasure which he could not return, or the drunken edge which he could not control.

Drawing a child to either side of him, he placed one hand on his son's glossy hair and settled the other lightly on his daughter's shoulder, his touch quieting them, and having achieved the stillness he needed, he said lightly to the pleasure and booze-edge in Catherine's eyes, "How much have you had to drink today, my girl?" Sent those words to her light as bubbles, and the cruelty was conscious and wanton, but he could not control himself and he knew that had he controlled himself in this moment, there would be other moments left in this day and in this marriage when he would have stabbed and wounded her. And he could not retract. He was years beyond retraction.

And Catherine's eyes winced, but she raised her glass in mock salute, and just before she drank, said with heavy and unmistakable irony, "Dear husband! My dear husband, I'm so grateful for your concern!"

And Johnny Graves groaned.

In a smooth motion, Johnny swung away from the corner of the desk—where he had been perched since before Will came in—and settled lightly in his chair behind the desk. There, with a creak of springs, he leaned back and regarded them all. With his even breathing lifting his massive chest beneath the white of his shirt front, he looked at them with the peculiar detachment of a man far gone in melancholy and, therefore, detached from all life. Yet, paradoxically, Johnny's detachment allowed him to feel an infinite and sad kindness toward all living things. He felt that infinite, sad kindness now, and looking first at Catherine, then at Will and the children, he thought suddenly, All this will end badly some day.

Disturbed by the thought, and clumsily trying to cover this most awkward of awkward moments, he heard himself say idiotically, "Can I pour you a drink, Will?"

"Sure," Will said, "sure, why not?"

He pushed the children lightly away and they moved quickly to their places at the other end of the office. But sending the children off is not a neat disposal, Will knows, and he knows there will be few moments in this marriage and family that will be easy and uncomplicated. No, Will thinks, nothing is neat. Everything—even the light gesture of sending the children away after he attacked their mother—has a complication, for the children see and understand and make this complex thing between their parents their own; even now it has settled in their hearts like sharp stones.

So thinking, Will inserted a finger into the watch pocket of his trousers, felt the warm metal there against his belly, and heard the faint, expensive chitter of the timepiece.

Johnny picked up his glass and in a quick gulp emptied it. Bending to the desk drawer, he fumbled for the bottle, brought it out with another glass, carefully poured Will a stiff drink, stretched forward past Catherine, who was still braced against the front of the desk with her head down and her eyes closed, to set the drink on the corner of the desk nearest to the corridor door where Will stood, then poured himself an even stronger one. Now Johnny knew that he would not move from this office for the rest of the night, that he would sit in this office drinking quietly until he could drink no more, and he would sleep on the couch and wake with foul mouth and throbbing head in the early light, and outside the office windows would be a soft and marvelous May morning, which might or might not save him, and if it did not, then he would be drunk for days.

Will came forward then, his shoulder almost touching his wife's as he took the glass from the desk and raised it to his lips. Catherine quickly rose at her husband's approach as though stung, moved off a few steps and stood there with her back to her husband and the desk behind which Johnny sat. For a moment the room settled into the silence of serious drinkers—three people drinking not for the pleasure of drink, but drinking to hold off the silence surrounding them and all that the silence contains.

Catherine wandered aimlessly to the windows, paced along the length of the long room, then turned, leaned against a wall at the farthest point from her husband that the room would allow. Johnny, seeing her watching Will and Will watching her, thought again, All this will end badly. Catherine paced the length of the room again—a dangerous moment—Will watching her every move, Wyatt and Virginia watching her. Abruptly, she sat on the middle sill, looked again at her husband, who sat braced against the desk facing her. For a moment, her eyes met Johnny's where he sat just behind Will. Then her eyes returned to Will's and she said, softly and directly to him, "Your children were very good today. They're becoming quite civilized, aren't you, chicks?" She did not look at the children, even though she addressed them, but kept her eyes on Will.

The children giggled nervously and Catherine smiled, but her eyes stayed fixed on Will, who did not move or speak. She watched him anxiously, for she had made an offering of love.

"I'm glad to hear that," Will said quietly, after a time.

Catherine smiled weakly. And she was grateful. But still the room hung fire.

He put one hand in his suitcoat pocket, felt there the gold-netted case of a forgotten fountain pen he had been searching for all day. Bringing the pen from his side pocket and transferring it to his inside pocket, Will repeated the words, "Yes, I'm very glad to hear that." He looked down at the glass between the fingers of his two hands. He had received Catherine's offering in the way you take something that you don't want but that is pressed upon you. In thirteen years of marriage he was nearly buried in offerings taken and set aside. Like that gold-netted fountain pen which she had bought and wrapped and put besides his napkin at breakfast. He had glanced at the package, then, while she eagerly watched, had opened it slowly, setting the paper neatly aside. There it had been when he opened the leather case—that remarkable, beautiful object glinting up at him. "Thank you," he had said almost immediately and had gone dutifully to her, touched her shoulder, bent down to her mouth, letting his lips linger on hers because he knew that would please her. He returned so little. What he did return was returned lightly in feather touches with his fingers on a shoulder, or feather touches with his lips on a bare neck that said, "I don't deserve what you offer," and what he returned was only enough to hold all this together: a marriage, children, a complex financial entanglement.

"Nobody peed in their pants, eh?" Will said, looking up at the children. "No one vomited on the shoe salesman, eh?" He looked again at his wife.

I bruise too easily, Catherine thought, I must pick myself up and not let myself bruise so easily. I must not be so given to him that I have nothing left for myself or my children.

That is what she thought now, but alone, later, she would regard her image in the darkened living room mirror and see that badge and beacon of booze—the drinker's red-tipped nose—and say aloud to that image, "Kate, darling, you're going to hell in a handbasket!" She would take out the combs and the heavy hair would fall and she would whisper, "Kate, dear woman, you're going to rack and to ruin!" Reflected in the dark glass, she would see Will's ghostly image appear beside her own, his features pale as her own, his white shirt front glowing in the old glass, and then his arms would be around her, holding her with one arm around her waist like a sash and the other across her breasts, and she would shudder as that hopeless love surged in her.

So she sat braced against the window sill of Johnny Graves's office and let go—stopped resisting Will long enough to realize that she was woozy, but not so woozy that if she stopped drinking now she would be sober and merely tired by the time they got home, and they would not continue this, but go silently and without angry words to bed, where, in the early light of the May morning, they would have their awful compromise.

So thinking, she said with great effort to Johnny, who looked up at her from behind the desk, "Johnny, come to dinner on Sunday, if you want. We've got a crowd coming."

Will, loosening his taut body, a loosening visible to the entire room, brushed invisible cigarette ashes from his trouser front and said quickly, "Yes, come early. Make it a day. Or come tomorrow if you don't mind sleeping on the library couch. We've got the Hoyts staying over until Monday."

Yes, Catherine thought, thank God for the Hoyts. Thank God for the crowd on Sunday. Thank God for all the people we use to fill up the void in which we live. God rest the merry gentlemen every one!

"Maybe I will," Johnny said.

"Oh, now he's playing hard to get!" Catherine said to Will. "He's keeping us in suspense. We'll be hanging at the windows dawn to dusk wondering if our Johnny's coming. Oh, we'll send the children down to the blacktop with flowers. You children will sit on the fence with bouquets and wait for Johnny, won't you?"

The children nodded vigorously.

"You see," Catherine said, "they'd adore it."

"All right," Johnny said, "I'll come tomorrow. Early afternoon." But he knew he wouldn't.

"Perfect!" Catherine said. "And now I want another drink and then I want to go home." She started to cross quickly from the middle window toward the desk, but Will's voice brought her up short in the middle of the room:

"No!" Will shouted, banging his empty glass down on Johnny's desk with a sharp, explosive sound.

Catherine winced and closed her eyes at the sound, but came forward so that she stood close to where Will leaned against the desk. She held her glass out, looking all the time at Johnny, who sat behind the desk, as she said quietly, "Pour me another one, will you please, Johnny? A short one, because my husband here thinks I'm getting drunk." She drew the glass back and turning suddenly to Will, who was not two feet from her, said, "How dare you! How dare you object to what I want! Do I object to what *you* want?" And suddenly bold, she set her glass down. "Have I *ever* objected to you?" She edged the glass toward Johnny, then turned to look defiantly at Will and moved so close that they stood almost eye to eye.

Will jutted his chin out and snorted, his small, compact body vibrating with anger, and he said in a voice awful in its deadly quietness, "Yes, my girl, you do. And often. Very often."

"That's so," Catherine said with a nervous smile and nervous eyes. "You're right. I do object. Strenuously." And she added slyly with the brilliant logic of an accomplished verbal brawler, "Which is why, if you haven't already guessed, I want another drink."

Will shook his head and said, "All right, damn you! have another drink! Have the whole goddamned bottle if you want!"

Catherine leaned close to her husband and said in a voice so low Will could barely make out the words, "Just because you have a little tassel dangling on the front of you, doesn't give you the right to *order* me to do *anything*!" Will snorted again and shook his head disdainfully, but Catherine's words had disarmed him, as she had intended they should.

Catherine turned back to Johnny, who held her eyes with his own. As she watched his thoughtful and concerned eyes, they pained all at once. He said, "I think the bar's closed for today."

At those words, Catherine seemed to hover a moment between the two men, one behind the desk, the other in front of the desk beside her. She became aware of the faint, exhausted smell of their Bay Rum aftershave and her eyes danced with amused power as she said to Johnny, "Cutting me off, eh?" With a brittle smile added, "Ganging up on me, eh?" Then, "Aren't you—oh, just a little, Johnny—interfering in my marriage?"

"Yes," Johnny answered frankly, "yes to all those questions." And he looked toward Will, who leaned on the desk with his head down, one hand across his eyes like a visor, as he massaged his temples and shook his head.

"I could impugn your character, you know," Catherine said, smiling.

"Yep," Johnny said, still watching Will, "you could, but that wouldn't make me open the bar." Will took his hand away from his eyes and smiled gratefully at Johnny, who returned the smile.

Then it was the three of them poised a moment in that rich, rose-colored, hopeful light that washed them head to toe, making their skin blush luminous and beautiful. They were no longer young, but far, far from old, yet shaken out now, cast in themselves, characters fully formed. That light colored them and made the daffodil yellow of Catherine's suit deep against the dark color of Johnny's desk and sharp against the deep gray of the carpet. Here, before Catherine in the persons of these two men, were the most important choices of her life: the choice she made and the choice she might have made. From the other end of the office, Wyatt watched them, not knowing yet—though he would know in time—that they were the most definite, palpable people he had ever known, that the force of them would not diminish with the years, that their force would, indeed, increase. They would remain to the end of their days—and beyond in Wyatt's memory of them—stunningly stubborn, magnificently selfish, and always, always, utterly and unalterably themselves.

Catherine's eyes swept over the children, who regarded her with troubled, serious looks and seemed ready to burst with something they dared not show. Little Judges, Catherine thought, looking at them, little Their Honors—and they get that from their father!

There was an uneasy stir in the room as everyone shifted slightly in place, followed by silence. From beyond the closed office door came the sounds of the firm beginning to empty for the weekend—muffled voices, doors opening and closing, muffled laughter—and suddenly everyone became aware of the abrupt, sharp sounds of car horns and the clatter of el trains penetrating the room from the window side.

Catherine sighed, gave it up.

"And now I really want to go home," she said. She looked at the children and said, "It would be very kind of you two if you picked up those paper airplanes for Johnny." The children dutifully started to rise.

But Johnny said quickly, "No, don't bother."

Catherine looked at Virginia and said, "Well then, who's got to powder her nose? This is your last chance before we get home."

She turned and looked sadly at Will, her face filled with an appeal that he acknowledged blankly. Then she brushed past him, put one hand on the doorknob and said, "Come on, Ginny." Virginia stood, followed her mother from the room. In the corridor someone called, "Kate Shaw! How *are* you? And is this Virginia?" Then the door closed and there was another silence in which Will looked thoughtfully for a long time at his son.

And Wyatt was afraid.

And then Johnny burst out, "Is it that bad? I can't believe it's that bad!"

Will was pale in the rose light, beautifully pale, thought Johnny, what with his black hair and his blue eyes. Will twisted his neck from side to side to relieve the tension in his body and replied, "Yes, sometimes, but not always." His tone was mild and low, and he lowered his head, ran a finger around the inside of his collar, looked at Johnny, and said, "You've seen it often enough. As a matter of fact, it was almost yours to handle." And he smiled widely, and chuckled, and Johnny colored faintly.

Again Will looked the length of the office at his son. Without forethought, without conscious calculation—or so Will told himself later—he said, "Ah, Johnny, it's the loneliest thing in the world!"

And Wyatt stared at his father and Will saw the tousled hair so like Catherine's in color and texture, the sweet face and vulnerable eyes so like his mother's, and the child perplexed him, confounded him. What does he know? Will wondered. What does he understand? And in that moment, Will let go of the line, cast off, began in that deep rose light the slow, slow drift away from his son, though Will did not know that he had begun to drift, and that the pulling away from Wyatt would, from now on, make the boy wild for possession of him and would lead to the inevitable showdown, the inevitable calling out, awful and leveling: a moment on the stairs in the twilight of a deep winter afternoon when Wyatt was fourteen and while Catherine lay drunk and howling, her back curled and pressed against the spindles of the bannister on the floor above them, in that stairwell that magnified her howls a hundred times. And Wyatt will stand in silhouette four steps above his father while Will stands exposed in the thin light from the landing window behind Wyatt—his gray, handsome, weary face upturned in awful revelation to the window light. Wyatt, the sobs heaving up from a deep place inside him where for years something has lived tensed and coiled and now is released, will say, "Why don't you love me? What have I *done*?" repeating that question over and over again, until his father does not know which sound—his wife's drunken howls or his son's broken sobs—is the more awful. But he will do this: touch the boy, stand on the same step and rest his hand on the boy's shoulder and say so softly the words seem breathed rather than spoken, "I love you, son, believe that I do." And that moment and that touch will mark the beginning of a tentative rapprochement that will continue, growing slowly over the next seven years but ending abruptly with Will's death a week before his son's twenty-first birthday; and in the empty years after that untimely event Wyatt will think, I was just beginning to get to know him, just beginning, and then one morning he was dead and his death was the one thing of all the things possible on this earth and in this life that I did not *expect*.

But now, in Johnny's office, Wyatt, at age seven, meets his father's thoughtful look and is afraid.

Then Will, in slow, deliberate, extremely orderly and calculated gestures, punctuated by many thoughtful pauses, lit a cigarette, held it in two fingers along his cheek, exhaling smoke slowly from his nose. Clicking his lighter three distinct times, he looked down at the carpet and the expensive gleam of his shoes.

Wyatt sat seething with his mother's passion and his father's detachment—at war even now in his small body. With great effort, he scooted forward on the chair through the soundlessness until he found himself kneeling on the floor looking into the case that covered the ship, the fingers of both his hands caressing in circular, smooth motions the brass-capped corners of the glass.

All his life he would remember Johnny Graves's model yawl *Irene*.

The stalwart beauty of her canvas stiff with invisble wind, the graceful thrust and curve of her timbers, the smooth varnished decks, the tiny wooden turnings of her rails, the miniature braiding of her lines, the infinitesimal brass mountings of her wheel—all those things he would remember.

The ship would sail into his mind, at age thirty-three, the last time he saw Johnny Graves standing on Madison Street in the twilight of a damp and penetrating March afternoon. The curved buttresses of the new First National Bank building thrust up five stories above him to disappear into the soaring, overpowering expanse of that enormous structure. Wyatt, wandering in preoccupation around the streets of the Loop, nearly ran into him, and starting to alertness, drew back.

The years had drawn out Johnny's squareness, dissolved the flesh from around the bones. He stood tall, thin, gaunt, in the gloom at the curb, holding a white-tipped cane and facing the lights of the traffic of Madison Street, turning his head from side to side, cocking it queerly now and then as though listening for something—perhaps the familiar idle of the engine of his car, perhaps his driver's voice. He wore thick, heavy glasses, behind which his pale eyes swam, and Wyatt stood a long time looking at him before he comprehended the accoutrements of blindness. He approached across the glistening, fine mud film of the sticky sidewalk, speaking before he touched Johnny's arm, saying quietly so as not to startle the man, "Johnny, it's Wyatt Parsons, Catherine's son."

Johnny seemed not to hear, though he stiffened slightly and kept turning his head this way and that as though in agitation.

"Johnny," Wyatt repeated firmly this time, "it's Wyatt Parsons, Will's son. You used to come to our house in the country."

But Johnny turned from the sound of Wyatt's voice, drawing his arm and cane away.

"I'm blind," Johnny said bitterly.

For a moment Wyatt did not know what Johnny meant, and then said stupidly, "But how are you?"

Again he touched Johnny's arm, and again Johnny shook off the touch and said angrily, "I said, young man, I'm blind!" He turned those pale, swimming eyes on Wyatt, eyes made huge by the thick lenses of the glasses. Wyatt looked at him in surprise for a long time and then, shaken and hurt, turned and started away, but was stopped by the west-flowing crowd moving like some enormous living entity all the way from Michigan Avenue, several blocks to the east, to the commuter train stations beyond the west boundary of the Loop.

"Boy!" Johnny called, perhaps hearing Wyatt's retreating footsteps, his eyes searching the blur, trying to find the shape of the boy among the many shapes. "Wyatt!" he called, and then waited, and then said to the air, for he could not be sure that Wyatt stood there, "Your mother—is she dead?"

Wyatt, only a few feet off, stopped, arrested in his flight. He had not expected this. He had not known what to expect, and now he had this. He froze with a clutching awful grief. He could not speak. He could only stare at Johnny, who was trying to form his face into something that was friendly but could not do it.

"Yes," Wyatt said hoarsely. "Yes, almost ten years now."

Johnny, speaking to the air, answered in a tone you use in talking to yourself. "That's what I'd heard," he said. He repeated it to the air, to the March twilight, which was only a darkness beyond his own darkness—"That's what I'd heard."

Then he faced forward again, and cocking his head this way and that, tapped the cane sharply, impatiently, in short bursts of sound against the sidewalk. And Wyatt thought that if he dared say another word, if he dared make another move toward Johnny, he might release some enormous spring coiled in the man that would catapult Johnny into traffic.

Why, Wyatt thought, suddenly comprehending, I might kill him if I persist in this! *I might kill him if I make another move!*

Hey, Liberal

Shawn Shiflett

Hey, Liberal is a story about the experience of students in a predominately black, gang-ridden high school in Chicago during the year 1969, approximately one year after the assassination of Martin Luther King, Jr. The novel, which deals with the complex problems of such a school situation, is a strongly paced story, with vivid characters and narrative movement, interesting situations, and many wildly funny "educational" scenes, as well as very serious scenes, plus keen observations about teaching and learning.

The two principal characters, Simon Fleming and Louis Collins, are both white and come from liberal, middle-class families. Their fathers, both Protestant ministers, were deeply involved in the non-violent civil rights movement of the early sixties. Though the story keeps centrally to Simon, the point of view moves frequently to other students, and to teachers, parents, policemen, an administrator, and occasionally to an overall point of view, so that we get a comprehensive narrative sense of what is happening to this school, these participants, at that time in our history. In the riot-convulsed school, the story carries one boy to suicide, another to death in gang warfare, a teacher to being treated brutally by police, and Simon through many bizarre and difficult experiences. In the midst of it all there is a teenage love affair. *Hey, Liberal* focuses on Simon's and Louis's struggle for survival, identity, and an understanding of the hostile environment in which they find themselves.

Shawn Shiflett was born and raised in Chicago and lives in the Lake View neighborhood on Chicago's North Side. He received his M.A. degree at Central State Oklahoma University and is currently a Story Workshop Director in the Writing/English department at Columbia College. He recently was awarded an Illinois Arts Council Artists Fellowship and has had stories published in *Nicotine Soup, Angels in My Oven, The Story Workshop Reader, Writing from Start to Finish,* and *Privates* magazine. He was featured in the 1985 fall issue of *Chicago Singles* magazine.

From *Hey, Liberal*

Louis

By Shawn Shiflett

So one day, on his way home from school, Simon is walking down Webster Avenue—long fast strides, staring straight down at the sidewalk as if thinking about vitally important business—when, suddenly, someone driving a red VW comes tearing down the street, slams on the brakes, does a complete about-face spin, grinds the gears back into first, and jumps the high curb right next to Simon without somehow busting an axle. The car dee-stroys someone's front lawn and stops just inches in front of Simon, pinning him up against a tall wrought-iron fence. He stands there with his arms stretched out to either side, like he's Jesus Christ on the cross, and with the screech of tires still in his ears and his heart pounding up into his head, he looks to see who the hell the madman is behind the wheel. Louis, grinning his bloodshot, stoned-out grin and wearing his beat-up, leather Air Force jacket, leans out the window and, just like Bugs Bunny, holds his hand up to his mouth as if chomping on a carrot.

"Ahhhhh, what's up, Doc?"

Simon barely managed to say, "What the...what the fuck's wrong with you?" but Louis just revved the engine a couple of times.

"Come on, liberal, I ain't got all day. Get in the car."

Neighbors peered out the windows of their newly renovated three-story, Victorian houses to check and see if there had been a wreck. Simon looked all around as if more concerned with who was watching him than whether his bones were still intact.

"Will ya get outa here, Louis?" He squeezed past the car's bumper and walked fast down the sidewalk; but Louis wouldn't leave him alone and backed the car up, then idled it forward right behind Simon. The car's right tires rolled along the sidewalk while the left ones stay-pressed everyone's parkway lawn.

"Come on, liberal, let's go. I ain't got all fuckin' day. I plan on being in California by midnight."

Without looking up from the sidewalk, Simon waved his hand down by his side, trying to shoo the car away as if it were a stray dog. He came to the end of the block and crossed the street, but Louis followed right along in the VW, the car bouncing on its shock absorbers as it rolled off the high curb of one block, then back up the high curb of the next block, continuing down the sidewalk.

"You're gettin' me mad, liberal, and do you know what happens when I'm mad? I do crazy things. Now, for the last time, in the name of Martin Luther King, get in this goddamn car!"

Simon's frantic pace slackened to a standstill. He looked every which way as if searching for what to do next. Louis stopped the VW right at his heels. A bearded man yelled out from the second-floor window of his home:

"Hey, you? What's the matter with you! Get the hell off my lawn with that car before I call the cops!"

Simon pressed his hand to his chest as if about to proclaim his innocence and disassociate himself from Louis, but Louis crawled halfway up out of the car window and pointed at Simon, shouting, "He made me do it! The liberal in the penny-loafers made me do it!"

"I don't care who made you do it, get the hell off my lawn before I call the cops on both of you!"

Louis flipped him the finger, "Ahhh, go suck your mama's dick, Harvey. You can't miss her. She's the one with tits on her back and hair on her ass."

The man disappeared from the window, and within seconds the front door of the house swung open, the man storming down the stairs toward the front gate. "OK, you guys want trouble, I'll give you trouble!"

You guys? Simon thought, What the fuck's he mean, *you guys?* With no time to think, he threw open the car door and jumped inside, not even shutting it before Louis peeled rubber on the sidewalk with one back tire and dug a trench in the lawn with the other. The car banged back down over the high curb, darted in between two parked cars, and zigzagged down the street for half a block, nearly causing two wrecks and two Simon Fleming heart attacks before Louis finally seemed to come to the enlightened conclusion that maybe he should stay on the right-hand side of the road. Simon sank down in his seat, his right arm braced against the dashboard.

"Jesus, will ya take it easy and watch where you're goin'? You know, I bet that guy wrote down your license plate. He's probably callin' the cops right now."

Louis calmly lit a cigarette with the lighter from the dashboard, slammed on the brakes for a stop sign, then hung a right onto Sheffield. "Who gives a fuck, liberal? It ain't my car."

Simon felt as if he'd left his stomach somewhere back around the corner on Webster Avenue, but asked, "Whose car is it?"

"How the fuck should I know. I stole it. Shit, I don't even have a license."

"YOU WHAT?" That's when Simon noticed there was no key in the ignition. The car was hot-wired.

"Oh, fuck, just let me outa here. I don't want nothin' to do with this. I mean...oh, fuck! Don't you know stealin' a car is against the law?"

Gobs of smoke sputtered out of Louis's mouth. "No shit, liberal. Look, no big deal, I been doin' it since I was thirteen. No one ever stops me 'cause I look old for my age."

It was true. The hairy stubble on Louis's face was that of a twenty-five-year-old man, not a seventeen-year-old boy; and his shoulders and chest were filled out, even though lately he seemed to have lost weight.

"Look, all I do is take it for a spin and then park it within a block from where I took it. So relax. I don't really steal it, I borrow it."

They hung left and headed down Fullerton. Simon looked at his lap and shook his head, "Oh, fuck. I can walk home from here. I live just two blocks down that way." But Louis zoomed right on by Simon's street.

"Relax, liberal, don't ya wanna go to California with me?"

Simon flipped his head up and glared at Louis. "Quit callin' me *liberal*!"

Louis melodramatically slapped his hand over his chest. "Oh! I beg your pardon! What exactly are you then, if I may be so presumptuous as to ask?"

Simon looked straight ahead out the windshield and grinned in spite of himself, sure that Louis would make fun of him for what he was about to say, but saying it anyway. "I'm a radical."

Gobs of smoke sputtered out of Louis's mouth as he laughed. Simon tried his best to stop grinning and glared at Louis again.

"Well, fuck yourself, Louis! Just because you don't get involved in the movement anymore and ride around on your fuckin' bicycle in your fuckin' underwear, you think you're so fuckin' great!"

For just a moment Simon felt in command of the situation, as if he'd put Louis on the spot; but Louis just shook his head and let out a long smoke-filled breath.

"Ya know, I don't know what I do to start these scandalous rumors about me, but the fact is, liberal, I was *not* riding around in my underwear. It was my bathing suit. All right, so it's a little weird riding around on a bicycle in your bathing suit in the middle of the winter, but not when you take into consideration that I had just smoked a nickle bag of grass, downed a tab of pure Ozly acid, and had been speeding my ass off for five straight days."

They continued down Fullerton, and Simon lost no time in launching into a lecture on the evils of drugs and how dedicated radicals should stay away from them. He didn't realize that Louis's exaggerated responses of "Really? No shit...you don't say...how about that" were Louis's way of mocking him, and by the time Simon realized it, he felt he'd been had. He slouched down on his seat and muttered, "Asshole." After a few more blocks they took a right, climbing the ramp leading to the Kennedy Expressway. Suddenly, Louis burst out singing:

> *We are liberals.*
> *We are fearless.*
> *We will talk a good game,*
> *But are really very tame...*

When he'd sing the chorus of his made-up song, he'd throw his head from side to side:

> *Ha-ha-ha-ha-ha-ha-ha,*
> *Ha-ha-ha-ha-ha-ha-ha...*

They darted in and out around cars.

"Jesus, Louis," Simon said, bracing his arm against the dashboard again, "will ya slow down!" But Louis just ignored Simon and kept time to his song by pounding the heel of his hand against the steering wheel:

> *We are liberals.*
> *We are fearless.*
> *Even though we always smile at you,*
> *Never doubt that we will rile you.*
>
> *Ha-ha-ha-ha-ha-ha-ha,*
> *Ha-ha-ha-ha-ha-ha-ha...*

Simon shook his arm up and down to emphasize his words. "Look, I already told you, I ain't no fuckin' liberal! I'M A RADICAL!"

Louis looked at Simon for what seemed to Simon like an awfully long time for a man who's supposed to have his eyes on the road.

"You really think you're a radical?" Louis calmly asked. "I mean, you really, really think you're a radical?"

Simon sneered at Louis, nodding his head, "Yeah, asshole, I really do!"

"Well, then here, you drive for a while." Louis let go of the steering wheel, dropped his arms to his sides, and grinned. The car started to veer over into the next lane toward a white Buick that looked like a luxury liner next to the VW. Simon's eyes bugged out, and he threw up his hands as if to cover his face from the oncoming doom. "ARE YOU CRAZY?" The man in the Buick let out a non-stop blast from his horn, and Louis yelled, "GRAB THE FUCKIN' WHEEL, LIBERAL!"

Just before the two cars would have collided, Simon lunged over and grabbed the wheel with both hands; he practically lay in Louis's lap as he steered the car back into the right lane. Having never driven before, he stiffened all over, realizing that the slightest turn of the steering wheel was immediately obeyed by the wheels of the car without question—his life now in his hands. At the same time, Louis floored the gas pedal, the VW catching up to cars in front of it so fast Simon had to swerve all over the three-lane highway in fairly heavy traffic in order to avoid driving right up someone else's exhaust pipe. He steered as best he could from his awkward leaning position, heat flashing through him, muscles tensing, eyes open wide with fear.

"LOUIS, I DON'T KNOW HOW TO DRIVE!"

The speedometer read 60...65...70. The VW shook all over as if about to break apart, but each time Simon let go of the wheel and tried to sit back up, as if challenging Louis either to take control of the car or let them crash, Louis would do nothing but grin or sing, the car veering off to the left, forcing Simon to lunge back over to Louis's side of the car and grab the wheel again.

> *We are liberals.*
> *We are fearless.*
> *We will have ourselves a ball,*
> *While you wait for us to call...*

Amazingly, there wasn't a cop car in sight. We're going to die, Simon thought, swerving the VW from left to right and back again. Cars honked at them from all sides. His arms grew tired. His back ached from leaning. His head began to sink down between his shoulders, a heavy exhaustion weighing him down.

"Please, Louis," Simon pleaded, "I can't do this anymore."

After a long pause, Louis eased his foot up on the gas and grabbed the wheel, the engine winding down. Simon collapsed back over into his seat and slouched down, feeling drained, breathing hard. They cruised along for a while, and then Louis gave Simon a couple of friendly pats on the knee.

"Now that's what it feels like to be a radical."

Simon didn't say a word. He stared straight ahead, a vacant look in his eyes as he watched jets cut through the sky, coming to and from nearby O'Hare Airport. When they hit the toll booth, Louis flew right by one of the automatic money-takers without paying, and Simon didn't even have enough fight left in him to think of protesting. Soon the whine of the car's engine lulled him. They passed suburb after suburb—Elk Grove, Schaumburg, Hoffman Estates, Barrington—then on out into farmland, the brown stubby stalks from last year's corn crop scattered like broken bones over fields to either side of the road.

He didn't notice that an hour had gone by or that the crazy twinkle in Louis's eyes had begun to fade. Louis started up a ramp as if about to call it quits and head for home, when, for some reason, he didn't cut the wheels sharp enough at the top of the banked turn. The right front tire hooked over the shoulder onto the dirt. He tried to correct himself too quickly and the car flipped, tumbling down the grassy embankment. To Simon it all seemed to happen in a dreamy slow motion, the grass and sky outside the windshield going around and around and the car throwing him every which way, until it finally came to an upside-down stop. He found himself sitting on the back of his head and shoulder blades, his chin digging into his chest and his feet somewhere up against the floor. It took him a moment to orient himself enough to find the door handle, then a moment longer to figure out how to use it upside down. He opened the door and crawled out, falling to the ground. He lay on his back in the soft dry grass and stared up at the sky. It all seemed so peaceful—sparrows chirping in a grove of trees on the other side of the field and the sun about to set, casting a warm amber tint over everything. And then he remembered Louis and bolted to his feet. A momentary headache attacked him. He stumbled around to the other side of the car, flung open the door, and found Louis sitting on his head.

"Hey, you all right?"

Louis didn't answer, just blinked. Simon pulled him halfway out of the car by his ankles, then yanked him up with a bear hug and leaned him against the car.

"You all right, Louis?"

Louis stood there like a zombie, his eyes cast down at the ground. "Get me home. I'm crashing."

"Whaddaya mean crashing? We already crashed." Simon bent down, trying to see into Louis's eyes. "You sure you're all right, Louis?"

Louis didn't look up. "On speed. I'm crashing on speed."

"You mean on *drugs*, Louis?" Simon asked. But Louis just stood there, staring down at the ground.

For the most part, the hill of the ramp blocked them from the view of drivers on the expressway, but just then a car coming up the ramp slowed down, the driver seeing the wreck down below. Simon looked back over his shoulder at the car and couldn't decide whether to feel rescued or trapped. When the driver saw that no one was seriously hurt, he continued on without stopping. Simon began to pace back and forth, throwing his hands up in the air and shaking his head. Oh, fuck, he thought, sooner or later someone's going to stop, and I'm gonna be thrown in jail for stealing a car, and it'll be on my permanent record, and..."Come on, Louis, I gotta get home! You're the one with all the big ideas! How the hell should I know how to get us back?"

Just then Louis glanced up at Simon, his eyes an empty, ghostly gray. "Don't think, just do it."

Simon took one look at those eyes and knew what he had to do.

"OK, Louis, OK." He gently grabbed Louis by the arm. "Come on, I'll get you home. Just relax."

As if helping a blind man, he held on to Louis's arm and led him up the embankment, along the ramp, over the bridge, and back down the ramp to the other side of the highway. They stood on the shoulder, and Simon stuck out his thumb to hitch a ride back to Chicago just as he'd seen it done in the movies. Sometimes he'd glance at Louis just to make sure he was OK, and for the first time he noticed that he was as tall as Louis, even though he had always thought of himself as shorter. Within minutes a car pulled over, and a computer researcher who liked to talk about the wonders of modern technology and the need for the United States to quit "pussy-footin'" around and drop the bomb on North Vietnam gave them a ride. Simon sat in the front seat, wishing he could let his mind go blank, but instead he found himself trying to keep up with a conversation he couldn't concentrate on. When he wasn't smiling uncomfortably at the computer researcher, he was watching the day give way to night all around him—cars' headlights coming on—or sometimes he would glance back to the back seat where Louis sat staring down at the floor, his shoulders and head swaying whichever way the car swayed. The houses and office buildings once again grew denser the closer they got to Chicago, an hour passing quickly. The computer researcher dropped them off at Fullerton Avenue, and after a short bus ride and a ten-minute walk they stood, much to Simon's amazement, at Louis's front door.

Louis slowly reached into his pants pocket and pulled out his house key. He handed it to Simon, as if the task of opening the front door were too great for him to handle.

"Don't let my mom see me. Just get me to my room."

Simon unlocked the door, and they entered the vestibule as quietly as possible. They stood there listening, until, from the kitchen in the back of the house, Simon faintly heard Muzak droning out of a radio, then the hiss of steam from an iron. It seemed to Simon that Louis's mother was ironing every time he came over, a drawn look always on her face. He hustled Louis through the living room and into his bedroom, silently shutting the door. Louis collapsed on his bed face down. The grayish-blue light from a streetlight streamed in through the window.

Simon stood over the bed, whispering, "You OK?"

But Louis didn't answer, not even waking up when Simon rolled him over and sat him up long enough to help him out of his leather Air Force jacket. Simon started to leave, but stopped when he noticed the shelves of books lining the walls. He walked over and read a few of the titles: *Crime and Punishment, War And Peace, The Idiot.* Some of the authors' names were just as ominous looking to Simon as the thickness of the books themselves. He cracked open the door, listening for the hiss of steam from the iron in the kitchen, and tiptoed back out of the house. On his way home his neck and right shoulder began to stiffen as if he were just now feeling the effect of the crash. He thought about confessing to his father what had happened, then decided against it and, instead, made his penance by avoiding stepping on the cracks in the sidewalk.

The next evening he sat in the living room, reclined back in the easy chair as he thumbed through the front section of the newspaper. Suddenly, he laid the paper down on his chest and asked, "Dad, do you know who Louis Collins is?"

His father, lying on the couch reading the sports page, looked up at him, a tired look in his eyes that Simon had noticed a lot lately.

"Who?"

"Louis Collins. He said you used to be friends with his father."

That's when Adam told him all about how Louis's father had been a Presbyterian minister involved in the civil rights movement, and that he had gotten killed a few years back when he and others had lain down in the middle of a construction site because they didn't believe high-income housing should be built where it would push low-income families out of the neighborhood. Somehow, a bulldozer driver didn't see Louis's father lying there and backed up his bulldozer, accidentally running right over him.

Simon jutted out his chin and asked incredulously, "You mean instead of getting out of the way he just laid there?"

"Yep, just lay there."

"Didn't scream or nothin'?"

"Nope, didn't scream or anything."

Simon leaned forward, the footrest of the easy chair folding back into the chair as he sat up. "But why didn't he get out of the way?"

"I guess it's because he believed in dying for his convictions."

"But Jesus!" Simon let out a short nervous laugh. "That was a dumb way to die, don't ya think?"

Adam just looked at him, the tiredness still in his eyes. "I don't know anymore. I used to think I knew, but now I just don't know. All I can say is that he was a very moral man."

He picked up the paper from his chest and began to read, then put it down again.

"But I do know this. I am not a nonviolent man. I can take on the discipline of nonviolence if I have to, but I'm not a nonviolent man."

Simon leaned as far back in the easy chair as it would go and gazed up at the ceiling. In his mind he imagined what it would be like to watch a bulldozer come right at you, the treads crushing your toes first, then the ankles, calves, testicles, the sides of your stomach splitting open, lungs popping flat, blood rushing up your throat and into your mouth, until finally the treads roll right up over your head, and all is dark. And Simon thought, Didn't even scream. *Didn't even scream.*

He didn't see Louis at school for over a week. There had been a time when he couldn't have cared less if he never saw Louis again, but now he seemed almost frantic to see him. And then one day, there was Louis, pulling up a chair on the other side of the table from Simon in the lunch room, that bloodshot, stoned-out grin on his face. He sat down and dug his fork into his spaghetti.

"What's happenin', liberal?"

Simon looked at Louis, as if really seeing the true Louis for the first time, and asked, "You OK?" But Louis just yelled, "Am I OK? Are oranges orange? Do airplanes fly? Do dogs bark?"

The lunch room continued to fill up with students, and soul music blared out over the PA:

> *Say it loud,*
> *I'm black and I'm proud.*
> *Say it loud,*
> *I'm black and I'm proud...*

On Tuesdays and Thursdays, Simon attended music class instead of art. Because of a schedule conflict, Louis transferred into the same class at the start of the second semester. He didn't even bother to show up for the first month and a half; but the senior counselor, well aware of the fact that Louis's Achievement Test scores were by far the highest in the school, only gave Louis a stern warning that he would not tolerate any more class cutting in the future.

Mr. Ellis, the music teacher, would often have the class watch a movie of Leonard Bernstein conducting the New York Philharmonic Orchestra so that he could slip out of the room and over to the teachers' lounge to get a cup of coffee or grade some papers. He was a short, plump man with an oversized head and thick leprechaun eyebrows that shifted up and down a lot. Standing by the door, he would hold his fingers up to his lips, look out over his bifocals, and in his deep, yet playfully seductive, feminine voice, tell the class, "I will be back in a few minutes. In the meantime I want you to be quiet like bumps on a pickle, like mice on ice, like sand on land."

Most students, sitting up on fold-away bleachers used for chorus practice, would stare blankly back at him, bored stiff; others would roll their eyes around as if to say, Mister, you are one weird fucker. No sooner would Ellis flip off the lights and shuffle out the door than the class would go up for grabs. A black boy would tune in the super soul sound of WGRT on his transistor radio and yell at the projector boy, "Turn the gotdamn, motha'fuckin' sound off, scrub, so we can hear us some fo' real music!" On the movie screen (where COBRA STONE

LOVE was scrawled in huge black letters), Leonard Bernstein, dressed in a tailed tux, would be working up a sweat as he conducted the New York Philharmonic Orchestra through one of Mozart's concertos, but all anyone could hear was the radio playing:

> *I'm a girl watcher,*
> *I'm a girl watcher,*
> *Watchin' girls go by.*
> *My, my, my,*
> *Here comes one now,*
> *Ummm, ummm, ummm...*

A black girl would pop her fingers and bob her head, stopping only long enough to tell some boys, "Well, if y'all think I look like a cow, this be one cow y'all know ya ain't nevah gone lay yo' skanky-ass hands on."

"Oooooo-weeeeee!" someone else would hoot, and then lots of laughs and slapping-five and the soft shuffle of cards from way down at the other end of the bleachers where all the blackjack players huddled around. But Simon would just sit in his usual spot at the very end of the highest bleacher over by the windows, slumped back against the wall with his feet propped up on the bleacher below him. He'd stare at the silent screen and reach his hand up to twirl a lock of his hair around and around his index finger, his mind millions of miles away as he daydreamed about a long-gone Little League baseball game when he'd hit two home runs or made an unbelievable, over-the-shoulder running catch in the outfield.

But then there was Louis. One day he jumped out of his seat the split second Ellis left the room, ran over to the chalk ledge across the room, snatched up the teacher's pointer, scrambled back to the middle of the room, and stood right next to the movie screen, somehow grabbing everyone's attention before they could turn on their radios, or take out their cards, or start signifying on someone. With a quick snap Louis cracked the long pointer in two over his knee, making a conductor's baton out of it, and flipped the other half back over his shoulder as if not caring where it landed.

Oh, fuck, Simon thought, sitting up and no longer playing with his hair, sure that Louis was about to somehow disrupt the status quo of the classroom and thereby destroy the shield of invisibility that Simon strove so hard to maintain. He grinned as he watched Louis, yet wished Louis would just sit down and behave. On the screen, Leonard Bernstein raised his baton for the Orchestra to settle down and get ready for some serious Beethoven's Fifth. Imitating the maestro, Louis did the same, his face the picture of stuck-up solemnity as he poised the busted pointer above his head. The music started:

> *Da-da-da-daaaaaa...*
> *Da-da-da-daaaaaa...*

Just as Leonard Bernstein swooped down with his baton, Louis swooped down with his, swinging his arms up and down in clean, precise strokes, his head lowered so that his long, straight brown hair hung down in his face and flopped around with each sudden snap of his head. His cheeks trembled, his eyes all afire as he'd direct to his left, then to his right, then to the whole imaginary orchestra, commanding his strings to start cookin' with one hand and his horns to cool it with the other. And then the music changed and his arms flowed back and forth like gently rolling waves, his eyes swooning. He was good, almost as good as Leonard. A black boy sitting on the top riser yelled out, "It yo' thang, hunky, do whatcha wanna do!" And still another more sarcastic black boy clapped loud and fast, "Bravo, white boy, bravo!"

Amazed that the class was actually enjoying Louis, Simon relaxed a little bit, as if because he and Louis were the only white boys in the class their fates were somehow attached to the same umbilical cord. He slumped back against the wall, but even though he still grinned, he could not completely let go of his uneasiness, suspecting Louis would find a way to push people in a way they did not want to be pushed.

After a minute or so of Louis's conducting, the class grew quiet. Like an angry god Louis raised his arms up above his head, his whole body jerking violently as he threw them back down to his sides again.

Da-da-da-daaaaaa,
Da-da-da-daaaaaa...

Louis, crazy insane Louis, was pulling the whole class into the music. Simon's head nodded back and forth, his fingers tapping softly against the bench he sat on. To him even the slashed shades seemed to undulate in time with the music, a soft breeze blowing against them through the open windows. But the more Simon found himself drawn into the music, the more he became aware of a tightening foreboding within himself as well as within the entire classroom. Louis was forcing them all to break their silent conspiracy not to learn. Soon, someone yelled, "Sit down, boy!" Other black students yelled for Louis to sit his gotdamn skanky, hunky ass down.

Ohhhhh, fuck, Simon thought. He looked out through one of the holes in the slashed shades, the sun bright and the waist-high prairie weeds in the vacant lots blowing back and forth. He thought, All they'd have to do is cut the grass, clear out those trees, stick in a backstop, and you'd have a real nice baseball diamond and...I'm not responsible for you, Louis. He glanced around the room and shook his head in disgust as if to show black students that he was no fool and would rather listen to Marvin Gaye's "I Heard It Through The Grapevine" or James Brown's "Say It Loud, I'm Black and I'm Proud."

But still Louis conducted, his eyes lost in his hair, his thick neck coated in sweat and his short-sleeved, brown-and-white-checked shirt growing wet across the shoulder blades. Finally, a tall black gangbanger stood up and slowly walked down the bleachers toward Louis. The room grew quiet except for the music from the projector. One of the gangbanger's friends, sitting up in the middle of the bleachers, yelled, "Oooooo-weeee, hunky, you done made Ernie mad now."

Simon slumped farther down against the wall to make himself as small as possible. Are you satisfied now, Louis? he thought. Ernie walked over and stood right in front of Louis. His palms were turned back bad-like, and his Afro pick was stuck in the back of his 'fro. Louis just went right on conducting, his head bowed. Like a father calmly explaining to his misbehaving son why he has to be whipped, Ernie said, "Now, hunky, didn't I tell ya to sit yo' ass down? Say, hunky, I'm talkin' to you!"

He took another step closer to Louis, but just then Louis flipped his head up, his teeth gritted tight in a snarling, sadistic grin and that bloodshot, stoned-out twinkle in his eyes:

Da-da-da-daaaaaa,
Da-da-da-daaaaaa...

The intensity of Louis's sadistic grin suddenly let Simon and everyone else in the classroom know that Louis was not only perfectly capable of taking care of himself, he was not someone to fuck with, either. Louis waved the busted pointer in and out in front of Ernie's face. As if taken off guard, Ernie backed up a step, then another, Louis slowly walking toward him. Not looking where he was going, Ernie tripped back against the edge of the bleachers, just barely catching himself from falling. The whole class laughed, and to save face and play off his fear, Ernie laughed, too, yelling, "Help! Help! Dis here white boy a crazy motha'fucka'!" He ran back up the bleachers, pushing his way through students to his seat and sat down again, holding his hands out in front of himself as if to ward off Louis.

"Be coo', white boy, be coo', I didn't know you was Frankenstein's mama." He laughed some more and held out his hands so that his friend next to him could slap him five. Louis just stood down below on the floor, still conducting, that grin on his face. Simon relaxed and shook his head, thinking, How the fuck do you get away with it, Louis?

Mr. Ellis walked back into the room and closed the door firmly behind him as if to warn people of his entrance. The only things he had taught the class all year were the difference between a major and minor chord, where to find middle C on the keyboard, and the lyrics to such oldy-but-goody classics as "Way Down Upon the Swanee River" and "Eating Goober Peas." He took one look over his bifocals at Louis, and asked in his deep, yet playfully seductive, feminine voice, "What is the meaning of this, Mr. Collins?"

Louis just went right on conducting the class, with his back to Ellis.

Students looked back and forth between Ellis and Louis with mischievous smiles, everyone waiting to see what would happen next. Even Simon grinned almost wickedly, the "us-against-him" attitude he felt toward Ellis racing giddily through his veins.

"Mr. Collins. I'm talking to you, Mr. Collins. That pointer is public property and wasn't put here to be abused."

Louis continued to conduct. Ellis walked over and stood to the side of Louis, keeping a respectful distance.

"Mr. Collins, I will not have you disrupting my pupils as well as my time. Do you comprehend me, Mr. Collins?"

Louis still didn't answer, swinging his arms in and out, his head bowed. The longer he ignored Mr. Ellis, the more Simon wanted to burst out laughing, and he began to bounce his foot against the bench below him. With a voice decidedly more stern and less feminine, Mr. Ellis held his hand out and said, "Hand me the pointer, Mr. Collins. I said, hand me the pointer, please." He slowly reached for the pointer, but just then Louis flipped his head up and whirled around. He walked toward Ellis, waving the pointer close to Ellis's face as if he wanted to cram the whole Philharmonic Orchestra right down Ellis's throat. Ellis backed up, his thick leprechaun eyebrows twitching and his mouth hung open. The class stomped their feet and whooped it up, someone yelling, "Oooooo-weeeeee!" Simon couldn't help but laugh, for once forgetting his fear of being at Dexter High School.

"I think you'd better sit down, Mr. Collins," Ellis managed to say, "I think—oh, my God—you're bucking for a suspension, young man—oh, my God. If you don't sit down this instant and behave, I'm afraid I'll have no other choice than to—oh, my God."

All of Ellis's "oh, my Gods" made Simon and the rest of the class laugh even harder. Louis backed Ellis up over by the windows right in front of where Simon sat. Without missing a beat of the music with the pointer, Louis reached over with his free hand and pulled up a shade, bright sunlight flooding the room. He leaped up onto a chair that stood beneath the window, his whole body silhouetted in sunlight, and waved the pointer through the final glorious moments of the movement. Ellis stood down below in front of Louis and looked up at him as if at a loss what to say or do next. With a flip of the wrist, Louis threw the busted pointer up in the air and climbed out the window, hopping down to the yard outside. He stuck his head back inside the room. Looking over at Simon, he held up his hand and waved his fingers.

"Bye-bye, liberal."

He swung himself over the waist-high, chain-link fence that encircled the yard, crossed the street, and started across the vacant lots. Simon sat up straight and craned his neck, he and everyone else in the class following Louis with their eyes. He's leaving, Simon thought, he's really leaving. He looked all around at everyone else, wanting someone to confirm that, yes, Louis Collins had indeed climbed out of the window and was now gone, but everyone he looked at looked back at him with the same elated smile of amazement as his own. The sound of thunderous applause erupted from the projector, and on screen Leonard took his bow. Ellis yelled out the window, "Come back here, Mr. Collins! You're bucking for a suspension! Do you hear me?" But Louis never looked back, walking his slow, lazy, uncoordinated walk across the vacant lots, until, finally, he disappeared around the corner of the DePaul Settlement House gym on Webster Avenue.

The excitement in the classroom seemed to walk around the corner with Louis; everyone settled down. Mr. Ellis just stood there looking out the window. Students smiled or giggled softly, watching to see what Ellis would do next. Knowing that Simon and Louis were friends, Ellis looked over at Simon, as if to ask, Why did he do that? He couldn't understand why his strategy of not pushing students to learn, in exchange for their remaining relatively civil in his classroom, had not worked as usual. He lived in constant fear that a student or another teacher would publicly accuse him of being gay, yet he found it beyond his control not to innocently flirt with some of his male students. Simon possessed just the right combination of innocence and youthful good-looks to suit Ellis's taste. Once, when the class had been sitting in chairs instead of up on the bleachers, Ellis had walked past Simon. Seeing that someone had written the words "blow me" in Simon's music book, which sat open on his desk, Ellis leaned over Simon, pointed at the graffiti, and, just to see how Simon would react, asked, "What's that mean?" He had been amused at the way Simon had blushed, grinned nervously, and shrugged his shoulders, refusing to answer even when asked what the words meant a second time. He often saw Simon and Louis come to and leave class together and couldn't understand why someone like Simon would want to hang around a "lost cause" like Louis. Just the other day, Ellis had patted Louis on the back as Louis started to walk through the classroom doorway at the beginning of the period, only to have Louis stop, turn around, and firmly say, "Don't you ever touch me with your faggot hands again or I'll ram my fist three feet up your faggot asshole."

Glad that no one was within earshot, Ellis had stood his ground, stating, "There are laws against accusing people of such things, young man." But the way Louis sneered back at him, then continued his slow, lazy walk into the classroom, let Ellis know that he would have to be extremely careful when dealing with Louis in the future.

When Ellis looked at Simon, Simon looked down at his feet and grinned nervously. How the hell was he supposed to know why Louis had stepped out the window? He always felt uneasy when Ellis looked at him, sure that Ellis was going to try and butt-fuck him the moment he got the chance. Ellis began to pull the shades up one by one, shaking his head as if he just couldn't believe what Louis had done. He picked up half of the broken pointer lying on the floor near the window, then walked over to where the other half lay by the blackboard. Trying to fit both ends back together, he mumbled, "Well, maybe it can be glued."

The projector boy had already turned off the projector, and Ellis walked over to the light switches, flipping them on. He sat down at his desk, looked out over his bifocals at the class, and, as if calling a truce, said in his playfully seductive, feminine voice, "Ladies and gentlemen, I'm going to finish grading these papers. As long as you're relatively quiet, you may converse among yourselves."

Simon once again slouched back against the wall behind him, twirled a lock of his hair around his index finger, and waited for the next period bell to ring; but now and then, whenever he thought about Louis, a silent laugh convulsed him.

Six months later, Simon was flipping through one of Louis's books and found a letter wedged in between two pages, a letter Louis apparently never sent:

May 3, 1969

Dear Gail,

...So I'm walking across this field that wasn't a field when you were here because Urban Renewal tore down a shitload of houses, and I can still hear fucking faggot Ellis yelling at me with his faggot voice, when, suddenly, I decide why the fuck not come out to California and visit you? I mean, what am I doing here anyway? In my mind I kept seeing you answer your front door that time your mom and dad were out of town, and all you had on was that red fishnet sweater that you could see right through. There was a sly grin on your face as you shook your hair out of your eyes and said, "Hi," grabbing my crotch and pulling me inside. Gail, I swear to fucking God, I haven't had a pair of tits to squeeze and suck as nice as yours since—honest injun. Even if I have to go all the way to California to cop another feel from you, it's worth it, and besides, I miss you a lot, you and that tight little sandpaper cunt of yours. Yeah, yeah, yeah, I know what you're saying: "Can't you ever be serious, Louis?" Look, Pizza Face, the world ain't worth being serious about—for someone who has such nice tits I can't understand why you can't see that. But I don't want to argue about it right now, just let me tell you what happened. I'm crossing this field, see, and I'm so fucking wasted on speed it's like...like I'm sure that if I just hurry up I can hitchhike from Chicago to San Francisco by late afternoon. So I get to Webster Avenue and thumb a ride to the expressway where I can get off under the viaduct at Fullerton and try to catch another ride down the Kennedy. I'm still standing there an hour later and the fuckin' jagoffs in empty cars are just whizzin' by. This one fuckhead even leans way over as he drives by and locks the passenger side of his car, like I might try and jump in while he's going by at thirty-five miles an hour. I mean be honest, do people do things like that in California?

So after a while of just standing there, my eyes start to stare at things, like my feet, or the sidewalk, or an empty potato chip bag blowing down the gutter. I start to notice all the dirt flying around in the air the way it always does under them stinking viaducts, and for some reason this car wash across the street with all these nigger attendants in green uniforms starts depressing the shit out of me. Suddenly, I know I'm crashing. The realiziation that I'm not going to make it to California to see you is too fucking much—I mean, shit, Pizza Face, this was the fifth straight time in a month I had started out for California, and only once did I barely make it beyond the suburbs. I could smell your hair the same way I could when we'd hug and the top of your head would tuck under my chin. I started staring hard at the drivers whizzing by, trying to make them feel guilty for not picking me up, but no dice. And then my thumb started feeling heavy. The next thing I know I'm sitting on the curb with my legs stuck out in the street, and all these fuckin' jag-off cars are honking for me to pull them in as they swerve around, but I can only hold my hands over my ears, close my eyes, and concentrate on your freckled face. I said to myself, Gail, please come get me. I'll do anything for you and I know you can hear me so please ride by in your little VW and pick me up.

But when I opened my eyes, you weren't there. I wanted to die, Gail. I mean, lots of times I think about wanting to die—yeah, yeah, yeah, you think I'm bullshittin', but I'm not, Pizza Face—sometimes I think I do speed just so I can think about dying when I crash. So I was sitting there so fuckin' depressed—even the thought of your tits revolted me and you know I never go more than five minutes a day without craving those tits of yours. Before I forget, when I finally make it out there this summer, can we fuck on your living room floor like before with you wearing that red fishnet sweater? Do your aunt and uncle have plush carpeting like at your mom and dad's house? If so, I hope you don't have your period again this time—ha-ha-ha. By the way, did your mom or dad ever ask you about the stain, and if so, what did you tell them—that you stepped on a mouse while crossing the room to change channels on the TV? I can still see you on your fuckin' hands and knees, scrubbing at it with a sponge, but no dice, Pizza Face, Mr. Clean had met his match—ha-ha-ha.

So anyway, I'm sitting on the curb crashing my brains out. I don't know why it hit me so hard, maybe it's because it was the fifth straight day I'd been speeding, but what the fuck, I did the same thing last week and it hardly bothered me a bit. I can't seem to get it together to pull my legs in. Don't get me wrong, I'm very fond of my legs, and I'm telling myself, Look, if you don't pull your fuckin' legs in, some jagoff's going to run over them, but I just couldn't budge them, like they weren't connected to my brain anymore. Did you ever have that happen? I mean, I *party* the hardest, I *fuck* the hardest, and I *crash* the hardest. I started feeling unbearably hot, but it took me a good five minutes before I managed to reach a hand up to unbutton my shirt.

The next thing I know I'm down at the police station with this itchy blanket around me 'cause some pig arrested me for indecent exposure. He told my ma he found me lying in the street under the viaduct "stark naked," as he put it, with the traffic swerving around me. It must have been the way he says, 'cause I don't know what the fuck happened to all my clothes. I must have ripped them off me or something. Who knows? So now my ma's been sending me to this dip-shit shrink once a week. I just sit there and talk. I mean, it's kind of stupid, but I act serious because it makes my ma happy, and it costs her a lot, and I figure I owe her that much with all the bullshit I cause her. So listen, Gail, I just wanted to say hi and tell you I really, really, really miss you and that even though I'm lonely I can understand why you moved out to California to live with your aunt and uncle so that you could get away from me. I just wanted to tell you that I'm sorry for all the fucked-up things I did to you and that I really do love you, and I'm not going to lie to you again and say I'm getting my head screwed on straight, because we both know I'm not ever going to have my head screwed on straight. Hope to see you soon.

Louis The Terrible

P.S. I got this friend, Simon. Do you know him? He's still a virgin and if I bring him out to California with me would you do me a favor and fuck him? He could use it. Will be waiting to hear from you.

If only he would apply himself, teachers would say; if only he would stop playing clown—the boy with an IQ of one hundred and sixty-four, whose Achievement Test scores rated among the highest in the nation. For Christ sake! he had letters from Harvard and Yale stating that if he would be so kind as to apply to their schools, they would be so kind as to accept him with full scholarships. What a pity, they would say, what a waste, what a Louis.

Regardless of the senior counselor's warning, Louis continued to cut class, sometimes for days, and other times he'd show up at school so burnt out he'd walk right by Simon in the hallway as if Simon were a total stranger. Sometimes Simon would find him sitting at a lunch room table with that empty, ghostly gray in his eyes. Simon would pull up a chair across from him, sit down, and with a deeply serious expression on his face, which he figured all revolutionaries should wear, say, "Why you mess with drugs for, man? Drugs only help the ruling class to keep the proletariat masses in line, because you can't educate the people or pick up a gun and fight for your freedom." But Louis would just shake his head tired-like, as if to say, Not now, liberal, don't lay that commie shit on me now. He'd pick up his carton of chocolate milk and go sit somewhere else, leaving Simon to grin uneasily and wonder what he had said wrong, or maybe he was just missing something altogether.

But during Louis's long absences from school, Simon would get to thinking about the times when there had been the bloodshot, stoned-out twinkle in Louis's eyes that Simon found himself drawn to, yet on guard against—like the time Louis and Simon stopped off at the A&P after school to buy a couple of cans of pop. No sooner had they passed through the automatic front doors of the store than Louis was shoplifting. He stuffed all kinds of things inside his beat-up, leather Air Force jacket: bananas, apples, broccoli, carrots—whatever he could get his hands on—canned lima beans, Campbell's Pork 'n' Beans, The Jolly Green Giant's Creamed Corn, Jello. He even stuffed some frozen peas down the crotch of his khakis (said he wanted them thawed by dinner time).

"Will ya fuckin' cut it out, Louis!" Simon whispered, pissed and scared as he looked every which way to check if anyone was watching, because Louis sure didn't seem to care. So as a last resort Simon walked ahead of Louis, trying to look nonchalantly over the different products on the shelves and pretend he wasn't with Louis; but Louis stayed right there on Simon's heels, walking crouched down like Groucho Marx. Whatever item his hands grabbed off of a shelf he held it over Simon's shoulder for Simon to see.

"Hey, liberal, you want some Rice-a-Roni? You want some chicken wings? You want some chipped beef?"

He shoved each item under his already bulging jacket. Simon just kept his eyes straight ahead, walking faster and faster. And then as he waited with his can of Coke up at the check-out counter, Louis snuck on out the front door and stood on the sidewalk in front of the store's tall windows. He pressed his nose flat against the glass, crossed his eyes, and smiled in at Simon. Slowly, he slipped a couple of chicken wings out from inside his jacket and held them up to either side of his head like ears, wiggling them back and forth. Fuckin' crazy jagoff must want to get caught, Simon thought, unable to keep from smiling himself. In desperation he stared down at his Coke on the conveyer belt and scratched his nose, then rubbed the palm of his hand against the back of his neck and stared at the DAIRY sign on the wall across the store—anything to keep from laughing and acting as if he knew the crosseyed fool wiggling the chicken wings. He fumbled getting the correct change out of his palm to give to the check-out girl, then half-ran half-walked out of the store and started down the block; but Louis stayed right on his tail, walking that Groucho Marx walk. One by one he pulled all kinds of food out from inside his jacket, holding each item up for Simon's approval.

"Hey, liberal, you want some Bisquick? You want some Rice-a-Roni? You want some pork 'n' beans?"

Meanwhile, the store manager finally realized he was being ripped off and ran down the block after them, yelling, "Hey, you two! Stop right there! Bring that back here right now before I call the cops!"

Simon started to run, then just as quickly stopped as if to give himself up, but Louis grabbed him by the arm and took off running, singing:

> *We are liberals,*
> *We are fearless...*

At first Louis pulled Simon along, but once Simon found his feet moving, he gave in to the crime and fled, smiling in spite of his fear. Bananas and apples and Campbell's Pork 'n' Beans spilled out of Louis's jacket as they ran, so that by the time they ditched the store manager and were back at Louis's house, sprawled out on the front steps, Louis's jacket was completely empty.

"You crazy asshole!" Simon yelled, his head bowed as he tried to catch his breath from running and stop laughing. "I swear to fuckin' God, you're a fuckin' banana. Now I'll never be able to go back to that store again." But Louis didn't seem to be listening as he patted his hands on his chest like a man who has misplaced something. Then remembering where he put it, he reached down the crotch of his khakis and pulled out a box of soggy defrosted peas. He held them up for Simon's approval.

"How 'bout some peas, liberal, you want some peas?"

Or there was the time Simon took the El downtown to Wieboldt's to buy a pair of pants, and Louis came along to pick up some books at Kroch's and Brentano's. First, Louis talked Simon into buying a pair of those bell bottoms that all the hippy kids were wearing, and if that weren't embarrassing enough for Simon, Louis dragged him into a bookstore. One thing Simon couldn't stand was bookstores—something about all those rows of books and the fact that someone was going to read them all and that someone wasn't going to be him. It took him six whole months just to read *Black Boy,* a book his mother had given him. So here he was in Kroch's and Brentano's—biggest goddamn bookstore in Chicago—and had only been downstairs in the paperback fiction section for thirty seconds when he got the jitters and started pulling on Louis's arm.

"Come on, Louis, let's get the fuck out of here. I gotta get home, OK?"

Louis gently shook his arm free and continued to scan the wall of books in front of him. "Relax, liberal, relax, you're always in such a fuckin' hurry." He started to pick books off the shelves: *The Electric Kool–Aid Acid Test, In the Penal Colony, One Flew Over the Cuckoo's Nest, Moby Dick.* At least Simon recognized the last one because he'd seen the movie three times on "Family Classics" on TV. Louis shoved every other book he picked up under his Air Force jacket, saying, "One for me and one for them; one for me and one for them."

Simon slouched his shoulders, looked up at the ceiling, and shook his head, thinking, Ohhhh, fuck. But by now he knew better than to try and stop Louis. He walked into another aisle and pretended he was by himself, picking up a book to scan through it. If Louis weren't giving him enough cause for anxiety, his ankles felt as if they were swimming around inside his first-pair-ever bell-bottoms, and he was sure that everyone in the store was sneering at him because he looked like a hippy. When he saw Louis head up front to the check-out counter, Simon shoved the book he was flipping through back on the shelf, walked over to the stairs, and stood with one foot on the bottom stair so that he could run up and out of the store just in case Louis got caught. Louis smiled at the black check-out woman, his jacket zipped up all the way to his neck and no more than a slight bulge showing from the four books stuffed inside. He laid the books he was going to pay for on the counter, and in a sweet voice said, "Nice weather we're having, huh?"

She didn't even look up at him, only nodded, adding up the books on the cash register. Louis paid for them. Just before he walked away, he slapped his hand over his heart—rather, over the stolen books—and with the same sweet voice said, "You have a nice day, now."

Again the woman only nodded without looking up at him, going on to the next customer.

Crazy fucker must want to get caught, Simon thought, shaking his head, yet he couldn't help but smile as he started up the stairs. By the time he reached the main floor Louis had caught up with him.

"You know, liberal," Louis said, "you're always in such a fuckin' hurry. I mean, what's your problem, you beat your meat too much or what?"

Embarrassed to the core of his fourteen-year-old soul, Simon socked Louis hard in the shoulder, "Fuck you, motherfucker! I don't beat my meat!" He raised his right hand and emphatically stated, "I swear on a stack of Bibles I ain't never beat my meat, so help me God."

They passed a man dressed in a suit and tie in the aisle, and Louis leaned over toward him, asking, "Hey, Mister, can you believe it? This kid says he don't beat his meat."

The man just walked right on by them as if he didn't hear Louis or didn't want to hear. Simon socked Louis hard in the shoulder again, hissing out, "Will ya shut up, Louis!"

They walked out of one of the front doors of the store and onto the crowded sidewalk. Even though the El tracks ran plain as day over the middle of Wabash Avenue, Simon tried to change the subject by asking, "Which way to the El?"

"Which way do you think, fool?" Louis asked, and then, right there on the sidewalk, he pointed at Simon, screaming, "Meatbeater! Meatbeater! Meatbeater!"

Simon backed off a few steps, grinning a shit-eating grin. Blood rushed to his face as he looked around to see if anyone was listening to Louis, who was yelling like a carnival barker, "Yes, ladies and gentlemen, step right up and see the gen-u-ine meatbeater. All ya gotta do is give him a nickel, step back (so he don't getcha pretty clothes all sticky), and watch him BEAT THAT MEAT!"

Before Simon could collect his thoughts enough to wipe the grin off of his face and just walk away, Louis yelled out his rhyme at the top of his lungs the way Marines yell cadence when they march:

> *Eight, nine, twenty-one,*
> *Beat your meat, you've just begun, say*
>
> *Beat your meat, baby,*
> *Beat your meat, baby.*
>
> *Eight, nine, twenty-two,*
> *Beat your meat till black 'n' blue, say*
>
> *Beat your meat, baby,*
> *Beat your meat, baby...*

Louis bounced up and down, shaking his head, and every time he hit the chorus, he'd stop bouncing long enough to eyeball some unsuspecting All-American citizen who just happened to be walking by.

> *Beat your meat, baby,*
> *Beat your meat, baby...*

Some folks took a quick glance at him, but most just kept walking, looking straight ahead. Simon tugged tentatively on Louis's elbow, saying under his breath, "Will ya shut up and come on, Louis?"

> *Eight, nine, twenty-four,*
> *Beat your meat right through the door...*

Simon socked Louis in the shoulder. "Will ya shut up and come on, Louis!" He yanked Louis by the arm, but Louis wouldn't budge, bouncing up and down again.

> *Eight, nine, twenty-eight,*
> *Beat your meat on roller skates...*

"Fuck this," Simon mumbled. As if urgent business demanded his immediate attention, he walked on down the block toward the Randolph Street El station; but even though he was shaking his head and looking down at the sidewalk, he couldn't seem to stop laughing, listening to Louis's voice rise above the crowd:

> *Eight, nine, twenty-ten,*
> *Beat your meat and do it again, say*

> *Beat your meat, baby,*
> *Beat your meat, baby...*

Or there was the time Simon was sitting in the lunch room with Julio, when Louis walked over to their table carrying his tray of food. Julio looked up at him and, for a joke, said, "Well, well, well, speaking of hunkies!"

Simon pointed his finger at Louis and snickered, as if somehow that would make him something other than white, but Louis just stood there and stared down at Simon, shaking his head.

"You know, liberal," he said, "I swear to God the fuckin' spics are acting more like niggers every day."

The smile dropped off Simon's face, a chill traveling up his backbone. He glanced all around the crowded lunch room to see if any blacks or Latinos beside Julio had overheard. But Louis didn't give a shit who the hell overheard. He leaned down over Julio, staring at him face to face.

"And another thing, spic, do not cook what you will not eat."

Julio stared back at Louis, as if searching for the right comeback. Simon wanted to bust Louis's goddamn head, whispering, "Will ya keep your voice down." But just then Julio let out a forced, continuous laugh, the kind of laugh Simon suddenly realized he had wanted to get out of Julio for a long, long time but never could. Louis let Julio go ahead and laugh and then pulled up a chair across the table from Simon.

"What's happenin', liberal?" He twirled some spaghetti on his fork, a grin on his face, as if he were saying, Calm down, fool, calm down.

Or there was the time a black boy was frisking Simon down for chump-change in the hallway between classes, when just then Louis walked by. He placed one hand on the black boy's shoulder for support, then proceeded to lift his leg, imitating a dog taking a piss on the boy.

"Thanks, man," Louis said right to the stunned black boy, then added, "Ah'm sho' you can dig where ah'm comin' from, brotha'."

Louis ran down the hall, stopping here and there to lift his leg on a locker, all the time singing:

> *Ah can't help it if ah'm a dawg,*
> *Bow-wow, bow-wow...*

The black boy stood there for a second, as if thinking, What the fuck..., then ran down the hall after Louis, whose voice Simon could hear floating up the stairway from the second floor:

> *Ah can't help it if ah'm a dog,*
> *Bow-wow, bow-wow...*

He's crazy, Simon thought, absolutely positively a banana. But

Simon couldn't stop smiling as he moved on toward class, his money still in his pocket.

And so it would be that during those Louis absences from school Simon would miss Louis. He'd call Louis up on the phone after school, asking, "Wanna do somethin'?" He'd forget about how Louis would scare him shitless or piss him off royal; instead, embedded in Simon's memory was Louis, walking that slow, uncoordinated, lazy walk of his down the school hallway with his untied rawhide shoelaces flopping all around his ankles; Louis, demanding, "In the name of Martin Luther King, get in this goddamn car"; Louis, slapping Simon on the thigh, saying, "Now that's what it feels like to be a radical"; Louis, in music class with that sadistic grin on his face as he waved the busted pointer in front of the gangbanger's face. Louis, Louis, Louis...

Late one afternoon, Simon walked over to Louis's house to find out why he hadn't been to school in three days. He found Louis in his small dark bedroom, the shade drawn and a strobe light flashing. On the stereo, Grace Slick of Jefferson Airplane sang about revolution; the smell of cheap Indian incense burning in a tray next to Louis's bed permeated everything. Louis lay on the bed, flat on his back, crashing his brains out, not moving a muscle. He wore dark sunglasses and stared straight up at the ceiling. His face had grown more and more gaunt and his clothes were starting to look baggy.

"Hey, Louis, where ya been?" Simon walked across the room to turn down the volume on the stereo so they could talk easier. The strobe light made him unsure of his steps, as if his feet might somehow fall right through the floor. Once he turned the volume down, he could hear the soft steady gurgling of an aquarium sitting on top of a wooden crate. He walked over and stood by the foot of the bed, smiling down at Louis.

"Didn't your mom tell you I been callin'?"

Louis just waited a second, then got up off the bed, gently brushed past Simon, and turned the volume on the stereo back up. He walked over to the bed and lay down again, the blue light of the strobe reflecting wickedly off of his dark sunglasses with each flash. A surge of anger rose up Simon's neck and into his face. He had been all ready to go out and have some Louis-type fun, but instead he was getting ignored. He stepped over to the stereo, reached to turn down the volume again, then decided against it, feeling as if his mind were somehow dissipating into the flashes of the strobe. I gotta get out of here, he thought, and opened the door, slamming it shut behind him. What the fuck did he care about that crazy fuckin' asshole anyway? He hurried past Louis's mother, who was wiping off the kitchen table with a sponge. He had never seen her dressed in anything but her blue houserobe and slippers, except for the times she came home from her secretarial job, and even then she always changed into her robe within a half hour. She hardly looked up from the table as she said, "I don't know, Simon, Louis's been acting funny all week; I can't do a thing with him. Maybe when they throw him out of school he'll shape up." She yelled at Louis's closed bedroom door, "Louie, how many times do I have to tell you to turn that thing down?"

Simon mumbled, "Bye," opened the back door, and shut it hard behind him. He took the backstairs down two by two and headed home through the alley, walking fast; but halfway down the block he slowed down and shoved his hands inside the pockets of his white Levi jeans. His steps became less purposeful, and he wondered why the hell people always grew tired of him.

Back at school, the riots went on. The Friday after Simon stopped off at Louis's house, someone pulled a false fire alarm. Classes poured out into the hallways, which soon became crowded as all hell with everyone yelling, screaming, and just waiting for something more to happen. Simon walked his not-too-fast-not-too-slow walk down the second floor hallway, his eyes focused straight ahead as he eased his way from one side of the hall to the other to avoid any groups of gangbangers who might just happen to be looking for something tall, white, and skinny to beat the shit out of. And then, just a ways down the hall, he saw the back of Louis's head and shoulders through the crowd. Louis was walking that slow, lazy walk of his in a straight line down the middle of the hallway as if telling every gangbanger within ten miles, *Here I am, motherfuckers.* Simon saw his friend walking like that and thought, You're dead, Louis. He wanted to yell, *What the fuck's wrong with you, asshole? Don't you know how to play the game?* But he didn't yell, because he was too goddamn fucking-A good at the game by now, and to fucking high hell with anyone who wasn't!

What happened next happened fast. Simon watched as Louis refused to step aside for three black gangbangers and instead tried to walk straight through them. With gangbanger quickness they threw him up against the lockers and were all over him, smacking him silly in the face and kicking him in the balls. Louis crouched off balance against the lockers and swung up at them wildly, letting loose some God-awful screams, "COCKSUCKERS! COCKSUCKERS! COCKSUCKERS!"

Simon stopped dead in his tracks, his mouth hanging slightly open. Black students ran past him and gathered around the fight, smiling, laughing, someone yelling, "HIT HIM! HIT HIM!" Already Simon saw another black gangbanger frisking a white boy for chump-change over by the wall only a few feet away. Gotta keep movin', Simon thought, as if trying to shake out of a trance, knowing trouble could spread his way any second. He turned around and walked back down the hall, feeling guilty as hell for not trying to help Louis. It's Louis's own fucking crazy fault, Simon thought, hoping Louis hadn't had a chance to see him; he asks for it. But as he hurried back down the stairs and through the first floor corridor with that not-too-slow-not-too-fast walk of his, he looked all around, feeling that he wanted to explain something to someone, but didn't know what, or to whom.

He didn't see Louis again for three days. Then one night, while he lay on the couch watching reruns of "Superman" on TV, the phone rang. Hoping the call was for him, Simon jumped up, ran from the living room into his father's office, slid in his stocking feet across the wooden floor to the desk, and picked up the phone.

"Hello."

Louis didn't even bother to say hello, just asked, "Wanna get stoned?" So after Louis had assured Simon at least ten times that you can't get addicted to marijauna, and, no, it doesn't kill your brain cells or make you a schizophrenic, Simon said OK. His hands grew sweaty and his face flushed hot, yet in the back of his mind he'd been thinking of trying dope for some time. He hung up the phone, threw on his blue Dexter baseball jacket, yelled to his mother in the kitchen that he was going to meet Louis, and ran down the stairs, hearing her yell at him not to stay out too late. He headed down the block toward Armitage Avenue where Louis had said he was baby-sitting for a divorced woman who liked to get high and always let him smoke some of her stash. He walked fast down the sidewalk, in and out of the glow of street lights, always light on his toes, listening, watching out for gang-bangers. He passed first through Corps territory, then into Latin Kings territory, and even made a game out of the danger, humming the theme song of the TV show "Mission Impossible" under his breath as if he were some sort of secret agent behind enemy lines.

When he reached the apartment building, Louis buzzed him in at the front door. He climbed the stairs two by two and was just about to reach the third floor landing when he looked up and saw Louis grinning down at him over the railing. His right eye was a little puffy, and a purplish, half-healed gash ran in and out of his eyebrow. Drifting through the open door next to Louis, Simon could hear the Beatles on the record player, singing "Fool on the Hill."

"Say, asshole," Simon said friendly-like.

Louis's voice took on a black dialect. "Well, if ah'm an asshole, feel free ta lick me clean jus' as soon as ah get outa de baf'room, hunky."

"Sheeeit," Simon said back, smiling. He punched Louis in the shoulder, his way of saying he was glad to see him. They walked into the apartment, and even though Simon already knew the answer, he just had to ask, "Damn, man, what happened to your eye?"

"What the fuck do you think happened?" Louis's voice was surprisingly quick, yet matter of fact. He didn't even look at Simon, just nonchalantly swung the door shut, turned away, and walked that lazy walk of his farther into the apartment. Simon followed him, studying Louis as if trying to decipher, from the sway in Louis's shoulders, whether or not Louis had seen him in the hallway that day. He knew that even if Louis had seen him, Louis didn't feel like talking about it, because after you've been jumped, there isn't anything much worth saying about it to anybody.

The bare brick walls of the sparsely furnished loft apartment were decorated with a couple of Thai rubbings of gods and an American flag with a peace sign in place of the fifty stars. An old couch draped with a purple-flowered Indian bedspread stood against the far wall; in front of it sat a coffee table covered with back issues of *Evergreen Review,* an "underground" newspaper called *The Seed,* and a *Black Panther* newspaper with a picture of Huey P. Newton on the cover. Huey sat in a tall, throne-like wicker chair, a harpoon in one hand, a shotgun in the other, and a look on his face that said, "Fuck with me at your own risk." On the other side of the coffee table an old wing-back chair and a huge pillow rounded out the living room area. The kids were already asleep inside their bedroom, which was made out of unpainted drywall, and to the side of the kids' room the mother's double boxspring and mattress lay on the floor. The whole place stunk of incense and scented candles. Simon took one glance around the loft and thought, Hippies must live here. He took off his jacket and plopped down on the couch.

"So where is it?" Almost unable to contain his anxiety, he leaned forward, wanting to hurry up and smoke the dope before he had a chance to change his mind. Louis sat down in the wing-back chair across the coffee table from Simon.

"Calm down, liberal, calm down. I swear to fuckin' God I have never seen a hunky in a bigger fuckin' hurry than you in my entire fuckin' life. Smoking pot takes a sense of grace, a sense of culture, a sense of cosmic dignity—all of which we're going to have to work on in your case."

Simon grinned, yet threw up his hand angrily. "Well, fuck you then, asshole! And look who's callin' who a hunky!"

He leaned back against the couch, trying to maintain a cool air, but soon he began to tap his fingers against his thighs or bounce his legs nervously. Louis picked up a Blood Sweat and Tears record album off the floor and placed it on his lap; then picked up a Vitamin C bottle off the coffee table, unscrewed the cap, and poured some dope out of it onto the album cover. Simon found himself leaning forward again, watching every meticulous move Louis's hands made. He brushed the dope back and forth with the flap of a match book, separating the stems and seeds from the rest of the dope. He took a box of yellow, banana-flavored rolling papers from his shirt pocket, removed two papers, licked the long edge of one of them, and glued the two together. The record on the stereo stopped, and all Simon could hear was the hum of the fluorescent lights at the other end of the apartment, the crinkle of rolling paper in Louis's hands, and an occasional car going by on Armitage Avenue. Louis creased the paper and carefully sprinkled the dope inside the fold, smoothing it out nicely and evenly with his fingers; but he did such a poor job of rolling the joint between his thumbs and index fingers it turned out bumpy and crooked.

"Well," Louis mumbled, twisting both ends of the joint tight, "I never said rolling was my forte." He licked the entire joint and ran it through his lips one final time to suck off any excess spit.

"Shit," Simon said, grimacing, and pointed at the joint. "You think I'm gonna fuckin' smoke that thing after you've greased it all up with your fuckin' mouth?" But Louis didn't even look up at Simon, just said, "That's the way it's done, liberal." They waited a minute or so to let the joint dry, and then Louis lit it. They passed it back and forth with Louis explaining how you have to hold in each drag as long as possible and push your gut down like you're taking a shit so that you drive the smoke into your bloodstream. Each drag burnt Simon's throat more than the one before it, his eyes watering, but he tried to hide his discomfort because the last thing he wanted to do was cough and give Louis a chance to laugh at him. When they had finished the joint, he slouched back in the couch and waited for the high to hit him.

"Do ya feel it yet?" Louis asked, grinning.

Simon shook his head and shrugged his shoulders. "I don't feel shit." He had expected the dope to instantaneously make him feel as if he could float around the room.

"Relax, liberal. It always takes longer the first time."

"Well, it better fuckin' hurry up, 'cause I got to get home in an hour."

"What yo' fuckin' hurry, hunky?" Louis asked.

"Fuck you, asshole, and look who's callin' who a hunky."

Louis threw his head back, a gangbanger sneer on his face. "Sheeeeeit, you not only looks like a hunky, and talks like a hunky, you gotdamn smells like a hunky."

Simon threw his head back and sneered like a gangbanger himself. "Sheeeeeit, only hunky ah see 'round here be you, bawh!"

Louis popped up from his chair, did a pimp walk around to the other side of the coffee table, and stood towering down over Simon with the palms of his hands turned back bad-like and an evil, gangbanger glare in his eyes, even though he was obviously trying hard not to laugh. Softly, yet firmly, he demanded, "Loan m'a dime, hunky."

Simon grinned and looked down at his lap as if hoping Louis would go away, then looked up, not sure he wanted to play this game, as if maybe (though he couldn't quite put his finger on it) there was something racist in it. "Will ya knock it off, Louis."

"Ah say, loan m'a dime, hunky." Simon hit Louis's thigh with an open palm, trying to push him away. "Will ya get the fuck outa here, Louis?"

Suddenly, Louis reached down and yanked Simon to his feet by his shirt collar, demanding, "All ah find, all ah keep, hunky."

At first Simon was startled and off balance, but when Louis started frisking him down for chump-change, he shoved Louis and sprang back a step himself, yelling, "Keep yo' motha'fuckin', monkey-ass hands off me, scrub, fo' ah dot yo' eye!"

There they stood, two white boys playing who could be the blackest, both of them squared-off on opposite sides of the coffee table with belligerent stances.

"Sheeeeeeit," Simon said, "you keep messin' wif' me, ah be forced ta take me some drastic action and wipe me some a dat white off yo' skanky-ass."

Louis doubled over laughing, the high from the reefer hitting him. He barely managed to straighten up long enough to let out a weak, "Sheeeeeit," before he doubled over again and fell to his knees.

"What de fuck you laughin' at, hunky?" Simon went on, pointing an accusing finger down at Louis. "You bes' not be laughin' at me; ain't no hunky evah laughed at me 'less he ready ta joust. Go ahead, motha'fucka'. If you so beau-coup bad, fire on me!"

Simon slapped his hands against his chest as if inviting Louis to hit him with his best punch. "Ah say, fire on me, hunky; jump into ma chest!"

Louis held his hands up as if surrendering. "Awwww, scrub, be coo'."

"Ah ain't no scrub," Simon said indignantly, "and ah ain't no hunky. Ah'm Stone ta de bone," and he beat his right fist proudly against the left side of his chest the way any member of the Peace Stone Nation would represent his club.

"Awwww, brotha'," Louis said, slowly rising to his feet again, "Ah thought we was partners."

As if Simon just could not believe this hunky's audacity, the evil gangbanger glare in his eyes intensified.

"PARTNERS!" he yelled, "PARTNERS? Me partners wif' a hunky? Ah ain't yo' motha'fuckin' partner. Ah ain't even yo' motha'fuckin' associate, much less yo' motha'fuckin' blood; and if you calls me yo' motha'fuckin' brotha' one mo' motha'fuckin' time, ah be forced to whup ya upside yo' motha'fuckin' head. Is dat motha'fuckin' clear? Now, dis here be ma brotha'."

Simon snatched the *Black Panther* newspaper off the coffee table and held it up so that Louis could see the picture of Huey P. Newton on the cover. He held it right next to his face and smiled a big toothy smile.

"See de fambly resemblance? Ah taught Huey P. everthang he know; jus' aks any soul brotha' on de South Side. Say, 'Excuse ma worthless hunky-ass fo' aksin', Mista' Black Afro-American, but who taught Huey P. everythang he know?' And they say, 'Why, Simon, dat who, soul bro' numbah one.' Go ahead and laugh, hunky. Dat's what ah be doin' all las' night when yo' mama be suckin' on ma dick jus' like it was a popcicle stick."

Louis cut his laughter short and glared at Simon. "Don't be talkin' 'bout ma mama. Las' hunky talk 'bout ma mama found his dick hangin' from de gotdamn antenna on de Prudential Buildin'. Go ahead and laugh, hunky, but it true. Dat dude ain't got no mo' dick; he done fucked his last hammer."

"His what?" Simon asked, forgetting he wasn't supposed to be white.

"His hammer, hunky! His hammer! Don't y'all know what a gotdamn hammer be? You know, he be walkin' down de street, leanin' hard on his hammer, when ah drives by in ma white Cadillac and says ta maself, 'Ain't dat de hunky who been signin' on ma mama, who ain't never done nothin' bad in all her sweet life 'cept clean de white folks' homes ta make ends meet?' Sho-nuff it be him, and ah jumps out ma Cadillac, push de hammer flat back on her ass, and den takes out ma knife (which ah carry fo' self-protection), and cuts de hunky's dick off. Weren't no big deal, dem white boy's dicks only be 'bout two inches long, as ah'm sho you know, hunky."

"Sheeeeeeit," Simon said, trying his best to sneer. But now it was he who couldn't stop laughing, and he doubled over forward, his knees buckling as if he were on the verge of collapsing.

"So de hunky be layin' dere, screamin' and shit, wif' blood drippin' down his pants. "Gimme back ma dick, motha'fucka'! Gimme back ma dick!" '

"Will ya shut up, Louis!" Simon plopped back down on the couch, still laughing, yet a sense of uneasiness came over him. He was sure of it: this game was definitely racist. But Louis went right on acting like a black gangbanger, bobbing and weaving his head and shoulders and pointing his finger across the coffee table at Simon when making a point.

"So ah gets ready ta jump back in my Cadillac wif' de hunky's dick tucked away in de pocket of ma tailor-made threads fo' safe keepin', when ah notice dat de white bitch jus' naturally spread her legs afta' fallin' flat on her ass on de sidewalk—might calls it a natural reflex when she finds herself on her back. So ah fucks de bitch wif' de dude lookin' right at us, but he ain't sayin' boo, 'cause he know he can't no way satisfy her pussy no more wif'out no dick. So he jus' start, cryin' and shit, and she be groanin' and shit, and ah'm humpin' like a dawg and fucks de shit outa dat bitch."

"Will ya shut up, Louis!" Simon threw himself out on the couch and kicked his legs up and down like a kid throwing a temper tantrum. He grabbed a small throw pillow and held it down over his face as if that might help him stop laughing.

"So den ah takes de hunky's dick down to de Prudential Buildin', parks ma Cadillac right in de middle a de street, and tell ever'one who be honkin' at me ta kiss ma sweet black ass, 'cause ain't nuffin' but hunkies honkin' anyway. So ah goes into de Prudential Buildin', takes me de el'vator on up to what de hunkys call de *observation* deck—sheeeeeit, ah gives dem somethin' ta observe awright—an ah crawls up on de roof, and climbs like a monkey on up de antenna, and sticks de hunky's dick over de top. It fit sorta tight, 'cause like ah said, it only be a two-inch dick; but ah stretch it out a little, and den it fit jus' fine. Den ah looks out ovah de whole gotdamn Chicago skyline wif' all dem big-ass skyscrapers where de rich hunkies makes all dere gotdamn money off black folk's sweat, and ah say, 'Dat what you get fo' talkin' 'bout ma mama.' Ah'm tellin' ya, ain't no one get Channel Nine tuned in fo' a long time wif' dat hunky's dick ruinin' de reception and all."

Simon took the pillow away from his face, in control of himself just as long as he stared up at the ceiling. Finally, he took a deep breath, looked over at Louis, and sternly said, "That's not funny."

All the air seemed to go out of Louis as he sighed and let his shoulders and arms go limp. He rolled his eyes around as if to say, Jesus Christ, liberal, you sure can be one big drag sometimes. He plopped back down in his chair, lit up a cigarette, took a deep drag, and tilted his head back, blowing out perfectly round smoke rings one right after the other.

"Well, what's all right with you, liberal? I mean, shit, you don't take drugs, you don't drink, you don't fuck, you don't read, you can't even imitate the goddamn niggers without feeling guilty. Fuck, liberal, I've known Baptists who were more fun than you. What exactly is it that you do like to do?"

Simon sat back up on the couch and thought about it for a second. He looked Louis in the eye and said, "Baseball. I like to play baseball."

Louis cocked one hand up behind his ear and leaned forward in his chair. "You what?" He knew Simon was on the school baseball team, but Simon had never talked to him about it, scared Louis would think it was dumb. Now something within Simon refused to let Louis undercut what he loved most, and he threw his hand up angrily, saying, "Fuck you, asshole, I play baseball!"

"Baseball," Louis said impassively, as if this he just could not believe. "The liberal likes to play baseball." But for once this was something Simon knew how to defend.

"Yeah, that's right, fuckface, baseball." Simon looked down at the coffee table, yet his eyes were focused on what he saw in his mind. "I like the feeling you get when you're out in center field, and you can smell the grass, and there's all these fuckin' dandelions, and the sun's real hot, 'cause it's summer, and from out in center field it's like you can see the whole game, and the infielders are all chattering, 'Hey-batter-hey-batter-hey-batter-heeeeeeeey-SWING!' I know it don't make no sense, but you get to where you can tell a batter's going to hit the ball at you before the pitcher even throws it. It's like everything gets real quiet inside your head and then—BAM!—there's that crack of the bat, and you're already runnin' back as fast as you can, 'cause you know just by the sound of the bat that the ball's comin' way the fuck over your head. So you follow it as it comes over your shoulder and run like a motherfucker; and just when you think there ain't no way you're gonna make it in time, you dive for it. It's like you're fuckin' flyin', and every muscle in your whole body is strainin' for that goddamn ball, and just like a miracle you just barely catch it inside the top of your web; then as you slide through the grass you know that this is what you play baseball for, this is what you always want, 'cause it's cool, man! It's fuckin' cool!"

Simon pantomimed the infielders crouching down, waiting for the batter to swing, then the outfielder running for the fly ball while looking up at it over his shoulder, diving for it and coming up with it in his glove. He was leaning forward on the edge of the couch now and looking across the coffee table at Louis to see if he was getting the picture, but Louis just sat there letting cigarette smoke out through his nose.

"Baseball," he said, just as impassively as the time before, except now his facade seemed forced, his eyes right on Simon.

"I mean, did you ever hit a baseball?" Simon asked, "I mean really hit one solid?" He stood up between the couch and the coffee table and assumed a batting stance, his hands gripping an imaginary bat. "I swear to God, ain't nothin' feels better in your hands than to grip a baseball bat nice and tight."

"I can think of a few things that feel better to grip nice and tight," Louis said; but Simon closed his eyes for a moment, shook his head, and held his hand up as if to block Louis's words.

"No, really, jagoff, there ain't nothin' feels better than when you hit a ball real solid." He assumed his batting stance again, looking straight ahead as if at a pitcher.

"It's like you're up at the plate; and the pitcher goes into his windup; and you're already steppin' into the pitch before the ball even leaves his hand; and you can feel the power in your body uncoil right up your legs and into your hips; and then your arms start to come around; and just at the moment when your bat meets the ball you flick those wrists and—BAM!"

For just a second he watched the flight of the imaginary ball that he had just hit, then looked at Louis.

"See, no one thinks I can hit a ball far 'cause I'm skinny, but it don't take no muscles to hit a ball far, it just takes wrists—quick wrists and timing. That's why I use a skinny handle bat, so I can get that quick wrist action and then—BAM!—there's that solid crack; and the ball takes off in a line drive down the left field line; but you don't look to see how far it's goin', 'cause that wastes time; you just put your head down and take off runnin' down the baseline; and if the first base coach waves you on, you go for two, then three; and if the third base coach waves you around, you head for home; and ya come barrelin' down the line like a motherfuckin' tank, 'cause ya don't know where the ball is, and ya ain't got time to look back; and, meanwhile, the other team's relayin' it in; and all you know is it's gonna be close 'cause the catcher looks like he's gettin' set to catch the ball; and your whole team is up off the bench, yellin', 'Slide! Slide! HIT THE DIRT!' So you get there just as the ball gets there, but you go in head first and knock the fuckin' catcher flat back on his ass; and just like a dumb shit he drops the ball and you score. Then your whole team is clappin' and screamin', and you slap-five with everyone, 'cause ya just hit a home run."

Simon pantomimed everything he told, even the slapping-five with his teammates. Louis leaned forward in his chair as if he wanted to get up and walk around, then he leaned back again as if somehow pinned there.

"Ya know," Simon went on, sitting down on the edge of the couch again, "the first time my dad took me to Wrigley Field I just couldn't believe how pretty it was. For some reason I thought it was gonna look black and white 'cause that's the way it always looked on TV, but Jesus! the outfield grass was so fuckin' green, and the infield dirt looked almost orange, and there was all that thick ivy growin' up the outfield walls, and everyone was screamin' and shit. I was only seven years old. The first time Ernie Banks came to the plate, he hit the first pitch all the way out onto Waveland Avenue. I knew right then I wanted to be a major leaguer. I mean, shit, when I lived in Cardinal Park everyone played baseball. First ya start out in the Peewee League, and then ya move up to the Midgets, and then Pony. So it's like everyone's on a team; and everyone wears their baseball cap to school; and you can tell what team someone's on just by how old they are and what color cap they got on; and it gets fuckin' embarrassing if you're in last place, but it's cool if you're in first. I was an All-Star for three straight years! I used to play baseball all day. I mean ya get to where ya play so much baseball you know what to do before it even happens: man on first—play's at two; bases loaded—force at home; watch out for the bunt—third base and first base pull in; steal sign on—shortstop cover second; full count—runners goin'; sacrifice fly—tag up and then dig for home. Two hands, always catch the ball with two hands; and keep the bat level; and when ya win, rub it in—Two! Four! Six! Eight! Who do we appreciate? Yankees! Yankees! Yeeeeeey!"

Simon had jumped to his feet, his hands above his head as if he had just thrown his baseball mitt into the air to celebrate his team's victory. And then the words were just there in his mouth. He looked at Louis, put his arms back down at his sides, and said, "I know how your father died."

He took Louis completely off guard, and their eyes locked, every muscle in Louis's face subtly changing from disbelief, to grinning, to anger, back to disbelief. He tried not to move, not to show any clue. He was ten years old when his mother had left it to his uncle to tell him that his father was dead. Louis had not cried then, nor during the wake or funeral. But three months later, he took the miniature pool table that his mother and father had given him the last Christmas—by far the nicest gift he had ever received—and dropped it off the back porch, watching it fall two stories to the yard below, where it cracked on impact down the center of the green, felt-covered surface. When his mother came home from her secretarial job later that day, she found him lying on his bed, crying. He told her what he had done, but when she asked him why, he could only shrug his shoulders, not knowing how to explain the logic of needing to break something he loved and break it beyond repair.

"So," Louis said, staring at Simon, his jaw twitching and his lips held tight. "So ya know. Whaddaya want, a fuckin' medal? It's not like it's any secret; it was on the front page of every fuckin' newspaper in the country."

He looked furious, furious with Simon, with his father, with the whole goddamn world. Simon sat back down on the edge of the couch, uncomfortable with the advantage he suddenly felt over Louis. For the first time that evening he noticed the dark circles under Louis's eyes, the gaunt cheeks, the eyes an empty gray.

"I just wanted you to know I know," he said, and then, trying to disarm Louis's anger by offering him a chance to hurt him back, Simon asked him something he had wanted to ask for a long time.

"Why do you hang around me anyway?"

For a moment Louis looked as if he would say the nastiest, foulest, go-for-the-jugular thing he could think of, but then he leaned back in his chair, contemplating. Finally, he said, "Because you're so fucking normal."

Simon knitted his eyebrows together questioningly. He glanced around the loft, thinking, Normal? Normal? He wasn't sure how to take that, for this was 1969, year of the "flower child" and hard underground rock and "Power to the People!" and "Off the Pigs," and somehow "normal" just didn't seem to cut it.

Both of them avoided each other's eyes for a while, nothing to break the silence but the hum of the fluorescent light and an occasional car going down Armitage Avenue. And then, as if trying unsuccessfully to shake the ghostly gray out of his eyes, Louis asked, "So, do ya feel it yet?"

Simon looked over at Louis, still preoccupied with digesting his new title of Normal. "Feel what?"

"The grass, liberal, the grass."

Simon rested back into the couch again, looked across the loft at nothing in particular, and shook his head. "Naw, I don't feel shit."

Korean War Novel, untitled

John Schultz

There was a great silence, a lid, that was put on the Korean War, directly after it happened, in a way that did not happen with the Viet Nam War. This lid of silence occurred partly because the Korean War lasted only three years and was extremely unpopular; Americans wished to regard it as an aberration, not as the shape of the future, whereas the Viet Nam War lasted ten or more years, time enough to divide the country. More than two and a half million people were killed in Korea, which is about a million more than were killed in all the years of U.S. involvement in Viet Nam, though more American soldiers were killed in Viet Nam.

   The time of the story straddles the months before and after the end of the Korean War, two years or so after the integration of blacks and whites in American army units. First Lieutenant Wilfred Woodson, a black man and a decorated career officer, takes command of the 163rd Heavy Equipment Company (Engineers) from Captain Baker, an easy-going reservist. The company is shocked by Woodson's gung-ho style of command, his careerist zeal. Principal characters are Pfc Asdourian, the 163rd's Personnel Clerk, a sharp, witty, energetic soldier; Cpl Masterson, Company Clerk, who becomes involved in a self-destructive struggle to maintain himself with the new CO; M/Sgt Ball, a rigid First Sergeant, with a mysterious past that is suddenly and devastatingly exposed; Cpl Warner, a senior medic at the 144th Medical Detachment and friend of Asdourian; Col. Taylor, Commanding Officer of the 68th Engineer Group; Pfc Rhodes, a deserter for two years; and others. The negotiation over the repatriation of prisoners of war continues at Panmunjom. With their constant demonstrations, rebellions, and escapes, the PWs housed in pens near the 68th's compounds create a tense, suspenseful situation. The novel deals with conflicts between soldiers and officers and between the United States army and the Korean populace, and with combat situations created by the PWs and guerilla, fires that destroy half the city, and mass PW escapes. Because many of the characters were involved in the early parts of the war, the novel becomes a story of the entire war.

John Schultz authored the short novel "Custom" in *3x3* and *4x4* (Grove Press); *The Tongues of Men* (short stories and novelle), Big Table, Follett; *No One Was Killed* (non-fiction novel about the Democratic Convention of 1968), Big Table, Follett; *Motion Will Be Denied* (non-fiction novel about the Chicago Conspiracy trial), William Morrow. The play-version of "Custom" was produced at the Body Politic Theater in Chicago. He originated the Story Workshop method of teaching writing and has continued to develop and broaden it. He chairs the Writing/English department and is head of the Masters programs in Creative Writing and the Teaching of Writing at Columbia College, Chicago. His text *Writing From Start to Finish* and *The Teacher's Manual for Writing From Start to Finish* are published by Boynton/Cook.

From *A Korean War Novel, untitled*

Responsibility

by John Schultz

During cherry blossom time, in April, in Pusan, spring 1953, in the large compound of the 68th Engineer Group, in the area of the 163rd Heavy Equipment Company, Master Sergeant Ball inspected the company area in the morning, afternoon, evening, and night, wanting to see each blossom and each tree from every possible angle and distance. The barbwire-enclosed compound contained the only trees of any kind in this city of hundreds of thousands of shacks and more than a million refugees. Stocky, strong-chested, square-faced, with grey-blond crew-cut, he reached up delicately to bring down, touch, and smell the sprigs of bloom. The very mountains that ringed the city on one side and pressed it toward the sea were stripped barren from the constant search for firewood. The fact that these cherry trees existed solely because of military protection, first Japanese, then American, pleased Ball. In the night, among the trees, he listened to the fire alarms, coming from anywhere in the jammed shacky city, savaging the night. Ball, because he was First Sergeant, had a small room of his own in the staff prefab, where it was possible for him to write by a small lamp after lights out at eleven, secretly, a biographical history of Roman commanders.

On this warm spring evening, after lights out, he strolled in Japanese shower slippers, gripping the thongs between his big toes and the next toe, wearing fatigue pants, white T-shirt stretched across his solid chest. He was thinking about Hannibal and Carthage, the First Punic

War, and Scipio Africanus the Elder and Scipio the Younger, historical figures with a freshened presence for him since the amazing appearance of his new Commanding Officer, a Negro, First Lieutenant Wilfred Woodson. Ball, as he saw it, had exchanged the shabby, easygoing command of Captain Baker, a civilian construction engineer in officer's uniform, for the command of a black man who wore the Combat Infantryman's Badge, had been a Ranger, had medals from the fighting in the first part of the war, and had taken a hundred Chinese prisoners once. This information caused a shuddering alertness to pass through the company and a strange expectation to rise in Ball.

From the first day of being commanded by "a man of color," Ball felt a sort of physical awkwardness, though the uncomfortability was more that he thought he ought to feel something special than that he actually felt it. Suspended between the *ought to* and his mysterious appreciation, he sought precedents in ancient history. Hannibal was a black man, and there were rumors in history that the Scipios had swarthy blood from being conceived and raised in Spain. Ball peered at pictures of Roman coins in his reference books, examining the profiles of the Scipios for negroid features.

This night he was stoically excited with imagining Hannibal floating his elephants across the Rhone River on rafts covered with sod. The sod must have been put there to reassure and pacify the elephants. Or was it because they wouldn't step onto, couldn't keep their balance on, the round logs of the rafts? He made a mental note to research the point. He was also trying to imagine the challenges of provisioning such an army in ancient times, an army of 50,000 men, of thousands of horses and other beasts, moving from North Africa, through Spain, France, Germany, and down toward Italy. There must have been little left stored or growing behind such an army. Did they buy it, or take it? How much did they bring in supply wagons? Ball tried to imagine the American army living off the land in Korea. Kim-chi every day...The war would not last long.

In the midst of such imaginings, on the embankment by the farthest latrine and its ammonia odors, on the edge of the ghostly blooming trees, in the vast hilly darkness sprinkled with lights that was Pusan at night, Ball discovered himself looking puzzled across the heavy equipment staging arena, at an odd conjunction of persons at the barbwire fence, in the corner behind the motor pool out of view of the rest of the compound. The soldier on this side of the fence, who should have been walking guard with his rifle on his shoulder, was pressed with his front against the fence, his back to Ball, with another person in white on the outside of the fence stooped over in front of him. There was a sort of jostling of both figures, as if they were somehow joined. The sight of the M-1 rifle leaning on the fence beside the soldier horrified Ball. He tightened his lips against the impulse to scream at the soldier, and wake every man in the company. He recognized the way the skinny little soldier stood stretched up against the wire, the uniform sort of dripping down his body. That was Pfc Kowalski. Ball hurried awkwardly toward the scene. Coming in his flapping shower slippers around the motor pool building, he saw Kowalski gripping the fence with both hands, shining erect red penis thrust through an opening in the wire into the mouth of a stooped over jo-san, whose head moved up and down, rather carefully among the barbwire loops, a kind of groan being pulled out of Kowalski. Ball loosed a hoarse whisper that shocked the air:

"Soldier! Kowalski!"

With a wrench of terror, Kowalski grabbed his M-1, jerked around toward Ball, jerkily stopping himself from pulling the trigger. The hushed horror of Ball's voice—"Soldier!"—hit Kowalski again. In the dark in the street beyond the barbwire, an excited chatter of voices met the woman as she ran away. Kowalski mumbled, "Sarge...," with a terrible ache in his wrenched chest, frantically leaned his M-1 against his hip, and stuffed the object of his satisfaction inside his pants and fumbled with the buttons of his fly. He was shrinking throughout his body with stammering terror of all the guilt and fear of retribution he'd ever known.

Having been on the point of orgasm, hot and frigid reactions cutting through him, he experienced the impulse, the urgent need, as if it came from outside and possessed him, to shoot Ball then and there. *Do it now* screamed through him. But nothing happened.

Imposing, with his hands on his hips and his white T-shirt stretched in the dark against the motor pool, Ball said, "Soldier, report to the orderly room at o-nine-hundred tomorrow morning, and report to the sergeant of the guard now, as soon as you are relieved." Kowalski watched Ball march away, the first sergeant's chin jutting above the ordinary level. Kowalski's heart thudded, like someone knocking on a door to be heard.

By the time a soldier came running on the double to relieve him, he was quivering from head to toe.

In the dark quonset barracks, chattering uncontrollably, Kowalski dropped his M-1 on his bunk and looked up and down the humps of men under OD blankets, yearning for a voice to talk with him. He felt that only a voice could warm him. He was jerked and pulled by the chagrined feeling that he should have been able to avoid discovery. He took his stack of comic books out from the shelf of the orange crate beside his cot and, fumbling with a pencil flashlight, began focusing the tiny beam on comic book frames of Superman, Green Lantern, Wonder Woman. He was on the verge of sobbing. When the jo-san was sucking him off, he'd been imagining behind closed eyes that it was Wonder Woman. Then, as he was holding his mother's framed picture on top of the lapful of comic books, a wave of darkness swept him into sleep. He slept the rest of the night, in his uniform with his boots half unlaced, having awful flinching dreams of doors opening and rooms falling away on all sides. In the morning, he woke with his cheek against the barrel of his M-1.

Through the company's regular morning schedule, he took each step forward in time, to the washroom, through calisthenics and hand-to-hand, to Supply to check in his M-1, now toward the mess hall, as if amazed, yet dully with no feeling at all, that the ground actually existed there to meet his feet. He ate with dread, swallowing with difficulty and thinly, mumbling only a few syllables to the men at his table, aching with the fear that he'd become different from them. There was so much time to pass away, stare away, pace away, before 0900 hours, when in an unbelieving daze, his stomach clutched like a cold fist, he presented himself at the Orderly Room, taking off his fatigue cap the moment he entered.

Sitting barrel-like behind his desk, First Sergeant Ball, at the sight of Kowalski, pointed rigidly with his right first finger across his chest toward the closed door of the CO's office, but said nothing. He beckoned for Corporal Masterson, the tall, loose-bodied, white company clerk, to come with him into Woodson's office, and instructed Pfc Teale to watch the Orderly Room and not to disturb them except in an emergency. Teale, hunched earnestly over his typewriter, caught the look in Kowalski's eyes. "Yes, sir," he said. Teale was ringing inside from the helpless look in Kowalski's eyes.

Through the opening and closing of the CO's door, the office on the other side flashed with color, brightness, and the feeling of power. The American flag drooped in folds down the standard beside First Lieutenant Woodson's desk, Woodson's dark head with close wiry hair looking sculptured, his brown face deliberately expressionless, crimson engineer's scarf filling his neck, his brown hands on top white papers, his green uniform sharply creased and besprinkled with colorful ribbons and shining insignia, as he sat behind his desk. Private First Class Kowalski heard Woodson say to Ball and Masterson, "We are going to dynamite that rock before noon," and knew it was about a large outcropping of rock in the final prisoner-of-war compound to be prepared. The determination of his fate seemed to be an embarrassing interruption in a more important conversation.

The new CO of the 163rd Heavy Equipment Company, First Lieutenant Wilfred Woodson, often felt that the other officers in the 68th Engineer Group, the white officers, talked eagerly and jovially with him, or with reserved carefulness, in ways that urged a continuous smile from him, and it was tiring, really tiring, as if struggling in nets in a dream. By Woodson's desk, First Sergeant Ball stood rigid as a strung bow, chest out. Whenever Ball addressed him formally, or stood at attention before him, Woodson felt power flow almost unbearably through his body. And that could be tiring too. He would have to work on relaxing his blond, grey-eyed First Sergeant. In short bursts of words, Ball reported that Pfc Kowalski, while on guard duty last night, had been discovered committing "sodomistic practices" through the fence. In effect, in actuality, Ball declared, Kowalski had put down his weapon and left his post.

"You mean, he was..." Woodson restrained the involuntary twitch of his hand toward his own behind "...in the rear?"

Ball flushed red in his square face, up to his ears and into his grey-blond crewcut, a glowing blush that Woodson had seen only two or three times in his life. He looked away from the too marvelous sight of Ball's face, while Ball explained in unbelievably precise language how Kowalski was receiving, through the fence, the oral attentions of a Korean woman. That funny humming feeling came into Woodson's gut, which meant that something he much desired was about to be made to happen. Corporal Masterson was staring at the wall above his Company Commander's head. Woodson was a little irritated by the way Masterson, the Company Clerk, stood loosely at attention with a yellow legal pad in one hand against his thigh.

Woodson was nervous about disciplining this fuck-up Kowalski and did not quite understand why he should be fluttering his fingertips on his desk and against his thighs under his desk, until he realized that he intended to do more than discipline him. Never waste a fuck-up. He was the personal commander of two hundred and forty-eight men. He was tempted—saw the possibility—to use this fuck-up importantly, to send a message to the two hundred and forty-seven other men, two of them right there in the office with him, Ball and Masterson.

"He ought to be hung for that," Woodson said to Ball, who still stood rigidly.

"Yes, sir," Ball said.

"At ease," Woodson said. "At ease, Sergeant."

Ball relaxed slightly, ever so slightly, standing on the side of the desk near the flag, moving his feet slightly apart, putting his hands behind him. Woodson savored the calm, ritual feeling of having his blond, grey-eyed First Sergeant standing at ease beside his desk. Ball had not so far in the first few weeks of Woodson's command flattered him, but did give hard, bright obedience.

"This is a grave offense, Sergeant."

"It is, sir."

Woodson knew that many armies of history and of the present would shoot a man for such as Kowalski's infraction. Disorder caused by the expressed sexual impulse was something that armies feared; they either imposed the disorder of their sexual urges upon occupied or conquered peoples, or rigorously suppressed and transformed those urges into an ecstatic warrior mentality. If there was one thing of which Wilfred Woodson was scholarly, even more so than of basic combat and construction engineering, it was what "best soldiers" meant. What was the spirit of a soldier, a unit, a commander, an army, a nation, that made it good or "best" in soldiery? What the fuck did they do in those puritanical armies, the ancient Hebrew, the Greek, the modern Chinese? Just take it out on the enemy? They stood a man such as Kowalski up, tied to a post, in front of his witnessing comrades, and shot him, to get the solemn thrill of discipline. Never waste a fuck-up. Woodson thought the North Koreans would have shot such a man. The Russians, like Americans, fucked anything they met. The Chinese were the "best soldiers" he'd ever heard of. They never rotated, didn't know what not-a-day-too-soon one-year rotation meant. Two and a half years now on the line in Korea, some of them. They had legs, they could walk right up those mountains and then run the rest of the way. They could patrol, my God, how they could move in the dark. Playing his fingers on his knees under the desk, Woodson was chagrined and admiring even now of how they'd slipped right through the wire piled in front of his company's trenches, no sweat, and dragged Johnson out of his bunk in the bunker, out the entrance before he knew what was happening, dragged him screaming in his socks and OGs, no hat, no gloves, in that awful cold, back along the path they'd cut through the wire. Flares went up and swung above them in the upended frozen paddies, the wind in the barren little ming trees and the piles of concertina wire, the sour smell of phosphorus, shadows swaying. The gook patrol just stood up in the middle of the wire, not fifty yards away from the trench, the three of them pressed close to Johnson, making a strange beast with many legs and hands, and Johnson screaming "Don't shoot, don't shoot." Second Lieutenant Woodson would have shot them anyway, if the captain hadn't yelled "Don't shoot," too. Then every fuck-up that thought he might be walked out the same way someday yelled "Don't shoot, don't shoot," up and down the trenches. Johnson was still screaming when they went over the ridge. Out of the darkness came the sound of Chinese reed instruments playing "There's No Place Like Home." Glancing at his fingertips on the edge of his desk, Woodson marveled at what his hands had been then, in the winter in the trenches, chapped, cracked, caked with dirt and grease, broken painful nails, cracks in fingers, chapped lips, chapped cheeks, raw forehead, legs chapped by the wind through his pants. Hands hurt all the time. Poured weapons oil on them once when he couldn't find Vaseline. That hurt too. Why think of Johnson just before facing Kowalski? Johnson's name showed up on a Red Cross POW list weeks later. Something about Johnson. How did the gooks pick him out? Fuck-up. Soft in there, wants to complain and be trampled, to bitch and be kicked. Wants to be used, to feel the surprise of wanting the knife. Fuck-ups get fucked.

In two weeks the Chinese thought they'd waited long enough for the Americans to forget their lessons. For two days running, Woodson pulled in the outposts, laying an ambush for Chink's next patrol. Sucked it right into his platoon's section of the trench. And nailed it. He killed one gook in the depression of the company's latrine in the bottom of the trench. That look, that fuck-up's surprise, just as Woodson pulled the trigger on the carbine, and then it was as if the gook'd bit into a lemon. Just a mask of a punched-in face. Bits of brains frozen in the dirt they pissed on in the morning. Four Chinese dead and one prisoner. We'd done it right for once. And he'd shook involuntarily from head to toe for an hour or more afterward, trying to keep it suppressed so his platoon wouldn't notice.

Hunched over in his quilted cotton jacket, the prisoner squatted on his heels in the trench. He shrank down and to the side every time the American Negro Second Lieutenant came near him, in the bright, cold sunlight of the amazing morning. Woodson smiled big and said, "You're going to meet my eyes, motherfucker," as he squatted beside the PW, lit two cigarettes with his stiff hands, and offered the PW one. The PW held the cigarette like a pencil and puffed without inhaling and did not look at Woodson. Woodson sat there to show him that he could decide on his death or his life, until the PW felt it, did a slow shift of his squinty slant eyes, met Woodson's eyes, smiled, and was taken away, maybe knowing that every oppressed minute of his life was a gift from then on.

That was almost a year and a half ago, a different outfit, a different tour of duty, and more than two hundred miles north on the MLR. Maybe he's in one of the PW compounds that we're working on over there at the foot of the mountain right now. Maybe I've driven past him when he was standing and staring out the wire. Fuck-ups get fucked.

With his booted toes on the floor under his desk, Woodson lifted his heels and jiggled his feet. Then he planted his boots flat. "Bring Pfc Kowalski in here, Corporal," Woodson said.

"Yes, sir." Licking his lips at the surprise of having said even those two words, Masterson opened the door, held it, and nodded at the anxious Kowalski on the other side. The slight Pfc, his starched fatigues oddly big on him, marched into the room, the plywood floors amplifying every scrape and thump. He faced about toward Woodson, trembling, saluted and said:

"Private First Class Kowalski reporting, sir."

It was the voice of someone who had been dead for ten hours.

Woodson returned the salute briskly, perfectly, negligently. Masterson lowered himself carefully into the chair on Woodson's left, holding the pad of yellow paper and a pencil, to keep some rough record of the coming event.

Woodson spoke with matter-of-fact accusation, not a hint of tongue in cheek. "You were sleeping on guard duty last night, Private."

"No, sir," Kowalski said, bewildered, shifting his eyes and head toward Ball, questioningly, protestingly, and Ball screamed, "Attention! Answer your commanding officer!" Corporal Masterson shuddered and closed his eyes.

Kowalski felt wiped out. "No, sir," he said, unsure if he actually heard the words come out of his mouth.

Ball screamed again, "No, sir *what*, Private?"

"I was not sleeping on guard duty last night, sir."

Woodson spoke evenly. "What were you doing, Private?"

Kowalski felt himself shrinking, unclean, slovenly, inadequate to speak before the entirely clean, strong, shining Negro First Lieutenant, in the sharply creased uniform. He so much wanted to please Woodson that he gargled on the impulse to shout "Kill! Kill!" because Woodson always smiled brightly and meanly, during the morning's bayonet and hand-to-hand practice, when "Kill! Kill!" was yelled savagely.

"What were you seen doing last night on guard duty, Private?"

Kowalski had not known that the mouth, his mouth, could get so dry. He was sure that no words could come out of it. "Sergeant Ball saw me leaning on the fence, sir."

Woodson shook his head briefly to indicate that Kowalski was not giving the right answers.

"Where was your weapon, Private?"

"Beside me, sir." Kowalski's mouth was so dry, like squeaky cotton, shivers went down his spine.

"In your hands, Private?"

"No, sir."

"Well, where?"

"Leaning on the fence right beside me, sir."

Then Woodson spoke in a monotone, his words full and rolling. "Where was your gun, Private?" He was punning on the Army hazing rhyme, in which fuck-ups were sometimes made to stand on a mess hall table and demonstrate with rifle and open fly, "This is my weapon/This is my gun/This is for shooting/This is for fun."

"I didn't say gun, sir. I said my weapon was leaning on the fence."

"Repeat the rhyme for me, Private. You know what I mean."

Kowalski's mouth moved in a stiff, cottony way, tears making him blink. "This is my weapon/This is my gun...." He moved his hand automatically to gesture toward his fly, and Ball screamed, "Attention! Soldier, you are at attention!" That meant no movement, no speaking, except to answer direct questions.

"This is for shooting/This is for fun..."

Woodson, before Kowalski finished, glanced toward Corporal Masterson. With slightly agog mouth, barely suppressed squirming, the Company Clerk scribbled in desperate bursts on his yellow pad. Masterson would be the carrier of the message to the other two hundred and forty-five men.

"Now what were you doing on guard duty last night, Private?"

"I had not left my post, sir." Kowalski wanted so badly, so beggingly, to have it over with. "I was having sex, sir."

Kowalski's frankness caught Woodson off guard and made him shift about in his chair and bring his hands up onto the desk, folding one on top of the other, as he leaned forward. So Kowalski wanted the game to be over, did he? "Were there women, jo-sans, as you call them, inside the compound, Private?"

The way Woodson persisted in calling him "Private" was distracting to Private First Class Kowalski. "No, sir," he said.

"Then you had left your post."

"No, sir." With no will or energy to give further explanation, Kowalski could not get over the quivering in himself of wanting to find out what Woodson wanted. He was frightened that Woodson appeared to want more than the simple facts.

"If you had not left your post, with whom, of which sex, and how, were you having it?"

"My eyes were wide open, sir."

Ball screamed, "Answer your commanding officer! With whom, which sex, and how?"

Kowalski knew, with a sort of narrow urgency, that he was pressed with the need to mitigate against the charge of having put down his weapon and left his post. Sleeping on guard duty and leaving one's post were comparable to treason or desertion under fire. There was always the feeling that men were shot for these crimes.

Woodson looked at his folded hands on the desk, gathering strength.

"You were having sex," he said.

"With a woman, a jo-san, sir," Kowalski said, now fearing somehow a charge of homosexuality. "I was still on duty, sir. The guard always walks along the motor pool there, sir."

Ball leaned toward Kowalski and in yet another short scream that hit the Pfc like a blast, said, "Explain to your commanding officer how you did not leave your post!"

With Kowalski at attention before him, Ball on one side, Masterson on the other, Woodson was overtaken by a feeling of relaxed power. He uttered words and desired reactions occurred among these three men.

"I was being...getting, sir...a suck-a-ha-chee job." Kowalski couldn't help but see it even now in the comic book frame, with Wonder Woman doing it to him.

"You went to a local house. You left your post."

"No, sir." A nausea tightened in the bottom of his stomach. "I stuck it—," he gestured helplessly, hearing himself near tears, toward his fly, and Ball screamed again, "Attention! Attention!"

With his hands at his side, Kowalski said, "I stuck it through the fence for the jo-san, sir," feeling as if, being at attention, he were sticking it now toward Woodson.

Woodson worked his lips to get every wrinkle of expression out of his face. "You were still holding your weapon in the prescribed manner, Private." Masterson heard that line, sick with how urgently he wanted to giggle, yet miserable for Kowalski, and broke his pencil lead; he looked blankly at the snap of it, and stared out the window behind Kowalski across the heavy equipment staging arena, down to the barbed wire fence. The traffic of Koreans on foot, in the dusty street on the other side of the fence, moved in both directions. Sunlight flashed off the shacks sided with flattened GI beer cans.

"My M-1 was beside me, sir." Kowalski was begging.

"In your hands." Woodson never gave an interrogatory inflection now.

"No, sir. Leaning on the fence, sir."

Out of the corner of his eyes Woodson watched Masterson, the sick, lax smile on Masterson's face. Woodson saw that Kowalski was close to tears. Tension left the room, like wings departing. Ball shifted, yet without moving. Given up, released from self-esteem, Kowalski could not understand the stir in his groin.

"Guard duty is a grave responsibility, soldier. I always think of it as a privilege to protect your fellows. Now," Woodson said, "we come to the matter of punishment."

He looked down at his hands folded one on top the other on the desk. The attention of the three men grew upon him. The awareness of listening spread out from him like a ripple on a pond, to the sounds of a typewriter being pecked by Pfc Teale in the outside office, to, seen through the window behind Kowalski, a hundred yards to the other side of the fence by the staging arena, an old Korean man in dirty white rags running stooped on tiptoe with a yoke across his shoulders and buckets swinging from each end of it. "You could be rolling barrels in the Pusan stockade," he thought deliberately out loud, "and mastering the stockade shuffle."

"Yessir," Kowalski mumbled.

He could see to it that Kowalski was given a summary or even a special court-martial. He could see to it that Kowalski was sent up for "six and two-thirds"—six months in the stockade, fined two-thirds of his pay, and busted to E-1, buck private; he could make it a long time before Kowalski returned to the States. But Woodson also knew that his interest in discipline went against the norms of the American army in this quasi-combat area that paid little attention to uniform, military courtesy, general inspection—"chickenshit," in short. The actual charge against Kowalski was that of putting down his weapon. If he'd held the M-1 at port arms and surveyed the area along the fence while the jo-san orally administered to his sexual needs, the charge would be less clear. During the shabby get-the-job-done command of Captain Baker, only two weeks ago, Kowalski would have received a disgusted reprimand, Woodson was sure. It was also Kowalski's first offense. Fairness and "warning" were the traditional punishment for a first offense; however, Woodson wanted more of this fuck-up, more reverberation. He wanted Masterson, Kowalski, and Ball to deliver a definite message to the other two hundred and forty-five men in the 163rd. Shape up, yes. And more. The three men in the room were waiting to hear what he would do. He himself was waiting to hear what he would do.

"Your pass privileges will be revoked for seven days. You will be confined to the company area for that time. You will serve your usual details. Stay awake, Prviate, and keep your hands on your weapon at all times. Do you understand?"

"Yes, sir."

The message would go out. The two hundred and forty-five other men in the company would regard the interrogation as a timely warning and the punishment as exemplary. Kowalski was bewilderingly relieved. His pants were damp in the crotch, damp with the feeling of having had the pitiful little jerks of an orgasm without erection. He felt a personal understanding between himself and Woodson. Only Company Punishment, seven days without pass privileges, no court-martial. He flicked a look at Master Sergeant Ball.

"Dismissed," Woodson said.

"Dismissed," Ball repeated, hoarsely.

Kowalski did a good about-face, then paused, bereft, without memory or purpose, as if his mind had been taken away from him, and could not remember how to leave. Then he saw the door and marched toward it, putting out a hand to go through it.

Pfc Teale, at his typewriter, chewing on a typewriter eraser, sneaked a look up at Kowalski as he went past and did not recognize his face.

Woodson watched the door to the outside office swing back and forth in shorter and shorter arcs, boppety-boppety flashes of Kowalski bumping desks and mailtrays as, dazed, he threaded his way. When the door came to a stop, and its unvarnished plywood stood between him and Pfc Teale in the outer office, Woodson said, with a laugh, a slap of his knee, to Ball and Masterson, "What a way to go, and didn't even get his rocks off!" as he swung his head from side to side.

He became aware of silence from the two white men. Standing by the flag standard, Ball touched the fingertips of his hands together at his waist and smiled slightly at the empty space. Woodson saw Masterson gaping at him and immediately felt that he should not have said what he said. The obedient Ball never said an approving word about anything, but now Woodson knew, from the sudden simmer in his viscera, that that was the game that would be played between him and the First Sergeant, the game of withholding approval. Woodson got to his feet with a bang of his chair. "OK," he said, reaching for his hat, "let's go and blow up that rock."

Marquette Park

Gary Johnson

Marquette Park tells the story of the volatile relationship between Claus Burling, a young dock worker, and his wife Gloria, and their mutual realization that their marriage is collapsing. Set in the Marquette Park area, a rigidly segregated South Chicago neighborhood, the story also tells how mounting racial pressure dramatically affects Claus, his immediate and extended family, and the friends and neighbors he has known all his life. Frenzied street fighting and mob violence break out when blacks, marching for open housing into Marquette Park, are met with bricks and bottles and swastikas and chants of "Niggers go home!" As the story progresses, the street fighting, woven through and counterpointing the family tensions, becomes the focus of Claus's rage. Within the intricacies of the family and the wider sense of community, the story is about the pent-up frustrations and consequences of not being able to see other points of view, of not being able, even for a moment, to walk in another man's shoes or understand his dilemma. To protect their turf from neighborhood change, Claus and his friends, over many days and nights of bloody confrontations, finally chase down, drag from a car, and beat and stab a black man, leaving him for dead. It is the Bicentennial summer of 1976.

Born and raised on the South Side of Chicago, Gary Johnson teaches creative writing in Chicago. His work has appeared in *Hair Trigger III, The Best of Hair Trigger,* and *Privates.* In 1980, he was a judge for the nationwide college literary contest of the Coordinating Council of Literary Magazines (CCLM). He is a 1981 winner of the Edwin L. Schuman Award for fiction at Northwestern University.

from *Marquette Park*

"Bachelor Party"

Gary Johnson

For three days fierce quarreling from the Burling household sailed out over the rows of peaked bungalows crowding Fairfield Avenue. From dinner table to bed, husband and wife hounded one another with room-to-room shouting that sent their two children to their separate bedrooms with nervous stomachs. Neighbors heard the shouting as they sat on their front porches, walked their dogs on leashes down the dark alley, and slept in their beds. Rising early for first shift factory and downtown office jobs, already irritable with the hot, sticky August nights, they considered calling police when Gloria Burling's screams of rage ripped through the early morning darkness.

On day three of the fighting, playing his usual game of screeching his tires and jockeying lanes, Claus Burling barreled along Pulaski Avenue in his high-performance Dodge Charger, downshifting abruptly so his chromed exhaust pipes growled low and mean. Working stick shift and steering wheel with his powerful arms, a cigarette hanging from his mouth, he squinted his eyes against the gray smoke searing across his face.

"Guess the wife likes to hear herself scream!" he yelled above his rumbling exhaust, the cigarette jumping in his lips. "Gets so bad, I just shut off my ears. Only way to survive in that house!" Slouched in the passenger bucket seat, Lucho Chrisanti, a dark, young-faced Italian boy who had just announced he was getting married, stared out his window, turned away from Claus.

81

"Ey, Lucho! Ya listening to me?" and he slapped Lucho's arm with the back of his hand. Lucho flinched, hunching his shoulders. "Been married ten years!" Claus yelled, thumping his thumb off his own chest. "I'm talkin' *experience*!"

Claus's arms and youngish face were paint-speckled from roller brushing a living room wall. In the final phase of his remodeling project, he'd spent a good part of the day alone with his thoughts. When he carried his folded, paint-splotched tarpaulin to the garage, Casey, his next door neighbor, warned him over the backyard fence to sell his house because blacks were moving into Marquette Park and devaluating the neighborhood. Claus scowled at Casey with a sick, frightened feeling. Why, Casey said, his sister a mile to the east had just sold out to blacks and had taken a financial beating the likes of which she might never recover from. To distract himself from the edgy, anxious feeling, Claus flicked his cigarette butt out his car window, rubbed his sweaty cheek on his tee shirt sleeve, and clawed the sandy-colored hair off his forehead.

"We was sittin' the other night nice and quiet after dinner. Got my legs up, sippin' a brewski—ya know, coolin' out—when the phone rings. Wife answers, and who's on the other end but Sara, this broad I knocked up *three years* ago! Crazy bitch dragged me to court. Been payin' child support ever since!" He shook his White Castle cup with a straw poking out its plastic lid at Lucho, who couldn't help but look at Claus with his eyebrows raised.

"Yeah, right," Claus said, registering Lucho's surprise. "Thirty bucks a week for some kid I ain't never seen! *That* sucks. I ask: 'So why you call me?' She says her check's late. I lay into her: 'What the hell do *I* hafta do with child support you know comes straight outta my work check?' Guess she wanted to stick it to Gloria, who got all bent outta shape. Screams I don't love her, ain't got no consideration for the kids; cries I don't wanna be married no more—all 'cause she hates being reminded of Sara." Claus sucked hungrily at his soda straw to relieve his dry-as-wood smoker's throat, his eyes flitting between his mirrors and the traffic around him. "Swear that phone call put me right back in the doghouse I was in three years ago. Wife'll *never* let me live down that affair."

Suddenly, a dark blue van swerved in front of the Charger and stopped dead in the street to make a left turn. Claus jammed on the brakes, shouting out his window, "Hey, where'd ya get your fuckin' license, jagoff—Walgreens?" and screeched into the open right lane. "Come on!" he yelled, shaking his fist above his roof. "Stick your head out the window, so I can see what a *real* asshole looks like!" Secretly he hoped the driver of the blue van would smart-mouth him, or better yet, give chase as the young "toughs" of the neighborhood liked to do. Then he could reach behind his seat for his sawed-off baseball bat—stubby, so he could swing it inside the car if he had to—slam on the emergency brake, kick open his door, and jump to the pavement to have it out right there in the street.

"Pricks like him keep my insurance rates sky-high!" he yelled, terrible thoughts of plowing into that van flashing in his mind, images that would bother him for the rest of the drive.

Up and down the block, heads turned to the roar and rumble as the gold Dodge Charger, rolling on wide black slicks, slipped through Saturday afternoon traffic, rear end jacked three feet off the street, its chromed hubs flashing the sun. Kids pointed and spun around on the sidewalk, drivers stared, and old ladies in babushkas standing on corners shaded their eyes and stepped back on the curb.

"And *you* wanna get married, Lucho?" he yelled, teasing the stick shift between gears. "Listen! 'Cause of the wife, I gotta *sneak* to the auto parts store (This pig's snarfin' gas—needs a tune-up BAD!) And with my own money yet. Left the kids home alone for a whole half hour. Any one of which'll set her off her nut. Yeah, 'cause she's workin' at the bakery all day." An eye of sunlight winked off the chrome bumper of the car ahead of the Charger and caused a piercing light to flicker painfully in Claus's head. Worried about a migraine, he blinked his eyes and rubbed his left temple. Then a sense of dread washed over him as he remembered his promise to take his family out for dinner. What? And drag their feud into public?

Lucho grinned a dimpled smile loaded with white teeth, dashed a hand through his thick black hair, and tattooed a snappy beat outside on the car roof with nervous fingers. "Man, that's rough...really rough," he repeated, "'bout your wife bein' on the rag and all...," uncomfortably trying to steer Claus away from the "war stories" of married life.

Here we go again, Lucho thought. All this free advice and last minute "Are you sures?" from friends, uncles, older brothers, his father, and now Claus, who had just picked him up hitchhiking home from his weekend gas station job. In four hours he'd be tossing down the beers at his own bachelor party, the surprise spoiled by a buddy who forgot *who* he was talking to. And next week at his own reception, sitting at the head table before a roomful of hairdos and sport coats, he'd be obliged to stop eating, lean over and give Becky a greasy kiss on the lips in order to calm the crazy relatives ringing spoons off their water glasses. And now he still had to endure eight more blocks of this heat wave dripping down his back, and Claus Burling's bullshit, which he didn't care to hear.

"My advice to you—seein' as you're bent on lettin' this little girl tie your dick in a knot next Sattaday...," and their eyes met as Lucho slid around the bucket seat grinning, "my advice is don't get caught. At nuttin', mind you! Wife catches me buyin' car parts, all hell'll break loose. And I'm already in the doghouse. Man, got caught big—BIG!" Claus sucked the straw until the loud slurp and glug filled the car, then pitched the cup out the window, where it bounced in the street, sparkling ice scattering across black tar like shattered glass.

83

"Don't get caught at nuttin' ya ain't supposed to be doin'! Like my new boss. Damn token nigger just accused me, ahhh..." He caught himself, realizing he should not talk about the loading dock. Jail for sure, he thought, picturing a unit of undercover cops bursting into his bedroom and discovering his stash of boxed kitchen appliances piled in the closet—the result of months and months of ripping off the dock. After Friday's shift, he found a folded flap of yellow-lined notebook paper sticking out the vent slot of his green locker. "We know you're stealing, Burling," the sloppy handwriting said. He crushed the note to his chest and looked around the crowded locker room, tingling with fear. Who the hell knew? Other guys threw boxes off the dock. At breaktime they'd sneak under the trailers by the truck wheels to fetch their booty and hide it in their cars. Gloria had always warned him his stealing would get him in trouble and threaten his job when he had three other mouths to feed. But she toned down her criticism when he presented her with state-of-the-art appliances which she proudly displayed on her kitchen counter. He couldn't tell Gloria about the note in his work locker.

"So if you're foolin' around, gettin' a li'l on the side—WHATEVER—cover your tracks," he said, believing Lucho was hanging on his every word and waiting for him to continue. "Like the outlaws do—scuff up the dirt with a branch to hide their footprints!" Lucho wished Claus would shut up, and turning away from him, he pretended to be concerned with something out his side window.

"Plus, where ya gonna live? Raise a family? Apartments suck. Rents and landlords are a pain in the ass. Expensive as all hell. And if you're planning on *buyin'*—well, lemme warn ya now: Neighborhood's goin' to hell. Niggers jumped the old dividing line east on Sixty-third other side of the viaduct, buyin' up homes like crazy! Whites selling out and splitting. If they jump the viaduct and start buying around St. Rita High School like I heard they been—shit, goddamn shines'll rip through here like a tornado, take the whole South Side end to end!" Claus flicked his cigarette butt out the window, scratched his head, rubbed his face, his hands constantly moving.

Though he tried to resist, Lucho found himself drawn into Claus's monologue. Not that it was news. Same stuff he'd been hearing all his life: how blacks owned the whole South Side—the huge parks, the beaches and lakefront—all except for Bridgeport and Canaryville, and the very place they were now driving, the Southwest Side. His dad and uncles always talked about this stuff in the backyard, sitting under the big old cottonwood trees in their green-and-white webbed lawn chairs, smoking and bitching about how things "useta" be: When you could jump on any streetcar and go anywhere ya wanted in the whole darned city—ANY TIME OF DAY, they always said—and not worry about nothing. Yeah, he'd heard it all. But suddenly it meant something when Claus asked where he'd raise his family. Boggled at the thought of having to decide, he gazed out the window at the four wide tar lanes of Pulaski Avenue, the jammed car and truck traffic, and the storefronts, banks, and parking lots.

"Prob'ly best to talk your wife into an apartment, Lucho. Niggers invade, you can split to the burbs. Where else ya gonna go? North Side with the fags and weirdos? Me, I gotta house for two years now. Worried sick I'll lose what I paid. Even if I sell tomorrow, can't afford that eighty and ninety thousand dollar prefab garbage they're building in the burbs. Ya sneeze and it falls down! Plus, it's a wasteland. Nothin' goin' on. Buddy of mined moved out to Bolingbrook. When we go visit, we don't never see no people. Blocks full of houses and cars packed in driveways. But no people! That's 'cause they ain't got no neighborhoods. Nobody knows nobody else 'cause they all moved from someplace else.

"A real neighborhood is where people sit on the porch in their shirt sleeves bullshittin' and drinkin' beer. Everybody talks to each other, knows the buzz, goes to the same church, shovels each other's snow and stuff. When ya go away on vacation, ya got eight or ten people keeping an eye on your house so nothin' happens. And once a year ya have a hell of a block party."

Claus shook out another cigarette and slapped the pack on the dashboard. "Or you could skip gettin' married altogether, Lucho." A black Grand Prix raced past in the left lane. All Claus caught was a quick profile of teased, cotton candy blond hair, and a bare sun-warmed arm thrown lazily over the wheel. The blood shot to his head. No way was no broad in no straight-from-the-factory-GM-reject gonna show him up! Especially with him sitting on eight hundred horses just waiting to bust loose!

"Hang on, Lucho," he warned, pulled second, and popped the clutch. The engine roared, sidepipes trilled as the fat tires slipped and spun and scorched the street with a shrill whine, and the whole machine, after this dramatic strength-gathering pause, leaped forward, trailing smoke for half a block. "Gotta catch that Grand Prix," Claus yelled, as Lucho, flung back into the bucket seat like a rag doll, recovered by grabbing the dash. "Looked like a real fox, too!" he heard Claus say, as the Charger gobbled up an empty lane of tar, everything beyond the windows flashing past in a blur as if rushing backwards. He's crazy, thought Lucho.

"Bitch!" Claus yelled, and banged his fist on his custom foam steering wheel, no bigger than a dinner plate.

Up ahead the Grand Prix squirted under the winking yellow light at Sixty-third, where, from the rooftop of the Capitol Cigar Store a twenty-three-foot-tall fiberglass Indian, sepia-colored arm thrust above his shoulder like a traffic cop's, glared down on traffic. Lucho's eyes popped wide, feeling not the expected nod forward of breaking, but the definite sensation of speeding up as Claus plied the pedal. The gold Charger screamed into the red light intersection at a clean forty-seven miles per hour, horn blaring, as something red and white smeared across its path in the form of cross-traffic. Claus locked up the brakes and swerved an *S* pattern through bumpers and quarter panels, then punched the Charger through daylight, leaving a tangle of stopped-dead traffic and a melody of angry horns behind.

"Yaaaa-HOOOOO!" Claus yelled at Lucho. "Ey, gimme *five*, my man!" Lucho, drained of all color, opened one squinted eyes, dashed his hand nervously through his hair, and wiggled upright in his seat in a futile attempt to spot the Grand Prix, which had given them the slip.

Red-faced and charged with energy, Claus cooled down his engine, checking all his gauges. The cop's blue lights splashed crazily in his mirrors a block later.

"Whud I do?" Claus snapped, squinting up at the blue shirt. The reality of the big tall cop pricked his paranoia about his loading dock thievery, and his heart raced in his chest.

"Come on, pal. If ya don't know what *red* means, mebbe ya should let your buddy drive this big toy, and we'll keep your license, huh?" His mustache jumped sarcastically at each word. "Where yooze guys comin' from?" the young face asked, eyes darting around the car.

"Didn't see it till the last moment, officer," Claus pleaded, now more composed. Glad he wasn't being nailed for speeding, he thrust his wallet through the window, the corner of a ten dollar bill sticking up behind the license.

"Take-it-outta-de-wallet-buster," came the cop's flat, mechanical reprimand, calling Claus on the attempted bribe. He noticed the blue Chrysler auto parts on the back seat and the white paint flecks on the driver's arm and face. Any paperwork associated with a traffic violation is stapled to the violator's license, which is then returned after a court hearing or after the fine is paid. As he stood in the street with traffic rushing behind him, the young cop—looking for weapons, contraband, illegal aliens, *anything* that might kick him upstairs to plainclothes—ran his finger back and forth over Claus L. Burling's plastic license, reading it like Braille.

My God! A regular piece of Swiss cheese, he thought, feeling the dozen or so raised staple holes of previous violations. A regular cowboy!

"Aw, officer. My wife...she's pregnant...and I'm...well, I'm just tryin' to get home quick, see...," Claus argued weakly as the cop marched back to his squad car. Traffic slowed as drivers, alerted by the flashing blue lights, gazed suspiciously at Claus, who glared back, thrusting out his chin. By the time the cop reappeared with the yellow ticket, Claus had worked himself up into a lather (damned broad in that damned Grand Prix!) and he popped off about wasting taxpayers' money by stopping a guy who blows *one little light*, when real criminals were, at this very moment, stealing the city blind.

"Listen!" the cop yelled, and stepped back waving his ticket book. "If I measure how far your rear bumper is off the street, and how wide dose tires are—I'm *sure* we could accommodate you with a few more violations, Mac!" And right there he made a mental note to secure Claus L. Burling's paperwork with three or five or six staples, 'cause he had had it up to here with this jerk already. "Belongs on the drag strip—not the street!" he yelled.

Claus rumbled up his side driveway—actually two narrow sidewalks running between the houses to the garage out back—fuming mad at the jagoff cop and dreading his wife Gloria, whose rusted-out station wagon he'd noticed parked in front of the house. Moments before, Lucho had jumped out with a "Catch ya later!" but not before inviting Claus to his bachelor party that evening. Now, as he cursed the minefield of kids' bikes, balls, bats, mitts, the lawnmower, and coiled garden hose scattered the length of his driveway, Claus began formulating an excuse that would get him out of the house. If he told Gloria about his dock troubles now, she'd jump all over him saying, "I *told* you so!" and just to spite him, refuse to give up the stolen appliances he had given her, which she used daily in her kitchen.

That evening the fighting from the Burling residence knifed through street sounds, kid shouts, even the monotonous "Mary Had a Little Lamb" jingle tinkling from the blue ice-cream truck creeping over the lumpy, tar-patched street. Like twittering birds, the children flocked around the truck, while parents, sitting on old pillows and folded newspapers, watched from their porches.

Most evenings, after dinner tables had been cleared, dishes washed, and leftovers smothered in plastic wrap, neighbors took to their front porches with sweaty beer bottles, coffee, and cigarettes. From their cement bleachers they gossiped, watching twilight dim above the jagged house peaks and the nightly drama of kids, cars, and bicycles come alive in the narrow cavern of brick houses called Fairfield Avenue, which was lined with tall bushy trees, parked cars, and a gridwork of sidewalks that framed the small rectangular lawns before each housefront. Women, bunched together on one porch, waved to groups across the street and to cars lumbering past. Wearing stretch shorts and smock tops, they talked about kids, food sales, and husbands, while leaning into Bic lighters with cigarettes pinched from long leather-like cases, until the mosquitoes sent them indoors scratching nasty little red bumps. The men, more solitary figures, hunched over elbows-on-knees on the first stair in sleveless tee shirts, fanned misty arcs of hose water across their tiny lawns, relishing their after-dinner smoke with a squint. As the silvery spray flew from the ice-cold nozzle, their minds wandered and dreamed, lulled by the hiss and sputter and sweet aroma of soggy grass and warm puddled sidewalk. And "things was OK" long as the women didn't try to drag them into conversation. The neighbors blamed the heat for all the shouts coming from the Burlings, half-listening as they sat on their porches and gossiped.

Claus, smelling of aftershave, rushed from bathroom to bedroom in a state of half-undress, slamming drawers, doors, rattling bottles in the vanity, hair slicked back wet from his shower. While snatching a shirt from the closet, he noticed the boxes of kitchen appliances stacked on the floor. Damn, he had to get this incriminating stuff outta the house!

"Yooooo *PRO*-MISED!" his wife screamed from the kitchen. "Ya promised we'd go out for something to eat. Not to worry about dinner. Here I work all day and still gotta fix something for the kids and me!"

He stopped between rooms and looked down the short hallway, past Carrie's, then Timmy's bedroom doors, to the kitchen, tucking his crisp white shirttails into his pants.

"Ey! Are ya through?" he yelled.

She sat on a kitchen chair cocked out from the table, shiny white slip hiked up to her crotch, soaking her aching feet in a white porcelain pan of water. Balled up under her chair was a pair of flesh-colored panty hose, and thrown across a chair back, her white uniform dress, soiled with streaks of cherry, prune, and apricot from the bakery.

"Easy for *you* to say! You're goin' out! I'll stay home with the kids—no problem!" she snarled, and lifted her red feet dripping into the pan. "Worked all goddamned day on my feet. But hey!"—she pointed all ten fingers to her chest—"I'll babysit!"

He shouted back down the hall:

"Alright already—enough! I tole ya it's a *last minute* thing I got invited to Lucho's bachelor party. Whadeya want—call off the weddin' too?" He stormed into the bathroom and snatched up the hair dryer.

"Asshole," she muttered, and began yelling again.

The whizz of the hair dryer muffled her words, and he began singing, "*Oh ya musta been a beau-tee-ful baaaeee-beeeeeee!*" patting his hair and grinning into the mirror—a winning smile full of boyish mischief—thrilled he would not have to stay home and suffer another night of her hair-raising mood. Was it his fault that Sara (that bitch!) called? That she, Gloria, had answered? Who the hell stuffed that note in his locker? How long could he keep it from her?

From the cabinet under the kitchen sink he fished out the fleecy lamb's-wool brush, and with one foot up on a chair, feeling her eyes burning on his back, he buffed his shoe a shiny black. At eye level on the counter, some of the stolen appliances were strung out in a line, and he smelled the putrid smell of propane exhaust from his forklift at work. The anxiety associated with that smell gave him a nervous stomach.

Watching him, looking drawn and tired and fed up, she smoked a cigarette, and glugged a bottle of Diet Pepsi into a tall glass of ice cubes. Just the sight of him pushed all her jealousy buttons. He looked good, *real* good. Crisp and commanding. White button-down shirt, tight black slacks that shaped the two moons of his ass round and true. Sexiness oozed out of him. And she would not be hanging on his arm tonight! Behind her red eyes and mask of anger glowed the unquestioning admiration and devotion of the past ten years. But she would not pay him the compliment or acknowledge that he turned her on while in the throes of this battle.

"Suppose ya sat around in your shirt sleeves watchin' baseball all day long?" she yelled across the formica table.

He changed feet, buffed, and shouted, "Tacked up more woodwork in the fron-*troom*. Finished paintin' it too. *Hosed* down the garage, and rodded out the goddamn grease trap. What the hell more ya want?" He looked at her, her wild eyes not listening as she loaded another round of buckshot.

"And ran to the parts store!" she yelled. He glared at her drawn eyes and sweat-shiny face over his shoulder. "Said ya weren't gonna put no more money in that car—you said...."

"If ya don't believe me, go DOWNSTAIRS!" he yelled, throwing down his foot and changing the subject to trip her up. "Smells like something *died*! Next time I gotta clean out that grease trap, I *swear* I'm gonna *hire* somebody." He stopped waving the brush and stared at her. "What de hell ya stuffin' down de sink—whole chickens and sides of beef? 'Bout gagged to death!"

He stood in the center of the room slapping the lint from his pants legs, framed by sink, stove, refrigerator, and counter, where all the incriminating trophies were laughing at him: the electric can opener, shiny chrome blender, carving knives in drawers and cabinets, crock pots, and the four-slice toaster. An overpowering urge told him to sting her with the news about the dock. Just to shut her up. Tell her about the note, and that he thought Ernie Sutton, the "token nigger" foreman who had just been made his immediate supervisor, was probably behind it. Then he remembered she always got pissed off when the extra money from selling the stolen goods ended up as high-performance car parts. So he simply finished slapping the lint from his pants, stood upright, and changed the subject, never missing a beat.

"And this goddamn heat—my shirt's sticking to me already!" he cried, and flicked open a shirt button.

Gloria sucked her cigarette and blew a spout of smoke at him. "You said the kids would have their baths and everything before I got home. And you weren't even here! You ain't done nothin'—nothin'!"

No way could he deal with this screaming bitch today. He'd clear out the stolen goods tomorrow—definitely.

She continued her tirade loud and clear as he loaded up his toothbrush in the bathroom. So loud the goddamn windows were rattling, he thought. He threw down the tube, stuck his head round the corner, and in a mild-mannered tone he knew would get her said, "Ey! Ya some kinda nut? Tell me, who sits around in their underwear with their feet in scalding hot steamin' water on a day like ta-day, huh? When it's so hot ya can't even breathe. Huh? Ya stupid?"

She gulped the last of her Pepsi, lowered the glass and whipped the ice cubes at him. The silvery rocks ricocheted off the wall and, ten feet away, off Carrie's bedroom door, then bounced and clattered along the linoleum floor like tumbling dice to the dining room carpeting.

"Hey! Watch the new rug!" he yelled, and stormed into the dining room, kicking the cubes off the carpeting and back down the hall. "You're delirious!" he shouted, and ducked into the bathroom, sensing victory.

"I AM NOT DELIRIOUS!" she screamed, as if she were about to be murdered.

In the yard, Timmy hung on the back fence by his skinny arms, making funny faces through the chain-link to the alley, his knees dangling just above the dirt, as sister Carrie swung back and forth on the gate. Three of his friends, feet planted on either side of their bikes, stood in the alley, absentmindedly bumping their front tires into the fence. They talked of being hot and bored with summer. Nothing to do—no place to go. Maybe they could grab towels and swim trunks and dive into the park pool. Was it boys' day today? Nobody knew for sure.

"Ma said wait back here for ice cream," Carrie said quietly, swinging out into the alley, the gate gently slamming into the wall of sturdy garbage cans. She giggled, knitting her shoulders, eyes fishing for encouragement from the boys, and then switched sides for the ride back into the yard.

"I don't *want* no ice cream," Timmy answered, and letting go of the fence, plopped into the dirt on his knees.

"Ya gotta stay here, Burling?" one kid asked.

Timmy jumped up slapping dirt from his hands. "Naw, I...she...I think my ma wants me to hang for a bit—that's all...."

"Maybe we'll go to Grandma's house now that Dad's leavin' to go someplace," Carrie said, showing the guys she knew more than her big brother.

With the sun setting in front of the house, the entire yard would soon be submerged in blue shade. A single flaming ribbon of bright sun cut sharply across the backyard grass and fence, backlighting Timmy and Carrie. From the alley, with their bodies rimmed in sunlight, their yellow heads shone bright as beacons. The three boys, in the shade of the huge oak rising above the yard and tiny garage, shaded their eyes and squinted past brother and sister to the house and the yellow curtains puffing out from the row of open porch windows, stealing glances at one another because of the shouting to which Timmy and Carrie seemed oblivious—Carrie gliding on the gate, imagining herself in a spaceship, Timmy kicking at the huge tree trunk, its gnarled roots snaking into the grass.

"I don't *wanna* go to Gram's," he said, karate kicking at the tree in a blur of movement. "I wanna...," and Gloria's scream "I AM NOT DELIRIOUS!!!" sliced through the air, "wanna maybe go to the pool and do flips off the springboard," he continued.

The three boys arched their brows and looked at one another. The kid with the White Sox cap and tiny spider bike who lived blocks away across Kedzie Avenue said, "Somebody screams like that in our house, I'd probably go see about it." "Yeah, Burling," said another boy who knew the gossip, but had never heard Timmy confirm it—to which Timmy, in a straightforward, innocent voice, asked, "What scream?" and stared them down until they all looked away and rolled their bikes nervously in place.

Just this summer he'd started spending long hours at friends' houses, where parents, won over by his bright smile and pleasant (though sometimes nervous) manner, set a plate for him at their dinner tables. He found himself packed into other families' station wagons for trips to the zoo and picnics in the woods. Some nights he called home asking permission to sleep overnight at a friend's and watch a horror movie on television, "'cause his ma makes great popcorn, OK, Ma?"

For three days he'd been ignoring the fighting between his parents, walking away to shut it out. When their loud voices, full of hate and anger, shook him awake in his bed, he pictured strangers yelling in the next room, pretend-people who had somehow gotten into the house. On one protective level, he had not heard his mother's scream. And even if he had, it meant nothing to him.

The boys heard the gate clang shut and Carrie scream. They turned to see her twisted around facing them, her right hand over her left shoulder caught in the gate latch behind her, her throat locked in a strangle-hold by her own skinny arm, and one foot helplessly kicking the air. Timmy dashed to the gate, flipped it open, caught her with his free arm and stood her upright. Her shocked white face pulsed shades of red as she cried continuously, never taking a breath.

"You're not bleedin' or nothin', Care!" Timmy shouted excitedly, turning her hand over and over with his dirty fingers. "Only scuffed up a little," and he rubbed the white chalky marks from her skin. She yanked her hand free and ran screaming to the house.

The boys couldn't help but chuckle when Timmy said, "She can be a real pussy sometimes—no shit!" Minutes later his mother's blond head was framed by the middle porch window as she yelled, "Timothy Martin Burling! Get your ass in here!" Then Claus burst out of the back door and galloped down the stairs, looking as if to strangle Timmy himself, his long stickman shadow flung up against the garage door by the low orange sun bowling down the slot between the houses, dazzling his white shirt and black slacks. "Timmy!" he yelled, pointing a finger, then hooking a thumb over his shoulder—which meant "In the house, buster. NOW!"—he continued to the garage. Rumbling down the side drive in the Charger, he never in his life wanted so bad to get silly, stupid drunk.

"See ya," Timmy said flatly. Without even looking at his friends, he took leave in the informal, awkward style of kids who know they will see their friends tomorrow and the next day and the next, to play out the rest of the endless summer. Cutting across the yard at a trot, kicking his dusty shoes through the clumps of just-mowed grass, ducking from blinding sun to deafening shade, he thought, Good, Dad's splittin'. Because he didn't fear his mother half as much—she was so pliable.

Red-faced and puffy-eyed, Carrie sat at the kitchen table in a trance that told Timmy his mother had already decided matters. Gloria had screamed Carrie quiet saying, "It's too damn hot to fuss!" and dismissed the little scene because no one was dripping blood and there was no sign of broken bones. But she jumped on Timmy as soon as the screen door banged shut.

"So what the hell is going on back there, mister?" she yelled, pointing over his head. He froze in the doorway, his little hands touching the woodwork at his sides. The kitchen table stood between him and his sister, a good length of linoleum floor between his grass-stained gym shoes and his mother's bare red feet. Though her face was twisted-up angry and her yellow hair flared out, he knew she wouldn't hit him. Something was missing in her voice. She didn't have the goods on him. Plus she was smoking a cigarette. She never swung with a lit cigarette pinched between her fingers, except when crazy with rage. He met Carrie's eye with a "Wait till later" look. Her bottom lip curled up as if she might cry again, and she looked down to her lap.

"We was jussss—"

"I *told* you to watch your sister. How many TIMES I gotta tell ya that?"

"Awwwww, Maaaaa..., we was...she was...I mean, *I* was talkin' to Jamie and the guys and—and, *really*, I didn't even know she was swingin' on the gate. She gots her hand caught and *ain't even* hurt. Right, Care?" he said to his sister, who stared down at her hand, petting it in her lap.

"Don't-go-swingin'-on-the-goddamned-gate-it-ain't-a-carnival-ride!" Gloria moaned progressively louder, exasperated with her daughter's false hysteria. "Now get outta my sight—both of you—before I commit a crime that'll make the front page!"

They scattered, a rush of feet, and Gloria, overcome with a sudden dizzy spell, staggered forward wiping her brow. "I'm gonna pass out," she said, leaning on a chair back. "This heat—I'm gonna hit the floor!" The screen door yawned open, then banged shut, and the kid sounds trailed out into the yard.

All at once she didn't know what to do. No one to yell at, no one to kick or boss around. She needed an audience to throw a fit.

Sweat trickled along her scalp; the dizziness seized her; the heat, come to strangle her, closing in. Here in her own messed up and cluttered kitchen, with the counters loaded with dirty dishes, open cereal boxes, pizza cardboards, and potato chip bags, she would die of suffocation. First door off the kitchen was Timmy's room—dark, musty, silent, with the shade drawn. She waded through baseball mitts and shoes and piles of clothes, muttering to herself about the sour smell, snatched up the big floor fan and set it up in the kitchen. The warm rush of air sent the dust balls tumbling across the floor, and she fell into a swivel chair that carried her in a half-circle, then snapped back, facing her to the table.

When she was depressed, she sat immobile, all energy drained out of her, usually in this chair at the kitchen table, in the only room in the house with which she felt a kinship, chain-smoking and drinking coffee and staring off into space. She lost both foresight and hindsight. The family felt her deadly silence in each and every room. Sometimes they would hear the kitchen noises, the dinner making and dish washing, and then find her slump-shouldered at the sink, mute and moody.

The husky, cigarette voice of Sara's phone call still knifed her, though it had been three days ago. "Well, can I *talk* to Claus? It's very important," the sarcastic bitch had said, not just jabbing but turning the knife too.

Now nervous and worried, her hand shaking as she reached to flick her ash, Gloria looked down at her thin pale arms, spread her knees, and let the fan blow cool air up her rumpled slip. Exhausted as she was from a full day behind the bakery counter, the countless customers, and three days of intense fighting with her husband, she could not push Sara out of her thoughts. She was sweaty and smelled of grease and vanilla, needed a shower, but couldn't move.

Gloria remembered as five years of pleasant memories their time in the cheap-rent Back-o'-the-Yards apartment on Wolcott near Forty-seventh Street. The worn-out couch, card table, and metal chairs in the kitchen, and naked bulbs dangling on long cords above the beds reminded her of simpler days "when we were just playing house," she told her friend Peggy. In winter the kids stood on tiptoes and finger-painted on the dripping, steamed-up windows. On dead-air summer nights the sharp crack of pool balls and the sound of a mariachi jukebox floated across the street from the corner tavern. As she watched her children grow above the counter top, she also sensed a closeness to Claus she hadn't felt since their very first year of marriage. Her heart raced with delight when, leaning over the back of the couch and looking out the front windows and down through the trees, she'd find him, just home from work, sitting on a car hood talking to the Mexicans. They liked him because he was big and strong, and he joked around and fixed their cars in the middle of the tar-patched street. Plus, he knew a few words of Polish. In Back o' the Yards, where generations of Poles had learned to hold their noses living downwind from the Stockyards and the stench, and where Mexicans were now beginning to settle, the Poles were respected as the clear majority. Gloria ignored the pleasant memories because they also triggered flashbacks of the day that bitch Sara appeared on her doorstep. A simple memory of the apartment's black and white checkerboard bathroom with its old-fashioned tub up on legs could send her off into bitter memories of Sara. There was a knock at the door that day—or was it the doorbell?—that odd, twangy doorbell of the second floor Wolcott apartment that sounded like a jew's harp. Three years ago...so long ago she couldn't quite recall....

"Maaa...DOORbell!" Timmy had yelled.

Startled from her thoughts, Gloria dropped the gritty sponge into the bathroom sink and rushed into the lamp-lit front room where the kids played on the dusty rug—Timmy on his knees, tiny butt in the air, dragging around a wooden choo-choo train; Carrie sitting cross-legged, having a heart-to-heart with a rag doll. Gloria felt odd, almost dizzy descending the dark staircase, the old wood groaning and snapping under her weight, the queer light hovering smoke-like down at the foot of the stairs. A shadow of a person flirted in the folds of the cheesecloth curtains stretched across the door glass. The organ theme of "Garfield Goose and Friends" floated down the stairs from her own living room, and the scratchy sound of the all-news radio station droned through the wall of Mrs. Rodriguez's first-floor apartment. When Gloria wedged open the door, her own white-cloud "Yes?" misted the chilled air.

A woman in black turned from facing the street and took a giant step forward. Her face, powdered a sickly white, on the verge of a smile, kept coming and coming, sharp eyebrows above close-set eyes, and forced Gloria to jump back and close the door between them.

"Your husband home?" the woman asked in a throaty voice. Gloria stroked her own throat. "Oh?—forGIVE ME!" the lady barked and slit her eyes. "My name...," and she paused, looked down to her boots, then to Gloria standing in the open wedge of the door. "My name is Sara," she said quickly, watching for a flicker of recognition.

"What can I do for—"

"And I'm here to speak with Mister Claus Burling," she said, ignoring Gloria's question.

She wore a black fuzzy jacket cut above the waist that ballooned at the shoulders, shiny black satin slacks, and pointed boots with spiked heels. Her makeup, rather than complement, seemed to offend her face: rust-tone rouge slashed her cheekbones, thick rings of mascara pinched her eyes into the back of her head, coffee-colored lipstick enraged her lips into the grimace of two swollen earthworms pressed together. "Sassy" popped into Gloria's head—an impression she would never forget.

Behind the mysterious woman, where the dreary afternoon sank more and more into the grays of evening, Gloria noticed a group of young Mexicans in flak jackets milling around an idling car, its headlights glaring off the street, black and slick with steady drizzle. Streetlamps flickered on, caged by naked tree branches.

The way she squinted her black eyes, Gloria knew this woman knew everything about her and her family, and probably Claus. She grew wet in the armpits, and the damp chill of the street blew across her bare arms.

After a standoff of staring between them, a slice of time Gloria could never recollect, the stranger said curtly, "Your husband owes me child support, honey. He's my son's daddy.

"What!"

Gloria blanched and moved to swing at her. But the woman dipped down the stairs as Gloria screamed, "Get outta here! Whore! Bitch! Get outta here—here!—outta here!" Wanting to give chase but weak in the knees, she fell against the wooden porch banister. Farther down the block the woman slid into a low sports car and roared off. Gloria mounted the stairs in a complete daze to the kids sounds and TV noise and puked in the half-clean bathroom sink stinking of Comet.

Claus's green cardboard payroll checks, minus that child support, laughed at her every two weeks. All consideration toward her husband stopped, and she concentrated her love on her children, hoping to teach them a bit of compassion. She picked them up from school, scared them into believing they should never cross a busy street without her guiding hand, fired babysitters at the slightest complaint of the children. For two years, Claus played the role of humble servant, exceptional husband, a homebody with no interests but his family. He garaged his monster car, stopped drinking and carousing, and, at the end of the second year, plunked down a tidy sum and took out a mortgage on a brick bungalow four blocks from the sparkling lagoons, stone bridges, and green open spaces of Marquette Park. Claus and Gloria believed that their dream house, and the sweat and work required by a bit of property, would gloss over their differences and instill a sense of family pride and togetherness.

He believed if he straightened up, or at least faked penitence, his wife would not squeal to his mother or his in-laws. That would be a bitch—especially her parents, who gave him little credit for raising *their* grandchildren.

If three be the number boasting superstitious power—three strikes you're out, the luckless third fellow on a match, the digit able to shake loose the devil in all of us—Claus really cashed in. In the third year of his repentance he became restless. He spent wads of money on his car, hung out more and more with the boys at the park hangout, and growled at questions Gloria might ask to determine where he'd been when he stumbled home reeking of beer and pot. She pleaded, he yelled; the children, confused and guilty, buried their heads in their pillows in their own beds to blot out the shouting, believing they were to blame for their parents' arguments.

Often Claus wondered why he did not feel any remorse for snaking his wife. The guys often laughed behind Gloria's back as Claus bragged over beers about a fling he had had with "this big-titted babe a while back," tipping his bar stool on two legs and rubbing his chest in a drunk and devil-may-care attitude. He got caught. What could he do? Feel terrible for the rest of his days? Hey, ya win some, ya lose some.

"Hey, don't get married, Lucho!" Claus yelled to the groom, who stood off to one side of the red felt pool table surrounded by a group of close friends. Easily spotted because of his rather tall height and bright white fishnet jersey, Lucho shook a half bottle of Jack Daniels over his head to salute the basement bachelor party, which was packed with friends who whistled and shouted to him over the pounding rock 'n' roll. Groups of guys crowding the open floor all the way back to the gray-painted stairs in the far corner raised their plastic beer cups to the wood rafters to return the salute. In the circle of light formed by the shaded pool table lamp, Claus leaned on his cue stick, talking intensely with one of the groom's uncles, a stout, balding man, cheerful and sunburnt from a week straight of country club golf.

"I hear what you're sayin, Rocko," Claus said, nodding agreeably. "My buddy Joe Parisi—who's here somewhere—why, Joe says his whole block is goin' nigger. And even whites who *wanna* stay ain't got no choice but to sell!" he said, his eyes wide with indignation.

"Young man," the uncle began, grabbing Claus's shoulder and coming close to his ear. "Lotsa whites wanna hold out when the neighborhood starts changing, hoping something is gonna reverse it. But it don't never happen. Smart ones get out fast!" He squeezed Claus's shoulder, moved his hand down to his waistband, and with his thumb hiked up his green golf pants. "Me? Retired out in Hickory Hills seven years now. Nice clean place. Can't live with them black bastards. That's a fact. In Chicago? Never!" Uncle Rocko took a hearty gulp from his plastic beer cup. Claus gazed down the long table at his opponent in a red striped shirt, who clunked pool balls into the wooden triangle rack. Eagerly shaking hands and smiling with friends seldom seen, he felt giddy from the beer and noise and crush of people, momentarily relieved of the problems that waited for him beyond the smoky gray basement: an angry Gloria and the accusation of his stealing on the dock. But the uncle's matter-of-factness, especially the remark that the "smart ones get out fast!" troubled him deeply.

"Why, makes me sick to this day," Rocko continued, patting his belly, "absolutely sick to my stomach when I think about those beautiful beechwood cabinets I hadda leave to those goddamn junglebunnies in the old neighborhood. Me and my brother just put in new linoleum, too. And remodeled the basement with knotty pine. Think they appreciated it?" Claus scowled thinking of all the hours and money he'd just sunk into his new living room.

Lucho threw back his head and swigged from the whiskey bottle, and the cheers from the large gathering of guys surrounding the pool table turned heads throughout the basement. Card players seated at tables that lined one long wall hurriedly turned in their chairs. Noticing the card players' reaction, the disc jockey, wearing headphones and wrap-around sunglasses, leaped up from his turntables by the furnace to see over the heads. A few men standing on the beer line before the cement wash tubs shook their fists in the air. Claus smiled dreamily at

Lucho, then felt the uncle tap him persistently on the shoulder.

"May sound prejudiced, but OK, so I'm a racist or whatever ya wanna call it. But I seen with my own two eyes the way them animals ruin everything." Rocko jabbed a finger an inch from Claus's nose. "Here's a fact: Ya can take the bunny out of the jungle, but you can *never* take the jungle out of the bunny!" Rocko jumped away from Claus with his hand raised as if taking an oath. "Ain't it the truth," he said. Claus laughed out loud while snatching up the cue ball rolling toward him, and then yelled to the gang surrounding Lucho:

"Booze him up good, boys. So he can really bang away at her on dat honeymoon!" And leaning over the pool table, he teased the cue ball with his stick and rammed home a breaker shot that scattered the colorful triangle with a sharp crack.

More and more guys tramped down the gray-painted stairs into the crowded basement, where the smoke swirled around four naked light bulbs and warped wood paneling bowed out from the cement walls. Some guys were arriving for the very first time, others returning from a ritual called "taking a spin," in which a carload of dopers cruised the side streets passing hash pipes and joints from front to back seats. Now they squinted through the smoke and, from their higher vantage point on the stairs, waved over heads to locate the "lucky man" swallowed up by the crowd.

Three distinct groups of men mixed at this bachelor party. The young-faced, clear-eyed, just-out-of-high-school gang swarmed around Lucho, toasting their hero and slapping him on the back as he roamed from group to group. The older married guys—the group to which Claus belonged—stood in circles, hefting beers, stomping cigarettes on the cement floor and yelling in one another's ears to be heard over the blaring rock 'n' roll. They talked, among other things, about the son in Little League, the pregnant wife, TV sports, cars, gambling, and home improvements. While mentally noting their friends' premature gray hair, yellowed teeth, and fleshy paunches rolling over belt buckles, they drew out wallets to show kid pictures and laughed at high school tales almost fifteen years old. To give Lucho a hard time, these young fathers shouted to him when he paraded past with his buddies.

"She a virgin, Lucho?" came a shout from a stringy-haired father in a faded Black Sabbath tee shirt, to which the groom turned and smirked, nodding "Yeah."

"Bullllll-shit!" someone else yelled to a chorus of laughter.

"Stags. Get the stags. Gotta show him the skin flicks so he knows where to stick it!" someone else volunteered. The younger guys blushed, smirking nervously at the sex talk.

In summery pastel shirts and slacks, the groom's father, a few uncles, and long-standing family friends stood among total strangers, clutching beers and nodding agreeably, shocked at the rowdiness of the party. Stories about World War II and how their parents survived the

Depression by eating potatoes did not seem to excite these wound-up kids. Soon these older men would leave these young folks to their "fun and noise," and retreat to the soft chairs and air conditioning of the upstairs TV room to watch the White Sox twi-nighter, and reminisce about Nellie Fox and Minnie Minoso and the other '59 pennant winners.

Sandwiches had been served, and except for late arrivals picking over the food table scraps, the second drunk was well underway. Glops of potato salad trailed away from the food table, where, underneath, in the angle between floor and wall, a thick red splotch from a shattered ketchup bottle climbed the wall. Overturned bowls of sloppy joe meat, beer cups, balled-up soggy napkins, greasy piles of paper plates, and slices of cold gray beef were heaped in the center of the table. Flies the size of raisins twitched on the two naked ham bones.

Claus was fast approaching the drunken state where he would black out from the beer, having skipped eats, except for two slices of pink ham pinched from the food table and gulped down whole. During a blackout he would still function, but recall nothing afterwards. He was desperate to shut off his troubled mind. "Five minutes. Just gimme five minutes alone with Lucho and I'll talk him out of it!" he yelled viciously from the pool table. "Tell him straight. Call the whole mutherfuckin' thing off!"

Guys ringing the pool table encouraged him with cheers and claps and laughter. But Claus, playing seriously to his audience, cursed and muttered and circled round and round the table, eyeing his next shot with a cigarette dangling from his lips. Cigarette ash was smeared across his unbuttoned shirt and his hair was plastered to his sweaty forehead.

"*Hell-no-you-won't-go*, Lucho!" he yelled through cupped hands, the same hoarse voice he used at Sox Park and the Stadium to shout down "crooked" umpires and "blind" hockey referees.

The disc jockey, hunched over his turntables, dazzled Lucho and his friends, who stood before his impressive pile of electronic equipment. Behind a pink shower curtain that hid the furnace, a blinking strobe light flashed, silhouetting the disc jockey. Everyone felt the pounding beat pumped out of five-foot-tall speakers. Guys standing on the beer line rapped their empty cups on their thighs. Card players absent-mindedly drummed the table, reviewing their cards. Others talking in groups bobbed their heads or popped their shoulders while gliding across the floor. When the older men begged out, grinning nervously and waving like celebrities as they mounted the stairs, the disc jockey cranked up the familiar hard-driving motorcycle jam, "Born to Be Wild," and lit a wick of energy that sparked the entire room. A wild cheer drowned out the music for one hot second.

Claus sank a two-bank shot, and thrilled with himself, he spun away from the table, mocking a guitar player by running his fingers up and down the cue stick held at port arms. Behind him in the corner, Scum

Landis, the long-haired neighborhood burn-out, played an air guitar with eyes closed, oblivious to the world. His fingers mocked the chords and one-note solos of the rock song so precisely it looked as if he were playing an actual guitar, though there was nothing in his hands. He spun in place, jerking and contorting his body, grimacing at the screeches and wails of the song, mocking the "moves" of his favorite rock stars he'd seen on TV or live onstage at the Auditorium. His hair whipped as he twirled in place, sweat pouring down from the red bandanna knotted around his forehead, tinted glasses slipping down his nose. The guys watching the pool game were now spectators for his performance and, clearing the corner, they formed a huge circle around him.

A few other air guitarists joined him in the corner, and throughout the basement guys spun out of groups, plucking invisible strings and running their fingers up imaginary guitar necks. Others, living the fantasy of the song, bobbed their heads with tough looks on their faces. The whole place shook, the *real* music deafening. A few guys mocked drummers splashing cymbals, others the lead singer, using a prop for a microphone. Those not jamming nodded in approval to the beat. But all were studies in concentration, so intent was their listening and playacting. Behind closed eyes they pictured themselves up on a glittering stage, lit with bright colorful spotlights, suspended above an arena packed with loyal fans, the crowd reaching for them, shaking fists and yelling—the pulse of the thundering beat and the beer buzz smoothing the edges of the rock 'n' roll fantasy.

> *Get your motor runnin',*
> *Head out on the highway!*
> *Lookin' for adventure*
> *And whatever comes our way!*

Stars for a moment!

The final sustained chord rang out, a flair of guitars and drums building to a dramatic climax. All the air guitarists shook and shuddered, twisting in agonized frenzy, fluttering fingers up and down invisible guitar necks, until the final note fell—BLAM! The music cut out, a roar went up, and fists shook in the air. Someone spun the groom around and, flashing a thumbs-up sign in his face, forced a beer into his hand. The air guitarists opened their eyes to the reality of the smoky gray basement, dropped their pretend instruments, and walked away, shaking off the fantasy. Charged with energy, Claus grabbed a full pitcher of beer from someone's hands. "Yeah!" he yelled to Scum Landis, who huffed and puffed as if he had just sprinted a mile, his long sweaty hair sticking to his face, dark sweat rings circling the armpits of his gray tee shirt. "What a mutherfuckin' song!" Claus yelled again, and chugged three-quarters of the pitcher before taking a breath.

The song triggered a slap fight by the furnace. Shouts and hollers went up as guys rushed to that side of the basement and formed a huge ring around Joe Parisi and Mike Dudek, who, crouched in boxer stances, jabbed at each other's head and face with open palms.

"Get him, Parisi!" someone yelled.

The disc jockey jumped in front of his equipment, spreading his arms to protect his investment, until a buffer of onlookers separated his set-up from the fight.

"Come on, Dudie! Crack him back!" came another shout.

Dudek, with a construction job tan on his arms and face, still wearing his work clothes and boots clotted with cement, charged across the floor, forcing Parisi backwards into the crowd. Dressed in black from head to toe, Parisi bobbed and weaved like a darting shadow. A gold chain, looped across the open V of his button-down shirt, sparkled and jumped on his chest as he moved, and he spit off to the side every chance he could with his eyes fixed on Dudek. All faces turned to the excitement. The guys on beer line were torn between rushing over and sacrificing their turn or bobbing in place on their toes to see. Across the basement the shouts roused the card players to their feet, a few popping up and knocking over their chairs, gawking with mouths open, poker hands fanned across their chests. Parisi jabbed lightning-quick as if to poke out his opponent's eyes, then jumped back spitting wildly, his feet switching constantly. Dudek lumbered about and swung his meaty shoulders in broad roundhouse wallops. At each stinging slap the crowd cheered wildly, their hungry eyes following the figures round the circle. Some opportunists waved dollar bills, hoping to coax a wager.

"Stomp dat Polack!" Claus yelled jokingly, shouldering his way into the inner circle, watching Parisi's black pointed shoes shuffle fast. Claus and Joe were like brothers, and constantly watched out for one another. Sweaty and rumpled, Claus leaned on his pool cue, watching the slap fight with fascination, aware a brawl could break out if tempers boiled over. All Dudek's tanned and muscle-bound jock friends formed the opposing inner circle of polo shirts across the way.

"Kick dat greasy Dago's ass!!" Claus yelled again as Dudek charged across the gray cement floor, his joke, loud enough for Dudek's allies to hear, confirming the game. A broad roundhouse slap knocked Parisi off-balance and set him stumbling to one side, threads of beady sweat flying from his face, as Dudek's follow-through slashed the air. The circle OOOHED and AAAHHED, pounding their feet and clapping. Parisi shook his head, stunned. Charging back, he cuffed Dudek on the ear. Powdered cement mix puffed up from Dudek's hair. The disc jockey, hoping to break the tension, spun the Stones' "Jumping Jack Flash," its violent beat simply washing out the crisp slap sounds of the fight and making the crowd yell louder. The football jocks across the circle visibly stirred as the slap fighters began cupping their hands into square fists.

> *I was born in a crossfire hurricane,*
> *And I howled at my ma in the driving rain.*
> *But it's all right now, in fact it's a gas!*
> *But it's all right—*
> *I'm Jumpin' Jack Flash!*
> *It's a gas! gas! gas!*

In the mile by half-mile sprawl of Park District sod and trees called Marquette Park, the greasers, dressed in grays and blacks, parked their growling souped-up jalopies in a long line around the horseshoe curve of Redfield Drive overlooking the lagoon, where they fender-leaned, passed quarts of beer, and flipped cigarette butts at the spaces between crawling park traffic. They would hoot and holler at the girls, yell at cars to pick a fight, and gaze with silent awe at a fat bearded biker cruising past on a chopped Harley, his Nazi helmet decaled with a bold Confederate flag just above the eyes. They'd chew the neighborhood buzz—who got busted, copped some decent drugs, or finally landed a job. Dealers from the hood pulled up and sold pot, pockets full of Quaaludes, speed, and foil-wrapped packets of cocaine right from their car windows. Senior citizens ambling through the fenced-in Park District garden knew nothing of this curbside drug-dealing hangout a stone's throw away from the lovely pruned rose bushes.

The jocks, less structured and more independent, scattered to the green grass fields, cement courts, and glittering black cinder tracks, colorful as clowns in numbered jerseys of their favorite pro heroes. Pick-up teams charged up and down basketball courts, chased opponents in tag football, and from chain-link backstops knocked softballs high into the air. After the game they sprawled in the grass in a loose circle, tugging at their shoe laces, and recalled newspaper box scores, outrageous TV replays, and their own past injuries. They'd pile in their cars and cruise past the greaser punks who always seemed to scowl as if they were being forced to sit on their fenders with nothing to do but stare at traffic. The greasers would glare back at the jocks, call them sissies, fags who wasted their energy chasing balls and getting all sweated up for nothing. They rubbed elbows only at social gatherings where sparks usually flew.

Lucho, one of the younger set in the park hangout tradition, did not readily make distinctions between his friends. Generally liked by all, he moved freely between both groups, shrugging off questions like "Why you hang with them jock straps?" and "What fun are those greaseball troublemakers?"

Now in the hot, crowded basement the circle of jocks and greasers yelled at the top of their lungs, shook their fists, and cheered, the tension ready to snap. Parisi bent at the waist to duck a punch thrown by Dudek. Dudek flew into the crowd and felt a hundred hands spin him around and shove him back into the circle. Mick Jagger blared from the five-foot speakers by the furnace:

> *I was drowned. I was washed up and left for dead.*
> *I fell down to my feet and I saw they bled.*
> *I frowned at the crumbs of a crush of bread.*
> *I was crowned with a spike right through my head.*
> *But it's all right now, in fact it's a gas!*

Claus grinned, his eyes smarting from the thick cigarette smoke, and nonchalantly unscrewed his pool cue in the middle. The fat, heavy end would make an excellent club to crack heads once the fireworks began.

Suddenly, the disc jockey cut the twangy rock 'n' roll guitars and cranked up a Gene Krupa drum beat. Dudek slipped on a beer puddle and Parisi slugged him square in the gut. Dudek doubled over and the circle collapsed into itself, a free-for-all of flying fists. Stabbed on all sides by bony elbows, Claus shoved his way into the mash of bodies. With his club raised, he was drunkenly yanking a fistful of polo shirts toward him, when a wild whoop and flurry of whistles paralyzed the brawl.

Everyone froze—a basement full of mannequins—as all heads whipped around toward the far corner and the tall brunette cautiously picking her way down the gray-painted stairs in spiked heels and flimsy black negligee. She stopped, awkwardly teetering with her feet on two separate stairs, and squinted through the hazy smoke and bare bulb light, looking more like a wary grandmother checking a spooky basement sound than a young stripper hired by the boys. Her bony knees were red from kneeling on scratchy carpeting to find a contact lens in the upstairs bedroom, where she had slipped out of her street clothes. Her rouged cheeks and painted lips were a bright glossy red. From the sea of startled faces and glassy eyes, wolf whistles, grunts, hoots and hollers flew at her from all sides. In a sweeping glance she noted the mild-mannered drunks, loud-mouth rowdies, and the trouble spot in back that looked like a fight breaking up. Six months of cock-teasing rooms full of drunken men had taught her to size up groups in an instant.

No one noticed the pair of size-thirteen shiny black shoes up on the top stair which belonged to Carlos, her chauffeur and bodyguard. On command he would fly down the stairs and karate chop any drunken slob who tried to handle the goods. But rarely was there a need for him to show his dark face and gold-tooth smile. Christina was a pro tease. The after-the-touchdown roar of the basement crowd sounded normal. And when the gang of five or six old men excused themselves and tramped down the stairs past him, Carlos knew he could cool out and call the office to check if any more stops had been added to the seven scheduled bachelor parties.

Her awkwardness left her when her spiked heels found the basement floor. "Hallo, boyzzz!" she said in a choppy German-like accent, waving and grinning. The guys closest to her radiated away to give her room, while those in back surged forward to see. Claus clawed his way through the crowd, yanking shoulders and spinning guys out of his way. "All *right!*" he yelled, standing in the first row, close enough to see the greasy blue smudges of her eyeliner. She playfully tweaked his cheek as she paraded past, careful not to break her long beautiful nails. He grinned, catching a whiff of her thick perfume, then flicked his tongue wildly, all to the rowdy guffaws and backslaps of those around him.

She handed a cassette tape to the disc jockey with a dramatic flick of the wrist, grabbed an empty folding chair, dragged it to open floor space, and called for the groom. Cries of "Lucho! Lucho!" went up until he was pushed through the crowd and stumbled up to her, round-shouldered and smirking with embarrassment, but still with his chin up in tough-guy defiance. She shoved him back in the chair, and standing before him, wiggled her hips to the bouncy jazz of her pre-recorded tape, spiced with a tango drumbeat. Round and round she circled his chair, flapping her arms and grinding her hips in stiff jerky movements. The boys loved it and howled madly, especially when she flicked open her negligee and it parted momentarily like a curtain to show her tiny, dixie cup-sized breasts.

The rowdiest drunks formed the first row around Lucho, giving Christina a ten-foot circle of gray cement floor in which to move. Many in the first row, including Claus, were down on their knees with their plastic beer cups on the floor. Behind them, cheering faces pressed together to see. And farther back, guys stood on chairs craning their necks. The pool table in back and card tables along the near wall were abandoned, while the beer line swelled. Onlookers grinned nervously, not sure how to take this bold dancer with the hook nose, teased black hair, and "legs for days." Lucho's father and the uncles set their full beers on the top-loader washing machine apart from the group, fumbled with cigarettes, and looked on with folded arms, turning to one another with wisecracks and nervous laughter.

Lucho sat low in the chair with his knees spread wide, trying to act cool and unaffected, though his face wore an almost pained expression. He watched her wiggle toward him, her crotch floating hypnotically at eye level, and when she spun away, he quickly glanced to the guys for support, pleading with his arms out. Most laughed at him and pointed at Christina. "That's what you're kissin' good-bye, Lucho, ma man!" Claus shouted, then yelled to the stripper, "Come to *me,* darlin'! He's just a boy, a mere lad. Be gentle with him!"

When the music switched to a blare of trumpets not unlike the theme for "The Tonight Show," she kicked one leg high in the air, pulled the black bow at her adam's apple, and the negligee slipped off her shoulders. A gasp hissed through the room. Claus pounded his fist on the floor. She spun around and snatched the negligee out of midair, twirled it high over her head like a toreador, and flung it at Lucho. He clawed it off his face as the room erupted in laughter. "Why don't ja hang it up for the nice young lady!" some smart aleck yelled. Balanced on spiked heels, she strutted stiffly toward Lucho, running her hand up her thighs and string bikini bottom with the gold crotch, along her rib cage and pointy breasts, and then ended up by fluffing the stiff, sprayed hair off her neck. Lucho's drunken eyes popped wide when she unbuttoned his shirt, jumped away, and coaxed him with hand gestures to take it off. And still moving to the music, she stooped to untie his shoes, then demanded his pants by undoing his belt and delicately easing down his zipper. A thunderous syncopated clap urged Lucho on.

He wiggled out of his pants and handed them to her with a look of total dismay. Triumphantly she held them high over her head, coaxing cheers, then flung them behind her. Nickles, dimes, and quarters splattered and rolled across the floor. She stepped out of her panties to hoots and hollers, amost falling when the heel snagged the elastic band, then shot the panties at Lucho sitting in his BVDs and one white sock in the cold metal folding chair. He scored a point by snatching up the panties and pulling them over his head like a sweatband, the shiny gold triangle of the crotch pointing straight up from his forehead. The boys howled louder and saluted him with their beer cups.

Totally naked, she danced toward him, grinding her hips with her hands behind her head, her knees spread wide as if she were bow-legged. Lucho watched her black bush gyrate toward him, wink, talk to, tease him. She urged him on by cutting closer and closer circles to his chair before spinning away. Then she ruffled his hair, rubbed his shoulders while slinking behind him, and let her nails trail teasingly across his face and lips. From all sides the boys yelled "Get 'er! Grab 'er!" Joe Parisi, standing above Claus, yelled, "Show us what you can do, Lucho!" Forgetting himself and very much confused by the elusive tease and the boys' threatening shouts, Lucho halfheartedly reached out for her. But each time he did so, she wiggled away, never allowing his hands to touch her. He dropped his arms like dumbbells, frustrated and confused.

Round and round she danced to a disco beat, looking at the floor and occasionally at Lucho, but rarely at the crowd. Abruptly she stopped three feet in front of him, whirled around, and in a blinking second, bent at the waist and spread the cheeks of her butt. Lucho squirmed in his chair, grinned and pointed at her again, looking baffled. She popped up, danced a small circle, and in the same spot mechanically bent over again. Grinning back at Lucho through her legs, her upside-down face pulsing red with the blood rush, she slowly ran her hands and blood-red nails up the back of her thighs and spread again.

Lucho raised his brows and squinted his eyes to focus. Leaning forward for a look-see, the guys directly behind him grabbed one another's shoulders and bunched together, grinning as if posing for a bowling team photograph. Christina danced a few more loops, fluffing her sprayed hair, snapped the waistband on Lucho's BVDs, and for a grand finale bent over and spread one last time. Claus shot out of the crowd and across the open floor on his hands and knees and playfully dived for her legs as if to tackle her. Christina leaped away, and the group, laughing wildly, converged on Lucho.

Carlos appeared at the bottom of the stairs, tall, dark and big shouldered, and handed Christina a stack of business cards. She slipped through the crowd, still stripped naked, avoiding the arms that drunks tried to slip round her naked waist, but always managed to deposit a white card in the same grubby paw. Lucho stood around in his underwear shaking hands and grinning, until someone fetched his pants.

Near midnight, making no sense as his talk trailed off into mumbles, Claus staggered from group to group, sticking his nose into conversations he did not understand. At first the guys encouraged him and, laughing good-naturedly, sent him spinning into another group with a slap on the back. But when, to find his legs, he leaned his full weight on every shoulder in reach and shouted for attention, the wall of beer drinkers, many laughing behind his back, parted and cleared a path wherever he staggered. He bullied a jock into a shoving match by the beer keg, trying to spark another brawl.

Then Joe Parisi distracted everyone. "Hey! Leave each other alone," he said throwing out his chin and his pelvis and briefly cupping, then releasing his crotch. "Let's go brick dat nigger's house on Hoyne across the tracks. By my grandmother's."

Joe Parisi's grandmother and her neighbors had been besieged by realtors all through the hot summer months to sell their homes. "Get your asking price now. Before the value of your property bottoms out!" the pushy phone callers warned. Whites, surrendering to panic and fear, set up appointments to show their houses, unwilling to fight what they saw as a losing battle against the expanding black community, which now stretched for more than five miles to the east, to the very shores of Lake Michigan. Parisi, deeply crushed when his father, mother, and two younger brothers sold out and fled to Elmwood Park, still tried to rile up people to stay and fight. Furious at the whites' apathy, he stayed behind with his grandmother in her asbestos-sided frame house, because he had just passed the policeman's test and would need city residency. Plus, he didn't want to leave the old neighborhood where he knew all the hiding places, hangouts, trouble-makers, and guys who'd never let you down, and where he dreamed of wearing a cop's uniform.

"Come on, whadaya gonna do when they wanna buy *your* house?" Parisi shouted, trying to present the threat dramatically to the guys at the bachelor party, many of whom were hearing it for the first time. "Six, seven blocks from this very party! And all yooze guys' houses.

And the park!" he said, quickly poking his crotch with two fingers, then pointing over his head. "You *know* the next thing, niggers is gonna wanna use Marquette Park!"

They plotted in the dark gangway between the houses where they could barely distinguish faces—Joe Parisi, Claus, Scum Landis, and three others—and had to periodically step aside and press against the brick wall to let the stumbling drunks leaving the bachelor party pass by. Car doors, engines, and drunken hollers echoed in the clear night from the street out front and the bright-lit alley in back where parked cars were strung out along the garage doors.

"Shape up, man. You gotta drive my car. We'll get coffee," Parisi said, steadying Claus by the shoulder. The only person Parisi trusted driving his car was Claus Burling. He'd make sure Claus was half sober for the "job."

"Dudek! Hey, Dudek!" Parisi called, and bolted from the gangway. Dudek peeled away from his crowd and stood alone in the tiny grassed yard.

"Wanna pick up where we left off, Parisi?" Dudek snapped, hands on hips.

"Nah, nah. Fair fight, Mike. I just wanna ask you: Heard somebody messed with your little brother last week."

"Yeah, coming back from Sox Park him and a couple of buddies got jumped by some shines. Guess they got on the wrong bus or somethin'."

"Wanna get even? Me and a couple of buddies gonna brick some nigger's house." Parisi spit to the side and fingered his crotch, then dragged on his cigarette, his face glowing orange.

"Naw, I don't think so, Joe." I gotta—"

"Come on. For kicks. Need your old quarterback arm. We'll get beers. Come on!"

Behind the 7-Eleven store on Marquette Road across from the park, Parisi set three empty beer bottles in a row, and with a plastic funnel and a red gallon gas can filled each three-quarters full. "Gotta make sure the wick is packed real tight in these babies. So when ya light and throw, gas don't leak all over your hand and arm," he quietly warned the row of faces watching over his shoulder. A buzzing alley light high on a telephone pole popped bright, flickered dim, then went out at random; the light and shadow which swept round the group made everyone jumpy.

"Cry-Pete!" Can't see *anything* through these damn brown bottles at night!" he cursed, as circles of gas soaked the sidewalk around the bottles. "Don't none of you drink Miller's?" he asked, referring to the moment's-before chugalug that produced the three empty Budweiser bottles. The group laughed, but Parisi hushed them immediately.

Off to one side Dudek sat on a wire milk bottle case, breaking bricks in half on the right angle of a raised cement stoop. In the street next to the store, Scum Landis played lookout in his purple Plymouth Duster, pretending to be fixing a flat with his trunk popped open.

"What we do about cops, Joe? Ain't many cars on the street this time of night," someone said.

"You kiddin'? First off, I know mosta the cops in this district—personally. And come on! Use your brain. Most of 'em grew up here. Think they wanna protect niggers who are gonna trash everything like the rest of the South Side? Huh? Hell, they'll probably whistle and applaud!" Still squatting over the bottles, Parisi flicked open his switchblade and slit a fluffy white rag into strips, which he plugged into the bottles. "Plus, bars are closing. Streets'll be crowded with drunks swervin' curb to curb. Cops be busy as McDonald's at lunchtime. You ready, Burling?" Parisi yelled. Claus sat behind the steering wheel of the Cutlass, munching a large submarine sandwich and coffee Parisi had ordered him to eat.

"Alright," Parisi said, jumping up and wiping his hands. Everyone looked down at the three bombs with the gas-soaked rags poking out of the bottle necks. "Two cars. We'll lead. Garage is second house off the corner. White with green trim. Ain't no corner house, so you can see it from the street—even before we turn. We pop one bomb in the side window, toss a couple of bricks—we're gone. Send those niggers packin'!" Parisi looked at the nervous faces which seemed to change expressions repeatedly from the alley light flickering behind him. "And no smokin', till we're done."

The black Cutlass stunk of gas from the Molotov cocktails pinched between Parisi's feet on the rubber floor mat as they drove through the long dingy Sixty-third Street viaduct under the railroad tracks. Parisi hung out his passenger window flinging empty beer bottles at the riveted viaduct posts flitting past. "YEE-HEE!" he yelled after each throw, and with his shoulders hunched around his ears, he ducked back into the car, away from the crash and flying glass. "See the size of that rat running along the sidewalk?" he yelled. "Gotta be close to niggers!" Claus did not answer, but concentrated on driving and sipping from his styrofoam coffee cup between his legs, both mind and body on remote control. "Rat the size of this here brick, Dudek!" Parisi yelled again, and turned around and handed a full-sized brick with long white paper napkin rubberbanded around it to the back seat. "Gotta little message for our nigger neighbors. Kinda housewarming gift!" Dudek had wrestled off his gray tee shirt and tied it around his head for a disguise. "Since you're the A-rab telegram man," Parisi laughed, "deliver that right through their back porch window, will ya, towel-head?" Dudek grinned from the back seat. "Hey, Scum Landis still behind us?" Parisi asked.

They whipped into the alley, headlights glaring off the targeted garage, Cutlass leading the Duster. Parisi hung out the passenger window, the wick of his gas bomb flickering madly, and with a mighty side-arm heave, sent it crashing through the side garage window, where it exploded into a yellow fireball in the black interior. Scum

Landis hurled another from the second car. It bounced off the window sash and splattered flames across the wood slat siding and into the grass. Both cars stopped behind the garage, hidden from view of the house. Dudek in his tee shirt headdress and the guys from the Duster hurled a volley of half-bricks over the garage peak, listening for the crash and boom. "Hittin' a tree!" someone shouted. "Big goddamn yard tree!" Dudek charged the back gate, the "telegram brick" with the rubberbanded note cocked back over his shoulder like a football. With a clear view of the house sunk in the shadows of a tall poplar, he aimed for the wall of back porch windows, dappled silver with alley light. The brick flew with a grunt, and he toppled headfirst over the chain-link fence into the yard, catching himself on the row of garage cans just inside the gate.

"Let's go!" Parisi yelled, and standing before the garage, smashed the last gas bomb on the cement, sending tongues of blue flame rippling up the checkered garage door. Claus nailed it as Parisi grabbed closed his car door and pulled in his legs, tires screeching half the length of the alley. At the end of the block the cars turned separate ways. "We got 'em!" Parisi howled. "Nice driving, Burling! Dudek, sounded like a TD! We *got* them goddamn niggers!" Dudek stuck his big chapped hand into the front seat for the handshakes all around, holding his naked stomach, scratched and bleeding from the barbs of the chain-link fence.

Within fifteen minutes, screams of fire trucks roused neighbors—both black and white—who huddled in bathrobes and house slippers to watch the flames leap high into the air and lick the huge poplar stretched over the tiny garage. The cockeyed flashing lights of the emergency trucks splashed on the crowd's sleepy faces, dark housefronts, and quick-moving firemen in black rubber coats. Policemen pushed back the crowd when word spread the garage might blow up because of a shiny new car parked inside. The black family who owned the garage complained to police they thought they heard gunshots shortly before the fire and handed the cop a brick they found thrown through their back porch window. Rubberbanded to the brick was a scribbled note which warned "NIGGERS BEWARE!" with a skull and crossbones.

At dawn Gloria found Claus stretched across the bucket seat of his Charger parked in the driveway, snoring peacefully with his head resting on his balled-up leather jacket. Her relief outweighed her anger. At least he hadn't wrapped himself, drunk, around a light pole last night. She closed the car door with a soft click, half hearing the mad chatter of the morning birds, pulled her yellow housecoat round her and tiptoed back to the house, the dewy grass cold and tingly on her bare feet. He'll be a real son of a bitch with his hangover. Either short-tempered, loud and overbearing, or withdrawn and moody, she thought. And her parents were bringing the kids back home this evening. She had dropped off to sleep on the couch, afraid to sleep alone in the big spooky house with the kids spending the night at Grandma's. But when Claus did not come home, she eventually crawled to bed in a stupor. To avoid his surly mood she spent the entire day at the Ford City Shopping Center with her friend Peggy, while Claus coughed and wheezed in a cloud of cigarette smoke before a TV White Sox game, and placed phone calls to piece together the drunk.

"Whadeya mean? Burned down *what*?!!" Claus yelled into the phone at Joe Parisi. "Course I ain't told my wife. Didn't even know we torched nothin'! What time the party break up? A stripper? No shit. Man, I musta really been out of it." Claus felt proud when Joe explained the scheme and told Claus he could see, from his grandmother's window, the charred hulk of garage collapsed on top of the burned-out car.

"Good, that'll teach them goddamn bastards we ain't gonna stand for them takin' over our neighborhood. Whadeya mean don't yell? Nobody's home."

Scum Landis said that Claus tried to tackle the stripper. Someone else said he picked a fight with a barrel-chested football jock. And he found out while he and Joe were torching the garage, Lucho and a few friends "pigged out" at Denny's on Harlem Avenue, where they found Lucho in the men's room hugging the bowl in the wheelchair stall, tomato sauce-like puke running down the front of his new white football jersey. Claus felt angry and almost embarrassed that he didn't remember anything after the "Born to Be Wild" air guitar jam, though he bragged he had had a great time. "Yeah, we really partied down, man—ya know? Really got wasted," he said, making it sound like an accomplishment. Now, still in his underwear, he had this head-in-a-vice hangover complete with cotton mouth and nervous stomach, which tumbled with fear when he noticed, out his front window, the late-model Plymouth parked across the street with two men calmly sitting and reading the paper. Ain't that the maroon car that's been there all day? he asked himself. A panic seized him and he moved behind the drapes. A stakeout. Undercover cops. Oh my God! All those stolen goods in the bedroom closet. Goddamn Tilden Transport really wanted his ass. Or did the cops know about the garage burning? How the hell was he to get all these appliances out of his house?

When Gloria banged in the back door, wrestling plastic bags from J. C. Penny's and Turnstyle, Claus's paranoia had him tricked into believing she could read his mind, knew all about the dock accusation and the garage burning. He yelled from the living room for her to make him something to eat. She ignored him. And he didn't press it. She figured he was in a leave-me-alone-I'm-licking-my-wounds-type mood—sometimes more dangerous than his tirades, because you could never tell when he might explode.

Toward evening the doorbell rang with an insistent plea: one, two and a half short bursts, then a long haul. "Claus, get some pants on!

Ma and Dad are here!" Gloria snapped, and rushed past him to the front door. First thing she's said to me all day, he thought. Was the Sara saga over? He jumped up, banged his knee on the coffee table, and hobbled to the bedroom, cussing under his breath, "Gets so a man can't even sit around his own house in his shorts!" and slammed the door. A thick belt looped over the doorknob leaped for its life, and the heavy Mack Bulldog buckle thudded on the bare wood floor. "The in-laws," he muttered, wondering if they had parked next to the friendly police officers in the maroon Plymouth, as he pulled on a pair of trousers. The children, back from their overnight stay with the grandparents, shouted "Ma! Hey, Ma! Lookee!" obviously showing off. "And the kids!" he muttered again as he slipped into his black dress shoes. He cracked the door and stood motionless, listening to conversation fill up the living room.

"Gloria, it looks *soooo* modern! A brand new room!" her mother bubbled in mock surprise, in that tone that never really revealed her true feelings. "Really nice," she repeated, gasping for breath. Claus thought of Uncle Rocko's "beau-ti-ful beechwood kitchen cabinets" and pictured blacks sitting around the Burling's refurbished front room watching TV. Still he had not told Gloria about the new threats on the neighborhood, or how he felt about them. But how could he with her on the warpath about Sara?

"Claus finished it this week. Well, all except for the rug," Gloria said. Claus jumped, knowing the next question would be about money, the how-much-did-they-soak-ya-for-it interrogation. Her old man would then deliver all his cock-and-bull stories about knowing this guy and that guy and *the* place to get everything at half price—all of this long after the fact. I steal! That's how I get my money, Claus thought of telling them, enjoying the looks of horror he imagined they would have on their faces. Yep, a couple hundred dollars worth of goods lets me buy all the drywall and spackle I need. And sometimes it buys food for your grandkids! He thought of the second secret he was keeping from Gloria: the accusing note stuffed in his locker vent slot. He shuddered. And the "cops" sitting in the street.

Claus popped into the brightly lit room squinting, his hands bulging the pockets at his sides.

"Hello, Claus!" the in-laws chimed in unison—Gram with her too-big naugahyde purse, Gramps in his bold plaid sport shirt. A smile crinkled Claus's face, a smile he felt was stupid but could do nothing about. What had been two rooms—living room and dining room separated by an archway wall—was now one big rectangular space. In the center of the room one big gold sofa and two facing love seats formed a huge U-shaped sectional, which opened toward the TV. Two brown corduroy Lazy Boy chairs sat next to glass-topped end tables. Above the sofa a bold painting on black velvet of the Golden Gate Bridge twinkled with red and yellow Italian lights. The grandparents felt as if they were in the middle of a showroom and stood helplessly marooned three steps inside the front door, unwilling to sit down. Gloria smoked a cigarette in the center of the sectional between her two children, who were bouncing on separate love seats, playing to each other. Claus stood alone looking at all of them, the rest of the house at his back. Gloria fueled the awkward moment by tossing him a dirty look, as if he were still standing in his underwear.

"I bet this remodeling job cost you a pretty penny," Gloria's father said, gazing at the new drywall, dropped ceiling, sculptured rug, and furniture.

"Well...,"

"And I bet ya saved a lot doin' it yourself...."

"Yeah, that and—"

"Where'd ya get the ideas?"

Claus stared at the floor tapping his foot. The old man constantly steam-rollered his way through conversation, never letting a word in edgewise. Gloria chewed out Claus the last time her folks visited. "Ya didn't say three words all night!" Again he said nothing.

"Here—catch!" he said quickly. "Got some ideas from this here magazine," and flipped it, pages fluttering in a mad racket, toward his father-in-law. He parted the drapes to check the Plymouth still sitting on the curb, then turned on his heel and shut himself up in the bathroom.

Sitting hunched on the closed toilet stool, he could hear Carrie with her shiny black Sunday shoes and hard heels, and Timmy in his new cowboy boots race around the house like dogs let off the leash. He realized he didn't, at this very trying moment, care one iota for his children. He felt beside himself, light-headed and woozy. He had floated in a trance-like fog all day long, catching himself staring off and then retrieving his mind back to a reality that at best seemed dream-like and distant. He hated not being in control.

Sunday, the supposed day of rest, and he felt weighed down with all these pressures needling him from all sides. Has Gloria put down her tomahawk over Sara? Was the new dock boss, Ernie Sutton, really coming down on him for stealing, or had some other worker, jealous of his profits, written that note? Who were those guys parked across the street? And what was the fate of the neighborhood, his house, his kids' future, when blacks were pressing to buy up homes—his home! "Pretty soon you'll have niggers comin' up your porch steps, ringin' your doorbell, and sayin', 'Howdy-do! Mind if I borrow your lawnmower?'" Joe Parisi had yelled into the phone this morning. Claus had stood in his underwear in his own kitchen, silent and scared, listening to Parisi. If blacks jumped the four tar lanes of Western Avenue, they'd burn up the few blocks to his house in no time. He'd lose the thousands of dollars he'd already sunk into this place. Hell, his whole property would fetch half of what he paid for it! Hungover, Claus was badgered by all these thoughts. But the immediate one—the in-laws—made him nervous because he didn't feel like being nice. Not now when he didn't have a hold on himself. A tenseness gripped his chest, and the muscles in his neck felt pinched. A high-pitched squeal rang in his ears.

Then, all at once, the presence of Gloria's objects in the bathroom overwhelmed him. He noticed her blue fuzzy slippers parked on the scale next to the white bathtub. On the tub edge in the corner next to the dried, twisted washrag were little soap wavers of various shapes and colors—by-products of many baths—that Gloria would melt down into a big square hunk of swirling color. On the towel rack inside the tub hung a pair of her panty hose that permeated the air with an unbearable sour smell, which choked Claus when he was lying beneath them in a tub of hot steaming water. On the window sill sat a dusty red plastic flower jutting from a pot with little square windows that used to release a rose fragrance. But the deodorizing gel had long ago been licked away by stale air and the hot sun that crashed through the frosted window. Footsteps approached the bathroom door. Claus turned toward them and confronted his own puffy-eyed, saggy-faced reflection in the full-length mirror on the back of the door. He cracked a goofy grin, but not feeling particularly funny, let his face sag into a frown and reached back to flush the toilet to give him more time alone.

"Claus, could you make a couple of drinks for Ma and Dad?" Gloria asked after a soft knock on the bathroom door. "After you're through, dear?"

"'Dear?' Where the hell'd she get *that* from...," he muttered, jarred from his thoughts, realizing how sweet she could be when she wanted something. He sat for a while longer on the stool, dreading the whole scene. Then Carrie scuffed up to the door and banged wildly.

"Daaaaa-dee! Gramps wants to know if ya fell in?"

Tell him to go to hell, Claus thought, but said nothing, opened the door, and brushed past Carrie and her startled expression to the kitchen. Two shiny glasses, a stack of party napkins, and a bottle of bourbon sat on the counter. Timmy came stomping into the room with his clunky cowboy boots and threw open the refrigerator.

"Timmy, go ask your mother what she wants to drink," Claus commanded. Timmy clomped out of the room and down the hall. Claus felt relief from the thunder when Timmy reached the dining room rug. Gloria made sure a bottle of bourbon was always on hand for her parents. "Sick-ass drink," Claus muttered, clinking ice and pouring.

"Nothin', Dad!" Timmy sang from the living room. Claus walked slowly with the drinks, the ice clinking in the cool sweaty glasses, and counting to ten, he took a deep breath and promised himself to be a good boy and a smile a lot.

"Claus, it's real comfortable," mother said from the sofa, running her hand over the bumpy tweed.

"Yeah, they'll hold up pretty well," father said matter-of-factly.

"American-made, ain't they?" It was more a statement than a question.

"Toss-up between this tweed stuff or leather. But I don't like sittin' on cold leather. And in summer ya sweat like a pig," Claus said, passing out the drinks.

"Claus, Peg told me somebody's garage burned down near her ma's house last night," Gloria said. "A black family's. Hear anything about it?"

Sweat broke out under his clothes, his stomach sunk, and a guilty smirk creased his face. "Naw, last night...ahhh...the bachelor party guys, we kindaaa...kinda kept to ourselves," he said cooly, handing a drink to his father-in-law.

"Ain't that where the neighborhood's changing?" the father-in-law asked. "Probably *arson* then!" He sipped his drink.

"Yeah, Dad," Gloria said. "Peg's ma is scared it's all gonna go black. And that she's gotta move. Says she's too old to be house buyin'—or sellin'."

"This stuff's been goin' on since I can remember—since the end of World War II, thirty years ago. Yeah, when everybody came home from the war looking for a place to live!" her father said, waving his hand. "Where's a white guy to go in this here town?" He took another sip of his drink and added as if in afterthought, "And what are *you* guys gonna do? That's less than a mile from here! Think of the kids!"

Claus tumbled into a chair with the distinct feeling of wanting to disappear. But now the room was waiting for the man of the house to answer a heavy question about the well-being of his family in the year 2000, asked by a man he had little respect for, but who also was the father of his wife. All through Gloria's conversation Claus had been saying "nigger" to himself every time she said "black." Gloria hated to hear that word, especially when the kids were about. So, playing along so everybody would get off his goddamn back, he cleared his throat and said to the father-in-law with charm and directness, "Gotta remain calm. See what develops. No sense gettin' all shook up over a few people movin' around—especially when they're buyin' up frame houses. Can't afford these beautiful brick bungalows like we got. Plus ya think these Lithuanians are gonna move? Not on your life." The mother came to his rescue, having not understood one word about the phenomenon of neighborhood change.

"Ain't ya gonna put slipcovers on...the new sofa and chairs? I mean...keep 'em clean?"

"No, Ma," Gloria snapped, knee to knee with her mother on the long sofa. "We don't care if they don't last for twenty-five years or not."

"But, Gloria...," her mother gasped, and looked to her husband for support, hand grasping her throat.

"But no, nothin', Ma...,"

Claus eased back into his chair, satisfied with his performance and enjoying the lull that allowed him to step off center stage. Gloria's father rifled through the Sunday paper, the bright lamplight reflecting the print off his glases. Gloria and her mother turned to current food sales. And the kids, giggling quietly, rattled dice onto a board game on the floor at the ends of Claus's outstretched feet.

It started slowly—that pressure above the eyes, and the way the lamplight looked kind of funny. Claus rubbed his brow and his whole body tensed. It could mean only one thing. He sat bolt upright, fingers cluthing the arm rests as if waiting for a verdict. And the little white dot appeared before his eyes. Wherever he looked, the spot glowed, as if a flashbulb had just popped in his face. His eyes darted around the room: to Gloria, the kids, and grandfather. The white dot was everywhere—on the white prefab ceiling, brown rug, smooth walls, and heavy gold drapes. He blinked and blinked telling himself, No, no...not now...not today....But the spot persisted, and he sunk into himself, a nervous tension messing his thoughts.

The room took on a strange presence. The sounds swirled around him, dream-like. The kids' giggles and laughs echoed, changed in pitch and volume, revolving slowly, then fast. The crinkling newspaper became a percussive cadence that melted into the rhythm of swirling sounds. Gloria's voice sounded like nervous talk in an empty, far-off room; her mother's squeaky, like the talk of a cartoon character. Still, it might be a false alarm. But he looked at his hands—and then he knew.

His hands were not his own, but someone else's, rubber-like, mechanical, not connected to his body. Nothing was in the room except these artificial hands, their presence overwhelming. He could see each individual pore, a blondish hair jutting from each pinhole. They turned in his lap and floated before him. He broke out in a sweat. His heart quickened. A queasiness melted his stomach and he felt he might vomit as he looked at Gloria and noticed the white dot glowing on her face. But she only had half a face—one eyes, half a nose and a mouth, hair lopped over one ear, the other half masked by the glowing dot. He blinked hard and looked to the sports pages held between his father-in-law's strong hands. The thick headline was a senseless jumble of letters and spaces! In a panic his thoughts ricocheted inside his head, mixing with the sounds, the yellowish glow robbing half his sight. When he closed his eyes, the dot persisted. He felt himself hovering above the new spacious room, his family ignoring him, clouds of clean steam puffing past his face.

His right hand, strange and artificial, now went numb. Then his arm. He tried to make a fist and watched the fake fingers fold into themselves. His fingers were numb; they couldn't feel the fabric of the chair arm. The glowing dot burst into a sizzling white spot, alive and electric like a frisky water droplet flashing across a hot fry pan. The room was on fire, the lamplight searing into his eyes and head, the sounds now razor-sharp. The pressure behind his eyes slammed the inside of his skull. He closed his eyes and the dot sizzled white hot in the blackness.

"Gloria...Gloria...," he called in a drunken-like slur, his numb tongue flopping round his mouth. Holding a finger before her face, Gloria hushed her mother and answered him snottily. "Whadaya want?" she snapped, until she noticed he sat funny, holding his head.

"Got a migraine," he whispered. "Could everybody..."

"Keep it down," she finished for him. "Of course, honey."

She led him to the bedroom like a blind man on her arm. After he eased down on the bed, she asked if it was a bad headache. "Everything's on fire!" he said softly, burying his head in the pillow.

Mother was down on her knees tossing the dice onto the Aggravation board game, her pearls dangling from her neck, when Gloria returned. "He's got one of those migraines again. So let's keep it down. You kids take off those shoes right now," she said firmly. "I gave him aspirin."

"Listen, we'll go if you feel...," her mother offered, reading her daughter's worried face.

"Nonsense, Ma. He's gonna just sleep till morning." Then she wondered if he would miss a day of work. His headaches scared her. Like a camera flashed in your face, and the flash won't go away, and ya can't see anything for a while. That's how he explained them. He would get the chills and hot flashes and heave his guts. Couldn't drive his car 'cause he couldn't see. Couldn't stand any noise or even a hint of light. Buried himself in pillows and blankets in the dark bedroom until morning. It made her feel like he was possessed or something, like some other presence was in the bedroom when she brought him aspirin pinched between her fingers.

Dinner was subdued, everyone aware of Claus's empty chair at the HEAD Of the table.

"So when was the last time he had one of these headaches?" Gloria's father asked, swiping a paper napkin across his lips.

"It's pressure, Pa. That's what he says. Pressure," said Gloria.

"What pressure is there at home with your own family?" her mother asked, smiling round the table, her eyebrows dancing as she fixed on the children. Timmy and Carrie sat swinging their legs and listening like little adults. Things'll be alright in the morning, Gloria thought, forgetting the weekend fight. And not thinking, she poured strong black coffee into Claus's orange coffee mug sitting next to his empty plate.

Failure

Gerald Nicosia

The plot of *Failure* centers on a young man of twenty-five who, having failed to achieve a teaching career and unloved by the women he loves, goes to Oregon to find Bonnie, the first girl he loved. On the couple's subsequent cross-country travels with a UFO cult, ending disastrously with the young man's imprisonment in a kook's mansion in Toronto, he is at last able to integrate his past, present, and future through the creation of a multi-leveled diary, which begins with his meeting Bonnie in high school.

On an individual level, *Failure* is about people who fail to use their talents and powers and are driven, in one way or another, to self-destruction. On a broader level it is about the crises of belief—in government, religion, social and political movements, and cults—during the sixties and seventies in America.

Gerald Nicosia is the author of *Memory Babe: A Critical Biography of Jack Kerouac* (Grove Press, 1983; Viking/Penguin, 1985). A native Chicagoan with a B.A. and M.A. in literature from the University of Illinois Circle Campus, he has published a great deal of literary criticism, as well as poetry and fiction. This f^2 publication is the first excerpt from his completed novel *Failure*. While living in San Francisco, he narrated the 60-minute public television documentary video *West Coast: Beat and Beyond*. Now back in Chicago, he has recently finished a play on the life of Kerouac called *Jack In Ghost-Town*.

From *Failure*

Goldbloom's Basement

Gerald Nicosia

The winter of my senior year of high school I came under the tutelage of Irv Goldbloom. That spring he had acquired a doom of his own; or rather, the seeds of doom that had always been twitching behind his black eyes had suddenly sprouted into a mad vine whose strangulation grip was rapidly dragging him away from any ordinary identity. His only salvation—and you wondered for how long—was not to fight it, to let the madness carry him wherever it would.

In plain terms, he had founded a chapter of the radical anti-Vietnam War organization, Students for a Democratic Society, at our high school. A patriotic, fat-assed prick, a big ugly blond named Goliszewski, in the Civil Air Patrol no less, decided on his own to "infiltrate" this SDS "cell" and report its "subversive activities" to the school administration, all of which he performed as well as any snot-nosed stoolie. As a result, Goldbloom was stripped of his office in the class cabinet and warned that if he persisted he would be subject to a police investigation. From that point on he was a marked man; everybody from the school superintendent to his own parents wanted his hide nailed up on a good Jewish cross for example. He had been a championship swimmer (his body small and streamlined as a shark's) and was now a National Merit Scholarship semifinalist, from a family filled with honored athletes and scholars. If a kid like him could sell out to the Commies, then there was no hope for the whole American youth—the gym coach said as much, he whose swim team fell apart this year because Irv would no longer compete. When your best apple goes bad, the spores of its rot have a deadly potency.

One day in the hall, Irv hailed Goliszewski, for his own purpose feigning friendship, and Goliszewski said, "There's no reason why we can't be friends. I'm sure you know I only did what I had to." Irv, who was six inches shorter and forty pounds lighter, connected so hard with Goliszewski's nose that he landed flat on his back. Goliszewski declined to continue the fisticuffs. Instead, he and his family sued. Under pain of not graduating him, the school forbade Goldbloom to continue in the scholarship competition, fearing they could never live down such a winner.

Something drew me to him. We had long talks, while never ceasing to be at cross-purposes. However much I admired rebels, I had little sympathy for his bullying tactics. And though I could tolerate any taste in art, if it was genuine (and so I tried my best to appreciate his strange record albums: the strung-out sound of the Fugs, the somewhat mellower Blues Project, Bob Dylan at his electro-kinkiest, Donovan at his silliest, Simon and Garfunkel at their tawdriest), he refused even to consider merit in the traditional artists I revered. And yet the first time I came to visit I knew I could never hold anything against him. Past the shelves of trophies, the framed and glassed family heroes on the wall, he led me up to his bedroom, whose domed ceiling had been specially built by his rich father to give the house a "Jewish touch." Their money, he told me, had come from his grandfather, a bootlegger.

Nobody could live up to all that without going crazy. The *Guernica* print beneath the dome removed the curse no more than the original work of art had purged of absurdity the brutality and carnage it portrayed. The creation of the original, as well as the hanging of the print, were both feeble swaggerings to disguise an all-too-obvious defeat (that of the human spirit in its claim to sanctity). Like all rebels, Goldbloom was on his way to finding that the end of all rebellions lies in a mirror-image conformity to the thing rebelled against— that there is no escape from the life we are born into but through death. Thus those hurt by his desperate (and futile) thrashings to recover his sanity had no more right to complain than as if against a whirlwind or seiche, those acts of God without self-knowledge, which carry out a destiny they never planned.

His parties were so overwhelmingly sad (to me) that I generally sat by myself and wrote poetry. One of the hip-cats (in '67 we didn't yet have hippies) came up to me and said, "If this were my party, I'd feel lousy having somebody sit around writing poetry." But Irv didn't mind. He'd look at me with those eyes that had the curious power of expanding (maybe it was just his thick glasses) and say, "That's all right! Do what you have to! Every way is the way." But the other people wouldn't leave me alone. Freddy egged me on to smoke a marijuana cigarette, a terribly wicked new dissipation back then.

When I didn't inhale, he snatched it away, yelling, "You're wasting it!" Another night, Freddy's friend—big, bloated, homely Jim Rushol, who had dropped out of school to roam about Kentucky—sidled over to tell me tales of the logging camps he'd worked in and the girls he'd met and fucked in cheap movie-houses and the farmers' daughters: "Well, everything you ever heard about them is true." He asked if I believed him that he'd gone all the way, and I said yes. "I gotta tell ya, it's one hell of an experience!" he boasted. But later, when I had gotten rather soused on the Israeli wine Goldbloom provided just for me and had begun to tell him some of my own troubles with Bonnie, he said rather sadly himself, "I have to warn you, Harry, not to believe everything people tell you."

But perhaps I was waiting for Bonnie, for I knew that eventually she would show up. How could she resist so much action, as she would call it: the spectacle of so many people cliff-diving to glorious extinction? Seeing her see me, I blanched, but she came hurrying over with a smile so warm I was forced to smile back and betray everything inside. She asked me to pick up Irene and Ellen; and in my Plymouth, with only one headlight and virtually no compression (so that every time you shut it off it threatened never to start again), we made the merry pilgrimage through the below-zero night. Irene asked me to stop at Freddy's house, but he wasn't home. Then Ellen wanted me to stop somewhere too, but Bonnie said, laughing slyly, "We've exploited him enough. Let's go back."

In the basement we found Freddy waiting for us. Pupils as usual dilated, he handed me a glass of wine, which they all made fun of me drinking, and said, "Drink deep! There's something special in this one!" Before I had a chance to be suspicious, big Bob Olson—handsome, zaftig science genius (thrown out of advanced chemistry for making plastic explosives, notorious throughout the school for his "midnight parts company")—came over to usurp Bonnie. Clasped in his bearhug, she meandered to the table where cheese and crackers were set out, enunciating gravely, "I'm going to have two crackers and a smear of cheese; that'll be my only meal all day." He patted her nonexistent hips and laughed, "Better make it two smears of cheese—you don't wanna look lopsided!"

I retired to my corner, next to the huge reproduction of a sleek military jet streaking over an incredibly dismal city—a campy reminder of Irv's run-in with Goliszewski. All that was missing from the picture was King Kong (who would, of course, represent Irv) scrunching a couple of skyscrapers. But perhaps he had even intended the omission as a sign that this King Kong had escaped from the jingoist nightmare that had spawned him into the real world of conscious choice. As if to prove there was no predicting this monster, he left his many closer friends and came to sit beside me.

"You're hung up on something," he said, reverting to his favorite role of strong man addressing weak, but looking only like a small-town boy posing as big-city. Yet you couldn't dismiss him that easily. He had as scorching a mind as any you would ever meet; his haunted eyes could easily look through your soul; the things he said would stay with you forever: "When you come into this basement, you leave reason and understanding behind. No use struggling to get them back. I don't let them in here. They won't solve your problems, anyway. I can solve your problems. What's troubling you? Come on, tell me about it."

But I was silent.

"Don't be like that! You have to lose yourself, man. Ego is an evil thing; it distorts all your relations. You have to pretend you don't exist; then there won't be anything you're ashamed to tell me."

But I still didn't answer. He let those laser eyes jab holes all over me, and I stared back with as much hostility as I could muster. Fortunately the others were turning out all the lights, lighting candles. In the darkness, bodies seemed to sway gently, and faces were visible only by their highlights, by the occasional eye-gleams like stars in a black sky.

I was not afraid of hurting him (you couldn't hurt him any more than being born already had), but I was not going to tell him I didn't like anything about this basement. I was not going to give him that strong a weapon against me. I had seen him take people, single them out, get them to say anything, and then take that sentence, that phrase, even a single word, and make it a sin they had to confess to, stab their heart with it till they cried for mercy. Poor Stan Bono had claimed the only thing he wanted out of this world was a decent piece of tail, a woman who would move under him and not be a "dead piece of meat," and Irv had thrown his simple fantasies back at him so twisted and diseased that he'd screamed he was a jagoff and would always be a jagoff and yes he loved his own hand better than any damn woman. "That's your ultimate fantasy!" Goldbloom had accused. "That's the end of your trip! Admit it! The rest is just camouflage! You're in love with yourself and you only need other people to show it off to!" "Yes! yes!" poor Stan screamed, "maybe I am, and if I am, what of it?" "Nothing! Nothing! Nothing!" Goldbloom barked back. "Nothing! Nothingness! You're going to die alone!" And Stan had left the room, broken in front of everybody he'd wanted so badly to impress, his hand over his face—and he never came back.

They had opened the windows, and biting blasts were being sucked in over the crusted snow outside, making the candle flames quaver perilously on the brink of an existentialist's grave. A couple gave up the struggle, then a couple more, and in the near absolute darkness those faces that still caught a shard of light wore horrible, devil-like expressions, richly sensual and lustful, and you thought suddenly. *Now I know what hell looks like. Now I know what it will be like if I ever get there. But perhaps I can avoid it. But not by going to places like this.* And all the while that mystic bastard was watching you, reflecting back your weakness condensed like a black hole, crushing you under the weight of your own inferiority, magnified by *his* infinite thirst for life, love of life, ACCEPTANCE.

They were smoking yellow, seedy-looking cigarettes that sent strange yellow fumes curling up toward the ceiling in the dim light. Trying to make herself look sexy and inviting, Ellen lighted hers from a large guttering candle. You laughed to yourself and thought, *I bet she gets lampblack on her forehead. She's no more inviting than anybody's sister. How she thinks she's really something! And all that talk about how they've got rid of their egos. They have more ego than you have, you sonofabitch and bastard fool.* There were five or six lying flat on the floor, on their stomachs, like a six-pointed star, their heads all facing inward within kissing distance of one another, but instead they were telling stories and sharing the cigarettes. Suddenly Rushol yelled loudly, "What do you call this stuff, I mean, beside maryjane?" and Freddy answered, "Shit!" "What else?" asks Jim. "Coffin nails!" "No, not coffin nails, that's an ordinary cigarette!" "Pot, grass," somebody else says. "No, I know that. I mean what's the word for what we're smoking?" From beside me Goldbloom speaks softly: "Joint." It's the first time I've heard that term, and it seems a perfectly apt description for the place I'm in.

They were funny people, weren't they? You wondered if you could ever be like them, and if you *were* like them, how would it be? Would you be conscious of yourself as you were now? It troubled you, and you looked for answers in their faces:

Don Yirsa, the actor, was there with a leggy chick you'd've given money just to touch, even then (red candy lips, nose so straight it hurt to look at, fluffy brown hair like Hedy Lamarr's). They were sitting watching *On the Waterfront* on a portable TV, but Goldbloom wouldn't allow them to turn on the sound, since he had his own weird music on the stereo, and Yirsa was explaining, "It's the first movie where they used method acting" and fondling her bare shoulder like he knows he's in the limelight, like the grand air of this basement hole gives him more strength than Joshua had when he felled the walls of Jericho; but already in his face you see he is collapsing, breaking himself on a world he'll never be able to fit into, clean-cut boy who wants to please, whom dishes don't mind being seen with, but whose clippety-cloppety horse they aren't going to ride off into the sunset on (and I really sensed this then, eight years before he showed up in Oregon on the lam from life and his vengeful dreams).

Leda Vane, a girl neither pretty nor not-pretty, sits waiting for someone to talk to her, her eyes glazed like an insomniac's (for she knows no one will). You get up and go talk to her, joke about the pretensions and folly of these upstart Coleridges, and because she is a poet, a very good one (in contrast to the many self-saying artists here tonight who have mastered only one thing: self-indulgence), she understands and smiles conspiratorially: "There's pain in all beauty, and black is the brightest color, and how can they see in all this blinding light?"

There's Bonnie, on the sofa with Olson, his arm around her, but she looks like somebody who's just missed one train, yet is confident another will be here soon. Expectant—she's waiting for the dawn, you think—and then you see it's that very waiting that's eating like vitriol at her face, making her oh-so-old before her time.

And Irv, his face like an outstretched hand, proffers a cold grip of humanity. Having destroyed static, he makes you see how grisly purity really looks—for which you can never stop hating him, and he knows it and hates you back.

Toward every one you felt an antagonism. You would never know what they felt like because you could never be one of them. All the time you were so close to them in the flesh, you were miles and miles away in your mind, which would always be in the same place. That was stability. You were a stable fellow. Your thoughts were with them now—like the wind in the forest or over a lake or on a plain, always visiting—and in a day and a night they would be in a new land, like the sun rising in a different country hours after it has risen in yours. But there was one place where they always came back to roost, an identity you were sure of and could never run away from (and it was only because these others lacked identities that they were always running away from the terror of their own vacuum). There was no doubt who you were: you were living and had values and thought you were pretty liberal-minded. You loved all people, but you did not like anyone who hurt you. You often felt insecure and lonely. Sometimes you doubted you had meaning. But here you were with people who acted more sure of themselves than the Conquistadores. You had come seeking a piece of their reality, the peace of their reality, to sustain yourself on, but neither their peace nor their reality existed. You were looking to find their way of life to see if it were any better, but the search was only worsening your old way of life. It came to you then, in one of those quick flashes like an eye passing in and out of a candle flicker: *Maybe a person can't change. Maybe, Goddamn it, in the end you are what you are made like they say in books, and if you are a cat, then you can never be a horse, and like that. Nobody can change. If you are not born one of them, you will die still not one of them. But the question is, Are you losing anything by it?*

Looking at Bonnie, you knew what you had lost. But what was the answer? Did Goldbloom have it? You believed in him because he was the truest man you knew and he was sincere and had the soul of a poet. He wrote well and knew a lot and believed in the philosophy of the East, or so he said, but unfortunately you had not got around to the philosophy of the East yet. The philosophy of the West was enough for you for a while. There was time to learn yet, and you were not sure you wanted to abandon the ways of your world and step into a frightening new world that might upset your old values. *A man lives by his values,* you thought. *Take them away and you kill him as surely as if you put a knife into his heart. Tell a man suddenly, like Irv is doing, that he must get rid of his old person and you will kill him. Irv is a murderer and doesn't care. He's trying to make a new world at the expense of other people. He still has an ego but he would like you to believe that he doesn't and that you and everybody else should change. That's a hell of a deal, isn't it? Not till you die do you find out that he has been faking and cheating you all along. But some day it will come to him and he will get his. It's a pretty damned equal world and you go around cheating all day long and in the end you are going to get taken yourself.* And suddenly you realized you had learned the lesson he had been trying to teach you all along: "What starts out sincere ends up deceitful. What was simple in the beginning is monstrous at the end."

A girl named Cindy was playing the piano, competing with the Beatles' *Sgt. Pepper's* album. Somebody had told me she had a crush on Irv, that she'd gotten him to date her but that he wouldn't make out (and now, remembering his love for Ginsberg, I wonder was he gay? He knew too much of the world's deceptions for a "normal" seventeen-year-old). Cindy beckoned to me to come over and sit by her on the piano bench; and making sure Irv could see, she extended my forefinger and guided it along the keys while continuing to play with her other hand. His eyes spat fiery rage—I couldn't believe it, he was really jealous! Suddenly he jumps up and rushes, not toward us, but toward the six-pointed group on the floor. Bombing down onto a cushion, he pulls Irene out of the group and sits her on a cushion opposite him, ordering her to cross her legs as he does his.

"The trial is about to begin," he says. The rest of those on the floor sit up and watch as though he is a gladiator and she is a Christian. All except Freddy, who looks worried. "Cool it!" he says, but no one, least of all Irv, seems to hear.

"Why have you joined hands with death?" Irv asks.

"Leave me alone."

"You've embraced the eternal meat wheel."

"That's sickening."

"How do you feel right now?"

No answer.

"Sickening! You feel sickening! But why do you feel sickening? Ask yourself that!"

Irene starts to cry.

"You want to be cured, but you can't face your sickness."

"I'm sick of you! You with all your answers!" she bawled. "What do you know?"

"What do *you* know? Do you know why you're here? Because you want to get rid of the evil that's in you! Because you came here to give it to us! Because you want to make us sick like you are!"

Sobbing hysterically, Irene ran and hid herself between the meat freezer and the wall. Irv pursued her with a vicious glee.

"Don't try to put it in there!"

"You're nauseating!"

"Don't put your evil in my freezer! I won't keep it for you! It won't fit in there! Throw it up! Vomit it! But don't try to sneak it into somebody else's life!"

"Butt out!" said Freddy, standing over them. "I'll take her home."

"You can't take her home! She's going to die here! It's the only way! Let her die so she can be born again!"

"I want to go home with him."

"This is a fucking bad scene," said Freddy, trying to push Irv aside, but he didn't budge. Freddy bluffed, "We're cutting out!"

"That's the word! Misery has to be cut out, with a sharp knife!"

"Listen, Irv, you're going too far——"

"You've fallen right into her trap, stupid! Misery wants to feed on misery to proliferate itself throughout the world. Get out of here!"

Freddy hurried up the stairs, passing Irv's mother, who was on her way down to see what all the yelling and crying was about.

"Silence, cunning, and exile are an exile's only weapons," Irv concluded. "You must learn to use them. You must cut through eternity with the same blade it uses to cut through you."

(In those days I didn't know he was cribbing from *Portrait of the Artist as a Young Man,* but I didn't need to. Even his syrupy voice could no longer hide his insincerity.)

Seeing Irene, poor ugly thing, collapsed in a heap of tears and unlovability, Irv's mother demanded, "Why are you always bringing sick people into this house?" Before he could answer, she caught sight of Bonnie, stretched out by herself on the couch, her Arizona sky-blue eyes now closed to everyone. Evidently mistaking her for the girl who was after her son, she charged over and shook her awake.

"Doesn't our family have enough problems already? Do I need a gentile girl coming into my own home to seduce my son and make him crazy? Because of you he missed his own sister's Bat Mitzvah!"

"There was too much snow," Irv pleaded, suddenly docile. "I was afraid of getting stuck."

"So you're stuck with her instead? A skinny *goy* who brings the whole rubbish heap with her? I want you all cleaned out, *right now!*"

Bonnie seemed finally to realize what was happening.

"You've got it all wrong," she said, but before she could finish explaining, Irv stepped in and kissed her.

"You can't keep us apart, Mother!"

Mrs. Goldbloom huffed to the top of the stairs, shouting over her shoulder, "But your father can!" Instantly the guests began making for the exits.

"Why did you say that?" Bonnie asked, still in no hurry.

"Because you wanted me to."

She looked ready to slap him, then coolly turned around and asked

Olson to take her home. Irv asked me to drive Irene, and I told him he could finish his own dirty work.

"You don't understand," he said. "I can't help her till she stops fighting me. She knows what she has to do."

Irene looked up like a dog that will do anything to stop your kicking it, even like the hand it would love to tear in shreds.

"All right," she said, her voice unnaturally calm. "I'll have the abortion."

Irv was radiant.

"Look at her!" he exclaimed. "It may be your only chance to see a saint, a person free of this world!"

What I saw was a face cracked open and laid bare the way no human face should ever be, and I thought of that jet plane on the wall and how it came into a place too high and too fast, seeing too many things at once to see the beauty of each building, let alone each person in that building. On the contrary, it grouped endless incongruities into one vast ugliness, which it shattered with a sonic boom—and Irv was that jet (King Kong being merely the projection of my own destructiveness, which had wanted to answer blow for blow). That was how Irv entered people's lives: armed to the teeth with his superior "weapons"—cunning, silence, exile—and commanding the ugly grid of all their lies and self-delusions. But from that vantage he was unable to appreciate the miracle of their very aliveness, the wonder of a personality that can spin so many falsities as well as truths, the glory of each fabrication (valid or not) as another snowflake of the great human design. If that were the only way I could enter Bonnie's life, by mangling the million possible Bonnies into a single one I could understand, then—God forbid—I would rather give her up.

On the Seventh Day

Betty Shiflett

On the Seventh Day is a novel about a family which, after a move from suburbs to city, undergoes a great many changes in response to pressures and opportunities of city life, at a time when the city itself, and the country, are undergoing large changes. It becomes the story of two families, the Abernathys and the Moraines. The parodic forms that occur within the generally realistic framework of the novel are used to explore situations, character motivations, attitudes, and personal and cultural myths.

Betty Shiflett's stories and articles have appeared in *Life Magazine, Evergreen Review, College English, f¹, The Story Workshop Reader, Writing from Start to Finish,* by John Schultz, *Fiction and Poetry by Texas Women, Privates,* and other literary quarterlies. She just recently completed a story collection. She received an Illinois Arts Council award to complete her full-length play, "Phantom Rider," which was also given staged reading productions at Victory Gardens in Chicago and the Bay Area Playwrights Festival. She is now completing a musical version of "Phantom Rider." Another play, "We Dream of Tours," was twice produced by Dream Theater at the Body Politic Theater in Chicago and played in Ann Arbor, New York, and other cities on that company's eastern tour. She teaches in the graduate writing program at Columbia College.

From *On the Seventh Day*

On the Seventh Day

Betty Shiflett

Sunday filled the Abernathy bedroom. Kate, withdrawn and meticulously over on her side of the bed, back to her husband, appeared to be asleep. Diagonally opposite his wife, the pastor of St. Mark's United Methodist Church, Maxwell Abernathy, hopped around aiming his other foot into his shorts, his amazingly lengthy frame compressed into a half-crouch that threw him off-balance into their frozen Sunday silence, bumping now and then against the foot of their bed. Kate stirred not a jot. The blue, daisy-sprinkled curtains, only inches away from her slitted eyes, sucked flat against the screen with a dull snap, then puffed out again with each breathless, upredictable release of stagnant air. To Max, the rhythm of those curtains seemed to be the "life-beat" of Kate's "hidden thinking." So what if she knew that he knew that she was awake? Instantly, his worries caromed off Kate and resettled on the sleep-robbing matter of this "emergency" joint meeting of the boards he was only informed about last night in one of Earl Greiber's casual mid-supper phone calls, an edge of sterness welded onto the buddy-buddy Chicago voice of the chairman of the trustees. A meeting slated without first consulting their pastor! Judas Priest, what was it this time! Too many social-action ("racial overtone") messages from the pulpit? Coffers running low? Or just plain not enough house calls chalked up this month? Let them keep their word about that assistant! With somebody to run the Sunday School and the Youth Fellowship, he could canvas the community for new members, maybe some live-wire ones. In six months, whether the boards wanted it or not, he'd show St. Mark's the meaning of social conscience!

The pastor's wife concentrated on not blinking back each time the white-daisied curtains shooshed insinuatingly across the sill—corrupting me, she thought for some odd reason— and almost made the mistake of smiling at their rhythm. But strict annoyance at being waked forbade it.

Summer Sunday—always 6:00 a.m.!—her thoughts idled against the rhythm of the curtains. Somewhere, somehow, there must be a man of the cloth who writes his sermon weekdays, nice and organized in his study. Saturday night wouldn't be too hard to take—stay up till dawn, for all she cared. But, of all Max's peers and liberal seminary classmates, she had yet to meet the gentleman. Neither did she know the clergyman who could put it off any longer than the Right Reverend Maxwell Purcell Abernathy, or hate himself less for procrastinating.

The curtains shooshed. Kate blinked. Earl Greiber's oily voice of last night muscled into the bedroom's already abrasive, spellbound atmosphere. Earl's invariable "Good news tonight, Katie! How's my girl?" (chuckle), then his brisk "Let me speak to your hubby!" followed by that *hissss* as he exhaled cigarette smoke, which seemed to issue straight through the holes in the yellow receiver. Now, lying upon her bed, at the center of her universe—with sunshine drilling over the tops of the cottage curtains onto her unmoving form, it seemed to Kate that the trustee's presence attacked her scant well-being, as she would have it assessed this Sunday morning, with a power that rendered tawdry the pristine daisies, squalid the pitiful puddle of costume jewelry, pearl and rhinestone, weakly glinting from the edge of her dresser, reflected in the down-tilted face of her mirror. Earl Greiber never disappeared punctually, but stood in your consciousness, his light grey eyes, pupils always at the pinpoint squinting against the bluish jetstream of his cigarette, as he considered you. Those eyes could also twinkle up like Ole St. Nicks', she liked to remind the pastor, when Earl—cherubic jowls, dimples and all—squared his shoulders in mental preparation for hefting some new mess of troubles for "Pastor Max."

"Let me speak to your hubby!"

Some added swagger to Earl's normal innuendo warned her that this was no perfunctory request, but a crisp command. She tried to telegraph this to Max, but she could tell that all he got was her tight little smile, as the awful phone left her hand and he shushed the children with a "sh-hhh" and a wave of his crumpled napkin. Wiping meatloaf grease from his long fingers, he reluctantly swiveled round from the table on his kitchen stool to reach over the heads of his daughters Sal, eight, Andie, six, and his son, five-year-old Doug. The children were perched on taller stools than their parents. So the children could eat at the same level as the adults, Max had measured, cut off, and evened the legs of two stools. Taking the receiver from his wife, he sawed the phone-cord playfully back and forth across his son's burr-cut, and Doug dodged and yelped in protest, and got a fatherly pat on the head to his deliriously joyful, mock embarrassment. He tried to cross his eyes, shaking his head "wrrrrr," his sisters tittering, each one envious of her little brother's gift for getting attention.

Kate wanted Max to pick up that phone and *return* the order: "Quit 'droppin' by' my manse with little gifts for 'Pastor's family' which you lay on my good-lookin' wife; I know you're checkin' up on me: 'Afternoons when Pastor's not at the church in that nice oak-paneled study we built him, is he workin', earnin' an honest livin'—or home, lazin' round the house?' " Wasn't it enough her entire kitchen, electric pencil sharpener, fry-pan, ice-box—everything that plugged in—sang the praises of Greiber & Sons' appliance shop on Milwaukee Avenue? Depend upon it, Earl had never less than two reasons for anything he said or did, and Max, eventually, felt the bondage of gifts only a little less sharply than she.

"How's it goin'?"

Don't lead with your chin, she wanted to tell him. She saw her husband's grin fly across the table and over her head in the direction of the wall-fan Earl himself had installed "for Katie." "You signed any hot contracts lately? What's up?"

In a stage whisper that got tiresome at meals during long church conversations, she told the kids, "For the fifth time, finish your string beans, if you want dessert!" With Daddy occupied, they sensed she might weaken and Daddy fail to notice.

It would take three or four well-brayed pieces of Earl's eternal "Good news," minor triumphs of usher board or trustees, St. Mark's bowling league score, his latest business coup, or wooden-limbed teen-age daughter's ballet recital before he could possibly get down to just the right timing to drive home a proper shaft. "I thought you'd want to know" from Earl meant "Get set," and Max's face, after that last guffaw, was beginning to show doubt, then worry, and sooner or later they'd see it grim. His emotional switches drew the children (who was she kidding? drew *her*) like steel filings pulled toward the sweep of a huge magnet. A person could be in another room and sense his mood.

"Fact of the matter *is*, Earl, I'd kind of imagined my stock was goin' *up* with them, if house calls this week mean anything. Is it the Golden Agers who've been buzzin' in your ear, or somebody else?" Max tried his best insulted laugh. "You know as well as I do, Earl"—a half smile, sincere appeal to reason—"that sons and daughters of old people can, understandably I'll grant, be insatiable. No one ever gives Mom or Dad sufficient attention." She recognized the deliberate tone shift, but was not ready for Max's unprecedented "What?" Barely a syllable, it seemed to stay even with the height of the adult heads, one on either side of the square table, and hovered just out of reach of the kids' understanding. Their father's silent intentness became the center of focus for their hushed curiosities. Then Max, ducking his head with that way of slicking his thick chestnut hair back from his forehead, reasserted himself in a plainer tone, "Earl, I just can't believe it's worth all this to-do!" Kate saw the kids' spoons and arms tentatively waver as the bleak look returned to Dad's blue eyes, and the big shoulders which had inched higher and higher during this conversation droop to a deflated slope. "Of course. If you think it's necessary. You know I'll be there."

Max, with a lackluster expression, passed the phone back to his wife, who put it in place behind her on the counter, a spot always too near the stove. When she turned back around, she saw him shoveling in food with a vengeance.

"Well, what did he say?" she asked, unable to wait longer.

" 'These old nesters ain't so easy to change, Max! Can ya blame 'em?' " he mimicked. ' "They're very fond of you, Max!' Seems the Golden Band prefers *home* visits, not 'just being talked at' about my 'new-fangled notions' whenever I 'smell coffee' and decide to venture out of my office...merely to go slummin' down to the basement for their meetings at 'coffee *an*' time. I don't need an Earl Greiber to tell me that!" he said out of one side of a crammed mouth. "That's hardly what it's about. He's got somethin' else up his sleeve, damn his eyes!" Kate deliberately glanced at the kids to suggest his outburst was inappropriate. "I'll say what I want!" he snapped. Then, ' "Emergency meeting' after Communion tomorrow!' They oughta be whipped for that!" Kate blushed for her unabashed gasp. ' "I'm not at liberty, Max!' " he whined, wagging his head back and forth in mockery of the way a grown-up might refuse children things.

"That's *all*?" she asked.

" 'Not at liberty!' " Max repeated the phrase over and over. For Earl had left the reason for the Sunday noon meeting of the joint boards of the church a top secret to be divulged only after Communion services.

"I don't know if I have any business as a Protestant minister of the gospel offering those guys the sacrament!" Max clanged the fork he'd just relinquished against his plate. "Highway robbery is what it is, 'Stick 'em up!' Makes me feel violated. Can't they leave a man anything?" His ruddy coloring sank to a dullish lavender while he thrashed about.

"Maybe it won't turn out to be so much after all," she offered lamely, unable to resist trying to soothe him.

"Couldn't be much worse, could it?" His words flew at her with the sting of sand.

"They couldn't— —"

"— —I wouldn't be too sure about that! You know how it is in the church; they make you so miserable you leave!"

"How can you talk like that?" she groaned, with a look around at the children, knowing very well how he could.

"Damn!", he added, "Wish I'd got the jump on *them*." If anger diminished, the melancholy he really felt was sure to return. Always one extreme or the other. She ached with helplessness before the riddle that was Max, with the turbulence of her feeling for him, and from an almost overwhelming desire to protect her children.

She persisted, unable to check herself, "Why don't you let us clear the table? You go read or something," actually forgetting dessert as she said it.

"Mom," Andie objected.

Worse for the kids, if I send them away. At best, she had only slowed down his process of getting himself together, perfectly characteristic of them both, she thought disgustedly.

"Lemme alone!" he growled. "Will you never understand, I have to explode *some*time!" At length, when Max had ceased eating and no one said anything, he balled up his napkin, shoved back his plate.

The meticulous Sal, with big grey-blue eyes, had no more arch looks for her brother, her cheeks almost as ashen as her father's. She was the most transparent to his swings of mood. Andie, her calm, sunny good nature quelled by forces she didn't understand, grew afraid, even of swinging the red canvas heels of her P.F. Flyers against the rungs of her stool, as was her privileged custom. Doug, ordinarily alert to all possibilities to annoy his sisters, crept under their maternal mien toward their father, and desired mightily to cry, terrified that he could find no reason for it that seemed his own. As a small community of three, no longer occupied in whining about having to finish their string beans, they huddled about the desolate table. Kate absently dished up the pineapple-upsidedown-cake, her afternoon's unair-conditioned project no longer a proud sacrifice. Under the moody adult silence, the children consumed their long-awaited dessert. "Elbows off the table! *Use* that napkin, son!" Max said bleakly and curtly.

In the living room around midnight, she watched his too quick mellowing, marked by a contrite but expansive "Well let's have their side of it, come what may. They're not perfect, Lord knows I'm not either, but least I can do is keep a reasonable mind; I *am* their pastor."

"It won't hold," she said. "They'll scorify you at the meeting tomorrow."

Max bounced his fist off a striped couch cushion hard enough for her to feel it two cushions away. Kate, with a leaden fury that their sanity depended upon the improvability of Earl Greiber's human nature, held aloft the damp hair at the nape of her neck to catch a late night breeze, and watched her husband's blue shirt, sweat-soaked between the shoulder blades, as it disappeared around the bend of the stairs.

"You're wasting a lot of undeserved faith on Earl!"

He turned, stooping over the bannister. "Don't you get it?" he said in low, tense voice, aware of his proximity to the sleeping children. "If I have to have this job, the only way I can operate is to believe what I do when I do it. Look, I have to be able to *work* with the man."

"Okay, okay," she said and began turning out the lights.

As they lay in bed in the ninety-degree July dark, the heavy and light smells of sweet elysium and petunias wafting up from the beds Kate had just watered around the back stoop, she could tell that he was once again coaxing a solution within his grasp.

"It couldn't hurt to have a talk with Earl *if* this blows over."

Her already overheated blood surged with impatience at his gullibility, and the words slipped out. "You never learn, You think dinosaurs like Earl Greiber are going to change."

"That's my *job*—changing dinosaurs into angels!"

"Until the next big stink he masterminds for St. Mark's?"

"You make me feel like I can't do anything right!—*what would you have me do*?" This last was wrenched out of him in bitter helplessness. He spun away from her, flopping flat over on his back like a gaffed fish. She had no answer, of course, only pride, an overweening need to be right—oh she hoped not!—and a deep revulsion for the situation that put her husband in this light. She whispered in splendid self-pity, "Just don't be fooled, hon; just don't be fooled." He flung himself out of bed leaving her to fall asleep alone. "Are you going to watch T.V.?"

"I have to work your barb out of my system some way!"

"By all means! *Any*thing, just so you don't write your sermon!" she said aloud to the ceiling as he left. For hours, she listened to the tinny burble of voices coming up the stairs. When he came to bed, her back was burning with heat from the mattress. She longed for reconciliation. Surely he knew she couldn't be asleep!

When the alarm went off, just as she felt herself sliding into real sleep, she was jerked into hot, headachy wakefulness and stranded there, beached on his motion and noise. The unappetizing dregs of last night's wrath were rekindled by the buzzing of the ivory plastic-coated G.E., thanks, Earl. This morning, it seemed, she was capable of contrition and great annoyance, even venom, in the same breath, and it was taking all her strength of will not to ask, Why, just this once, couldn't he get his sermon done on time? Why do it only last-minute on Sunday morning?

Look at him, slamming and bulging around in this tiny, breakable room—wants to make sure the kids don't miss a thing. Whap! Another drawer. Pastor Abernathy's preaching cuff-links weren't in the top one either. One more like that and the bureau would collapse in a pile of maple kindling, pennies, matchbooks, and slips of yellow paper with very important phone numbers and addresses. The papers and old receipts would land on top of the heap, naturally. No way to lose them. She'd tried.

The bed — custom-tailored, vast, and a gift from Max's father—

ground the floor with its castors. Kate called it the "centipede bed" because it never seemed to stay put against the wall, but sneaked away on its twelve screw-in legs. Now they chattered as he torpedoed an outside corner of the mattress with his two hundred pounds, and started to polish his shoes. His weight and the swing of his arm brushing shoe leather dipped the mattress with each bounce. It would have been easy to let go, sidle up against him, run a lazy arm around his waiste, let him cradle her head in his rangy lap. A fitting way to end a whole night of not touching. Only a sheet between, wadded and pink. But everything in the room was frozen, nailed down, or pasted up—except those items Max bullied into motion. Disturbing the dead. Obscene! Only the curtains breathed slyly in-and-out. She felt like a chunk of concrete. Move a toe?, out of the question; let the mattress heave! A size-13 1/2 shoe rocked the floor. And for each slam, every wallop, a shard of her cement flew against the quiet plaster. The tight place began to lump up and roll around below her ribs. Sometimes not tight at all, just a snaky flush that ripped through her belly and left her damp and giddy. Or she'd end up kneading the flesh with her fingers where the crazy thing had passed by, wanting to pluck it out.

As if it had been on a spring coil, Max's corner of the mattress swerved up, rolling Kate to the precipice of the bed by the windows. He ploughed over to the closet, finding every loose floorboard even in sock feet, jangled an incredible number of coat hangers, and dragged out his best suit-coat. Kate thrashed irately onto her stomach, angling toward his side of the bed. Dropping the mask of sleep, she watched him, her nose dug sideways into his pillow. Hang on.

Wondering why the hottest day of the week always fell on Sunday, Max shook his head once before pushing his arms into the coat, then shucked it off and, slapping it back on a hanger, laid a small bet with himself about how much longer his wife would take to thaw, heat and all. Why should she be the "injured party," anyway? He'd noticed long ago that high temperatures weren't much help to Kate once she'd decided to freeze, so—twenty-four hours and a break in the weather. Reasonable leeway.

> "Make it one—for Paul—and one more—
> for Silas—"

Kate heard him start up that old camp song, almost coated with woodsmoke from the big fires they used to sing around, with the kids, up at week-long Family Camps. The kids' enchanted eyes would shine at her beyond the lovely flames, when they sat on the other side, across the circle of logs that served as seats, feeling big and acting independent. Max moved around inside the log circle where sat the many families gathered here before lights-out, "lining" them the words to the old, old "rounds," gesturing with both hands when they should "come in," each group, each time. Sing loud, sing soft, those hands would say, for Max loved to lead the singing.

With a sleepy moan, she rolled over enough to risk a direct glance, and he was grinning at her as though he rather enjoyed the sound of his own voice.

> "One for to make-a-my heart rejoice.
> Can't you hear those lambs-a-cryin'? —"

At the door he gulped deeply and looked back at Kate. That ragged pause cut clear through her. To prove she hadn't heard it, she flopped over again, face to the window wall in a stolid line of legs, rump, arms, and skimpy nylon. A pale ribbon from the bow at her breasts wrinkled around her neck and fell on Max's side, which was to say, her backsides. He thought about grabbing her, maybe playing rough, for a second. She's got nice angles after three kids. And her hair's still dark and sweet. Before he could get on with his daydream of playing hookey from the pulpit, and the "emergency" meeting of the boards, colored with a twang of remorse about all that banging that probably had waked the kids, the earlier certainty of her jawline caught up with him, the eyes frankly open, *Don't talk to me.*

Back turned against her husband's hardening stare, Kate jacked her top shoulder up a little higher and concentrated on not listening.

> "Oh Good Shepherd,
> Feed my sheep."

His words, his voice, resonated up the stairwell as he went down, and Kate felt the bedroom was closer than ever with her husband. What he really wants is for me to hop up and fix his breakfast.

"If you want—," he was wailing now from the kitchen,
"To get to Heave*n*"—pronounced hum on the final *n*,
"Far beyond—"
Too high for him, she gloated.
"—the distant shore—" A skillet smacked the grill.
Then, in a very slow bellow, "Stay away from those *long-tongued* liars—" Kate flounced off the bed and jarred out into the hall so hard her feet tingled. She panted against the newel post, enjoying the way its pedestal dug into her hip as she leaned over, contemplating the abrupt drop to the bottom of the stairwell. After a dramatic pause, Max resumed in his sweetest, deliberately churchiest tones:

> "Oh Good Shepherd,
> Feed my sheep."

Danger of tears surprised Kate and doubled her pique.
"That soggy old song—not fair!" A pitiful whisper. A barrage of cabinet doors swung open and went "*fump!*" as Max drummed them

shut.

"He must have thirteen hands!" She bent over the rail, undecided, and listened while Max played the kitchen like a console. The spring on the oven croaked—the door snapped up short—

"Kicked it, I bet!" The electric mixer mumbled, faded out, then took off. Kate headed down in her see-through "Baby-dolls," ignoring all windows and neighbors. At the bottom step she instinctively reached out to rescue whatever must be scorching in the kitchen, then let her arms drop when she saw Max turn from the stove, where three blue rings of flame spurted too high, having no pans or skillets to cap them. He was just transferring a pleasant-looking omelet from her biggest frying pan to a place setting for one at the table.

"I got cold." He indicated the three burners and pulled a long wink, her cue to giggle.

"That heat's no joke!" She swooped over to shut it off, and snagged her elbow on a low button on his shirt-front, for an instant throwing each of them off-base with the other. Kate stared at the innocent-looking pearl button, damned if she'd look up. "Salvage your eggs," she said, and he moved away. Each one knew the day together had begun, like it or not.

Then Max's baritone hit the old refrain:

"I said,

'One—for Paul,

And one more—for Silas—' "

She flew at getting everybody off to church with an intensity that frightened her. "I'm careful not to make a habit of a practical turn of mind," Kate liked to remind one and all, but Sunday morning made practicality not only a virtue but a necessity. What (besides "elbow grease and muscle") massaged Doug, with his sore toes and prickly heat, into good clothes or any kind of shoes? If Sal, to outsiders a placid-faced Madonna, but actually a junior *prima donna* "already strung up" with problems of "what to wear," decided to have a go at either her brother, wretched with heat rash, or Andie, who worshipped her older sister beyond reason, Sabbath breakfast could easily degenerate into the best brawl of the week. Kate shelved all queasy thoughts about her "holy triangle"—herself, Max, the church—and what in hell they were coming to, and jumped into matters at hand.

No shortage of matters existed. And since Max had holed up in the living room with a lapboard and an officious brace of Bibles and reference books, those matters were all hers. Predictably, nobody had any clean underpants. Kate dropped the strip of bacon she was coaxing from the package, clattered down the steps to the basement in clogs—"Hey!, you courtin' a broken leg?" Max yelled. She ransacked the dryer, reflecting on the merits of getting organized as she checked underwear labels for sizes. In the middle of her second trip down to press a sash for Sal, Max yelled that her bacon was smoking him out of the living room and out of his mind.

"You've got legs, turn the fire down yourself!" she bawled up at the basement ceiling. Five minutes later, raking the charred strips into an empty milk carton, she felt vindicated. "How's everybody supposed to get fed?" she asked of no one in particular. Andie floated down in her nightgown and camped on a stool at the kitchen table like a baby Buddha with her eyes closed behind a screen of brown tangles still moist from the pillow. She'll evaporate the minute I pick up that brush, Kate guessed, diving for the hairbrush on the counter.

"Do my barrette, Daddy!" Sal pestered her father across his lap-board, absently jabbing his writing elbow with her pink bow-clip.

"Doug-las!—-Front and center!" Aghast at the hour, Max remembered his son had been up forever, still in his pajamas, blocking the door to his room with a shaky Lincoln Log house. Kate exploded breathlessly up the stairs and poked her head in at Doug's room, knowing he'd pit Lincoln Logs against time and neckties. "Get dressed so Dad can fix your tie before he leaves!"

Max climbed out from under his books with a sermon outline in his pocket and raced to leave ahead of the family wave. Larry Bach, the Sunday School Superintendent, called to report he'd been locked out of the church. Pastor Abernathy, trying to leave the house at a dead run, was forced to stoop in front of the pier glass while smoothing a stubborn collar which showed every sign of betraying him in the pulpit. Suddenly he slapped his chest, searched the pockets of the light coat draped over his arm, and on his way out accused his wife of hiding his *Book of Common Worship.*

"Don't you know it's Communion Sunday?"

Setting her spoon on her saucer, Kate aimed for the back of his head with sarcasm that surprised even her as she reminded the high priest, "I've little enough reason to use your *Book of Common Worship.* Perhaps you've noticed I rarely conduct funerals, weddings, or baptisms. Indeed, I have not yet been able to qualify for my ordination vows, though to do so and thus relieve you partially of your onerous burden is my most cherished desire." Before the last words were out, she knew she'd gone too far, too near the mark. He paled, mustered a few words about "another copy which had better be on my desk at the church," hesitated, then rushed the front door. That pinched look settling in around his eyes told her he really did worry about a professional takeover, whenever and wherever in his life she dug her interests in. Yet he wanted her to be "interested."

Max threw the screen against the bricks. Kate hung on to her coffee cup and counted the flies that trickled into the entrance hall. Shaken and empty, she sat around until it was too late to wash the dishes.

Their arrival at St. Mark's after a brief journey on foot, Pastor

Abernathy's girls looking like pastel butterflies, occasioned flurries of Sunday smiles on the lips of parishioners. Today, despite her fears of the impending "emergency" joint meeting of the boards to take place after services, Kate understood the greetings to be in the main friendly, unlike the pointed remarks in the past—"I always wanted to see the color of the hat you'd wear"—which had made her feel set aside as a prize enigma. With heat melting down her pale yellow dress at belted waist and underarm, she tried to return their smiling greetings in kind. Doug, at her side, looked as if he could bite the first sweet old lady who came near.

In Sunday School, the pastor's wife muddled through her twitchy, but small, class of Junior Highs with the help of a fatally naive teacher's manual, and had to put down a wellspring of kinship with Max's lack of preparation. She didn't run into him until later in the choir room, after she'd smothered herself in a glassy black robe and lined up at the door with the others for the minister's send-off prayer. Breathing in this small, humid room was shallow. The squat choir director wiped his forehead and rapped his music stand. Max, standing poised before the decorously closed door that shut out the throng of worshippers drifting through the narthex into the sanctuary, lifted his hymnbook, which concealed the few sermon notes he'd scrounged, and unleashed a prayer for a "worshipful approach" to the anthem about to be performed, which meant he devoutly hoped certain ladies in the choir would not swing their purses down the center aisle during the processional just this once, dear God! Kate, noticing Hey! that Max had forsaken his robes, teased the idea of stopping off at the john and removing everything except shoes and robe. But the processional, jockeying now into the broad narthex, made the next hour and fifteen minutes palpable reality.

Ensconced on the deacons' bench between a modernistic Communion table that always struck him as an aircraft carrier and the chunky stained-glass cross mortared floor-to-ceiling in the front wall, the Reverend Maxwell Purcell Abernathy surveyed his people. At eleven o'clock, prismatic gold, crimson, and purple danced from the cross, dazzling at least two-thirds of the congregation but painfully blinding every eye in the first seven rows. Seven rows of faces squinting and cringing before the cross did not displease the pastor, who sat drumming his fingers impatiently on the dark red hymnal. Beginning with the eighth row, the "third degree" quality of the light refractions played out gradually to colored sunbeams which fell harmlessly across faces and lapels, but only the balcony cast a shadow which offered total escape. He steeled himself for the pugnacious, chin-raised set of Earl Greiber's blond-grey head. People on the aisle turned to gape at the choir trailing jerkily toward the chancel and their pastor. Max felt they were marching on him personally, bat-armed robes, handbags, hymnbooks and all. Don't come an inch closer! he thought, as they stumbled two abreast up the single step to the pews on his left. Kate, the fourth soprano trickling over the gold carpeting, scarcely met his eye at this moment when they customarily gave each other the gift of a joke through a "blank" meeting of the eyes. This exchange, without tip-off to choir or congregation, had long been a cornerstone of solemn Sunday fun, a reward, maybe, after all that fuss back at the house. Today his wife's face was still and cool, the high cheekbones and arched brows just bordering on haughty. *Not today*, that face proclaimed. Instead, he blessed Grace Elmquist at the organ for holding up her end of the bargain with a decent cadence in the teeth of an ominous time lag which he knew had been perpetrated by two aging basses who, when they opened their mouths to begin any hymn, habitually came in late but strong, dragging down most of the choir voices: "Holy, holy, holy, Lord God Almighty...God in three persons, Blessed Trinity!"

Inevitably, the processional halted with the choir in place to one side. The front pews were vacant, except for a few children and old ladies who still liked to see the minister and the service. Max rose and, into the descending but by no means perfect hush, pronounced the Introit over the heads of the congregation squarely to four ushers whispering behind their white carnation boutonniers in the little blue alcove at the rear. Only the potted palms that flanked the blue walls appeared to hear him, though he spoke quite distinctly. Adding a silent prayer that Sal, Andie, and Doug, doubtless whooping it up right now in Junior Church in the basement, might grow up to have finer sensibilities during services than these eternally juvenile ushers whose indifference so rebuked the "minister" in him now, he was appalled to notice how his eyes, the whole time, systematically ransacked the pews for Earl.

On his left, four rows this side of the balcony, he spotted the Greiber pew. Left to right he counted them. The three males, like book-ends with Earl on the center aisle, guarded their two females in the middle. The Greiber women, as was their habit, gazed indiscreetly at their pastor. Earl's wife, Portia, would be steadfast throughout the service: Wherever in the chancel Max chose to move, her rosebud smile would follow. Pale Judi, on the other hand, chained to her parents, never joining the other teens in the balcony, looked more dispirited than ever, already turning her gaze inward. I hope she finds whatever she needs in there, Max blipped, trying to keep his eyes off Earl, who, on the aisle, was shamelessly pumping the hand of a skeletal usher, Chester Roth, just then returning from the front pews where he'd been adjusting windows for an elderly couple. The flattered Chester allowed his bony hand to be snared in chairman Earl's two square paws as if the trustee had got hold of something precious; then, on Earl's release, Chester stalked with stilt-like gait, radiant, up the aisle. Upward from the base of his heels, Max felt a rush so utterly strong that he marvelled at the sensation that he himelf was watching from a back pew, in a sublime state of wonder, to see what he, Max Abernathy, would do in the chancel if Earl struck up a fresh conversation with Harry Loomis, just now scuttling self-importantly on his final return trip to the big double doors at the rear of the congregation. Taking his own good time, Max noticed. To the pastor's relief, Loomis' journey went uninterrupted by Earl. Outside the open windows a distant power mower cut off. The sounds of feet scraping and pages rustling seemed to leap and jump at Max's ear, while into the relative silence the chairman of the trustees, with a brief flash of dark-framed glasses, turned and poured upon his pastor a look of cooly delivered, unfathomable earnestness. Max spun on his heel and moved briskly up the shallow step to the chancel, the immense Bible awaiting him on the Communion table for the reading of the first scripture, and then to his pulpit.

Was it possible, he wondered for one bottomless moment, that such small events as he'd just witnessed, seen for what they were, could seize the direction of a man's life as surely as one glimpse of the veil-rent interior of Israel's Ark of the Holy Covenant was said to strike a man dead? Could such events pitch a man headlong into a drastically different aim for his life and the value which he placed upon the lives of others? For that instant he felt himself once more pulled, with infinite force and attraction, to throw it all up, this high-minded business of "the ministry," a calling seated as it was in the notion that all types of human nature can be changed; if some *can't*, then the best efforts of *his* imperfect nature, pitted against such odds, were doomed to fail. This doubt he knew no minister could afford. By comparison, the troublesome question of assigning to Christ accurate proportions of divinity and humanity became merely a riddle solved by the simplest of theological equations. But with only a glimpse of that lightning stroke of thought, he swiftly resolved never to give in to Kate's impatient ways, her implicit demands that he reject, out of hand, the chief tenet of the course he'd set his life upon. His unravelling of "original sin" required the faith that almighty God never made the man that couldn't change. *It shall remain*, he vowed, grasping the smoothly carved oak trim enclosing his pulpit. Ascending to the pulpit gladly, he viewed his congregation for a second time this morning, now with a fonder, somewhat more sweetened eye.

From her favorite seat in the airless choir loft, at the end of the front pew overlooking the congregation, Kate could with impunity be on view for parishioners while she watched her husband, in profile, at work in his pulpit. With heart-wrenching amazement, she observed the big-framed Max moving cleanly and easily in the new seersucker suit, as if the grace of his flowing robes, though they'd been temporarily cast aside, had not deserted him in this his Communion Meditation. He didn't even look hot, she thought, as she tried to arrange limbs and suffocating robe so they never touched each other.

"Working at the Noontide" was the sermon title coyly announced in Kate's bulletin. Her old warning signals told her that her husband was moving square into the danger zone. Every adult sweltering in those pews was probably thinking, just as she was, *This better be good*, if it was about civil rights, because there had been city council talk about a high-rise that would bring blacks into their neighborhood. There had never been a black face in the congregation. They had Max in their cross-hairs, all right.

She could tell that now his eyes fixed the congregation without lingering on the Greibers. Those blue eyes of Max's were clear and guileless during "point one" on his hard-won outline, increasingly stormy and electric as "point two" began first to simmer and then to cook, and somber and brooding for the overdue windup, leaving the congregation (that portion it was possible to affect) wrung-out, titillated, and reproved by his nicely climaxing homiletic skill. Most of the older men looked purplish and a great many of the younger women misty-eyed. His sermon about having the courage of your Christian beliefs, "Stand up and be counted!", even in the "heat of the day" had, at this tender point in Max's relationship with his congregation, been interpreted by them (correctly) as referring mostly to civil rights. She winced at the sight of Earl's pink, knowing face.

But inexorably, the power of an audience had exerted its draw upon Max, and his needs and their desires (for what?, for a little drama in their lives?) had once again meshed. The very breath quivered in Kate, shallow, reluctant to be expelled. Yes, he was a "not bad at all" preacher, and she still admired and thrilled to that, even while she wondered where "that" was taking them. Max would get a *hiding* when this was over. Within their property and terror-ridden hearts, she knew the congregation could only translate Max's sermon as a demand to "let the niggers into our own backyard!" Her blood raced uncontrollably. And she remembered the step-up of warmth this morning with which she and the kids had been greeted.

Where would they go and what would they do if things kept on this way? Max could not hold out against Earl forever. Kate set to reviewing Max's off-again, on-again readiness to quit St. Mark's "one day" and try a city pastorate again, though there were "Earl Greibers" there, too, they knew from experience. Any contemplation of momentous change for themselves and their brood filled her with delicious trepidation if not a downright tizzy.

"Will the elders please come forward?"

Two of them, Christine Sobrick and Doris Malvert, women Max and she had invested a lot of time in, walked down the aisle to face Max directly across the communion table where each, along with all the others, would receive from the hands of their minister "the bread and the wine" laid out on silver plates under snowy napkins while Grace Elmquist slid her sweet organ tones into "Break Thou the Bread of Life, Dear Lord, to Me." From coffee-klatching and study groups, Kate knew them. Even when they brought their small gripes about him to her, they adored their handsome Pastor Max, though when it came down to voting, these token women officers, her friends, that Max had driven himself so hard to get elected, were no better than their husbands' politics.

Rounding out the second verse, the breathy voices of the choir promised, "...Then shall all bondage cease, all fetters fall...," and for a moment Kate, too, floated on that wide pool of deepening solemnity spread by Max's sonorous injunciton to "Come to the table with pure hearts." She glanced down at the uneasy faces of Chris and Doris. Were they remembering their "theology sessions" led by Kate, her relish interpreting "Pre-Communion Confession"? Then Kate glanced at Max. That proud set of head, shoulders, and those long legs which, close together, held his body at attention, seemed to be saying to the congregation: "Come! Won't you walk on these waters with me? We'll risk it together." (You don't have to be perfect, but we do have to get those blacks into better housing.) In that stern and amiable spirit he addressed them with the warnings that Jesus gave to his disciples shortly before his passion, when "the Lord spake in parables" about the Kingdom of Heaven.

Max laid the tip of his long index finger to verse one, chapter twenty-five of St. Matthew, printed on the fine translucent vellum of his pulpit Bible, now dwarfed as it lay open upon the vast oak table, and lifting sober yet warm blue eyes to the congregation, began the scripture reading with the parable of the foolish virgins who went forth to meet the bridegroom, but taking no oil to trim their lamps, had to go out to the oil merchants, and missed the bridegroom. " 'Watch, therefore,' admonished Max, in Jesus' own handy words to his disciples, " 'for ye know neither the day nor the hour when the Son of man cometh!' " On the heels of the foolish virgins followed the "unprofitable servant," who, in fear of his master's wrath and greed, had not risked investing the one talent given him on his master's departure, and who was cast into "outer darkness." And the last story: When the Son of man comes to separate the sheep from the goats, and sinners, terrified and baffled, protest, " 'Lord, when *saw we thee* an hungered, or athirst, or a stranger, or naked, or sick, or in prison?' " to these sinners his implacable reply will fall, " 'Inasmuch as ye did it not to one of the least of these, ye did it not to me.' "

When at last Max leaned forward supporting himself with a lengthy hand on either side of the golden-sheaved Bible, and his clear baritone rolled into prayer—"Let us humbly confess our sins before Almighty God"—Kate felt the pull of his words more than anyone else in the sanctuary had a right to!

In the teariness and mystery of her desperation, she was busily calling upon all her reserves to greet the drama gathering from every corner of the sanctuary, from every "dark corner" of her heart. Earnestly she tried to conjure the kneeling Jesus robed in deep wines and whites and blues as in the church-famous picture, for it was all she had: his brown locks long on his shoulders, hands clasped on a cold, forbidding table-like rock—at prayer in a blasted garden, pleading for his mortal life, his blue eyes, so much like Max's, saying "Let this cup pass from me." Max's voice immediately amended from the pulpit,

> " 'For in the night in which he was betrayed, he took bread, and blessed, and brake it, and gave it to the disciples, saying, 'Take, eat; this is my Body, which is given for you ...' "

Kate's torment always increased as she strove to produce the ultimate and proper thoughts and images of Christ crucified, rather than the old, mistaken childhood picture and visions: her kind Lord hiding from her fierce looming molars, he being tossed in their path by her awful tongue, until, as her own early Sunday School teacher had taught her, "You have killed him." She tried harder than ever not to let the miserly thimbleful of "wine" whistle down the back of her throat, but to force this sacramental "drop" to slow down long enough so that she might savor Christ's blood shed for her, her own glory of redemption, without that invading imagery of cannibalism. She felt her Christ and Max's fate—*their* fate hanging in the balance—deserved something better, more filled with meaning, but she could never elude the pull of those old childhood images. ' "O Lamb of God!, who taketh away the sins of the world,' " Max's voice rang out. ' "Have mercy upon us,' " mumbled his congregation. But even as Kate, impossibly childlike, impossibly moved, flinched with each bruise of the body of Christ inside her murderous mouth, Max continued from the Communion table, lifting high the silver chalice:

> " 'After supper, he took the cup, and gave thanks, and gave it to them, saying, Drink ye all of it; for this is my Blood which is shed for you. Do this as oft as ye shall drink it, in remembrance of me.' "

Elders, with their sprinkling of women, stood at the ends of pews in what Max called the "fig-leaf position," hands limply crossed above the crotch, awaiting silver plates of cubed Wonder Bread passed hand to hand. Tiny "wine cups" ringed with Welch's Grape Juice clinked musically into the shining Communion service. Judi Greiber's subterraneously troubled eyes blinked up at Max from the sheer force of his roving glance. Faithful to the liturgy, the minister was now ready to be served after his flock. He took bread from the plate which Doris timidly offered; his jaw, Kate noted, once the white cube had passed his lips, perfectly unmoving. Just then, Earl Greiber leaned across his daughter Judi, eclipsing her, his raised bulletin shielding the lower portion of his face as he whispered lengthily to his wife, whose plump hands all the while remained folded in her lap. Now what does *that* mean? Kate would have given a pretty penny to know what Earl was saying.

The "sacrament of the wine" complete, the congregation's last notes of "Tis Midnight and on Olive's Brow" (with blasphemous Abernathy humor known in their household as "On Old Olive's Brow"), singing of Jesus at the Mount of Olives in Gethsemane, settled evenly and peaceably upon the air below the vaulted ceiling of oak timbers:

" '... for others' guilt,
the Man of Sorrows weeps in blood ' "

Kate with her vigilant index finger staunched a tear at its brimming: Always a sucker for Communion, she was stung with a backlash of resentment for Max's prowess this past hour in forcing her to suspend anger. But already, with his arms uplifted and generously thrust forward over the heads of a wilted and penitent congregation, he was intoning the Benediction. On the lagging notes of the "Sevenfold Amen," his final syllable catching the sleepy choir so that only Kate's voice stood out, the service ended with much the same indifference as it had begun, but now with a great babble of voices and chucking of hymnbooks into pew racks.

The irrepressible ushers stomped down the side aisles during the Benediction, ready to snatch leftover bulletins at the first trumpet of the recessional. One of their number streaked behind the backs of the people seated in the last pew in time to throw open the double doors for the choir whose members began clammily to disrobe in the narthex while others still recessed down the center aisle. Children scrambled to freedom from every sector of the church. Doug, freshly escaped from the basement and Junior Church, skated into the choir room and tried to chin himself on his mother's arm, upsetting her balance as she was stepping out of her soggy robe. "Don't drag on me!" she cried. But into the packed narthex he had already disappeared with friends. After the farewell handshake with the minister, a tradition Max despised (but which today yielded no Greiber hands for him to shake), families blinking in harsh noonday sun regrouped as usual on the steps outside and started quarreling over early lunch and a trip to the forest preserves versus sweet rolls with coffee in the church basement's Fellowship Hall, late dinner, and washing the car.

Max, turning from noonday brilliance back into the vestibule, shadowy by contrast, endured a swift dropping sensation from collarbone to gut accompanied by the incongruous notion of blindness, as he sifted the shadows ahead of him for Earl. "Losing my vision, like old Eli!"

147

His wing-tips rang on polished tile as he passed quickly through the artificially lighted narthex and stopped at the big double doors, arrested by the scene at the opposite end of that long flat aisle under the high and massively oak-ribbed ceiling. Veritably at the "foot of the cross," the church officers gathered, milling more and more away from the pulpit side, beginning to fill the first two pews. Through the echoing emptiness, the further reaches of the nave, their voices floated up to him like exploding bubbles.

Having sensed his disquieting presence at the back, some turned in their pews to stare, with a jolt, as the long, well-shaped fingers of his right hand cupped over the back of the last pew where he had stopped, suddenly upon entering, apparently taking his ease now, his coat unbuttoned while with the other hand he jingled pocket-change, his tie a stark wound on the splash of white shirt.

No. Not one of his women officers — they were easier to educate than the men, more open — had seen fit to boycott this fateful meeting. Well, he thought, we had some hope for them. Now the minister bedeviled himself for the thousandth time: Why were the men so difficult? So cantankerous? So terrified of change? Just then the chairman of the trustees ceased talking with Larry Bock, the Sunday School Superintendent, abruptly turned toward the pulpit side of the sanctuary, his blocky face three-quarters visible, and squinted up at the cross, studying it for a moment in a proprietarial yet adversarial way, which Max remarked as he strode forward. Neither fear nor adoration was in that look. The naked knowledge of it sank keenly and coldly into the minister's heart, and with it, all his mildest hopes resumed, now on a sharper note, their long, slow process of withering and decay. What do such men seek from the church? he asked the gilt false organ pipes affixed to the chancel wall opposite St. Mark's Hammond electric. *I will perish here.*

Through the floor, he could hear the Happy Fellowship Hour raging in the basement. Kids, probably his, up on the stage banging on the baby grand, or tearing around the folding chairs and tables at ninety miles an hour. He straightened that noose-of-a-tie around his neck, preparing to meet the trustees and elders.

* * * * * *

At home, later that afternoon, Kate had already fed the kids peanut butter sandwiches and was wiping the kitchen table when Max came striding in the front door, his eyes blankly puzzled, lips tight-set. Angrily he whipped off the red-striped tie and slung it over the banister on his way upstairs to change clothes. In the kitchen, along with their bologna sandwiches, the couple chewed over the results of the much dreaded "emergency" meeting of the joint boards of the church, the cause of Max's tardiness. These hopelessly "practical," self-styled "men of the world," Kate knew, not content merely to strike sharp differences of opinion with their pastor over his "brash" talent for social-minded projects ("Inasmuch as ye have done it unto one of the least of these my brethren, ye have done it unto me"), used also any real or imagined shortage of cash to keep their man in line. Kate thrilled to the clash and clamor of battle, her wifely pulse quickening, though she knew there was apt to be big trouble if she didn't perfectly tread the thin line between disinterest and compassion. She herself could never tell where empathy for Max left off and a desire to "critique" and "run things" began. It was a trap for both of them if she did not give the sympathy he deserved, or seemed to judge his problems not so difficult to bear.

"Every summer, same old thing," Max growled. "'Low on funds!' they say. Whiners. Does Mr. Chairman Earl Greiber make out his Benevolences/Home Missions check while he's revvin' up the Buick for his 'summer cottage' up in Wisconsin? What I want to know, which one runs his business the way they pretend to run a church?"

He paused, in a fume, while Kate tried to calculate her way across the tightrope.

"Then every summer they *will* get edgy when funds are normally low; start dancing up and down they're so happy, claiming our 'Giving is falling off!' because of social issues I'm pushin' direct from the pulpit."

"You really feel it's worse this time?" she ventured, sensing immediately she'd taken a wrong tack.

"'The consequences look serious,' my foot! *Let* them 'stand up and be counted'!" She started to speak, but he glared her down: ' "You're a man with a family, Max! We thought you'd want to know.' "

"*Some*one spoke up!" she said, as if to make it so.

"No-body!", he emphasized, letting his sandwich arm down against the table's edge with such force it set their iced-tea glasses tinkling.

"What about the women?", she dug a deeper hole, pushing the plate with the extra sandwich toward him. He pushed it back at her.

"What are they good for?——sit there and look agonized? I *almost* felt sorry for them, seeing as I worked hard enough to get them on the boards. You got any more tea?" he said, rattling naked ice cubes wrathfully in his empty glass. Turning to the sink for the tea strainer, Kate could feel her husband's unseeing stare searing away just below the red halter ties on her back. "That Earl even had the gall to say my 'gloom-and-doom racial sermons' scare members away! Why, next thing we know, 'Pastor's salary will be affected.' Good riddance, I say!" She brought his tea. He paid no attention to her bare arm crossing in front of him, but lurched toward her, thumping his stool against the floor once more. "You know why a man like Earl Greiber joins the church? Ever wonder why he's not content just being a heathen spending his money? Three guesses!" He laughed what the kids called his dirty laugh, his new focus upon *her*, demanding response. Kate stepped backward, shrugging, her stomach tightening.

"Friends? Power? Adoration? Come *on*!", he motioned as if directing traffic. "He can live without all those. What's something only the *church* can give him?"

"What?" she said.

"Earl Greibers can't live without their privilege of *corruption*. He needs a whole congregation and all its goals to prove it. An' you know *why*?"

"No." She fell deeper into the trance of his fury.

"He's got to play it close to the vest, so he sees 'dollar-for-dollar.' Not only where his investment's going, but exactly how it's working for *him*. Him, his kids, his family and community, his *image* of himself as a power — — he has to see it reflected around him every minute. He thinks *I'm* impatient, when he can't sit still on an 'investment' two seconds before he has to see it comin' back? That's his radius, his whole brain and being is described by that circumference, and inside there he has to re-create everything by corrupting it!" Kate, as if in obedience, straddled her stool and sat down, breaking her trance. Looking at the flat, inward turning hurt just behind the blue surface of his eyes, she saw he'd reached a dead end, his stamina gone. Now there'd be something else to take its place in his life. But *what?* Afraid of not knowing the answer, she reached over and gripped his inert hand with hers, protectively.

"*Some* are more broad-minded," she began.

He raised blazing eyes to hers. "Well that's not the way it looks from here!" His long stiffened finger thumped the table. "I'll ask you not to forget that!"

Driving that last inch to get what she wanted (his attention?, proof of her own authority?) had provoked her into saying something she didn't believe and couldn't defend. She clinched suddenly cold hands between her tanned thighs until her shoulders ached from sitting rigid. Through the big square window opened to a neck of lawn, their white garage opposite, she saw Andie drop to her knees to pet the dachshund and tease Gretchen's sparkling black nose, the dog suddenly wriggling against her in a paroxysm of pleasure that toppled the child backward, and the two gave themselves over to each other. Kate suppressed the pang that she really felt, thinking: Well at least they know what they're doing!

Pretty soon Sal prissed through the kitchen door on her way to answer friends at the front door, and Kate made herself slump a little on the stool, activating the snake's customary rough zig-zag path exactly as the queasy itch in her stomach early this morning had predicted. Two little boys, one of them Doug, swung on the icebox door until she swatted at them to stop. Max finally held the salt shaker up to west light saying, conciliatorily, "Our best families may be a little 'me-first,' but they make good on their pledges, you'll see!" and cracked the table top with the glass shaker.

"Fine. I hope you're right," she murmured, as Andie and dog burst through the back door, thundering the length of the living room. Pastor Abernathy's troubled gaze still roamed a back yard crowded with a donated wooden playhouse and rusty swing-set. Kate felt remote to those clear blue eyes, with their just plain baffled expression. A prickle, an odd chill, shot across her brown arms.

When she got to the dishes at last, she heard him flop on the couch in the living room with a forlorn groan. Scouring cold grease from a skillet, she thought with an uneasy shudder that every time she tried to help, *she* got hurt. Then Max's space in the front room dissolved into profound silence save for the eloquent crackle of Sunday papers and the smartly snapping sound of the dog's long ears as she shook her head just before curling up to sleep.

Sometime later he dropped the comics in a tent onto the rug near Gretchen and snored with his mouth slack. Children of all ages pranced in and out. During high-decibel TV commercials or a whirlwind chase of children right past his nose, Max thrashed a bit, and twice, bolting upright and staring about in horror and misery, moaned "Oh my God!" in a piteous voice, and pitched down again. Finally he gave up. In foul humor he cleared the room of kids and roared for his wife.

Kate, all this while, had kept track of her own kids and a half dozen more, answering the phone, and fighting disappointment when none of the calls justifed rousting her husband out of his slumbers. The itchy twist in her stomach drove her to bury herself head and shoulders in a sudden siege of weeding among the tall spider plants in the bed bordering the garage. Seizing handfuls of pale-stemmed elm seedlings, she concentrated her stomach muscles against the itchy twist of the snake. When Max called, she came to him with muddy fingers.

He sat on the couch in a stupor, flushed, a sunburst of upholstery wrinkles planted on his cheek.

"You don't ever get enough sleep, do you?"

"Then for God's sake why did you let those kids loose on me? Whose side are you on?" He felt raunchy, all right, and started throwing the orange-striped bolsters he'd used for pillows back against the couch any old way, as if he couldn't get them far enough away from himself. For some crazy reason, at this worst of all possible times, she caught herself mentally forming words to open a serious conversation. But what did you say first? Honey, I've had this weird itch in my stomach for six months, and if you don't get it out ...? Then, oddly, she plunked down beside him, her bare thigh close enough to be repelled by his sweaty Bermudas and the steamy damp hairs on his shin.

"Any of those phone calls for me?"

"A few messages I took. Nothing to wake up about."

"Well, I thought we'd hear from Larry before now. He was purple this morning, waitin' for my key to let him in!"

"He's not in Earl Greiber's league, but he's always sniping," she said. "What now?" A momentary blanching reaction passed over her husband's face at the mention of the chairman's name, but Kate doggedly refused to show regret. She squatted on the rug folding newspapers, which suddenly seemed crucial. "I don't see why it would hurt you to put *all* these in one spot instead of sailing them page by page over a whole room!"

"Well that's just because you don't know how good it feels to sail 'em—and don't play mother to me today. It's Sunday!"

Kate grabbed the papers and made it to the kitchen before he could see her face. Max fumed out the back door and fell into their only lounge chair. The kids had given it to him last Father's Day. That same afternoon the dog chewed the seat, and now, as Max tried to straddle the hole, he swore profoundly but softly at the red dachshund just then easing her sad nose around the corner of the house. A few years back Max had cursed himself roundly for a sloth from Sunday lunch straight through Monday dinner. With Monday evening, the fog of meetings, counseling seances with couples already plying divorce suits in the courts, and apologies to chronically inflamed parishioners took over. Apology came hard to Max, and for the rest of the week, he never knew what hit him until his Saturday night lethargy about sermon writing set in again. He tried to focus a little objectivity on this week's Greiber upset. But he knew the bastard had the jump on him now. Up came Doug with a softball under his arm, but left on a shrug and a head shake from his father, who was feeling very low in himself because of the "kick-in-the-teeth" he'd just received from the boards. Doug's request merely deepened his mood of impotence and dread.

Standing at the kitchen window, Kate saw the boy's eyes go dull as he cut across the lawn. When *can* he find time if not on Sunday afternoon?

But Max hadn't missed his son's face, the carefully guarded eyes that said, This happens a lot, but I won't care. He could still see those eyes, that head of soft brown hair looking large on the small neck as Doug obediently recrossed the lawn moving away—from his father! Nor did the clink of the gate extinguish that look Max expected to see for the rest of his life.

Kate appeared on the back stoop.

"I forgot to tell you," she said. "The Bergsons are coming over after supper. Don't ask my why. They called. Something about how nice it would be to get to know the Abernathys as 'real people.' Wonder what they've been reading?"

Max brushed by her on his way in for a book. "Then they'd better go where there's some real people—wherever that is."

"You'll be jolly company! Why don't you take Doug over to the park and work off some of that spleen before they get here? And I don't mean on him!"

"Why don't you let me figure out how to improve my own outlook on life? I'm supposed to know all the angles."

"That slipped my mind," she said as he started upstairs with the latest, a dark blue volume of Kierkegaard's *Sickness Unto Death*. Ah yes, Fear and Trembling, she warned herself, but nevertheless yelled at the sound of carpeted footsteps expiring overhead: "Somebody has to pull this place together!" She waited for that to take effect.

"Just don't get yourself in a snit over the Bergsons," he sounded off from the bedroom. But she rolled the Electrolux out of the hall closet anyway.

Cleaning house under pressure ordinarily turned Kate into a human dynamo, but after she'd chased dust pussies with the vacuum nozzle for half an hour, and battled the boa constrictor suction hose up the stairs, she was sweating like a hog. Fearing her temper on seeing Max still immobilized on the bed with the eternal book, she tried to acclimate to the blast of late afternoon heat rising from the stairwell, then dragged the screaming monster across the bedroom threshold. To prop himself up, reading the essay on "Forms of Despair," he'd crammed both pillows into a crack that continually widened between bed and wall. The west sun had a stranglehold on him to boot.

"I'd pull those blinds if I were you," she blasted, going on all fours to vacuum under the bed.

"You're not me. I'm fine."

With a mattressful of heat radiating between them, Kate steadied her weight against the bed to pull herself up, and felt that skittish beast slide another inch from the wall.

"Do you *want* me to fall?" He tried to scoot the bed back, and only shoved it forward. "They're not going to invade our bedroom!"

"Well, they can't help seeing it when they come up to use the john, unless I lock all the doors!"

"Next thing—you'll be washing curtains and expecting me to hang 'em while the door bell rings. You vacuum every day, anyway!" This last was far from the truth, though Max would have sworn it.

"Rave on!," she said, "Aren't you ever going to change?", whipping her magic nozzle inside his closet.

"I'll damn well be dressed before you are!" That was a fact, and they both knew it, but he'd belted it out loud enough to carry a block.

"Shh! The girls have friends in their room!"

"Don't hiss at me!" He was braying full tilt now, and decided to go a little further. "If you really crave peace, why don't you say something sweet to me for a change?" His voice, over the puny vacuum noise, rolled like thunder. To Kate he was all teeth and jaw. She found no reasonable answer, though, and came near tears of annoyance with herself for taking his question to heart. Afraid of whimpering if she said anything, while Max desperately glared, she dragged the vacuum into the hall, heart pounding, her lips set against the dangerous twitching in her face, and closed the door, soft and peaceful.

In the bathroom, sweet self-pity mounted along with a fateful presentiment that nothing in this world ever again would be right, as she carefully spread the plastic shower curtain to hide the ring in the tub. A stir of breeze along the tops of the Dutch elms drew her to the narrow casement window that often revealed the family's most private ablutions to the neighbors across the street.

"Yo-o-o—Sal! Andie!" From the front porch below, a child's high voice strung out the neighborhood signal. She heard Sal raising the window in the next room:

"Whadda ya want?" Then a whisper to the kids playing dolls on the floor:

"She would have to show up now!"

"Don't go down!"

"Say you can't," they advised. They began to buzz about what should be done in lower voices.

"Already little bitches," Kate surmised. "Every one of them's had a good teacher." She swiped a grayed sponge at the water spots proliferating on the mirror, then grabbed a hand towel to polish it, and found streaks of her own face looming toward her in the glass.

"God! That'll have to change before they get here. I can do better than that." Vaguely but deeply disgusted, she felt the snake whispering in her stomach, unbuttoned her shorts to ease it, as if it were actually a physical affliction, and traced Max's footsteps from their room up to this door, where they paused. For a fact, she didn't remember closing it. He knocked, waiting, knocked again. "One of you kids in there?" He rattled the knob, teasing. Had no idea he was talking to his wife. Just needed to piss, bad, she bet. Couldn't see her doubled up over the white porcelain, pressing a fist into her belly, and a dirty scrub sponge against her mouth — as if she could keep that snake safely turning and twisting, knifing inside her belly, bottled up there so it would never get out and thrash her life, as she knew it, to bits and pulp.

Eventually she straightened up. She clapped both hands, one with the sponge in it, over her ears to cover the roar in her voice: "I'm—*coming*! Can't you see I'm coming?" Dropping the sponge under the lavatory, working her shorts button into place, she even managed a certain kind of smile for her husband, humming,

> Stay away from those long-tongued liars,
> Oh good shepherd,
> Feed my sheep.

In the following excerpt from the same novel-in-progress, *On the Seventh Day*, Kate Abernathy pokes fun at herself in the process of examining some myths and fantasies about white women and black men. This is a mentally conducted and highly parodic investigation waged by Kate, the heroine of the full novel, known in this piece and so nicknamed herself, as Lady Kate. "The Miracle of Lady Kate—AN IMMACULATE CONCEPTION" is written in the form of a woman's confession to her diary of an event so bizarre and personal that the lady in question can risk no other mortal ear.

This piece falls in the latter half of the book, while the preceding title-piece excerpt, "On the Seventh Day," is the opening chapter of the novel. As to the occasion of "The Miracle of Lady Kate" within the movement of the novel as a whole, our heroine, Kate Abernathy, after she moves with her family to the city, has become involved in a lengthy clandestine affair. On her thrice-weekly trips to her lover's apartment for their meetings, she is regularly importuned by a black janitor from the basement steps leading to the boiler room of Charles' labyrinthine apartment complex. He calls to her from his basement den, his doman, "Got the time?" After a few weeks of trips back and forth, carried out in a high state of secrecy because she lives with her family in the same neighborhood, Kate naturally begins to imagine the logical but, of necessity, fantastical outgrowth of the obvious elements inherent in the situation. The following excerpt records the resulting parody, *imagined and mentally authored by Kate*. This piece is one of the many different kinds of parodic forms that occur within the realistic framework of the novel.

From *On the Seventh Day*

The Miracle of Lady Kate—
AN IMMACULATE CONCEPTION

by Betty Shiflett

In today's episode, we find Kate, clad in shorts and pink halter, purloining Persian lilacs, daringly picked for her lover Charles over an alley fence (thanx to the kindness of a willing bush!), just before entering Charles' building.

No sooner had she secured the fluffy purple Persian lilacs and tucked them safely behind her palm like a workman's cigarette, so that prudish eyes might gain nothing save the back of our Kate's hand, than she JUMPED at the sight of a pure white Dixie cup lolling in the breeze on its conical axis atop a slanting red Dempsy Dumpster garbage bin. Dazzling! thinks Kate.

Why does the Dixie Cup importune our Kate?

The Dixie Cup is perfect for Charles' bouquet, Dummy! Kate plucked it from its hot position in the sun, presenting it to a far hotter place in the scheme of things (as we shall see).

But where would Kate get water?

No sooner had she invited that sore question than the shadow of a Black Man fell across M'lady's path, across the red hot Dempsy Dumpster!—in a manner of speech, across the *world*!

(Mild Kate! Steady Kate!)

Here follows an entry from "The Daily Diary" of Lady Kate— *taken up mid-account.*

And no sooner had I found him casting his unholy shadow upon my path (yea, Diary, darkening the very bricks of that smoldering alley!)

157

than I spied the black yawning doorway through which he'd sprung. It was the basement of none other than my dear Charles' precious building! (Remember, Diary? That yellow brick monstrosity I took you to last year to read Charles something juicy?) The Black Man's eyes were dark portentous fellows; you should have seen the way they glowed in his face!—but who would believe he'd pluck the *Dixie cup* from my startled grasp? Pleased to report, I saved those fallen lilacs every one! (Though as how to rescue my tender plans for Charles that afternoon, I remained at a loss.)

"*Watah?*" he bayed, "You wants *wa-tah?* Step right down, got plenty wa-tah inside!"

Words cannot describe his smile! With his big callus-sharp paw he took my arm as assuredly as if it were a trolley stanchion or light pole placed there for his service! And though I writhed, kicked, and squealed—"Take your hands off me!" (it's a wonder no one heard!)—by this disgusting bit of elbow leverage did he draw me like Alice through the rabbit hole (only in this case the rabbit was black!) down three steps into a vast room, uncommonly bursting (quite running amuck, if you ask me) with leaden-hued pipes. Their dreary up-and-down and crosswise clamor emanated from one huge, shabby, asbestos-covered cylinder that squatted festooned in cobwebs—sunk in shadow at the extreme rear of that place, pulsing with a redly feeble glow.

"Don't touch me!" I spat.

Yes, Diary, *spat!* and wished to spit more than *words!* But unhand me he would not, requiring only one big paw to drag open his furnace door—whereupon broke out a ROAR, a BELCH of smoke, and a BLAST like a fiery rebuke! Such unwanted heat on my cheeks and bare legs! My heart slid even deeper into my new white pumps at the sight of flames lashing in a most enterprising manner over a bed of glow-bright coals, so long and wide that in spite of myself (as he dragged me closer) they seemed—as now does my precarious life on this earth—to have no beginning and no end!

I landed a slap on his cheek, which he brushed away.

"You hear dat?" he snarled, and slammed the door, putting a damper to that horrible gale. "Dat's de howl whut heats dis en-tire buildin'! Whut heats de air white folks breaves! An' watah fo' to bathe deysefs wif! How you reckons dey gonna stay so *white?*"

Now I confess to you, all this wearisome while I kept my lilacs at my bosom, though withered with an unearthly heat (the lilacs, Diary, not the bosoms). They might have been the blasted vestiges of my dear Charles who, amongst his papers and books, sat somewhere in the whitely populated regions above, at his desk enthroned. For little hopes had *I* that we'd ever meet again o'er trifles half so sweet as these Byzantine blossoms pillaged in the full tribute of their perfumes! Not once for the duration of his "lecture" did he loose his grip upon my arm, nor I upon my lilacs!

"Cut it out!"

I was sick of his flesh on mine! And banged him in the knee with the spike of my new white pump for good measure! Watch this: Seizing upon my ankle did he thus attach himself by no less than *two* tender limbs, wrist *and* ankle! forcing me to hop about on one foot at arm's and leg's length (if you see what I mean). Then momentarily, he let go my arm in order to remove my left pump. Diary, it embarasses me to repeat this: He squeezed my toes one at a time (according to some sinister satisfactions of his own) until, spent and worn to a frailty, I forfeited, for the moment, my fiery defense. Standing there on one poor foot, one-shoe-on and one-shoe-off, my heel cupped in his palm, my bare leg and foot extended at his disposal (fortunately I was wearing shorts, the white ones), I permitted him, somewhat more tranquilly, to continue, though I quailed for my dear children who should be motherless if all did not fare well.

"You sees, Honey-chile, dis sys-tem," he swirled his striped janitor's cap at that crazed roadmap of pipes overhead, "don't come to Black Mens all one time. Heh-heh-heh! Important wisdoms, dey comes to Black Mens one-at-a-time ... sly-like. 'Cause dey knows when whole bunches of 'em smack ya down *hard*, you gone shake yo' nappy haid 'No!'—say, 'Ain't truckin' wid no Trouble!' an' dives yo'sef belly-face down, a'countin' ebbry quibberin' bone in yo' body, waitin' fo' dem whisperin' footsteps ob Trouble to *de-part!*"

Now, Diary, I would not have thought it possible, but by snatching up my wrist once more and hauling in on my ankle, he drew me closer!—hop-hop-hop—then letting go my ankle, he tried to wrap that gigantic paw around my derriere. My slender build was no match for his maniacal strength, and I was soon to feel the iron muscles of his chest!—alas, poor Charles! He produced a key ring, using only one hand to find a key, which he then brandished under my nose. (It was kind of neat!, the way he did it by *touch*; but I wouldn't want the least misunderstanding on *that* score.)

"But when yo' wisdoms insinuates demsefs one ... by ... one, why, you jes' natcherly cain't *hep* yo'sef! You swallows 'em down, all dem new idees whut you should not be gittin', payin' no 'tention to 'em 'cumulatin' in de bery pit ob yo' Black Soul ... steady changin' you from de bottom up! Till sure as Christmas come to li'l pickaninnies on cold mawnin's, hit's too late! One mawnin' you wakes up wid-out one scrap lef' ob yo' Black Mind an' Soul whut ain't *dif-frent!*"

Diary, I had to *sneeze*. Those keys excited my nose!

"Now to look at me, ya wouldn't think I'se de niggah what own all de watah an' heats *in dis buildin'!* Now would ya, Honey-Chile?" *(Honey-Chile!)* "Well, Black Mens don't *git* dey con-trols ovah-night!"

Sigh! Some Horatio Alger-type story, I knew, would follow; but with the wisdom born to Women, I was able to dissemble, here and there, mildly favorable response to his rag-tag, illiterate tale.

The keys!

"*Fust* come de keys whut Ah fines on de sidewalk spawklin' in de sun. Lyin' by de pawkway undah Ole Cottonwood like de Debil hissef drop 'em—con-*ven*-ient! Old Cottonwood, shibbrin' his branches an' a-dancin' up dem green leafs! he be tellin' me: 'Pick 'em up, fool! pick 'em up!' So Ah picks 'em up. What de Hell!"

Diary, when he shrugged, his gray work-shirt tightened dramatically across his barrel chest, determined to pop a button above his stout belt-line where the rusty skin peeped through. Then with a majestic effort, he sucked flat his frighteningly powerful nether regions. Oh, Diary!

"When ya cain't own one mizzable thang wuth *ownin'*—it hurts ya here in yo' gut!"

With won-der-ful detachment, he patted himself along his bulging zipper-line!

"So say to mahsef—"

He jerked me back against the bulge.

"—say, 'Meybe when Ah fines whut dese keys unlocks, *den* will Ah own me sumpin' puf-fect!'"

Diary ...! Can you hear me if I whisper? (*That bulge was growing!*) But so as not to excite him, I prudently murmured, "Pray *do* go on!"

"So takes de fust key. See here? He be long an' skinny an' flat!" Diary, when he stuck *that* key under my nose, I screwed my courage to the sticking point—I owed it to my children!—and tried my gentle hand. (Won't say *where*.) I had it on good authority one should placate them. But know what? Strange as this may seem, I really couldn't say if he appreciated it; *he never missed a beat with that tasteless tale of his*:

"Ah scratch mah haid wid dis long, skinny flat key (lak a dumb niggah), but Ole Cottonwood, he be shimmerin' an' a-shakin' up dem green leafs! a-tellin' me: 'Stick 'er in de Dodge, fool! Try de Dodge!' ... an' *dam* ef Ah don't see dis here blue Dodge Dawt spawklin' at de curb! ... shinin' huh whitewalls an' glittren' huh chrome! Woman! You shouda seed dem bumpahs! Dey wuz mighty cheer-ful! An' layin' up in huh back windah—*what you think Ah spies?* Spies me a rifle butt! Peekin' out ole long skinny box, an' *smoove* lak a baby's ass!"

Lilacs in hand, I daintily pursed my lips to restrain a yawn—I disapprove of firearms—but he deliberately mistook me! and brought those pinkish lips next to *mine* so the vibrations from his mumbo-jumbo tickled like tissue paper on a comb! (It just doesn't seem possible I was too petrified to turn my head.)

"So! ... sticks de fust key in de lock ob de blue Dodge Dawt—'Glory Hallelujah, God-dam! got me a new car!'—turns de key, go scritch! Say, 'Dat lock *rusty!* Need mah drink ob oil!'"

He whisked from his hip pocket a grimed copper oilcan with a long thin spout protruding like an insect antenna.

"Dis here oil need a li'l stirrin' up!"

He shook the bulb of that oilcan until it sloshed satisfactorily back and forth next to his big fat ear; he had all the tricks and stage props necessary to show me his unspeakable intentions!—a regular showman in janitor's clothing! (Diary! ... do you realize that after all I've gone through, *I*, your long and most intimate confidant, *may need vindicating?* Diary, you may become an important document! Think about it!)

He held his oilcan before him and twirled it in his fingers in "Cosmic Inspection."

"Dis here am de col-lect-ed greases whut am sweated an' squeezed outen de po's an' skins ob po' Black Mens out bendin' dere backs an' a-bustin' dere balls a-workin' undah Ole Man sun *all ober dis Worl'!*"

(In *tone*, he approached a certain primitive eloquence. Those buttery Southern accents imparted double mirage-like meanings, but I had given up the struggle to fathom *a word he said*, and was barely able to lean my poor head drunkenly on his grimy chest for a teen-cy respite.)

"Takes de flat skinny key out de rusty lock, sticks dis here oil spout *in*, gibs 'er mah drink ob oil, sticks de key back in—'Hey! mah oil work *fine!*'—opins de shiny blue do' ... sniffs!—smell too new! Don't need dat! Don't need no white men's car smellin' *bad* lak dat! Got mah puf-fectly good Ole Caddy whut Ah dribes on Sunday." (Dig his "limo," Diary.) "So whut, she got huh lef' side stove in, front fendah to *back* fendah! (She be drippin' watah to huh fust red light.) Ah sits cool! peerin' an' a'peevin' 'roun' mah steerin' wheel, holdin' mah ears 'cause Ole Caddy Darlin', she lak to backfire up a storm! Skeercely kin Ah see dat green light turn, 'cause *steam* be heavin' up so fierce undah Caddy's hood, a-foggin' up mah windshield—but she run jes' fine! Blue smoke a-fumin' out huh tail; sound lak ar-til-lery firin' up huh sweet ass! (Heh, heh!) No suh! Don't need no ole white man's smelly car to get *me* places! ... So *slams* de shiny blue do' ob de Dodge Dawt; takes mah *second* key—"

Now Diary, lean closer. There's something I've been putting off telling you: He didn't really say "*second*," he said "*secon*"! (If you follow my decoding.) But I get so tired writing things out the *hard* way.

"See dis here brass key—whut got de roun' haid? Now Old Cottonwood, he set up dat shiverin' ob de leafs sumpin' *frightnin'!* Tellin' me: 'Stick 'im in de *third* do', on de *fif* flo', on de right-hand side, fool! In de *big* buildin'!' Well, looks up yonder, an' dere am dis big—tall—wide—yaller buildin' fulla windas: *where de white folks lives!*" Diary, he really said "*libs*," not "*lives*," but I was afraid you'd never get it. Anyway, I covered my ear with the hand that held Charles' lilacs but allowed my free one to remain you-know-where, just for safekeeping.

"*Don't waste no time!*" he brayed, dropping his oilcan on my pink halter! my *right* breast, the slightly smaller one as you will doubtless remember, and right you are, Diary Ole Girl!, his big paw was sure to

161

follow.

"... Takes mahsef up to de *fif* flo', Honey-Chile!—"

This small "endearment" I merely ignored.

"... Stick mah key in de *third* do' " on de right-hand side!"

(Yes, really "*thuhd* do' " and "right-*han*' " side.)

"Got dis big, long red carpet undah mah feets! ... Feelin' fine! Jes' lak white folks!"

(His constant harping on our ancestry!)

"... *Turns* dat brass, roun'-haided key in de roun' brass lock on de *third* do', on de *fif* flor', on de right-hand side. ... Go scri-i-tch! *Dat* lock rusty! Need mah drink ob oil!"

(Screw his oil, his oil, his oil! ... He's got his hand on my breast and he wants oil???)

"... *Pulls* de key out de rusty lock! Sticks dis oil spout *in!* Gibs 'er mah squirt ob oil, *sticks* de key back in ... *opins* de do' to de 'paht-mint——Woman! Whut you think is *dere?*"

I shook my head vigorously. How should I know what's in his old "*'paht*-mint"?

"Gots Per-sian rugs to wahm mah feets. An' coluh TV fo' to sweeten mah silences! Whut you thinks Ah sees in dat 'paht-mint' sittin' on huh soft, roun', white couch-deevan-*so*fa?"

"Safety first" is my motto. I grabbed that paw of his and shoved it DOWN! (Can't tell you where, Diary.) I let him know what he could do with his old hand! (But, Diary, I really don't think excitement is good for them. Ridiculous—soft-white-couch. *Yekkk!*)

"... Why, it be some old *white* woman! (jes' lak you) sittin' on dat white couch-deevan-*so*fa in huh strap-less red satin *evenin*' gown, an' huh diahmon' necklis an' cloud ob long black feathas whut she be floatin' evah-which-way roun' huh nice white neck an' two white bosoms! ... She whitah dan you." For once, he looked me (coldly) straight in my green eyes. "Huh hair be blon'."

Diary, he was a *shrewd* man. I felt my raven locks (formerly the source of so much pride!) blackening by the "secon'."

"Old White woman, she fix me wid huh cold, giltterin' eye (huh eyes be *blue*), an' she say, real snotty-like, rustlin' huh feathas and pattin' huh TV on de haid like a baby, 'Come sit by mah coluh TV, Big Boy, an' le' me hold dem pre-ci-ous balls!'

(Diary, level with me; do we talk like that?)

"... Shakes mah haid, 'Naw! Doan need no old white woman hep me keep mah balls wahm!' "

("*Warm!*—Warm, warm, WARM!)

"... 'Got mah puf-fectly good ole black gal whut works lak a *dawg!* (Fucks huh when Ah pleases!) She keeps greens on de table fo' mah chilluns, cornpone on Satday, an' doan ax de preacha ovah too much, to slobbah up de chickin whut she kill on Sunday. (Fucks huh when Ah pleases, *if*—heh, heh, heh!—ole preacha doan git dere fust!)"

(Diary, what is "*slobbah*"?)

"Now Ah axes you, woman, how come any Black Man need *mo'*?" Diary, his wink changed to a hideous glare!

Consumed with fear, methought to soothe his inflamed animal breast by placing my small white hand—yes, yes! the one with the lilacs!—delicately upon those clammy old *"men-things"* down there in hopes of mollifying him (somehow his zipper had crawled down). Tell no one, Diary! It worked!

"... So shet de do' *hard* on dat ole white woman wavin' huh feathas roun' at me. Huh blon' hair be shinin', huh diahmon' necklis spawklin', an' dem two white bosoms bouncin', but Ah says, 'So long, ole white woman! Yo' paht-mint smellin' *real* nasty. Don't need you. Switch on yo' coluh TV, keep you comp'ny!' Ole white woman, she be lookin' right sorry. (Be jes' lak you! White wemens be all time fallin' off yo' chairs an' spillin' out yo' windas to get ten inches ob good black dick!)"

How does that make *you* feel, Diary?

But cheer up. These small white hands had done their job, and I perceived him in a weakened condition. Never in a thousand words, Diary, could I convey to you the sour expression with which he wrestled that beatific look of ecstasy off his stubborn face! I was encouraged to increase (imperceptibly) the pressure of *both* hands, Charles' wilted lilacs being hardly a bother. I might yet come out unscathed!

"... So *leaves* out de front do' ob dis big wide tall yaller buildin'. Takes out mah thuhd key ...

(Doin' your own translations, Diary?)

"... 'Lookie here, dis ske-le-ton key! Got plain, long, skinny body (lak mah ole black gal)!"

Diary, if they don't have a higher opinion of their own women, how can they expect to have a higher opinion of *us?*

" 'Dis key look lak he don't opin *nuthin'*! Too damn weak,' Ah sez, 'an' too dumb! But Lawd, Lawd! Ole Cottonwood bustin' hissef all *o*-vah dat block! Jouncin' up his leafs lak he gone reach right down an' *smack* dis here niggah wid one dem hebby branches! Tellin' me, 'Fool, fool, y'all done *refused twice't!* Take yo' las' key, fool! Stick 'im in dat hebby gray padlock whut you sees lockin' up de base-mint ob dis buildin'!' "

Think, Diary! A grown man taking orders from a tree!

" 'Beggin' yo' pahdon, Ole Cottonwood,' Ah sez, cubberin' mah nappy haid wid dese black hands 'cause he bein' mighty *playful* wid dem branches, 'Dis ole dumb, skinny, weak key cain't take on no white man's hebby padlock! *Look* at hit!' " Naturally, Diary, that key was right back under my nose! "Ole Cottonwood branches be cold and still—lak he *in*-sulted. 'Fool, foool ...,' Ah hears whisperin' way up in his top branches, 'Ah ain't givin' you no mo' free ad-vice!' "

(On the other hand, Diary, I must say the Cottonwood showed more sense. These people just take, take, take.)

"... So *takes* dat dumb, skinny, weak ole key, stick 'im in dat hebby glum gray pad-lock whuts lockin' de do' to de basement ob dis building'!"

Diary, when he pointed his oilcan at that grimy concrete floor—yes, yes, with the hand I had so meticulously shoved down you know where! (I had my children to think of)—I was *shocked* to see my dainty white pumps forced so close to his lumpy, grease-stained boots! Oh, Diary, I hope you're never in a position of real powerlessness!

"... *Turns* de key, go—scri-i-i-ttcchhhh!!!—'Mah Lawd! dat lock rusty! Need mah drink ob oil!'"

(Oh boy, the "secret of life"!)

"... *Takes* de key out de rusty ole padlock! Sticks mah oil spout *in* ..."

(In—out, in—out!—Is that all he thinks about? Don't their mothers ever tell them ...? Or do they just put these kids out on the street to pick up what little they can?)

"... Gibs 'er mah squirt ob oil! *Sticks* in mah key!...."

(Key, spouts, you name it! but never! Diary, never. ...!)

"... Flings opin de do'! say, 'Lawd! Lawd! *Dis* de buildin' where de *white folks lives*! Dem pipes whut you see runnin' up de ceilin' thithah-an'-yon—wid watah an' wahmth fo' to keep white folks wahm an' clean— is *dere* pipes! Puf-fect!' Ah sez. Natcherly, Ah thanks Ole Cottonwood mos' *kindly* 'fore Ah commence to studyin' dem pipes," waving his arm at that gruesome maze of plumbing. (Diary, he prefers trees!)

"... Now Ole Joe, he be ver' *famil-i-ar* wid dem pipes!"

(Diary, when he tapped his chest on that naked V of black skin where his shirt burst open——tremors rushed up and down my spine!)

"He know *eb*-bry one—where she go! whut she do! in eb-bry 'paht-mint, fo' eb-bry white man an' white woman whut needs 'em!" He jabbed his oilcan at the ceiling, then with the other hand, jangled his keys at the ceiling, too, like castanets! stumping his squat thumb resoundingly against that chest of *steel!* proclaiming, "Ah knows!"

Diary, That Black Man was *strong*!

Suddenly he dragged me by the raven locks back to the shadowy wall by his furnace, dexterously produced from his breast pocket a fat cigar, *nipped* off the tip between his big ugly teeth, and with a single hammy hand proceeded to ignite it. (That man had incredible agility with his fingers when he wanted to.) I saw by the infernal glow of his stogie a strange flock of words and pictures scrawled on the soot-caked wall over an otherwise invisible, dome-shaped knob or dial, its series of tiny numbers now grease-smudged due to the over-zealous rubbings of our janitor's affectionate fingers.

"Mah thu-mo-stet!" he breathed, tapping it with the wet, slimy end of his stogie so the sparks just flew! Well, Diary, it seems he meant that clock gizmo they put on walls. Big deal. You know, the thingamabob that regulates your heat? But spouting his mumbo-jumbo, he patted this one on its head. With what a smile, Diary, he was fondling that knob! Listen!:

"Ah kin tuhn 'em *up*, or tuhn 'em *downnn*. Ah kin cook 'em till dey swimmin' in dey own sweats—or Ah kin freeze 'em solid in dey beds! Ah been habbin' me some ber-ry intresin' '*spear*mints wid dis here knob!"

(He's been having some interesting "*chewing gums*"?)

My mind became galvanized with an awesome, "blue-print"-type picture that laid out the honey-combed habitations of hapless whites housed in this enormous, evil yellow brick! Then, painfully, I recalled certain erratic temperature changes my tender skin had suffered (after a brisk tryst) under the boiling-hot-to-icy-cold needles of my dear Charles's shower! Woe is me! thought I. For a joust of any kind between my sweet-scented Charles and this execrable Fiend, I had good reason to avoid! And what of my motherless children? These troubled thoughts raced through my mind as I tried, unsuccessfully, to return his gesticulating hand (won't say where ...) But button up your overcoat, girl! We can squeak through this thing together! Diary, would you hold my hand? My sweet correspondent, are you with me to the bitter end? Oh, it *aggravates* me to think how much Womanly Fortitude I pumped into that Monster!

"Woman!" he crudely interrupted my thoughts by tapping once more on his darling knob with the slimy butt-end of his stogie, making orange sparks rain, "... when Joe gits read-dy he gone take his fuhnace downnn!"

Now get this, Diary.

As he stuck that soggy butt back between his lips—twisting his thermostat knob "spearamentally" and keeping an eye on *me*, his cee-gar pulsing brightly as his furnace—I thought on all the other unpleasant small disasters (in this yellow brick monstrosity) that my sweet helpless Charles endured: balmy summer days when his steam radiators wouldn't shut off, snowy winter mornings with that blue tide of Comet frozen in his tub.

I tell you, Diary! Most of us never know what it's *like* to be in the grips of a larger power! As if I weren't cupping his (quote) "pre-ci-ous" old "balls" right! Then he jangled those keys—and did I start! Visiting Charles and all, I'm alert to warning noises. He pressed his hard old bulges perilously nearer to me—thundering!: "When Ah takes mah fuh-nace down, *how dey gone stay so white?*"

Well, Diary, I shouldn't hesitate to say, my fate was imminent. I just *knew* the rest of my life would be ... er, well, *you* know, ah ... "colored?" by this experience.

But now a foreign feeling stole over me.

Diary, how's a lady to know where Duty leaves off and Adventure begins? (That's always confused me, and I dare say I'm not alone!) You see, I'd led such a sheltered life (except for wee trips to Charles'), never having tasted life's more "savory experiences"—well, what does

Charles know?—that I began to worry in an unaccustomed way about my children! I reasoned: If their mother, say, by her unsullied example, practically removes all the "difficult choices" from her children's lives, well, how can they ever get enough "practical experience" telling Right from Wrong? What guideposts will they have in this vale of tears? You don't have to point the way to me *twice*. I saw my duty and I did it. I owed it to my children, but—

The rest I would not confide to anyone but you....

"Wa-tah? Y'all still wants wa-tah?"

He then dragged me to the furnace and, just as I feared, opened it with a ferocious, fumy laugh. And when he threw his head back and guffawed around that stupid cee-gar, Diary, I twisted, writhed, and *strained* (Charles' lilacs in one hand, the other—oh, never mind) to find what this insensible madman wanted, for surely otherwise my progeny were DOOMED!—I was dizzyfied—what with that hot bed of coals, their red dancing reflections on his face, and the salty, thick sweat juicily shining up all those creases in his powerful neck ... oh, Diary—ahhhhh ...

I mean ...

I think ...

I hardly know *what* I did ...!

Did I *ask* him for wa-tah?

"Wa-tah?" I heard him say again. "You still wants wa-tah?"

My defeat was sealed!

True enough, on these white breasts my lilacs had entirely keeled over, gruesome furnace heat having done for them what my attentive hands could not. Then, from the grime-infested floor he plucked that vile white Dixiecup, that turncoat, which I now realized to be my TRUE SEDUCER! and darned if he didn't grab up his oilcan! (it had made such a sweet clank dropping, I'd hoped never to see oilcan *or* Dixie cup again) and squirt thick, black oil furiously from can to cup.

"*Look!*" he raged, holding aloft the now besmirched Dixie cup, "nothin' tuhns wid-out mah oil!"

Goody! So I just let him BLOW. I mean, what's a Lady to do???! As to his crummy you-know-where, if you're still interested, Diary, I am tenacious, and I had not let go—Somehow, Charles' lilacs got caught in the zipper ...

Nonetheless, I kept my grip on them, sad as they were (or, should I say, loyal as I was?), while I honestly tried not to listen to his dumb ... Diary! I just wanted to finish and be done with it! ... Yelling his head off about how "nothin' moves or shines" without his OIL—blah-blah-blah—jangling his keys for emphasis, waving his red-tipped cigar butt *up—down*!

"Not a wheel *tuhn!* Not a cog go *'roun'!* Not one stick ob white folks' fur-ni-chur gone *shine!* ... NO! Not eben dat rifle butt lyin' up so fine in some old white man's smelly car!"

Honestly! You'd think they'd get it out of their systems.

And then, Diary, *darned* if he didn't dash that Dixie cup full of oil over my poor, shriveled-up Persian lilacs!

"Dem posies ain't *puf*-fect!" he fumed, pointing that antenna spout at my lilacs. "Ole White man upstairs be wantin' his posies *puh*-fect! Too *dry!* Needs mah drink ob oil!" he said, glaring piteously upward. (Charles must surely be alarmed! We keep a tight schedule.) He then charged at me with his oilcan! "Dem posies too *dry*, Hon'-Chile!" Over and over, Diary, he squirted me with these sentiments, then grabbed those dumb lilacs from my oily bosoms and crushed them in that strong Black Hand (the lilacs, Diary!) as he stomped our defenseless Dixie cup with his clodhopper boot! Not that I care to defend the cup; perfidy is its own reward. Now it would never hold lilacs for Charles! Then, on the heels of the Dixie cup, he tossed my black, dripping lilacs into the furnace! The flames flared!—feeding that ferocious HOWWLLLL-L-L-L.... I saw nothing, heard nothing, felt nothing: except—Diary, I'm sad to report—barbequed lilacs, and those mean, roving hands smearing oil around on my once-white bosoms....

Then overhead he raised his copper oilcan, guzzling oil straight from the antenna spout and, roaring drunk, tore out the door laughing, leaving poor me without one drop of hot water to clean myself up! WHAT TO TELL *CHARLES?*

P.S., Diary—

I do, on the other hand, have this second, confusing memory—it's so slippery! I'm not sure which is WHICH! Please to help sort things out. (I've done a few favors. Remember when we changed all those names, just to make *your* life simpler?)

Later ... I cannot for this mortal life recall where, or when, but I think I might have been lying with Charles (the room seemed terribly hot), or was it my liege, in the baronial bedroom? Never mind, it seems I'm flat on my back toward some purpose. I heard this rumbling mumble (he never could spit the words out), but with a sort of sonorous croon (if that strikes you as possible) he says to me in this mumble, like he's laying on some kind of *"miracle"* (remember, Diary: can't see, but think I *smell* him *over* me ... and oh yes, Diary! ... now it's coming back ... I feel so clearly, on my bare shoulder blades, the grit from his darned old basement floor): "Ole white woman," (these were his exact words) "fo' yo' pains, you gits ten inches ob mah good black dick!"

Honestly, Diary, I'm that depressed. What can it mean?

The Pink Lady Primer

Beverlye Brown

Although the Victorian ideal of the "angel in the house"* was a particularly virulent version of ladyhood, mega-sellers like Helan Andalin's *Fascinating Womanhood* and Marabel Morgan's *Total Woman* indicate that the idea of the Pink Lady is still alive and well. The public fascination with figures like Nancy Reagan and Princess Di also indicates that Pink is still perking happily along. How perfectly Pink of Nancy R. (whose attention to *la toilette,* table linens and china seems to be her forte as First Lady) to publicly proclaim in 1980 that she had never for a moment regretted giving up her career, that her life had only begun when she married Ronald Reagan, and that she had never wanted a thing in this world but a husband, a family, and a house with geraniums and the window box. Shy Di, of course, has done every right thing a Pink Lady could do. She dropped out of high school to attend cooking school; slept under a picture of Prince Charles even before they were formally introduced; charmed him (like a "warm little puppy" as the British press so prettily reported) when she at their first meeting taught him to tapdance on the lawn; passed the muster of not only the Queen and the Queen Mum but the royal physician, who pronounced her to be a "young lady with an unblemished past"; was married in the most sumptuous wedding dress at the most romantic wedding of the century; and then—ever svelte and fashionable—produced not only two Princes but enough press coverage to make the mouths of Madison Avenue's savviest savants water.

*Coventry Patmore's paean to ninteenth-century womanhood.

Pink Ladies have always been prolific, perhaps because they have been a popular solution to the notion that woman's nature is particularly troublesome and therefore, like a bad little jack-in-the-box, ever prone to pop out and plague mankind. Certainly from Eve's time to our own not only woman's meddlesome curiosity but a host of ills supposedly endemic to the female of the species have been well chronicled. Virginia Woolf warned that enough ink had already been spilled discussing what the Victorians called the "woman question." The *Pink Lady Primer,* however, is dedicated to the premise that poking fun at some well-worn views of women is not only good for a giggle but good for the geese and ganders, still legion among us, who believe in peachy, pearly, persistent Pink.

Beverlye Brown, who currently teaches at Eastville College in Dallas, Texas, has taught courses in writing and literature in high school, university, graduate school, and private workshops. Her fiction has recently been published in *Texas Writers*. She was born in Chicago, Illinois, and has lived in the North, the South, the Southwest, and the Midwest, all locales where Pink Ladies abound.

From *The Pink Lady Primer*

*Everything You Always Wanted to Know About Who and What Is and Isn't Pink: The Sunshine Inspiration Committee's Guide For True Ladies Everywhere**

Beverlye Brown

PINK RELIGION, POLITICS, AND MONEY—
PINK POOP ON THE PINK RPM'S
THAT MAKE THE WORLD GO PINKLY AND PRETTILY
ROUND

> In Which the Sunshine Inspiration Committee (sometimes known as SIC) Discusses Deities and Doctrines, Bills and Frills, Hypergamy, Hysterical Historicals, Modern Magpies, Big Busts, Little Asses, and WHAM THE WHIM† Day. Also Mentioning Grover Cleveland, Jeanette Rankin, Sonia Johnson, Phyllis Schlafly, Margaret Thatcher, Ella Grasso, Mrs. George Bush, and Ferraro née Zaccaro.

The Pink Lady's religion is simple. She is Pink and thus attends (with prim composure and a pretty hat) the church, synagogue or cathedral of first her Father's and then her Husband's choice. Since

---

*Unfortunately the *Pink Lady Primer* includes a great deal of information most certainly distasteful to Pink. UnPink unpleasantries concerning Pinkless Emancipated Women (PEW) as well as some Pink pleasantries concerning Pinkly Unconditionally Feminine Females (PUFF) are included as Pinknotes at the foot of the page. SIC says a PUFF will fluff you up when feeling low, but a PEW should be read only on days when you are feeling particularly peppy and in the Pink.

†See earlier chapters for discussion of Women's Horrible Infernal Movement.

Eve (the first woman on record) ate the apple (the earliest WHIM debacle on record), Ladies have had the good sense to leave theology to Gentlemen who invented and therefore understand it. Secure in the knowledge that God takes care of Pink Ladies, she does not fuss and fume over doctrines, dogmas, deities and deacons she is congenitally unsuited to diddle and dabble with. Remembering Samuel Butler's dictum "The souls of women are so small, one wonders if they have one at all," and Helen Bell's remark to Emerson "To a woman the consciousness of being well dressed gives a sense of tranquility which religion is powerless to bestow," Ladies practice church chic staying Pinkly put in their pew looking as pretty and pious as possible.

The Pink Lady's economics are even simpler. She has none, but she does abide by the following four rules of thumb:

1) The Pink Lady does not make money, she marries it. PEW 1 Remembering Mama's dictum that it is as easy to fall in love with a rich man as a poor one, she is proficient at hypergamy, the practice of marrying up, so that she will be well taken care of at all times.

2) If times get hard, she does not undermine her Husband's confidence with false economies. She buys her yearly fur, upgrades her jewelry collection, refurbishes her home and her haberdashery, and plans an even posher vacation than the previous year's, knowing that Hubby will appreciate that she appreciates that he can still cut the mustard money-wise.

3) If finally forced to economize, the Pink Lady shops the following sales: January clearance, Washington's Birthday, Ides of March, Easter Honey Bunny, Merry Month of May, June Summer Fling, Fourth of July, August Angst Alleviation, Labor Day, Halloween, Thanksgiving, and pre- and post-Christmas sales. When cash flow is fitful or flat, the last thing a Pink Lady's Husband needs is to see her, the house, or the children frumpy and frowzy. So in addition to the above advertised monthlies, she shops daily for bargains to lighten the financial load in the Pinkest manner possible. PUFF2

4) The Pink Lady does not pay bills, balance checkbooks, or carry cash (except mad-money pinned to her lace chemise or the silk lining of her purse). She carries only credit cards, the bills from which are mailed to her Husband monthly. If she overspends, not wishing to worry Hubby, she intercepts all bills and neatly files them, as Juliette

---

PEW 1. Jennie Douglas, the first woman employed by the U.S. Mint in 1872; Maggie Lena Walker, the first woman bank president in 1903; Betty Friedan, organizer of the First Women's Bank and Trust Company in 1971 and others of their ilk have caused tons of trouble telling women that making money is more fun than being someone's honey.

PUFF 2. Sometimes, as did socialite Jan Williams of Houston, the Pink Lady will economize just for fun. Jan's birthday "costume party" offered a prize for the best-dressed woman with an ensemble under $150. "Some people thought we should have set the limit at $100 and really made it tough. But I was afraid if I did that, no one would have taken it seriously. If the limit was $100, a lot of them wouldn't even have tried." The Ladies, proclaimed "adorable," "clever," and "original" by Mrs. Williams, stunned Mr. Williams, host of the party, who said, "These are women who easily could spend $20,000 or $30,000 a year on clothes. I know it's hard to believe that they would possibly look good for just $150, but I tell you they looked wonderful. It was enough to blow your mind." SIC says Ladies can work miracles when they truly try.

Low, the founder of the Girl Scouts, advised, in stacks marked: "This Year," "Next Year," "Sometime," and "Never."

Except for WHIM-WHAMS, Ladies stay out of politics. True Ladies agree with Grover Cleveland: "Sensible and responsible women [sic Ladies] do not want to vote. The relative positions to be assumed by man and woman [sic Lady] in the working out of our civilization were assigned long ago by a higher intelligence than ours." PUFF 3 Not only Ladies, but most real politicians understand the relativity of realpinkpolitik. The former mayor of New Orleans, Moon Landrieu, put it in charmingly quaint vernacular, "Women do the lickin' and the stickin' while men plan the strategy." A Texas politician echoed this sentiment when he pictured Ladies in politics in their helpful and supportively Pink roles as part of the "beaver brigade." And that handsome man, the former mayor of New York, Mr. John Lindsay, in reply to the query of why there were no more women commissioners in his administration sallied most succinctly, "Honey, whatever women do, they do best after dark." Pink Ladies congratulate President Cleveland, and Messrs. Landrieu and Lindsay for knowing how to WHAM the WHIM with wit and charm. PEW 4

Pink Ladies, grateful for all the help they can get, have been fortunate in receiving assistance from true Gentlemen with WHIM-WHAMS. PEW 5 In 1887, Senator Vest of Missouri, speaking against the suffrage, put the case for Ladies beautifully:

> For my part I want when I go to my home—when I turn from the arena where man contends with man for what we call the prizes of this paltry world—I want to go back, not to the embrace of some female ward politician, but to the earnest loving look and touch of a true woman [sic Lady]. I want to go back to the jurisdiction of the Wife, the Mother; and instead of a lecture upon finance or the tariff, or upon the construction of the Constitution, I want those blessed loving details of domestic life and domestic love.

PUFF 3. If only the WHIM understood the defeminizing of politicizing as does Argentina's President Raul Alfonsin who notes, "Negotiating with women is very difficult. I prefer to negotiate with Mr. Thatcher."

PEW 4. On the other hand, women politicians are noted for their crudities. (Would they knew their French and were noted for their delicately edible before-dinner *crudités* instead.) Pat Schroeder, WHIM congresswoman, says things like "Hi there, I'm that radical you've all heard about who doesn't shave under her armpits and leaps over staircases screaming obscenities. I keep both children in the freezer and my husband is short, has feathers, and goes 'cluck-cluck.'" Ella Grasso, who in her own unfortunate words became "the first Lady [sic woman] governor who was not previously a governor's lady," also quipped, "I'm having trouble managing the mansion. What I need is a wife." SIC supposes they intended these gaucheries to be amusing. They are, in fact, a fine example of unLadylike and noxiously rude humor.

PEW 5. Would that the very first WHIM in Congress could have been WHAMMED before she arrived. Jeanette Rankin, sent to Washington in 1916 by the state of Montana, showed her bad judgment by promptly voting against entrance into WWI. Unfortunately, she also showed her slatternly stamina by being again in Congress years later to vote against WWII.

More recently, the WHIM was firmly WHAMMED by the Gentlemen of the State Legislatures who roundly downed the ERA. U.S. Senator Orrin Hatch, a distinguished Mormon, ably refuted Sonia Johnson (booted out by the Mormons for her unLadylike shenanigans and billed on the cover of *Ms.* as "The Woman Who Talked Back to God") by declaring in a Senate debate on ERA:

> It's implied by your testimony that you're more intelligent than other Mormon women, and that if they were all as intelligent as you, they would all support the Equal Rights Amendment. Now that's an insult to my wife."

Would that more Gentlemen would take such care to protect the fair and WHAM the WHIM with so admirable a flair.

But despite WHIM-WHAMS effected with both Pink and Blue shazam, from the suffrage, to ERA, to Geraldine Ferraro, women have persistently marched on the Pink Body Politic. Hysterical historicals (suffering no doubt from what the prominent Victorian physician Dr. William Alcott defined as "cauliflower excrescence of the uterus") and modern magpies (suffering most probably from the "raging hormonal influences [which] subject them [women] to curious mental aberrations ..." as described by Dr. Edgar Berman, personal physician to Vice President Hubert Humphrey) have meddled in and muddied the political waters. PUFF 6 Therefore, it is now incumbent on Pinks to use their talents to restore political balance by demanding that WHIM politicos be, as Ruth Mandel in "The Trouble with Women Candidates" has pointed out, "not too young, not too old; not too voluptuous, not too prissy; not too soft spoken, not shrill; not too ambitious, not too retiring; not too independent, not too complaining about being excluded; not too smart, not uninformed." In other words: NOT. Ms. Ferraro may have been, as Edward Robbs, GOP campaign manager, pointed out, "the biggest bust politically in recent history," but her candidacy set perilous precedents. T-shirts reading "A woman *is* the ticket" and "Finally a Ferraro," plus the sad sight of Mr. Zaccaro seated by Joan cheering Gerri on add up to Pink Ladies needing, as did Vice President Bush after the debate with Ferraro, "to kick a little ass." PUFF 7

The Sisters will therefore adopt April 1 as WHAM THE WHIM DAY, at which time each Pink Lady Chapter will celebrate with its

---

PUFF 6. Dr. Berman wonders, "Suppose that we had a menopausal woman president who had to make the decision on the Bay of Pigs?" *Entre nous* Ladies, SIC says, if we were on red alert when she was on red alert, the Pink could scarcely avert being seriously hurt.

PUFF 7. Ms. Ferraro was not advised by Pete Teeley, Mr. Bush's press secretary, to avoid sounding "screechy and scratchy" and called "crabby" and "bitchy" for naught. Barbara Bush, a proper Lady who quietly needlepointed purses while her husband campaigned, put it more poetically by dubbing Geraldine something that "rhymes with rich." Like Mrs. Bush, Ladies must utilize Pink political rhetoric to put the political WHIM in their proper places.

own April Fools WHIM-WHAM. (Perhaps a Pink "Over the Rainbow Party" ushering in a "new age of harmony between men and women" [*sic* Ladies and Gentlemen] modeled after Mrs. Schlafly's postmortem ERA *soirée*). PUFF 8 All Pinks will happily hoist the Pink-White-and-Blue on April 1 and in support of a Pink New Deal will determine from the bottom of their Pink Hearts of Hearts to keep WHAMMING the WHIM with the Pinkest of Arts. Remember:

THE PINK PAC PACT

Rouse the Pink Public
Martial Pink Pride,
Forge new Pink pathways
For Pink's true and tried.

Have Pink Privy Councils
Print Pink Privy Seals,
On Pink Ships of State
Make the Pinkest of deals.

Wave great big Pink pompoms
Tout Pink values dear,
Lift all our Pink spirits
With Pink we'll not fear.

With partisan Pinkness
We'll wend our Pink way,
The WHIMS we will WHAM
And win the Pink Day.

PINKLISTED I—ATTILA THE HEN AWARDS

Men perspire, Ladies glow, and pigs sweat. Accordingly, for their gross inattention to feminine hygeine, the sic presents the following Attila the Hen Awards to:

1. Margaret Abbott, the first American woman to win an Olympic title in 1900;
2. Annie Smith Peck, suffragette, who climbed Mt. Huscaran in Peru to plant a "Votes for Women" banner at the top in 1908;
3. Trudy Ederle (the girl President Coolidge should have called "America's Amazon" rather than "America's Best Girl"), who swam the English Channel in record time in 1926;

PUFF 8. Pink Ladies, devoted to Pink politics, are not generally concerned with partisan politics. But since Mrs. Schlafly, a Lady who knows a mandate when she sees one, is a loyal Republican, and since the Republicans did have the pluck to chuck the ERA, the Pink Lady Sorority is sending Mrs. Schlafly an itty-bitty porcelain Pink-and-white pachyderm, a commemorative trinket she will relish in the years to come as Pink Ladies progress down the Path of Pink.

4. Babe Zaharias Didrikson, who won more titles in sports, including AP's Woman Athlete of the Half-Century in 1950, than any other person, male or female, in this century;
5. Wilma Rudolph, known at the Paris Olympics as "La Chattanooga Choo-Choo," the first American to win three Olympic gold medals in 1960;
6. Wyomia Tyus, the first person ever to win the 100-meter dash in two consecutive Olympics in 1968;
7. Billie Jean King, the first sportswoman to earn $100,000 in 1970, and Chris Evert, the first sportswoman to earn $1,000,000 in 1976;
8. Maria Pepe, twelve years old, the first girl to play Little League baseball for the Hoboken Little League in 1972;
9. The Yale University women's rowing crew, the first women ever to march into the office of the P.E. director wearing *only* "Title IX" emblazoned like scarlet A's on their chests to demand equal shower facilities in 1976;

AND

Helen Wills; Alice Coachman; Maureen Connolly: Althea Gibson; Tracy Austin; Martina Navratilova; Nancy Lopez; Patty Sheehan; Hollis Stacy; Beth Daniel; Donna de Verona; Donna Caponi; Sandra Palmer; Patty Berg; Kathy Whitworth; Shirley Muldowney; Robyn Smith; Tenley Albright; Carol Heiss; Peggy Fleming; JoJo Starbuck; Dorothy Hamill; Mary Lou Retton; Mary Decker; Joan Benoit; and Valerie Briscoe-Hooks—to name but an unfeminine few—for their failure to realize that Ladies are good sports but never play sports where they risk getting their attire most deplorably dampened.

MAJOR MALE MENTORS—
MONITORING FOR PROFESSIONAL PINKS

In Which the Sunshine Inspiration Committee Discusses Genetically Feminine Behavior, Giant Steps for Mankind, No-Nos for Ladies, Comparable Worth, Looney Tunes, Martin Luther, Shakespeare, Ronald Reagan, Boy George, Dorothy Parker, Weddings, Luggage, Bric-a-brac, and Pedestal Power—All in Pursuit of Pink.

Numbers of Ladies under the pressure of professional roles have actually—Heaven help us!—metamorphosed into women. PUFF 1 If you are temporarily working outside your Home, one of the first mainstays against such a disaster will be to find a Major Male Mentor and Monitor, a Gentleman on the job who knows how to encourage atti-

---

PUFF 1. So much trouble could have been avoided by heeding Martin Luther's dictum: "Women should remain at home, sit still, keep house and bear and bring up children."

tudes and behavior that are genetically feminine and are for Ladies everywhere, in Neil Armstrong's terms, a giant step for Mankind. It will be a relief, not only to Mentors, but to all Gentlemen in a working environment, not to be placed in the stressful position of dealing with women. PEW 2 Too long have the WHIM tried to emulate (and in the process emasculate) Men. "Some of us are becoming the men we wanted to marry," says WHIM Gloria Steinem. Accordingly, the Sisters must take a militantly Ladylike stand to establish Pink Quality Control Circles which will abolish the pushy professionalism practiced by the WHIM.

The following are definite No-Nos for Ladies on the job:

1) NO briefcases—They look masculine and in the hands of a Lady like a silly attempt at seriousness.

2) NO networking or "old-gals' groups"—Old gals should stay out of groups; the less attention called to bags and sags the better.

3) NO female mentors—Women in a position to mentor will obviously be leading you in an unLadylike direction.

4) NO pension plans (containing IRAs, diversified investments, etc.)—Everyone knows that a Man's work is from sun to sun, and a Lady's work is never done. Therefore, Ladies do not need retirement programs. Husbands have retirement plans in which Ladywives share.

5) NO handling of important papers—Stocks, bonds, investor portfolios, computer programs, legal briefs, administrative memos, corporate strategies, etc., are off-limits to Ladies unless you are typing them for your Gentleman boss.

6) NO dressing for success—Whatever that is in your office, leave it to the WHIM who do not understand that Ladies dress for HIM. Whatever look your Dearie doesn't find dreary is right for you. Ladies can look short, tall, curvy, slender, slightly slinky, demure, exotic or homespun. Whatever in *His* eyes will adorn should definitely be worn.

7) NO degrees—Ladies do not take ACT, SAT, GRE, GMAT, LSAT, MCAT, or DAT; and they do not receive a B.A., B.S., M.A., M.B.A., Ph.D., LL.D., M.D., or D.D.S. Ladies are not concerned with advancing in the corporate culture but with life as a corporate wife.
PUFF 3

8) NO unLadylike squabbling over money—The concepts of "comparable worth" and "equal pay for equal work" are double-trouble for

---

PEW 2. Said WHIM Virginia Gildersleeve, a founder of the U.S. Navy women's corps in World War II, "If the Navy could have used dogs or ducks or monkeys, certain of the older Admirals would have preferred them to women." As well they should, SIC says, as well they should.

PUFF 3. Mrs. Sarah Josepha Hale, the sage Victorian editress of *Godey's Lady's Book,* famed prcedecessoress to such picturesque periodicals as *Ladies Home Journal* and *Better Homes and Gardens,* points out in her publication *Woman's Record or Sketches of All Distinguished Women from the Beginning Till A.D. 1850*: "The greater the intellectual force, the greater and more fatal the errors into which women fall." Dr. Grayson Kirk, former president of Columbia University, points up the wisdom of today's young Ladies who agree with Mrs. Hale: "It would be preposterously naive to suggest that a B.A. can be made as attractive to girls as a marriage license."

all Ladies and Gentlemen, to say nothing of the economy which would be left in rubble. As President Reagan's economic advisor, William Niskanen, pointed out, equal pay for equal work is a "medieval concept"; and as Civil Rights Commissioner Clarence Pendleton made clear, comparable worth is "the looniest idea since Looney Tunes." PEW 4

At the office as everywhere else, Ladies exercise Pedestal Power. Here's how to get it:

1) Personal appearance is paramount. PEW 5 A Pink thing of beauty is a Pink joy forever, so pay particular attention to the following:

   a. Every Pink Lady must frequent a beauty salon a minimum of once a week. If your hairstyle becomes too casual, you have not been suffering sufficiently under the dryer. A weekly three hours at the beauty parlor reduces tress stress while developing stamina that every Lady needs.

   Have a weekly manicure. Nightly repairs will ensure Pink (or clear gloss) perfection.

   b. Makeup is, of course, a must for a Lady in any place, public or private, where Gentlemen are present. Less for some Ladies, more for others, depending on your individual camouflage needs for maximum beauty prestige.

   d. Do not wear glasses. Dorothy Parker, a Lady who knew a lot about Gentlemen, said, "Men never make passes at girls who wear glasses." If you can't see, ask a Man to guide you.

2) When required to participate in staff development, ask for something Pink that is pertinent to working ladies, such as:

   a. Special consultants from La Lobe on earring etiquette;

   b. Information on the latest in foundations (garments, that is);

   c. Movement strategies; that is, a charm school or modeling agency consultant for instruction in correct walking, sitting, standing, position of hands (when at rest), etc.;

PEW 4. Would that Barbara Walters, who began as a secretary and became co-anchor with Harry Reasoner on the ABC evening news (to the tune of $1,000,000 per year) and later interviewer of celebrities (to the tune of heaven knows what a year), had read the funnies and understood Mr. Pendleton's pronouncement on monies.

PEW 5. SIC says Christine Craft, the only woman in history to be awarded $400,000-plus in a lawsuit for *not* looking pretty on the Kansas City nightly news, points up the harum-scarum heights to which the WHIM "right" to look a fright on the job has risen.

d. Fashion consultants (Saks Fifth Avenue, Bonwit Teller, Bergdorf Goodman, Bloomingdales, Neiman-Marcus, or reps from your favorite fashion fortress are vital) for advice on the building of your personal wardrobe. Wardrobe and appearance constitute the only true empire of any Lady and are therefore the rightful recipients of her empire-building attentions. Designer labels are encouraged on every piece of Lady's clothing. From stem to stern every Pink Lady must present herself (to use a bracing Male metaphor) as classy and cosmo as a Cadillac, as majestically magical as a Mercedes, as ravishingly regal as a Rolls, or at the very least, as peppily prestigious as a Peugeot. No quibbling about expense is acceptable. All is attainable if resources are properly budgeted.

e. Remember: the goal of all Pink Lady toilettes is to look feminine. Mannish or unisex dressing, even when in vogue, is *very verboten*. (Who knows what ill effect the advocacy of androgyny may have on the production of progeny?) Coco Chanel said, "A dress made right should allow one to walk, to dance, even to ride horseback." WRONG. SIC says, a dress made right should allow one to look pretty—period.

3) Office decor for Ladies should be as genteel and pastel as possible. It is soothing to a Gentleman that your presence be as useful but unobtrusive as possible. Display pictures of Husbands, Children, or Gentlemen friends prominently. However, bric-a-brac, doodads, and assorted bibelots that Ladies are likely to clutter about should be kept to the barest minimum.

4) Staff meeting behavior for Ladies should be quiet, reserved, and reflective. Adding comments in soft almost inaudible tones is acceptable, but never speak until all Gentlemen have expressed their opinions. If the matter under discussion is particularly important or controversial, it is best to say nothing. If you must say something, say it in only the most quiveringly hesitant tone. Remember, silence is particularly golden for the Pink. Therefore, normal Ladies do not normally speak unless asked a question or directly requested to comment.

5) Sit and stand in a demure manner and utilize no wild gestures. Drop words like "Darn" and "Gosh," and use expressions such as "Dear me," "Mercy me," "Gracious goodness," "I'm sorry," "I apologize," "It's all my fault," "I'll do better next time," and "Oh my, oh my, but I'm only a girl."

6) While observing all the Ladylike amenities mentioned above—BE EFFICIENT. Nothing is more trying to a Gentleman in a

hurry than a Lady in a disorganized flurry. Remember: cool, calm and collected with nothing neglected may get Him elected to just the position he has been pining for.

Most importantly, remember that while working out, homework becomes not less but more important. Absolutely spic-and-span is the Pink plan that will keep your Man happy. Guests to your Home should be able to compliment your seven-, or at least five-course daily dinners and floor clean enough to eat off of. SIC says a Lady's closets and drawers show the condition of her soul. God forbid that any Pink Lady should go to glory with hers dirty. Your children too will need extra attention for child-abuse prevention. This means teaching Sunday School, attending PTA, being a Cub Scout, Brownie Scout, Den and Room Mother, helping with homework and listening nightly to all their pet projects, problems or plans. PUFF 6 Also, as SuperPinkWoman [*sic* Lady], never go to bed grubby thus neglecting Hubby. Even though a tad tired at the end of the day, put on his favorite perfume and a nifty nightie, then turn out the light and keep his interest turned up bright.

One final word of admonition. Not all Pink Ladies are fortunate enough to be married; if not, they should begin immediately to strive toward that blessed end. As the nineteenth-century theatrical agent Elizabeth Marbury noted, "A caress is better than a career." Above all, remember Professor Alfred Marshall's advice to Beatrix Potter who relinquished a career drawing Peter Rabbits for a life of married habits, "If you compete with us, we shan't marry you." PEW 7 Those who do partake of marital bliss, guard unceasingly against being so caught up in your temporary take-home pay that you forget the sound advice that once shrewish Kate gave to the Ladies of Padua after she had been properly tamed by Petruchio:

> Such duty as the subject owes her prince
> Even such a woman oweth to her husband;
> And when she is forward, peevish, sullen, sour,
> And not obedient to his honest will,
> What is she but a foul contending rebel
> And graceless traitor to her loving lord?
> I am ashamed that women are so simple
> To offer war where they should kneel for peace
> Or seek for rule, supremacy and sway,
> When they are bound to serve, love and obey.

PUFF 6. "All that I am, I owe to my mother," said George Washington. Ralph Waldo Emerson agreed, observing, "Men are what their mothers made them." Imagine how the failed mothers of Nero, Genghis Khan, the Marquis de Sade, Hitler, Mussolini, Ozzy Osborne and Boy George (to mention an unfortunate few) must have felt at producing bad boys of such mind-boggling proportions. Never forget: *Mothers* are responsible for their offspring. Be sure you make *yours wunderkinder* the world can be proud of.

PEW 7. Unmarried newspaperwoman Nellie Bly, despite her editor's forbidding "Absolutely and irrevocably no. This is something only a man can do. Forget it Nell, this jaunt's not for you," went around the world in seventy-two days in 1889-90 carrying only a small alligator satchel. Not only her insubordination but her scandalous lack of luggage were most unLadylike lapses. SIC weeps to think of all the WHIM ambition responsible for so much Pink attrition from Nellie's time to our own.

SIC says *touché* and advises Ladies yet unmarried to put the spirit of Petruchio's wife into your life. You may then gain the affection and admiration of not only your Male superiors at work, but dates with a matrimonial mate and a *très chic* wedding in June under the moon or at high noon. Remember:

> Mentors who monitor Pink Lady jobs
> Take care not to let you be WHIMsical blobs;
> So one day from all the professions alarming
> You'll be rescued and married by a dashing
>   Prince Charming!

PINKLISTED II—ODDESSES

Fashion, family and homemaking moxie are the normal and natural feminine arts. Accordingly, Mary Phelps Jacobs, a New York debutante who stitched together two lace hankies and some ribbon to make the first bra, and Julie Newmar who patented panty hose "to make your *derrière* look like an apple instead of a ham sandwich" are to be commended for their attention to Pink Lady toilettes. Others like Hannah Wooley who founded the science of home economics and Bertha Plugi who invented parakeet diapers are also deserving of the highest Pink pluses and plaudits for their attention to domestic detail. The importance of decorative and domestic pursuits for the Pink Lady cannot be overrated. Elizabeth Cady Stanton, the most influential writer of the nineteenth-century WHIM, said of Susan B. Anthony, the most influential WHIM speaker of the period, that Susan often brought information to the Stanton residence that would "turn any woman's thoughts from stockings and puddings." SIC hastens to remind the Sisters that a concentration on stockings and puddings has kept many a Pink Lady of wavering understanding from falling prey to aberrant and abnormal activities. Thus the WHIM must be taught to heed the great Milton who said, "Nothing lovelier can be found in Woman [*sic* Lady] than to study household good"; and the admirable Joseph Addison who called Ladies "beautiful romantic animals, that may be adorned with furs and feathers, pearls and diamonds, ores and silks." Therefore, the SIC firmly raps and zaps the following undomestic and/or unfashionable WHIM:

1. Emma Willard, who founded the Troy Female Seminary in 1821 and taught algebra and geometry by carving potatoes and turnips into pyramids and cones instead of cooking them. (A culinary course was, of course, Miss Willard's correct curriculum.)

2. Carey Thomas, who founded Bryn Mawr in 1885 to show that "women can learn, can reason...without having all [their] time engrossed by dress and society." (How thoroughly undomesticated and *déclassé* can you get?)

3. Elizabeth Miller, who made the first pair of pants for women and Amelia Bloomer, who wore them at the first Women's Rights Convention in 1848, in New York where a local paper reported that the gathering was attended by misfits (why else would they wear bloomers?) such as "divorced wives, childless women, and some old maids."

4. Dr. Mary Walker, who declared corsets "coffins" and wore men's trousers, who refused to marry and manage a household, and instead received the Medal of Honor for her surgical services (how inelegantly employed could a Lady be?) during the Civil war.

5. Jane Addams, who instead of setting up her own private housekeeping, set up the first settlement house, a public domicile, in 1889, for working girls to gather and gossip in the evenings.

6. Amelia Earhart, who rather than placing her keepsakes prettily in a vine-covered cottage, sold them to finance her flights and then flew off, *sans* husband, to become the first woman to fly the Atlantic in 1928.

7. Ellen Swallow Richards, who originated ecology instead of applying her cleaning skills to her own home where, SIC says, the world would have been better served by her efforts.

8. Henrietta Chamberlain King, widow of the owner of the Texas King Ranch, who instead of babies, bred bulls, developing her own breed, the Santa Gertrudis, thus becoming one of the most ill-bred of all the once-wed WHIM.

9. Rosa Parks, who instead of sticking to her stitching as a Lady seamstress, refused to be Pinkly and submissively seated on the bus (according to the Gentleman bus driver's directions) and thus in 1955 started a nationwide free-for-all that called most unLadylike attention to herself and other WHIM whose un-prim, out-on-a-limb behavior was most shockingly unPink.

10. Yvonne Braithwaite Burke, who instead of staying home where she belonged (especially in her indelicately delicate condition), was elected to the U.S. House of Representatives in 1972 and then became the first woman to apply for and receive maternity leave from Congress, a WHIM who, like all the above-mentioned unmaidenly mavericks, has deeply grieved and peeved the Pink.

MORALS AND LAURELS—
HISTORICAL AND CONTEMPORARY CONTRETEMPS AND THEIR SOLUTIONS

In Which the Sunshine Inspiration Committee Discusses Adam and Eve, Fateful Imprudence, Unfounded Impressions, The Great Chicago Fire, Flappers, a WHIM Poetess, Dear Abby,

> Crucial Junctures, Mamas, Low-Flying Pheasants, the Girl Scouts, Nature Naturing, Close Encounters of the Pink Kind, Pink Encounters of the Close Kind, Ingrid Bergman, Katherine Graham, Betty Ford, Richard Nixon, Gentlemanly Sensibilities, Clever Endeavors, Married Bliss, and THE CURE FOR AMERICAN SOCIETAL DECAY TODAY.

And now Ladies, though painful to peruse, it serves us but ill to leave unconsidered the root of all the WHIM evils of history and the current upheaval and sad state of the world today. SIC must agree with Thomas Hood:

> When Eve upon the first of men
> The apple press'd with specious cant
> Oh what a thousand pities then
> That Adam was not adamant!

But alas poor Yorick, our first Father was understandably led astray, and the result is that we must now contend with noxious gases in the air; the demise of the dollar; the high price of oil, truffles, and *chateaubriand*; and the altercations between navies and nations that bedevil our breakfast and disturb our *demitasse*. Oh, if Eve had only stayed put and not ventured out alone. But indeed she could not because her very nature was flawed, and in a weak moment, like a bad little jack-in-the-box, out it popped to plague us all through eternity.[PEW 1]

Oh to what transgression has led the first *folie à deux* indiscretion. Today, the WHIM seems particularly prone to the "thoughtless enthusiasms," "spurts of passion," "fateful imprudence," and "unfounded impressions" described by the eighteenth-century poet Alexander Pope as indigenous to woman's character in matters traditionally ceremonial but now no longer necessarily matrimonial. Early in the twentieth century, Mrs. Claude Beddington, famed London hostess, Pinkly pilloried the morals of WHIM flappers. She decried:

> ...the present young girls smoking cigarettes incessantly; drinking not only with their meals, but cocktails on an empty stomach; using latchkeys, driving motor cars without even a chauffeur on board to chaperone them, sitting crosslegged

---

PEW 1. Accordingly, a host of the WHIM, beginning with the errant Eve, have since antiquity wreaked havoc: Pandora and her wretched box; Helen hammering down the gates of Troy; Guinevere smashing the Round Table to smithereens; Marie Antoinette agitating the French with her ill-timed remarks concerning baked goods; Mrs. O'Leary incinerating Chicago with her unsupervised cow; and due to their inefficiency and meddling, Rosemary Woods and Katherine Graham prompting President Nixon's resignation.

in skirts shorter than a Highland kilt, and riding to hounds astride. PUFF 2

Mrs. Beddington pointed out not only the immorality but the impracticality of such behavior when she observed that "a woman's great charm is her unattainability. Who ever enjoyed hitting a low-flying pheasant?" But the flappers flapped on, unperturbed, to their own and the public's detriment.

Later in the century, the WHIM poetess Edna St. Vincent Millay wrote:

> What lips my lips have kissed and whose and why,
> I have forgotten,
> And what arms have lain under my head till morning.

True Pink Ladies would firmly wallop such a trollop, but Miss Millay, blithely unshamed by such brazen behavior, insisted in other lurid lines that she would "burn my candle at both ends" though "it will not last the night." Unfortunately, it apparently lasted sufficient nights for the formation of her "Alumni Association," to which Mr. Edmund Wilson, a member, along with many others of her cast-off amours, joked that he belonged. SIC can only tremble for such fallen flowers and lament the "liberation" that has led in all areas, public and private, to the American Societal Decay we see all around us today. PEW 3

Oh how many of the world's woes could be cured by Juliette Low's catechism to the Girl Scouts, "Don't let any man make love to you unless he wants to marry you....Don't be afraid to say you won't play at nasty rude things" and by Dear Abby's advice to the lovelorn, "Be good. Stay nice. Don't sell yourself short and someday your prince will come." Certainly Pink Patron Saint Princess Di's Prince came. As one Mother put it, "He [the Prince] dated actresses, beauty queens, and rumba dancers. He's been everywhere in the world, could have any girl he wanted...." But he chose Shy (and sweet and pure) Di because, as another Mama remarked, "I don't care if it's 1940 or 1980, there are certain standards that just don't change....And I'll always believe that despite women's liberation and the so-called sexual revolution." Brava,

---

PUFF 2. Mrs. B. would have approved of the boarding school for young ladies described by Captain Marryat in his American travelogue of 1839, whose headmistress, not wishing to expose her charges to the immodesty of "legs" and desiring to "...preserve in their utmost purity the ideas of the young ladies under her charge...had dressed all the four limbs [of the pianoforte in the drawing room] in modest little trousers, with frills at the bottom of them." Mrs. B. would have also approved of Duke University in the fifties which forbade coeds to lie prone on the campus grass and draped male bathroom appurtenances with white sheets to protect the delicate sensibilities of Lady students residing in the Gentlemen's dorm during summer session.

PEW 3. Sydney Biddle Barrow, ballyhooed in the press in 1984 as the "Mayflower Madam," demonstrates the depths to which the once mightily Ladylike have fallen. Descended from Plymouth Bay colonists and listed in the Social Register, even Miss Barrow's pedigree did not save her from shockingly unPink behavior.

Mamas, Brava. PUFF 4

Indeed, as Princess Di and Mamas everywhere are well aware, Ladies can become, instead of perpetrators of the world's ills, "preceptor[s] of morals and keeper[s] of the keys" (*Anita Colby's Beauty Book,* 1959) when women's faulty morals become Ladies' lovely laurels. We have only to learn when to say no, avoiding woe, and when to say yes to a caress. A Pink Lady says "NO" to nature naturing naughtily in Close Encounters of the Pink Kind: "close calls" that no true Lady can condone or encourage. (Pink security depends on premarital purity, let no blemish diminish it.) A Pink Lady says "YES" only to Pink Encounters of the Close Kind: mating only after proper Pink dating and waiting. PEW 5 William Acton, the Victorian medical authority, explained the nature of correct Pink Encounters:

> I should say that the majority of women [*sic* Ladies]—happily for them—are not very much troubled with sexual feeling of any kind....As a general rule, a modest woman [*sic* Lady] seldom desires any sexual gratification for herself. She submits to her husband, but only to please him. PEW 6

Whereas Close Encounters of the Pink Kind are not refined and much maligned, Pink Encounters of the Close Kind are the ties that bind and should be designed with Pink enterprise to fill your hubby with sweet surprise. In other words, unmarried, a Lady must be inviolably chaste; however, once wedded, chaste must be erased posthaste no matter what a Lady's personal taste. For even though you, the thoroughly Pink Lady Mr. Acton describes, will *not*, your Husband most

---

PUFF 4. How much better off the world would be if we could still celebrate the virtues of young American Ladies as did the author of "The American Girl" in *The Young Lady's Offering of Gems of Prose and Poetry* of 1853:

> Her eye of light is the diamond bright
> Her innocence the pearl,
> And these are ever the bridal gems
> That are worn by the American girl.

PEW 5. Would that Ingrid Bergman, Nastassia Kinski, Gae Exton, Jerri Hall, Farrah Fawcett, and Jessica Lange who filled baby carriages before their marriages had done less mating and more waiting.

PEW 6. Someone should have apprised Betty Ford, a first Lady noted for a most unLadylike lack of reticence and rectitude in her public utterances, of Mr. Acton's advice before she blurted out: "They [the press] have asked me everything except how often I sleep with my husband. And if they had asked me that, I would have said, 'As often as I can.' " Mrs. Ford would have done well to heed the advice from *All for Love* that Tattle gave to Miss Prue (after she promptly replied "yes" to his proposition): "You are a woman [*sic* Lady], you must never speak what you think. Your words must contradict your thoughts, but your actions must contradict your words."

certainly *will* be interested in *tête-à-tête* for two *a la* Blue Boy style with you. PUFF 7

Now chaste Cinderellas, do not blush and blanch. A true Pink Lady is never besmirched when dallying with her darling according to his dictates and delights. SIC sympathizes with Ladies who still long with poignant Pink nostaliga for the time when we were advised, if overcome at a crucial juncture, to utter a genteel, mouse-like, squeaky "eek" and swoon quietly away. Oh, would that we could return to a time when neither expletives nor explicits concerning Pink physicalities were ever spoken in polite company. A time before Kinsey in the fifties and Hite in the seventies when the discussion of not only such delicate dilemmas as "crucial junctures" but even "multiple crucial junctures" the topics of research, public forums, and articles in women's magazines. But due to the unbridled shenanigans of the WHIM, our Gentlemen are tempted at every turn—and Gentlemen will be Gentlemen, you know. Therefore, more earnest and energetic efforts are required of Ladies today in *l'amour billets-doux* for married doves to sweetly coo. Any lady worth her Pink salt will use all her power of Pink pretend to ensure that married Blue lesiure is filled with all the Pink pleasure that Hubby will inevitably come to treasure. As Coventry Patmore wrote in the Victorian masterpiece *Angel in the House,* you must be "so wise in all [you] ought to know," but "so ignorant of all beside." PUFF 8

In more modern Pink parlance, you must be full of pretty Pink pranks, but nothing too frank or rank. This means, Ladies, that you must know a great deal you ought *not* to know but know that you *must* know in order to know with certainty what *to* know. You must also determine what you know that your Husband would *approve* that you

---

PUFF 7. In addition to being vital to your Mate's well-being, Pink Encounters of the Close Kind are also part and parcel of your civic and religious duty. SIC reminds us all of the myriad Mothers whose advice to their virginal Victorian daughters was to lie quietly on their wedding nights, comforted during their ordeal by the knowledge that they were doing their duty to the Empire.

Even Pope Pius XIII in his 1956 encyclical called a woman [*sic* Lady]

> that gentle creature to whose delicate hands God seems to have entrusted the future of the world ... the expression of all that is best, kindest, most lovable here below.

Ah, how bright may shine our little candle if only our natures are Pinkly channeled and handled.

PUFF 8. A Gentleman versifying in *The Mother's Book* (1831) put it perfectly in a poem entitled "Female Charms":

> I would have her as pure as the snow on the mount—
>   As true as the smile that to infamy's given—
> As pure as the wave of the crystalline fount,
>   Yet as warm in the heart as the sunlight of heaven.
> With a mind cultivated, not boastingly wise,
>   I could gaze on such beauty, with exquisite bliss;
> With her heart on her lips and her soul in her eyes—
>   What more could I wish in dear woman [*sic* Lady] than this.

know, as opposed to what he might be *shocked* that you know, and then let him know that you know what he *wants* you to know with the most *knowing knowing going.*

One last word of warning: be wary, Ladies, when you marry, for as the daughters of Eve, it is ever easy to deceive and grieve. The Victorian art critic John Ruskin, who saw a Lady as a "queen in a walled garden" with "home always around her," awaited his Bride and the future Mother of his Children with eager anticipation but was shocked into celibacy at the sight of hair in places unbeknownst to him when she disrobed on their wedding night! More artful "knowing and going" would have forewarned Mrs. Ruskin to take care in dealing with a man of such delicate sensibilities. Mr. George Bernard Shaw described a similar shock he received as a child:

> I had been brought up in a world in which woman [*sic* Lady] the angel, presented to me the appearance of a spreading mountain, a sort of Primrose Hill. On the peak there was perched a small, pinched, upper part, and on top of that a human head. This, to me, at the period of life when one is young and receiving indelible impressions, was a woman. One day, when I was perhaps five years of age, a lady paid us a visit, a very handsome lady who was always in advance of the fashion. Crinolines were going out; and she had discarded hers. I, an innocent unprepared child, walked bang into the room and suddenly saw, for the first time, a woman not shaped like Primrose Hill, but with a narrow skirt which evidently wrapped a pair of human legs. I have never recovered from the shock, and never shall.

Who knows what evil lurks as the result of such rudeness and lewdness? Take care Ladies, lest impulsive immodesties mock the mood and mode of your married Pink abode.

Always remember:

Armor for Armour

Mother, Mistress, Matron, Temptress
All these roles we must fulfill,
Then Jill for Jack a perfect partner
With peerless Pink will fill the bill.

But WHIMS and whims are ever present
Huddling 'round the chastest dame,
And nature naturing all defenseless
May tremble, maimed, defamed and blamed.

Then e'en the freshest sweetest flower
Must fold its leaves and shrink disdained,
If a loose and wanton hour
Doth its virgin blooms profane.

Thus 'round nature's tempting tempest
Place a guard of Pinkest Pink,
Married bliss thy chiefest armor
To Pink *amour* thou then may wink.

Then Ladies' laurels fresh and lovely
Are ever yours to have and hold,
The world thus saved by Ladies' labors
Knows all that shines is Pure Pink Gold.

The Author Is Dead! Long Live the Author!

John Schultz

The truly promising direction for contemporary fiction writing to take is toward a synthesis of fictional systems and a breadth and generosity of content and emotion, with a full commitment of the mind of the author in the perceiving, imagining, and telling of the story. This is a risk-taking venture in all of its aspects, to rescue verbal fiction for readers and, in the words of Robert Frost, to save prose from itself.

From the Bible to stories being written or told orally today, from Shakespeare to Gogol and Kafka, from Fielding to Joyce and Proust, Homer to authors of modern times, the written literature of fiction that has survived has been that which provides a vivid, compelling experience of story as told in language, developing character, points of view, event, imagery, narrative, dramatic relationships, authorial intelligence, and the fullness thereof, with plenty of inviting room for the reader or listener. Much contemporary fiction tends to reduce and trivialize these major classic elements of fiction.

Contemporary fiction is overall drained and too much squeezed by reductive versions of the constraints of Impressionism, Latter-day Impressionism, and what is called Post-modernism. As a literary movement, the career of Impressionism began in the last half of the nineteenth century with the work of Flaubert, James, Conrad, Wells, Crane, Chekhov, and many others, and has been pretty much dominant (in English-speaking countries anyway) since that time. Impressionism, following James' principle, sought to make *active* those elements that had heretofore been inert or had become inert in fiction.

To make fiction more active was presumed to require the withdrawal of the overt authorial presence from the space of the story and, in the storyteller's place, to make new demands upon the reader, concentrating attention on developing the illusion of the present reality of the story event through sense impressions. In many of the most successful examples of this genre of fiction, the voice of the author and his or her imaginative seeing are strongly, vigorously, even supremely present, and the author is also working for the reader very positively in the manipulation of time and the choice of a variety of points of view. James developed a complex conversational style to tell his seeing of the story, and we feel the attentiveness of James' internal listener during the act of writing.

Latter-day Impressionism (1950-present) reduced Impressionism to the slogan "Show, don't tell," which insofar as it sought, in its "seeing" dimension, to give a vivid, authentic experience for the reader, free of authorial prejudice, is a great half-truth; but because it is only a half-truth, when applied as a whole truth, it leaves out more than half of the potential of fiction. Too often, especially in creative writing programs where much of contemporary American fiction writing training occurs, the beginning writer, at a formative time, is subtly and powerfully admonished to make sure that no presence of a teller or author shows in the story. This requirement of making all signs of authorship disappear from the work ties your hands behind your back and requires you to pretend the story is not told by you or any author, suppressing distinctive voice, imagination, perception, invention, in short, excluding voice and mind of the author from the story. "Show, don't tell" deserts important aspects of the authorial function that were actually well fulfilled, in identifiable ways, in Impressionism itself. "Show, don't tell" undercuts its primary purpose of providing a vivid presentation of the story event because the teller must do the imaginative seeing of the story, the imaginative selection of what is to be told and what is to be left out, and only the teller's voice can do the telling of it. The teller's voice must inescapably carry the teller's intelligence and attitude with it. When the writer leaves out the teller-reader relationship, which includes the underlying teller-listener relationship, she or he is suppressing the intelligence which the teller alone can bring to the story to benefit the reader's involvement in dramatic story-movement.

The authorial need and function continue wherever successful storytelling occurs, no matter what pretense or rationale governs the admissibility or inadmissibility of the author's presence. It is not for nothing that many of the great Impressionist stories were done in first-person, or even in multi-first-person points of view, or in story-within-a-story frameworks, which gave the author a device for being able to address the reader directly, as in works of Conrad, James, Faulkner, Robert Penn Warren and others. We need only mention the first-person story-within-a-story framework of Conrad's Marlow stories, James' *The Turn of the Screw*, the multi-first-person points of view of Faulkner's *As I Lay Dying*, and the first-person and third-person points of view of *The Sound and the Fury* with the author directly addressing the reader in the famous appendix, or, in Robert Penn Warren's *All the King's Men*, the reporter Jack Burden engaging the reader with such strength of cynicism and sentiment. In K. A. Porter's "Noon Wine," we find the author choosing points of view and vantage points, moving from one to another, and compressing passages of time. In the great Impressionist third-person stories, other devices of parenthesis, parody of a form, persona of a point of view, "stream of consciousness," implicit theatrical structures, or simply a definite attitude on the part of the voice of the author, are used to enable the writer once again, through whatever chosen device, to get the sense of telling the story to a reader. In a story such as Hemingway's "Hills Like White Elephants," a fine example of the withdrawal of the author from the authorial space, the author is nevertheless keenly present, over the reader's shoulder, so to speak, in perceiving and selecting what will be told or not told, acting as a kind of theatrical director in the reader's mind toward the action. The change has occurred in the placement of the author and in the kind of constraints on the author's function. The distinctive laconic voice of Hemingway's early style works as an expression of the author's mind and of the two characters who keep much of their story suggestively suppressed.

However, the "Show, don't tell" story-event of Latter-day Impressionism all too often spends its effort in expunging signs of authorship and all too regularly publishes the shadow of a story. The author as human authority as well as the author as ecclesiastical authority is to be vanquished and erased, much as a religious or political movement seeks to erase the evidence as well as the function of its competitor.

Some of the more interesting contemporary American fiction comes out of the Post-modernist counter-reformation (1960-present), which re-includes a parodic version of the authorial presence, in a kind of closed system in which the major elements of fiction are under the sometimes brilliant though often belittling domination of the ego of the writer. Here the writer establishes an incorporated storyteller, as in E. L. Doctorow's *The Book of Daniel*, in which the author's direct relationship with the reader is one of fancy cynical footwork, but the framework is set to permit the inventive use of point of view, sometimes shifting from first to third person within one sentence, to tell the poignant and compelling stories of the Isaccsons' two children, with a driving perception of the moral faithfulness that frequently characterizes children between the ages of three and twelve. The Post-modernist system, frequently appears to require that the authorial position become occupied by a stand-in, costumed in a vaudevillian or bureaucratic guise that frustrates the full function of the storyteller's point of view, thus trivializing reader, characters, and story. Parody of forms which carry an inherent address to the reader is practiced vigorously in Post-modernism. In the most exuberant, outrageous versions of the Post-modernist system, the writer as ego invites the reader as ego to join in the parody of whatever, with self-parody becoming the most successful form.

Whether contemporary fiction is Impressionist or Latter-day Impressionist, with displacement of the author or with the pretense that the author has ceased to exist or been permanently exiled, or Post-modernist with its closed system dominated by the parodically ecclesiastical ego of the writer, there is frequently a lack of range and honesty of emotion permitted the characters, a lack of generosity of feeling and perception, a lack of seeing and imagining of life in the magnitude in which it is experienced by the individual. In Post-modernist exercises, even laughter, which is sought magnetically by most human beings, turns too frequently into a snigger. The neglect of the above elements avoids the "common secrets" of human experience, those feelings and motivations that everyone recognizes but seldom talks or writes about, but which have always been the stuff of good story.

Much of what has passed for experiment in contemporary fiction has been simply a sort of breaking up and re-shaping and manipulation of the furniture of Impressionist approaches, in either the original or Post-modernist guise, with few writers actually moving outside these particular rooms in the house or theater of fiction, but many chafing to do so.

The key word in James' Impressionist principle is *active*; the key principle is to make or render *active* those elements of fiction that had heretofore been inert, or had become inert. When we read the liveliest of the eighteenth-century novels, we find nothing inert about the relationship of the author and reader. This liveliness, of course, intrigued many of the Post-modernists. Presumably the author-reader relationship is also an element that should and could be rendered dramatically active. Yet, in recent literary history, some of the Post-modernists seem to have set out to reverse the principle by attempting deliberately to make *inert* what has heretofore been active and dramatic in fiction, and so fashioning the elements of their fiction as a parodic counter against Latter-day Impressionism's mannered pretense of making the story active by expunging all marks of authorship.

We have a literature of fiction, Impressionist, Latter-day Impressionist, and Post-modernist, in which the teller has been too long suppressed, seemingly exiled, or altered into an arrogant comic, but the ego of the writer, not so strangely, has become too much present, too much in conflict with the characters and the story, making too many diminishing choices and cheap invitations for the reader, with too little actual fun, too little seriousness, too little risk taken toward finding significance, too little compelling experience of the story. The authorial presence must be distinguished from the ego of the writer, which can seek a kind of negative enhancement of her or his position through the diminishment of characters, voice, and story.

In these three prevailing fictional systems, the space of the fictional theater of composition in the author's and reader's minds has become so diminished, so narrowed, that reader, characters, author, story, have little elbow room for maneuvering to gain the power of their separateness yet interrelatedness, even interchangeableness, in providing the experience of story. This interchangeableness occurs with the reader's identification and accommodations with the elements of story, permitted paradoxically by the distinctiveness of the author's telling. In the author's fictional theater of composition of the mind during the act of writing, in which occurs the author's hearing of his or her own voice and awareness of the internalized listening that is involved in the developing story, the readers have become atrophied, much in the service of casual ulterior interests. These internalized readers, so crucial to what the author will permit and how the author will shape the material, have become hecklers standing near the exit door, embarrassed by strong emotion no matter how artistically successful is its representation, requiring immediate moralistic titillations and preventing any deep experience from developing for the characters, the author, the story, and other readers who, not wishing to be embarrassed by the hecklers, are becoming restlessly inattentive and are looking elsewhere for the satisfaction of story.

If the classic elements of story have been plagiarized and tritely developed too often by television and film, garnering large popular audiences, we as writers of fiction must not, out of self-spite, forsake our birthright and assume that those classic elements of fiction have lost their power and validity for imaginative exploration and creation in verbal literature. It is the sheer pervasiveness of television and film, the fact that they are actually popular media, and occasionally artistically successful, that makes verbal literature become a bitter endgame among small groups, run by ecclesiastically and, yes, self-spitefully exclusive rules. In these endgame pursuits, writers seek superiority over their characters and readers and over the story itself, i.e., a belittling superiority over all of the elements of story and of contemporary life, over which they have no such domination. The reader is left only the alternatives of joining the ego of the writer in this endgame, enjoying it according to the gusto or agreement of wit, or the reader can choose to forsake the reader's function altogether. The area that the endgame groups allow themselves for their artistic skirmishing is ever shrinking, probably because that is a way for the participants to keep the area closely controlled.

Contemporary literature is too frequently reductionist, and attempts almost overtly, and seldom protests otherwise, to minimize the classic elements of fiction. When you read the following list, your mind will probably clamor with favorite exceptions. My purpose here is not to put together a catalogue of exceptions or partial exceptions, but to set forth and discuss the directions in which the exceptions are or should be moving. It is not enough to say that there would be trash in any age and, we hope, exceptions to the trash. We have reached a point in the historical development of fictional technique and permissions, where the health of the body politic of writers and readers is as important as the health of the partial exceptions to the ailments which are set forth in the following list.

> 1) There is an identifiable tendency, almost a requirement in some quarters, to reduce and trivialize content and emotion, avoiding the "common secrets" of our experience. What's left out of the story becomes overwhelmingly absent.
>
> 2) Too often the permissions for voice and style are narrowed in an inauthentic edited economy of language. This reduces the presence of voice. Voice engages author and reader. The consequent suppression of the mind of the teller in the telling of the story reduces invention.
>
> 3) There is a generalized suppression of the storyteller's point of view which suppresses the storyteller's imaginative opportunity and reduces and nearly misses entirely the dramatic relationship of the author and reader.
>
> 4) There is a tendency in contemporary literature to reduce perception, portrayal, and rendering of character, complexity and entity of personality, range and variety of it, the full development of which has become one of the major, unique potentials of print literature.
>
> 5) There is more than a little tendency to narrow and suppress the point of view of character or characters, excluding the dimension of exploring more than one character's point of view in a scene or story. Among those writers chafing to open up the rooms of the house of fiction, there may now be a partial exception in a counter-tendency to explore shifts of point of view. Honestly explored, this counter-tendency should increase the realization of character in story.
>
> 6) Because of the above reductions, avoidances, and trivializations, there is a tendency to smother

dramatic exchange and development among characters.

7) As the above tendencies become a mob attacking the potential of story, we find story itself greatly reduced, i.e., the development of meaning in the dramatic action among the elements of story becomes thin. Skimpy also is the presence of the authorial intelligence and imagination which can find or let emerge or not stand in the way of the action among the classic elements of fiction.

8) There is a tendency in contemporary fiction to opt for writer ego-manipulated meaning rather than seeking to discover the independent wisdom of the story in the interplay with authorial intelligence.

Sometimes contemporary fiction does all of the above in the name of suggestiveness and economy, sometimes in the name of ideological persuasions about aesthetic philosophy concerning point of view and how we come to know what we know. Yet economy, when practiced well, has nothing to do with length or brevity, because some of the truly "short" stories of our literature are indeed quite brief, yet deliver the fullness of a vivid development of all of the elements of fiction. The act of writing a story is a discovery of meaning in the action of author's and reader's minds experiencing the action of the story, which is, any way you cut, slice, or hack it, an experience of the author's mind put, to one degree or another, into print. If most of the story is left out, what is the reader finally to do?

If we investigate and develop the strengths of oral and written literature, we will find ourselves with stories that carry within themselves compelling space for the reader. The following dimensions are unique to verbal story, whether oral or written, and can be developed intensively in written fiction with more depth than in other media. As we locate these unique dimensions, we no doubt also locate the human need for them.

1) The storyteller's point of view, including the physical point-in-space vantage points of characters.

2) Access to the internal points of view of characters in the story.

3) The manipulation of time within story movement to discover compelling story movement, which also discovers meaning.

4) The use of language itself as the medium, which can only be done by a speaker or teller/writer.

Through voice and perception, the mind of the teller becomes peculiarly present in the imagination and language of the story. The special nature of story movement allows for a uniquely flexible manipulation of dimensions and sense of time. Storytelling has the capacity for using summary, compression of patterns of events, moment-by-moment, linear, and non-linear kinds of story movement, and allows for great detail, breadth, and complexity of experience. It has the imaginative potential of first-person, third-person, even of second-person, and of collective plural "we" and "they" points of view, plus the ability to go into the points of view of more than one individual in one story. Filmmakers have complained about the limitation on developing character's points of view in film, which is the major reason film uses music.

Virtually with its own wisdom, the story movement in verbal fiction organizes and makes sense of the material. The author finds and sets it forth. Then the reader takes the author's place, in the act of reading, and re-creates the story, with many identifications and accommodations of her or his own.

Because the elements of story emerge from different capacities of mind and brain, significant fiction writing ability does not survive damage to any part of the brain, while other artistic capacities, such as painting and playing of music, do survive damage to certain parts of the brain. This makes fiction writing a peculiarly holistic activity. Story movement will have the feeling and even the practical effect of being separate from the writer, of being or becoming independent, though paradoxically it is also a dynamic artifice shaped by imaginative intelligence. This occurs in much the way that the old stoneworker or toolmaker "saw" the figure or instrument in the stone to be shaped. The author shapes the story, for better or worse, depending on how much she or he is aware of the independent movement or artifice residing integrally within the material. Yet form may also, as Baudelaire observed, have an independent power of its own to call forth content. Such is the dialectic complexity in the wholeness of storytelling.

We often find that what's left out of a story was more interesting than what was put in, that, actually, the real story was left out, while a tired or mannered repetition is put in its place, dealing obliquely and shallowly with the "commitment" of the characters and author. The novel needs, in some essential way, to be dramatic. Unless people are bound to each other by some constraint or commitment, their lives are non-dramatic. So it is with characters in a story. The commitment may be social, economic, political, religious, emotional, involving the "contractual" constraints of marriage, family, children, sexual love or lust or lack of either, survival, job, institutions, tribe or other group, or the constraints and ironies of one's contracts with one's self. In stories that deal with military, war, or holocaust-type experience, the dramatic constraints of commitment are immediately evident and felt, which may be why we permit strong emotion in war stories and why war stories attract readers. However, the commitment can be voluntary or involuntary, new or old, or come by chance. The charge of the author is to find the commitment. In some way, the commitment of the author is to the exploration itself and involves danger and dramatic risk for the characters and the author. The outcome is at risk, which involves the familiar and the unexpected in a thousand ways.

The content that takes the artist's attention and presses to be realized often exerts force toward innovation of form and technique. The novel, which was a market-shaped form to begin with, required sufficiently widespread literacy and technology for its distribution, and the factual world of the story combined with the way it is told has always been of special interest. There is no reason, other than the impulse to genre suicide, for the novel to surrender the world of dramatic fact to verbal non-fiction or any other kind of reportage.

Impressionism, Latter-day Impressionism, and Post-modernism sought invention through exclusion or suppression of some of the classic elements of fiction, most obviously through exclusion of overt authorial presence or through suppression or undercutting of characters, reader, and story, and through parody of form. If we continue to accept all previous exclusions and to try to invent through the principle of exclusion, we end up with only the opportunity of excluding or suppressing what remains of the visualized and meaningful story itself. This has been attempted by some of the so-called language poets, in their attitude toward narrative in poetry, when they assign the story almost entirely to the reader's supposition, association, and invention, so that different readers will discover different stories, having only a fragmentary train ride in common. In inventing through such exclusion, they still recognize the reader's need for story. The final exclusion possible is that of language itself and we could argue that this too has been tried, or at least emptiness within a scant language framework has been tried. What is left?

Most contemporary literature still proceeds within the range of permissions of Latter-day Impressionism and Post-modernism. We need now to venture into and reclaim the imaginative space of the author. We need to open up these two closed systems.

We need to examine why we read. Why should we read fiction at all? Why should we seek the experience of story told with language? Orally told stories, in oral cultures, using verbal imagery, formulaic techniques, and vivid gesture, provided and provide (in past and present forms) a wholeness of experience of teller, audience, and story not achieved by other media. In oral cultures, the experience of the story helps teller and audience gain the warm, entertaining sense of belonging to themselves and each other. Stories can be told by the traditionally skilled storyteller, or be partly acted and partly told by players in a theater, dance, musical form. The listening audience, with its response, exerts influence on the shaping of the story. Today, in oral storytelling and in theater, we see that the coldness or warmth of the audience subtly and powerfully affects timing and every other nuance of the piece.

All of this changes with written literature, but the major elements in the theater of composition of the mind, for author and reader, are still there, though developed in a way that is peculiar to the experience of the medium of print. In print literature, the potential relationship of the author to reader, which can with greater or lesser effectiveness be connected by the undergirding of the teller-listener relationship, is usually one-on-one in the privacy of silent reading, though it can also be the voice of the story to a group in an out-loud reading, or a reading to the group by members of the group, as in Story Workshop classes. In these situations, readers as listeners may still, in indirect or direct ways, exert influence on the shape and outcome of the experience of the story.

We read and seek story in order to belong to ourselves and to a sense of others. We read to be taken out of ourselves and, paradoxically, into ourselves, while being carried into an imaginative state of mind of experiencing the story. We read for story; to be in relation to a teller of a tale; to meet the mind of the author in the voice of the author, in what the author imaginatively perceives and tells; to find out about human experience and potential; to belong to ourselves through high entertainment. We seek the wholeness of the imaginative state of mind in the experience of story, whether while reading fiction or listening to orally told or read story, or seeing and hearing visual-aural telling of story in theater or film. This experience of story is an almost perfect dialectic, interpenetration of subject and object, producing the imaginative state of mind. We are able to discern separate parts of the experience, at the same time that we find them joined in actuality without seam or welding.

We read to find out about human experience and potential. We daily seek stories both to escape from and to come to the best approximation yet of the sense and nonsense of our lives. New or freshly perceived content (the "common secrets"), and ways of perceiving and telling it, characterize every literary advance, i.e., the reader reads for a kind of authoritative gossip, and for style, structure, invention. Verbal fiction offers "common secret" experience of an order that cannot be got in any other way. "Literature," said Ezra Pound, "is NEWS THAT STAYS NEWS." The novel, of all art forms, has always thrived on trying to cope with the concrete, urgent complexity of life, creating the most dynamic artifice of human relationship and ambience in the movement of language.

Oral literature possesses direct, bodily present voice and gesture in the relationship of the teller to the listeners. The teller necessarily demonstrates in every way a clear respect for the listener and the quality of the listener's participation, and the listener for the quality of the teller's performance. Both teller and listener are participants in the achievement of the total effect. Oral literature uses strongly defined, repeated structures, or loose improvised structures, both with vivid imagery, to enable the story movement to carry the reader into understanding. Warmth of social experience and immediate accessibility to language and storytelling techniques characterize oral storytelling. With all, orally told stories in oral cultures must be memorable, i.e., one must be able to recall and retell them with dependable accuracy, though they may also change or be altered from teller to teller. Stories are told in all cultures. Story was a major way in which a people found and affirmed who they were and carried on their wisdom. Oral literature was often capable of handling complex material with its strongly defined narrative structures, imagery, narrative sequence, and formulaic techniques. Oral storytelling, when done well, possesses incomparably compelling immediacy.

In print literature, early novelists sought to leave room for a counterpart of the strengths and immediacy of oral storytelling, the author's relationship with the reader being conceived as the warm, immediate, important relationship of teller to listener. This is the authorial space that needs, in our own inventive way and with our own characteristic manner, to be reclaimed, along with the dimension that I call the storyteller's point of view. Print literature is capable of developing massive, subtle detail within complex frameworks that cannot be held together, in a recallable way, for the teller and listener of oral story. Print literature is also capable of powerfully developing the physical voice of the author in the telling of the story, using metaphor, verbs, point of view, and other devices in place of the oral storyteller's expressive gesture and acting, all of which helps give the sense of the warm advantages of the teller-listener participation in oral story. In print literature, there is the opportunity for exploring the privacy of the relationship of the author to the individual reader. Print literature offers the reader choice and mobility of engagement, which is not always to print literature's advantage. In order to achieve dramatic immediacy for the reader, authors of much of the written literature that has survived have developed physical voice in writing, the engagement of author and reader, and vivid imaginative seeing of character, event, and story movement.

Writing, to be writing, must be speakable. Phonetic writing in particular is a secondary form of speech; its graphic forms represent elements of speech; it gains its meaning from speech. We often say that we "speak" to the page, or the writing "speaks" to us; or we feel, to one degree or another, that a piece of writing has more uniqueness of voice than another piece of writing. Writing, because it is held in sequence in print, possesses a unique past-present-future progression.

We can turn from this page to previous pages to later pages. Both on the page and in the general process of realization, writing becomes a kind of sustained speech, infinitely revisable. In being transferred from an oral-aural-gestural medium to a visual medium, language loses some of the unique powers of speech, such as immediacy, exchange of response between speakers, gestural abstraction, eye contact, tone, closeness, warmth, capacity for lightning-quick improvised strategies for whatever demand is felt. It gains the potential for massive and subtle development of detail and patterns organized within past-present-future progressions (structures, plots, movements) that would fall apart in speech and not be efficiently recallable to either listeners or speakers. Nevertheless, the author who achieves vivid, compelling immediacy and precision in writing for the reader, seeks written counterparts for those capacities of speech that cannot be directly realized on the printed page. Vivid imaginative seeing usually comes first and produces a precision in speech and gesture which connects dynamically to writing. Such writing can have its concrete elements of imagery and patterns recalled with fair accuracy.

This transfer between speech and writing requires constant, almost automatic attention to the two medias' connections and differences. In mature writers, speech and writing may so much overlap that the author, making constant transfers between the capacities of the two media, will "speak writing" and "write speaking." Henry James' complex conversational style is a good example. Robert Frost emphasized the importance of this connection of speaking and writing when he said: "A dramatic necessity goes deep into the nature of the sentence. Sentences are not different enough to hold the attention unless they are dramatic. No ingenuity of varying structure will do. All that can save them is the speaking tone of voice somehow entangled in the words and fastened to the page for the ear of the imagination. That is all that can save poetry from sing-song; all that can save prose from itself." Freud, among others, also emphasized this dramatic nature of writing: "Writing was in its origin the voice of an absent person."

Speech is a way to voice, speech is a part of voice, but voice in writing is more than speech, drawing upon the peculiar powers created by the partial overlapping of the two medias' capacities. Voice is gesture and gestural counterparts, voice is culture (including the personal background of the teller), voice contains the powers of the unconscious and the conscious and the possibility of style. Voice is also the movement of a telling/writing through time, the economy of which is to use what it needs and to leave out what it does not need. Voice is the articulation of all perceptions in verbal expression, written and oral (including the so-called non-verbal which we want to get into writing too). Without voice and imaginative seeing, author and reader have nothing to play with in the theater of the mind during composition or during the act of reading or hearing the printed story.

The author, as Plato said of communication, seeks to transfer thought, imaginative seeing, imagery, and story to another mind, the mind of the reader. Imaginative seeing is visualization, conceptualization, abstraction, but it is also, and begins with, seeing in the mind right now as clearly and with as much impact as one sees in a vivid dream. Imaginative seeing is inherently inventive. Because of seeing-in-the-mind human beings are able to conceive and anticipate the spatial and temporal and other relationships that they need and desire so urgently to communicate to other human beings. The author and the reader must do the seeing of the story. No one else can do it for them.

The more the author is aware through the readers in her or his mind of the accommodations that the reader necessarily makes in understanding the story, the more the author concentrates on telling a story sufficiently vivid and distinct in itself to maintain depth and breadth of experiential meaning. The chemistry of this creation and transfer occurs in the theater of composition in the author's mind. This theater of the mind includes concrete and abstract imaginative seeing of people and events, inner speech, internal listening, voice, form, tense, points of view, and sense of address, with the full personae of address all playing their parts. It includes, in a reworking of the terms, author/teller, readers/listeners, characters, structure and movement of story. In some literature, particularly in the early novels, we see visible signs in print of all of these participating components of the compositional theater of the mind. There is the first person plural in the beginning pages of *Madame Bovary* to welcome us to the full play of Flaubert's theater of composition of the mind, with its techniques for manipulating time, patterns of experience, and point of view to get to meaning and movement in what will be a third-person story. The surrounding tense of the theater of composition of the mind is the present tense, so that we find the signs of it in novels where the author addresses the reader directly, but tells most of the events in the past tense.

In modern writing, many authorial elements are probably excluded from the final forms that meet the reader. Nevertheless, wherever the story is successful, the suppressed elements, which may actually be placed differently rather than suppressed, are functioning and still essential to the realization of the story in the process of its coming into being in the writer's mind. When authors seek to suppress the actual functioning of these elements in their minds during the composing process, the end result, the story made available to the reader, suffers. This occurs in Latter-day Impressionism with its pervasive attempt to erase the author and is only jokingly improved with the sometimes overbearing clown that we occasionally call the author in Post-modernism.

To develop the unique dimensions of verbal art in the storytelling of the novel, we need to reclaim the teller's function, place, and responsibility in telling the tale. First, we must recognize that in the most successful of imitative, Impressionist representation of a flow of imagery and talk, there is an author perceiving, inventing, selecting, and "telling" the story in his or her voice. Actually, the Impressionist author sought a different space, over the shoulder or to the side of the reader, in some cases. If a story works, we pay attention to it and to how and why it works. Where most hidden, in Latter-day Impressionism, the writer, if not the author, is most at labor, if only in the constant activity of covering his tracks and wiping away his fingerprints and doing away with the distinctive character of his voice. How much, in the way of such myriad attentions that seem more petty than subtle, can we demand of the reader before the reader goes away?

The reclaiming of the authorial presence, in a not necessarily parodic way, does not require a belief in omniscience, in God, or in a "rational" ordering of life, the three of which are not necessarily coincident with each other, in any case. Nor does it require a disbelief in any of these kinds of faith. Nor is it necessarily royalist in its sentiment. The Post-modernist parodic re-appropriation of the "authorial presence," often more the ego of the writer enhancing itself at the expense of the characters and the reader, has been done in the way that people joke about something they are coming tentatively to accept. Actually, the system of Post-modernism occasionally seems to be an enclosed, non-dynamic system, a system of boxes elaborated within and from boxes, sometimes with wonderfully outrageous gusto. However, the attempts of a fictional teller to apply a parodic or grotesque view systematically and belittlingly, so that no feeling or experience is allowed its own magnitude, exposes the Post-modernist construction as being removed from life, an artificial system for learning and experience, which is incapable of dealing with the range of emotion, event, relationships, dialectic, and outcomes of the experience of living. At the very least, fiction should be a dynamic artifice of language capable of coping with the stuff of life in a heightened way, attracting the reader's participation and sense of discovering or extending the boundaries of belonging to one's self and others.

Nothing is more naturally and distinctively human than our capacity for perceiving and creating artifice. Nothing is more human, more a part of human life, more crucial to it, than the making of instruments and art. These are not removed from life, but created by our capacity for imaginative seeing and dialectic in the subject-object relationship. When Post-modernism carries a rejection of meaning to the point of needing to avoid the stuff of life itself, it reveals what is apparently a deliberate lack of life-giving purpose. Its artifice ceases to possess the attractiveness of a "golden bird set upon a golden bough to sing..." Art is about life, mind, spirit, and meat, whether some artists may wish it to be or not, because it is imagined and perceived only by living creators and, in turn, imagined and perceived only by living receivers and appreciators, who have only their own lives and imaginations to use in creation and appreciation.

Occasionally the Post-modernist seizes upon the abstractive distancing of language from reference and seeks to break language off from its lifeline connection to the building of story and meaning from seeing-in-the-mind. Language is by no means simply an obedient servant but expresses the outcome of story in its encounter with the powerful intentions and perceptions of the author's seeing-in-the-mind. Actually, language is able to move far into abstraction without breaking this connection. This "distancing" allows word meanings to change in context with other words and in context of forms and audience, and for abstract, oblique, irrelevant, deceitful, half-truthful, non-sensical (playful as well as no-sense), very flexible manipulation of meaning to occur. When I reject use of the word "livid" because its reference for the reader could be to "bluish" or "reddish with anger" or "extremely angry," I am demonstrating that I feel the need for words to have as much precision of reference as possible. In the telling of story, as in other forms of discourse, the relationship of meaning to language, though imperfectly understood, is broad and powerful. In the author's and reader's minds, story is a major outcome of the pressure of seeing-in-the-mind to be realized in language.

It is not the God-like or ecclesiastical universality of the author that we need, but the author's heightened individuality of voice, with clear respect for the content, characters, movement, and reader of the story. It is the author attempting to find the "truth" of all these participations, including the author's own participation and attitude in what we call story. It is the author's capacity for exploring individual characters' points of view, with the potential of collective and rhetorical points of view. It is the author no longer in conflict with, no longer belittling, the characters, the events, the reader, the story itself. It is the author assuming the role that the author has always had in retelling and reinventing the stories of our lives, rediscovering the material of the "common secrets." It is the author committing voice and imaginative perception to the finding of the story and its wisdom, which is, as D. H. Lawrence observed, always wiser than we are. It is the author seeking the reader once again.

The novel has never been anything but flawed, never a paradigm for a fully organized and rational order of life and the universe. The very attempt to make the novel conform to the beat of an enclosed, exclusive system, such as the completeness of the parodic Post-modern system, is an exercise that removes the story from the reader and puts the ego of the writer in place of the author and in conflict with the characters, the story, and the reader.

Writers in their writing, and editors and teachers in their range of permissions, appear to choose either Latter-day Impressionism or Post-modernism and do not see the possibility of synthesizing systems, past and potential. The Impressionist story is one powerful possibility, with the author present in the imaginative perception and the voice and style of the language, and as an over-the-shoulder or on-the-side narrator. In the work of the great Impressionist authors, the individuality of the authorial presence invests the work from beginning to end, with many such authors choosing persona and point of view structures that allow them to address the reader directly or using dramatic techniques that remove the author from the immediate space of the story. Nevertheless, the great Impressionist authors realized that without the author the story goes into the grave, never to be experienced, just another untold story misting about in eternity. The Latter-day Impressionist story is another possibility, with narrow point of view, in which the writer keeps her or his hands behind the back, attempting to suppress any sign of authorship in voice, perception, or attitude, while actually suppressing the space that the storyteller would give the story and the reader. Then there is the Post-modernist ego of the writer acting as a sort of satirizing schoolmaster, inviting us into the closed system of his or her parodic universe. Post-modernism, particularly in its parody of form, is an inviting possibility. There is the Dickensian system, in which the author's dominion is central, genial, sentimental, satirical, reproving, straightforward by turns in its moralism, with the story occasionally allowed wisdom implicitly at odds with the ego of the writer. There are the systems of Defoe, Fielding, Sterne, and Balzac. There is the powerful compression and dramatic chronicle or epic movement of von Kleist's authorship, the courage of Kafka's attention to the commanding logic of dreams, of Gogol's exuberant respect for the independent movement of story as it occurs within clear authorial space, and of Christina Stead's significant modification of Impressionist techniques, her strong use of storyteller and characters' points of view, dramatic development among characters, and narratival rhetorical forms, in *The Man Who Loved Children.* Moving into the authorial space will allow us to reclaim social realism, appropriating a wide range of important contemporary content.

Versions of the parodic approach are one possibility, versions of the withdrawn or disguised or incorporated author are another, but there are other potentials less explored at this point in the development of fiction and audience. These have to do with the exploration of the storyteller's point of view and voice, which includes the flexible manipulation of the dimension of time, exploration of characters' points of view and access to inner points of view and personae of voice, and development of dramatic relationships among characters and the other elements of fiction. The most advancing potential remaining to us is that of invention through synthesis, rather than through exclusion of elements, recognizing that synthesis is not going to produce a novel exactly like any of the forms of the past, nor something that is patched of those forms, but something that partakes of all of those systems at the same time that it creates instruments and likenesses that didn't previously exist. The key principle is that of telling the story actively and dramatically. Such synthesis involves reclaiming author and reader space. Aesthetic ideologies are no more forgiving or inclusive than religious or political ideologies, but we could, if we would, let the stories of a hundred systems bloom.

Contemporary fiction sometimes seems to be spellbound, as in a dream, with the author, the reader, the story lying in a coffin, the dreamer leadenly unable to move. If we tell the spell backwards, we may release fiction into movement and discover the author very much and necessarily at work where least expected to be found. The authorial need and function continue wherever successful storytelling occurs, no matter what pretense or rationale governs the admissibility or inadmissibility of the author's presence.

The Author Is Dead! Long Live the Author!

I propose an opening up of the long forbidden rooms in the house of fiction and a throwing open of the grounds around the house as well. I propose an open system in which author, characters, reader, events, movement, and structure of story are released from their house arrest and allowed to find space and relationship each with the others. To do this, the author must be returned from exile, to act for the whole, to keep the vandals off the grounds, and to be present for the release of the crazy aunts, starving feral children, and the exposing of skeletons and other evidences.

The author must seek the reader again, which means seeking actual "friendly" readers capable of appreciation that makes significant shaping possible, in the way that Louis Bouilhet was an all-important reader for Flaubert, Leonard Woolf for Virginia, and Phil Stone for Faulkner, the way a great master or perceptive friend may be a reader for a writer. I will argue that there is no author without the reader, just as there is no talk without a listener, simply because when we talk "alone" with ourselves, we are listening, and when we write alone, we are reading, internally listening to, and responding to and shaping what we write. Without the capacity for internalized readers, the writer could not write. The listener-reader in the writer is space that needs to be reclaimed in fiction, to give space for other reader-listeners who will pick up the story to experience it. Writers need to look at this audience in themselves and realize that the needs of readers, the disposition of readers to read, their education and development, have powerful bearing on the future of verbal storytelling.

The ideas in "The Author is Dead! Long Live the Author!" are my responsibility and began in my personal struggle with literary ideologies many years ago when I wrote in my journal, "We must find some way to get the teller back into the tale." The works in the following bibliography bear importantly upon subjects in the essay.

Basgoy, Ilhan. "The Tale-Singer and his Audience." *Folklore: Performance and Communication,* ed. Dan Ben-Amos and Kenneth S. Goldstein, Mouton, 1975.

Booth, Wayne C. *The Rhetoric of Fiction.* Chicago: University of Chicago Press, 1961.

Chao, Yuan Ken. *Language and Symbolic Systems,* Cambridge, England: Cambridge University Press, 1968.

Clarke, Kenneth and Mary. *A Folklore Reader.* New York: A. S. Barnes & Co., 1965.

Diringer, David. *The Alphabet,* 2 vol. London: Hutchison, 1968.

Gardner, Howard. *The Shattered Mind.* New York: Vintage Books, Random House, Inc., 1975.

Gelb, I. G. *A Study of Writing.* Chicago: University of Chicago Press, 1963.

Gordon, Caroline & Tate, Allen. *The House of Fiction: An Anthology of the Short Story with Commentary.* New York: Charles Scribners Sons, 1950.

Havelock, Eric A. *Preface to Plato.* Cambridge, MA: Belknap Press of Harvard University Press, 1963.

Jacobs, Melville. *The Content and Style of an Oral Literature.* Viking Fund Publications. New York: Viking. 1959.

Langer, Suzanne. *Feeling and Form.* London: Routledge & Kegan Paul, 1953.

Lesser, Wendy. "The Character as Victim: Norman Mailer, Renata Adler, and Anne Bernays." *The Hudson Review.* Vol. 36, No. 3, Autumn 1984.

Lord, Albert B. *The Singer of Tales.* Originally published by Harvard University Press, 1960. New York: Atheneum, 1965.

Malmgren, Carl Darryl. *Fictional Space in the Modernist and Post-Modernist American Novel.* Lewisberg, PA: Bucknell University Press, 1985.

Newman, Charles. *The Post-Modern Aura: The Art of Fiction in an Age of Inflation.* Evanston: Northwestern University Press, 1985. (Originally published in *Salmagundi,* No. 63-65, Spring-Summer 1984, Skidmore College, Saratoga Springs, New York.)

Ong, Walter J., S.J. *Orality and Literacy.* London and New York: Methuen, 1982.

Paivio. Allan T. *Imagery and Verbal Processes.* New York: Holt, Rinehart and Winston, Inc., 1971.

Rosenberg, Bruce A. "Oral Sermons and Oral Narrative." In *Folklore: Performance and Communication,* ed. Dan Ben-Amos and Kenneth S. Goldstein, New York: Mouton, 1975.